$6.75

Import Liberalization and Employment

Walter S. Salant & Beatrice N. Vaccara

The consequences of liberalizing United States trade policy have been the subject of much talk in recent years but of relatively little serious study. Policy makers have generally been presented with widely varying guesses rather than with substantiated evidence and conclusions.

The purpose of this study is to help reduce reliance on guesswork by providing a systematic examination of one aspect of the problem: the effects on the level of employment in the United States to be expected in the short run following unilateral reduction in the tariff or other import barriers. After reviewing the market forces that are set in motion when import barriers are reduced, the study presents estimates of the quantitative effects on employment that occur in the United States when imports increase and displace domestic production by specified amounts. Then it deals with the stimulating effects on employment that might be expected because of the rise in exports resulting from the increase in imports.

The concluding chapter points up the difference between the effects of a liberalized trade policy on the total economy and on the industry whose protection is reduced, and it analyzes the significance of the findings for public policy.

IMPORT LIBERALIZATION AND EMPLOYMENT

Import Liberalization and Employment

The Effects of Unilateral Reductions in United States Import Barriers

by WALTER S. SALANT
and BEATRICE N. VACCARA

The Brookings Institution · *Washington, D. C.*

Library of Congress Catalogue Card Number 61-10751

Printed in the United States of America
George Banta Company, Inc.
Menasha, Wisconsin

THE BROOKINGS INSTITUTION is an independent organization engaged in research and education in the social sciences. Its principal purposes are to aid in the development of sound public policies and to provide advanced training for students in the social sciences.

The Institution was founded December 8, 1927, as a consolidation of three antecedent organizations: the Institute for Government Research, 1916; the Institute of Economics, 1922; and the Robert Brookings Graduate School of Economics and Government, 1924.

The general administration of the Institution is the responsibility of a self-perpetuating Board of Trustees. In addition to this general responsibility the By-Laws provide that, "It is the function of the Trustees to make possible the conduct of scientific research and publication, under the most favorable conditions, and to safeguard the independence of the research staff in the pursuit of their studies and in the publication of the results of such studies. It is not a part of their function to determine, control, or influence the conduct of particular investigations or the conclusions reached." The immediate direction of the policies, program, and staff of the Institution is vested in the President, who is assisted by an advisory council, chosen from the professional staff of the Institution.

In publishing a study, the Institution presents it as a competent treatment of a subject worthy of public consideration. The interpretations and conclusions in such publications are those of the author or authors and do not necessarily reflect the views of other members of the Brookings staff or of the administrative officers of the Institution.

Foreword

Estimates of the effects on employment of reducing tariffs and other barriers to imports have varied widely ever since the subject has been publicly discussed in quantitative terms. The various methods used to estimate these effects have been inappropriate or obscure or both. The question of what decreases in employment might result in the short run under given conditions seemed to us to warrant an effort to develop a method of estimating them and to trace through some of the indirect effects of reducing import restrictions. The contribution of the present study lies largely in its analysis of these short-run effects and in the development of a method of estimating them. It is significant that the decreases in employment resulting from tariff reductions are found to be considerably less than is often assumed.

Brookings presents this study as an important analysis of a technical and significant subject. The book is designed for both professional and nonprofessional readers, although it may be found to require the sustained attention of both groups.

The study was initiated and directed by Walter S. Salant. The Institution is especially grateful to him and to Beatrice N. Vaccara, his co-author. The Institution is also grateful to members of the Advisory Committee and others who have contributed through their comments, criticisms, and suggestions.

The study was financed out of funds for general support contributed by the Ford Foundation.

The views expressed are those of the authors and do not necessarily represent the views of other staff members, officers, or trustees of The Brookings Institution.

Robert D. Calkins
President

January 1961

vii

Authors' Preface

In presenting the results of our research, we have attempted, perhaps defying the experience of others, to address two audiences. We have tried to provide a thorough account of our work for the specialist. At the same time, we have tried to make our general methods, our results, and their implications clear to the interested nonspecialist, first by making it possible for him to omit four chapters without losing the continuity of the exposition or anything that he will regard as essential, second, by avoiding the technical language of economics in the other chapters, and, third, by confining the explanations of many statistical intricacies to the appendices or the four chapters that nonspecialists may omit. We hope that the only sacrifice involved in this effort to make the book comprehensible to the nonspecialist has been the time and energy of the authors and not precision of statement or rigor of reasoning.

We recognize that despite these efforts, a careful reading of the book will require the devoted attention of any reader. The difficulties appear to be an inevitable result of our decision to examine a part of the complex repercussions of a reduction of import barriers, a decision we made partly because we think the results provide a good case study of the intricacies involved in following through and estimating quantitatively the effects of any economic change. Since these difficulties are inherent in the problem and the decision to explain it, all we could hope to do was to ensure that mere unfamiliarity with the technical language would not be an added obstacle.

The reader may be impressed with the large number of assumptions that we have made in deriving the estimates. If he feels inclined to object to their number, we can only say that any estimates of comparable complexity must be based on many assumptions. If there is anything unusual in this aspect of the study, we hope it is not the number of our assumptions but our effort to make them explicit.

The effort to present our results and our methods clearly yet precisely and to appraise the effects on the estimates of economic changes that have occurred since the statistics underlying them were current have greatly lengthened the time required to prepare the manuscript for publication. Throughout this period, Robert D. Calkins, President of The Brookings Institution, and Ralph J. Watkins, Director of Economic Studies, have been understanding and helpful. For this we cannot express our appreciation sufficiently.

From almost the beginning of this study, we have had the valuable and conscientious assistance of Mrs. Carolyn Teixeira Jackson, who, with unfailing good humor, did nearly all the mountainous computational work that was not done electronically and managed to check and keep track of innumerable details and, at the same time, understand and not lose sight of the conceptual structure of which they were a part. Mrs. Eva Jacobs skillfully did the research necessary to derive the employment-output relationships for non-commodity-producing industries and prepared the memorandum that underlies the part of Appendix D that relates to these relationships.

We have received help from many others, too. The Bureau of Labor Statistics has allowed us to use unpublished data and has cooperated with us in other ways. In particular, we want to express our thanks to W. Duane Evans, Assistant Commissioner of Labor Statistics and Sidney Jaffe, Assistant Chief of the Division of Prices and Cost of Living, Bureau of Labor Statistics for their help at an early stage of the study in explaining some of the more intricate differences between variants of input-output relations and advising us about the choice of matrix. Jack Alterman, Assistant Chief of the Bureau's Division of Productivity and Technological Developments, provided indispensable assistance in estimating 1953 output in 1947 prices from data on 1953 shipments and inventories in 1953 prices. He has also advised us about the correct use of data on output per man-hour in connection with the appraisals made in Chapter 10. The late Faith Williams, when Chief of the Bureau's Division of Foreign Labor Conditions, provided unpublished tabulations of foreign trade data.

We also wish to thank Maxwell R. Conklin, Chief of the Industry Division of the Bureau of the Census, for providing unpublished data on shipments, inventories, and employment necessary for our estimates.

The Joint Economic Committee of the Congress, then known as the Joint Committee on the Economic Report, kindly permitted us to use material on United States merchandise exports in 1953 that was tabulated at their expense. Charles Goor of the International Bank for Reconstruction and Development assisted us in aggregating the data for 1953 trade between countries.

We had helpful conversations with Wilhelm Anderson and his colleagues in the Foreign Agricultural Service of the Department of Agriculture and with A. K. Cairncross, J. Marcus Fleming, Arthur Hersey, and Walther Lederer, who advised us about the choice of some of the assumptions that had to be made regarding exports. Karl Fox advised us about the suitability of our assumptions regarding the short-run responsiveness of agricultural production. They, like others who gave us advice, are, of course, not responsible for the use we may have made or failed to make of it.

In addition to this help from experts who, at the time, were in the United States Government or international agencies, we have benefited from the advice of Sydney Netreba, whose own brief but effective earlier work in the Bureau of Labor Statistics on the problems we were studying enabled him to warn us effectively of some of the dangers that lay ahead.

We wish especially to thank the members of our Advisory Committee, Professors Edward S. Shaw of Stanford University, Thomas C. Schelling and Arthur Smithies of Harvard University, and Bert G. Hickman of the Senior Research Staff of The Brookings Institution for their careful reading of one or more drafts of the manuscript. Their many penetrating comments and suggestions have immeasurably improved the finished product. We also want to express a debt and take this opportunity to pay our respects to the late William Adams Brown, a member of the Advisory Committee and a scholar of the highest integrity and character, who made several useful suggestions and whose unfortunate death while this study was in progress unquestionably deprived us of many more.

Marshall A. Robinson, now Dean of the School of Business Administration, University of Pittsburgh, but until recently at The Brookings Institution, allowed us to exploit his skill in economic exposition by reading all the chapters other than the four marked as "skippable" by nonspecialists and offered editorial suggestions that improved the exposition at several important points. Herbert C. Morton, Director of Publications at The Brookings Institution, made suggestions that improved the exposition in general and the early chapters in particular. Hormoussis G. Georgiadis, now Assistant Professor of Economics at Princeton University, while a Brookings Fellow hard at work on a difficult doctoral dissertation, generously took the time to read Chapters 1 to 4 and Chapter 7 carefully and to make valuable criticisms and suggestions for improving them.

The process of editing and otherwise preparing for the press a manuscript that presented unusual mechanical difficulties was performed by Miss A. Evelyn Breck of the Brookings staff with characteristic skill and good judgment. The difficult task of preparing the index was performed by Mrs. Jean Kyle.

To all these people we wish to express our great gratitude.

Walter S. Salant
Beatrice N. Vaccara

December 1960

Contents

TABLES AND CHARTS

PART
I

Introduction and Background

CHAPTER 1

Introduction

DESPITE THE HISTORICAL difference between the two major American political parties on the tariff issue, our last three Presidents, two Democratic and one Republican, have favored reducing United States tariffs below the levels established by the Tariff Act of 1930. They have argued that a reciprocal lowering of tariffs was desirable in the long-term interests of the United States, for both economic and international political reasons. In 1934, shortly after the low point of the great depression, Congress granted the President's request for authority to negotiate reciprocal reductions of tariffs by passing the Trade Agreements Act, but it granted the power for only three years. Since then, it has extended the power eleven times but always for short periods and generally with increasing restrictions.

All three Presidents have felt it necessary, except perhaps in 1945, to anticipate strong protectionist resistance to extension of their tariff-reducing authority and have made concessions to it in advance. The result has been that the powers they have obtained have generally been more limited than those they implied were desirable in the broad national interest.

The main explanation of these compromises between the presidential views of the national interest and legislative performance is undoubtedly to be found in the fact that liberalization of foreign trade policy may have transitional economic effects that are painful, even though they may be necessary to achieve a desirable long-run purpose.

These transitional effects have been the subject of much talk but relatively little serious study. Policy-makers have been presented with guesses regarding the economic effects of changes in import barriers, guesses that have varied greatly and in fact have disagreed even about the direction of the effects.[1] On the one hand, protectionists have predicted that a lowering of import barriers would have alarming adverse effects. One has said that it would create a major business depression, another that a radical reduction or abolition of tariffs on chemicals alone would leave the chemical industry with "no choice but to close down several billion dollars' worth of our modern plants," and another that 5 million of the employed in this country are directly exposed to and vulnerable to import competition while 15 million are vulnerable directly and indirectly.[2] On the other hand, some advocates of lower tariffs say that a reduction of our import barriers would stimulate employment, or imply that it would by saying that employment would be reduced if these barriers rose. Thus, Secretary of Commerce Weeks, in testifying before the House Ways and Means Committee said: "Let those who advocate the defeat or weakening of the trade agreements program count all the cost. Even though some of them may think they are shielding some business from some competition, their action, if successful, would jeopardize the job security of more than 4½ million American workers whose living depends on world trade."[3] Thus the range of possible effects presented to policy-makers and the public is wide, and the actual effects have remained unknown.

While short-run effects should not dominate decisions about long-run policies, it is a fact of life that these effects—or beliefs about them—have often dominated decisions in this as in other fields of public policy. This fact alone would be a sufficient reason

[1] The only careful empirically based study is one made by the U. S. Bureau of Labor Statistics for the Randall Commission. It estimates the number of "United States Workers Producing Goods Equivalent to Import Increases in Case of Temporary Tariff Suspension." See paper of this title in *Staff Papers Presented to the Commission on Foreign Economic Policy* (February 1954).

[2] See "U. S. Urged to Maintain Protective Tariff as Safeguard for Nation's Economy" by Howard R. Huston, Vice President of American Cyanamid Company in *Journal of Commerce* (Nov. 30, 1953), and testimony by O. R. Strackbein in *Causes of Unemployment in the Coal and Other Domestic Industries,* Hearings before the Senate Committee on Labor and Public Welfare, 84 Cong. 1 sess. (1955), p. 194.

[3] *Renewal of Trade Agreements Act,* Hearings before the House Committee on Ways and Means, 85 Cong. 2 sess. (1958), Pt. 1, p. 37. The 4½ million figure is an estimate of workers "engaged directly or indirectly in production or service for export, or in the distribution of imports, or in the first factory processing of imported materials." It relates to our total foreign trade, not to the portion of that trade that would be affected by the defeat or weakening of the trade agreements program.

for finding out more about the nature and magnitude of these short-run effects.

Consideration of such effects is not irrational, however. Short-run employment effects do affect the economic welfare of individuals and communities and therefore are a legitimate concern in the decision-making process. What weight should be given to them depends on their nature and magnitude; it cannot be judged until these matters are investigated. It is no more justifiable to assume that their magnitude is negligible than to assume that their existence is irrelevant. Yet few economists have devoted much attention to the economic and social costs of the dislocations that tariff reductions can cause.[4]

This study is intended as a contribution to our knowledge about one of these short-run effects: the effects on the level of employment in the United States that might be expected if the United States were to make a unilateral reduction in its tariff or other protective barriers against imports. Although, as will become clear later, the study does not provide a single numerical answer to the questions that policy-makers are likely to ask—at least in the form in which they are likely to ask them—it does suggest that magnitudes such as those mentioned above are greatly exaggerated. Its results also throw light on other factors relevant to decisions about changes in import barriers and to proposals for easing the process of adjustment to such changes.

Another benefit in studying short-term employment effects is that the mere effort to estimate them forces one to clarify ideas and reveals clearly the importance of some factors that might otherwise be overlooked. Indeed, close examination of what people mean when they refer to "employment effects" shows that the very concept of such effects is by no means unambiguous. For clear thinking about the policy questions involved, it is important to distinguish several such concepts, all of which are relevant to

[4] Among those who have considered them seriously are Professors Edward S. Mason, Seymour E. Harris, and Don D. Humphrey. Mason's views may be found in testimony given in September 1956 and published in *Administration and Operation of Customs and Tariff Laws and the Trade Agreements Program,* **Hearings** before the House Committee on Ways and Means, 84 Cong. 2 sess. One expression of Harris' views is in *Renewal of Trade Agreements Act,* Hearings, Pt. 1. Humphrey also considered these problems in the latter hearings but did so more fully in his comprehensive book *American Imports* (Twentieth Century Fund, 1955).

some policy question but each of which is relevant to a different one.

First, some people have in mind the effects of trade liberalization on production and employment in the country as a whole, assuming all influences unrelated to liberalization remain the same. This concept is relevant to the effect of liberalization alone on general business conditions. It takes into account the stimulating as well as the depressing effects and focuses on the balance between them. These stimulating and depressing effects include those not only on the industries producing the import-competing goods but on their direct suppliers and also on their indirect suppliers, and the effects of any resulting change of exports, and of any other changes in production caused by these changes. It excludes, however, the effects of forces unrelated to liberalization that might also happen to occur at the same time.

Second, people may have in mind the effects only on the industries at the "final" stage of production of the import-competing goods, while still assuming that everything unrelated to the reductions remains the same.

A third concept is the total change of production and employment in an import-competing industry during a period of time in which import barriers have been reduced, taking into account not only the reduction of import barriers but other developments affecting the industry. For example, general growth of markets due to population growth would mitigate or offset the adverse effects of a lowering of barriers; a general decline of business activity would aggravate them; and changes in technology or consumers' tastes might do either.

So far as actual layoffs of individual workers in an industry are concerned, still another concept is relevant: the net effect not only of liberalization and other factors affecting total employment in the industry but the rate of normal "separations" from its payrolls, such as the turnover due to retirement, death, normal shifting to other industries, and other normal causes. Because of these separations, it is possible to reduce the labor force of an industry without firing anyone, simply by failing to replace those who leave in the normal course of events.

It is obvious that the net change in employment and the rate at which employees are actually discharged depend not only on international trade policy but on other factors as well and are more closely related to the human problems of hardship than the first two concepts. All are useful, but they relate to different questions and therefore serve different purposes.[5] The estimates with which this study is chiefly concerned relate to the effects of liberalization alone, although crude estimates of other factors causally unrelated to it are presented in the final chapter for purposes of comparison.

Although the short-period employment effects, which are the subject of this study, are relevant to decisions about *changes* in the level of import barriers, it is important to bear in mind that they are only one among several relevant considerations. The longer the period contemplated, the less important are the transitional effects of changes from the existing level in relation to the considerations that determine what level is the most desirable one to maintain in the long run.

In stressing the importance of other considerations, we take a view that accords with the traditional view of economists. The influence of tariffs on the volume of employment has generally not been regarded by economists as one that should be decisive in determining a country's policy regarding import barriers, except during great depressions of economic activity. This does not mean, of course, that the level of employment has been a matter of indifference to economists, either recently or in the earlier days of the "classical economists" who first perceived the advantages of foreign trade. The reason short-run effects have traditionally received little attention is that classical economics assumed—or deduced from prior assumptions—that any unemployment, including that created by reductions of import barriers, would be temporary because unemployment would itself set in motion market forces that would eliminate it.

Today, few if any people accept the idea that market forces alone can always be relied on to restore full employment within a period of time that society regards as satisfactory. But some of the market forces set in motion by unemployment do tend to restore it. Moreover, governments can adopt policies seeking both to encourage these forces and to discourage opposing market

[5] It is possible to distinguish several more concepts, based on different combinations of causes and categories of effects. The concepts distinguished above, however, are the ones most commonly used and most commonly confused, and are the ones that appear to be most relevant to public policy.

forces that tend to cause unemployment to cumulate or persist. Even when changes in commercial policy have the immediate effect of causing unemployment, therefore, we may safely retain the traditional conclusion that they need not result in long-run unemployment, provided that policies to overcome the shortcomings of automatic market forces are in fact pursued. Our major departure from the traditional position is that we insist on this proviso.

Since employment effects are not a major consideration determining the desirable long-run levels of import barriers, what have been regarded as the major considerations? A brief review of them will indicate what lies outside the area of this study.

Foremost in the tradition of economics has been the effect on the allocation of given quantities of labor, capital, and other fundamental productive resources among different possible uses and the efficiency of their application and thereby the effect on the total production of the trading countries concerned.

Second are the effects that protection has on the relative prices of imports and exports and thus on the distribution of world income among the trading countries, also under conditions of constant total employment.

Third is the effect on the distribution of income among labor, capital, and other factors of production within a country, again under conditions of constant total employment.

Fourth is the effect of a country's import policy on the development of new domestic industries, a consideration that bulked large in the early history of the United States and that is again receiving great attention in connection with efforts to speed up the economic development of underdeveloped countries.

These four are all long-run economic considerations. The question of protection has also been considered from short-run points of view. Thus a fifth consideration is its effect on national economic stability. Barriers to imports, by reducing economic ties with the rest of the world, tend to make a country less vulnerable to income fluctuations originating elsewhere but tend to increase the effect of initial changes in domestic spending. Thus, for fluctuations of domestic origin, imports are an automatic stabilizer.

A sixth aspect of import policy, discussed intensively since World War II, is its relationship to our foreign aid policy. Trade has been proposed as a substitute for aid to countries that have difficulty in earning sufficient dollars and as a means of providing markets for export industries in developing countries.

Beyond these economic considerations has been the effect of a country's import policy on its military power and other aspects of its national security, a question specifically considered as long ago as 1776 by Adam Smith in his classic *Inquiry into the Nature and Causes of the Wealth of Nations.*

This study does not deal with these problems. That fact is emphasized in order to make clear that the study is intended as a contribution to only one aspect of United States tariff policy. The reader should be forewarned that when he has completed the reading of this book—if, indeed, he does—what he has learned will not automatically provide him with an adequate basis for judging the relative merits of raising, lowering, and leaving unchanged the level of protection against imports.

The effects that this study seeks to measure are effects of only some of the market forces that liberalization would set in motion. Before defining these forces and the effects we seek to measure more precisely, it is desirable to explain the broader background in which they operate. This is done in the next chapter, which considers, non-quantitatively, the market forces that are set in motion when import barriers are reduced. This completes the introductory part of the book. Part II deals with the employment effects that occur in the United States when, as a result of reductions of import barriers, imports increase and displace domestic production by specified amounts. (Although the analysis and estimates of Part II refer to reductions of domestic production that result from reductions of import barriers, it may be noted that they may also be used in connection with the effects of any reductions of domestic production that have a similar composition, whatever their cause.) In Part III we estimate the effects of these specified increases in our imports on our exports and the consequent stimulating effects on employment. Part IV brings together the employment effects of the displacement of domestic output and of the stimulus given to output by exports. Part V summarizes the empirical conclusions of the study, and explores their significance for policy.

Chapter 4 in Part II and Chapters 6, 7, and 8 in Part III deal with the logic of the estimating methods and, to some extent, their statistical application. These chapters are necessarily more technical than others in the book. Nonprofessional readers who are not interested in these matters may skip these chapters, which constitute more than one third of the book, and still obtain a consecutive and fairly complete description of the findings. They will, however, pay a price for skipping them: They will not fully appreciate the necessary limitations of the findings, and they will therefore assume an obligation to exercise greater caution in using them.

CHAPTER 2

How Liberalization Affects Output and Employment

I N THIS CHAPTER we shall survey the economic forces that may be set in motion in a nation's economy when its import barriers are reduced. A reduction of these barriers has immediate effects on relative prices, on output, on employment, and on incomes, and these immediate effects have further repercussions. Since this study concentrates on only a portion of the domestic output and employment effects, an appreciation of the variety of possible effects—some alternative to those examined in the rest of this study and some additional to them—is necessary for perspective. A survey of these effects will also help the reader to distinguish the forces that are included in the quantitative estimates to be presented later in the book from those that are excluded.

The chapter is divided into four parts. The first section considers what happens to price and output in the industry whose protection is reduced, which we shall call the "liberalized" industry. (What is really liberalized is the government's treatment of the imports and not its treatment of the domestic industry. This term is therefore not logical, but it is a convenient abbreviation.) The second section provides a broader view of the forces that are set in motion and some of their possible effects in shifting demand and the allocation of labor and capital between the liberalized industry and other parts of the economy. Probably the major force set in motion by a reduction of import barriers is the shift in spending from domestic production to imports. In the third section, therefore, attention is transferred from the broad view taken in the second section to the potential income-induced effects of such a shift on total output. The fourth section of the chapter shows how the effects estimated in this study are related to those examined in the third section and thereby paves the way for presentation of these estimates in the chapters that follow.

Effects on Prices and Output in the
Liberalized Industry

The first effect of a lowering of import barriers—whether it takes the form of a tariff cut, a relaxation of an absolute limit on the quantity of imports, or a reduction in an administrative or other barrier—is to permit Americans to buy a given quantity of the imported commodity at a lower price or to buy a larger quantity than before at the old price.

When competing foreign goods become available at lower prices or in larger quantities, American buyers will consider shifting their purchases from domestic to foreign goods. Whether they will actually shift their purchases depends on how domestic prices react. Domestic producers may lower their prices, raise them, or leave them unchanged. What they do depends partly on the degree and character of competition that prevailed among the domestic sellers of the competitive product before the import barriers were reduced and partly on how much the total costs of domestic producers vary as the level of their output changes.

We shall consider first the case of a domestic industry consisting of one firm that enjoys a monopoly in the domestic market because of a high level of protection. If the monopoly does not reduce its prices when its protection is reduced, it is bound to lose at least some of its business and therefore must reduce its output.[1]

But what if it reduces prices through fear of losing many of its customers? It may then avoid losing any of its previous business and may in fact be able to acquire additional business. In such a case, output will not decrease, and may actually increase. There is nothing to guarantee this result, however, for the price that is most profitable under the more competitive conditions, although lower than before the tariff cut, still may not be low enough to prevent loss of some business. If it is not, output will decline.

Suppose the commodity, instead of being sold by a monopoly, is sold by competing sellers, but that their competition is partly

---

[1] Here and throughout this study it is assumed that changes of sales are reflected in changes of output rather than of inventories.

or largely on a nonprice basis, taking the form of competition in quality, advertising, and other factors that establish customers' preferences for particular brands. Each producer then has some, perhaps a substantial amount, of business that is not readily enticed away when domestic competitors make small price reductions.

Now consider what happens when imports of a similar product become available more cheaply. There are two possibilities. If, at their old price, the domestic producers would lose mainly the business that is easily enticed away by price cuts on foreign products and would be left mainly with the business that is firmly attached to their products, they will reduce prices little or not at all, or may even raise them. Although the demand for their product has fallen, what is left has also become less sensitive to price changes at the old price. This decreased sensitiveness limits their incentive to cut prices when demand falls and makes it worthwhile for them to accept some loss of business.

The result may be different, however, in the alternative case, where a fall of import prices would cause the domestic sellers, if they kept their original prices, to lose their less price-sensitive customers, *i.e.,* those most strongly attached to their product because of brand or quality considerations. It is not difficult to imagine such a case. Several producers may sell goods regarded by their own customers as superior in quality to those of domestic competitors but inferior to a more expensive imported product. If a cut in tariffs makes that imported product cheaper than before, although still leaving it more expensive than the domestic product, customers who place a high value on quality would shift to the imported product if the domestic price remained unchanged, leaving the domestic producers primarily with the customers who are easily enticed away by price changes of domestic competitors.

In such a situation, a producer has a two-fold reason to reduce prices. First, by doing so he can minimize the loss of customers to foreign competitors. Second, the price sensitivity of the domestic market that would remain at the old price is greater than before the reduction of import barriers, thereby increasing his incentive to compete with his domestic competitors on the basis of price. If the increase in price sensitivity is small, a producer has no incentive to cut prices by enough to offset fully the loss of business at the old price. Accordingly, he cuts his production. If the price sensitivity becomes great, however, it may be profitable for a producer to cut prices by amounts sufficient to permit maintaining or increasing his production. Costs may prevent such a decrease in price, but they will not necessarily do so because, before the cut in import barriers, the trade of the less price-sensitive customers made it possible and profitable for a seller to charge prices above the additional short-run costs attributable to the last units of his production.

The effort of any individual competitor to minimize his loss of business by cutting prices will succeed partly at the expense of others. All domestic competitors face the same situation, however, and all may cut prices. Demand for domestic output as a whole can be maintained, therefore, only if prices are cut enough to provide a market stimulus at least equal to the loss of market that would have occurred at the old price. Whether prices will be cut this much, and therefore whether output of the domestic industry is decreased, maintained, or even increased, depends on how much demand falls at the old price, on how price sensitive the demand for domestic output becomes, and how costs vary with variations in output.

Thus, in the case of predominantly nonprice competition, output is maintained or increased only if the customers whom the domestic sellers would lose to the foreign competitor at the original prices are those not easily enticed away by domestic competitors. We have also seen, however, that this condition alone, although necessary to prevent a decrease of output, is not sufficient to do so. It merely means that the remaining market becomes more sensitive to price changes at the old price. An increase in this price sensitivity is not enough to cause producers to maintain or increase their output. That result requires that the increase in price sensitivity be sufficient to permit sellers to earn, from the larger volume of business, at least as much additional net revenue as they would lose from the cut in prices.

It is doubtful that there are many protected industries in which a cut in import barriers would cause a loss of the less price-sensitive customers and a consequent increase in price sensitivity sufficient to cause most producers to maintain or increase output. We may conclude that for most protected industries with predominantly nonprice competition, a cheapening of competing imports will result in decreases of output.

Under conditions of intense competition among a large number of sellers wholly on the basis of price, reductions of import barriers will necessarily cause domestic producers to reduce their prices and output. Under these conditions, even small decreases in the going price resulting from additions to the available supply would force domestic producers to meet the lower price lest they lose all their business. Even if producers do meet such price decreases, however, they will still have to cut their output. The reason is that, under conditions of intense domestic price competition, each seller's price was already—before the reduction of import barriers—very close to the additional short-run costs attributable to the last units of his production. At lower prices he would lose money on the business that was marginal before and will therefore be unwilling to supply as much output as before. Nothing has happened, however, to reduce the total amounts that buyers are willing to take. The result, therefore, is a decrease of domestic production and a rise of imports. Thus, we may conclude that, where there is intense competition wholly on the basis of price, the initial tendency of domestic buyers to shift from domestic to foreign sources for their supplies of the liberalized commodity will result in an actual shift, with a consequent decline in output of the domestic firms.

Reviewing the three general types of selling conditions that we have just examined, we can draw the following conclusions: (1) A cheapening of competing imports may or may not cause a decrease in the output of the domestic industry where the domestic product is sold by a monopoly or near-monopoly. (2) Although it may not cause a decrease of the industry's output where the domestic sellers compete to a large extent on a nonprice basis, it is likely to do so. (3) It must cause a decrease in the output of an industry in which many domestic producers are selling identical products.

This reasoning suggests that the combination of a decrease in domestic output of the liberalized industry and an increase of the competing imports may be regarded as the typical response to a reduction of import barriers.

A General View of the Effects on the Economy

A reduction of import barriers does not always affect the output of every industry or even the total output of the economy in the same direction as it affects output of the liberalized industry. Suppose, for example, that the liberalized import is a raw material, *e.g.,* wool, which enters into the domestic production of another commodity, *e.g.,* woolens. A fall in its price may cause a fall in the price of woolens, causing a transfer of buying from competing products, such as cotton goods, to woolens, thereby causing an increase in output of the woolen industry but a fall in the output of the competing cotton goods. Thus, liberalization may give rise to price-induced shifts of demand between products that have themselves not been subject to reductions of import barriers.

If cotton goods are produced mainly at home, the fall in their output will reinforce the fall in the output of wool, and their combined declines may outweigh the increase in output of woolens.

If cotton goods are obtained mainly from abroad, however, the increase in domestic output of woolens may offset the combined decreases in the domestic output of wool and cotton goods, so that there might be a net increase in total domestic output.[2]

These price repercussions may also work back to the resources used in production, further complicating the effects. If production of an import-competing commodity uses a specialized resource, a decrease in demand for the product resulting from a reduction of its import protection may cause a fall in the price of that resource. If another domestically produced commodity uses the same resource, the cost of producing the second commodity may fall, its selling price may fall, and its output expand. Thus, a reduction of barriers to imports of wool might reduce the price of domestic land used for raising sheep and might thereby stimulate domestic production of other goods that use such land. Here again, changes in relative prices create the possibility that output and employ-

---

[2] It may be noted, however, that the decrease in imports of cotton goods might cause a decrease of exports, which would strengthen the tendency for output to decline.

ment may expand elsewhere, offsetting the contraction in output of the import-competing commodity, with the possibility arising this time because of a change in the price of one of the factors used in production and a shift in its use.[3]

We must also note the possibility that a reduction of import barriers may lower prices in import-competing industries that have sales of significant size relative to total spending or may increase the range of buyers' choice. Such changes may induce domestic buyers to increase their total demand for goods and services at their pre-liberalization level of money income. An increase in total demand opposes the forces of contraction caused by the shift of demand from domestic to foreign supplies of the liberalized commodity. In some circumstances such an increase could be large enough to cause a net expansion in the demand for total output.

In addition to these changes in domestic buying, which are all induced by changes in domestic prices, a reduction of protection that increases imports affects the economy through its international transactions. If the country's international payments were in equilibrium before, the increase in its imports increases the earnings and incomes of foreign countries and also causes an outflow of gold or short-term capital (or a fall in the price of the liberalizing country's currency). Unless these changes are offset both at home and abroad, they exert downward pressure on the incomes and prices of the liberalizing country, thereby tending to reduce its imports and stimulate its exports, while the income, prices, and imports of foreign countries tend to expand and their exports to contract. These tendencies may be prevented from operating by policy actions (*e.g.,* domestic stabilization measures) or by institutional conditions (*e.g.,* price rigidities). If they operate, they may not be sufficiently strong to restore either equilibrium to international payments or full output and employment in the liberalizing country, but they work in that direction.

Thus we see that many forces are set in motion by a reduction

[3] Where production of two commodities involves significant use of a common resource, tariff, technological or other changes in demand or supply conditions affecting the production of one have caused opposite changes in production of the other. Professor Don Humphrey points out that increased domestic production of cattle, soybeans, and dairy products has displaced domestic production of wool and has increased wool imports, and that increased domestic production of rice has tended to increase the ratio of imports to domestic production of sugar. See his book *American Imports* (Twentieth Century Fund, 1955), pp. 87 and 88.

of import barriers. They often exert opposing influences on output and their net effect may be to increase as well as to decrease total buying of domestic goods, and thereby of domestic ouput and employment.

To trace out further repercussions would involve complications that need not be considered here. The influences that have already been discussed are sufficiently complex and different in direction to prevent us from making unambiguous generalizations about the direction of their net result in any particular case of liberalization. Some of these forces, however, take a relatively long period to accomplish their effects. Let us, therefore, concentrate on what appears to be the most important short-run influence on the level of total domestic output: the shift in spending from domestic to imported goods and its income-induced effects.

Effects of Shifts in Spending on Total Spending, Income, and Output

As the preceding discussion indicated, the usual result of a reduction of import barriers is a reduction in the domestic output of the liberalized product and an increase in its imports. The initial effects of such a shift are often referred to in public discussions as though they were the total effects. The initial effects, however, cause changes in income which, if not offset, may cause further changes in spending on domestic and foreign goods and in output and imports. A broad picture of how liberalization affects employment and output must include an account of these income-induced effects on output.

It should be noted that income-induced effects are not the only forces that affect total national output, imports, and other elements of national income. Although a fall in the demand for the output of a product or industry generally, after a short period of inventory adjustment, reduces actual output (except that of agricultural commodities with a long production period), the resources thus thrown out of work may be absorbed elsewhere. Their absorption may result from such market forces as wage declines in specific industries or a general decline in the country's prices and incomes relative to those of other countries, caused by a deteriorating balance of payments and a consequent tightening of credit or fall in the foreign exchange value of the currency, or it may result from the fact that the lower prices add to the purchasing power of some types of financial asset holdings and may thereby stimulate spending. If the resources thrown out of work are not thus absorbed and are of substantial magnitude relative to the whole economy, the government would take them into account in its general fiscal, credit, and other economic policies and might take curative action, if it has not already taken preventive action. Thus actual output might not decline. It is nevertheless important to know what further effects on the demand for output an initial tendency will have if it is not offset by such market forces or policy actions, and what determines how great these effects will be.

This section first analyzes the initial output effects and then analyzes those further effects that are induced by the resulting changes of income. It seeks to make clear that, if the initial changes are permitted to cause further changes in output and income, the final effects of the income changes on total output and total imports, as well as on other components of spending, may differ substantially from the initial effects.

Primary Changes in Output

A shift in spending away from a domestic product decreases the output of the industry producing it. Thus, if the import of bicycles is liberalized, the output of the domestic bicycle industry will fall. The bicycle industry, however, is only one of many industries whose output is used to make bicycles. It may only shape certain parts and assemble the bicycles, buying other parts from other industries. In any case, it must buy from other industries the materials it uses in the parts it makes for itself, the coal it uses to heat its factories, the electricity it uses to run its machines, etc. We commonly call these other industries the "steel," "coal," and "electric power" industries, but, insofar as they provide goods or services to the bicycle industry, they are engaged indirectly in the production of bicycles. If the bicycle industry reduces its output, it will buy less from these other industries, and they will reduce their outputs. Their suppliers in turn will be affected and so, in turn, will *their* suppliers. Thus, there is a widening series of effects on output throughout the economy.

The output effect on the import-competing industry—the bicycle industry in this example—we shall call the *primary direct effect*. The effects on the output of its immediate and remote suppliers we shall call *primary indirect* effects. They are necessarily in the same direction as the primary direct effects.

It should be noted that the primary indirect effects on output in this example are induced by changes in the output of the bicycle industry that are communicated to other parts of the economy by changes in purchases of one industry from another for use in current production and not by changes in the income and spending of the workers and stockholders whose labor and capital are employed in it or in the spending by industry for capital goods. For convenience they will be referred to as "output-induced" rather than "income-induced."

Similarly, when a shift of spending from domestic to imported goods causes a primary decrease of domestic output and when the direct and indirect suppliers of the liberalized industry use imported materials, the decrease of their outputs induces a reduction in their imports that is a partial offset to the increase in imports of the liberalized product. Thus, the increase in imports of bicycles is partially offset by an output-induced decrease in imports of rubber by the tire industry, which supplies the domestic bicycle industry. The increase of total imports is therefore less than the increase in imports of bicycles.[4]

Income-Induced Effects of Primary Changes

The primary direct and indirect changes of output cause changes in the income of the businesses and workers producing it, and these income changes normally lead to changes of spending

[4] All these primary output-induced changes are included in the primary or "autonomous" changes that are "multiplied" by subsequent changes of income. They are part of the multiplicand to which economists apply the "income multiplier." The additional changes allowed for by the income multiplier itself include only *income*-induced effects.

in the same direction, which in turn lead to further changes in output, employment, income, and spending. Such income-induced changes in spending are not confined to United States residents. Increases in United States imports raise the incomes of exporters in foreign countries and the dollar earnings of those countries. These changes abroad normally may be expected to lead, directly and indirectly, to increases in United States exports. Our final preparatory task is to see how these income-induced effects on output modify the primary effects.[5]

To see how initial shifts of spending from domestic production to imports affect total national output, we shall consider the initial shift as having occurred spontaneously, *e.g.*, because of a change in tastes, rather than because of a change in commercial policy.[6] Similarly, if a fall in the price of imports causes an initial increase in total demand for output, this increase may be treated as if it were a spontaneous increase in spending out of a given level of real income. In this way we can take into account some of the major effects on the demand for total output that result from a reduction in prices without taking price changes explicitly into account.

In examining the effects of the changes of income initiated by a shift of demand, we must distinguish different possible domestic and foreign reactions to income changes. We must also distinguish between cases in which a shift of demand to imports is and is not

[5] International aspects of income-induced changes have been analyzed by Lloyd A. Metzler in his articles "The Transfer Problem Reconsidered" in *Journal of Political Economy*, Vol. 50 (June 1942), and "Underemployment Equilibrium in International Trade" in *Econometrica*, Vol. 10 (April 1942), Fritz Machlup in *International Trade and the National Income Multiplier* (The Blakiston Co., 1943), Thomas C. Schelling in *National Income Behavior* (McGraw-Hill Book Co., Inc., 1951), Pt. III, and James E. Meade in *The Theory of International Economic Policy*, Vol. 1 (London: Oxford University Press, 1951), Pts. II and III.

[6] Spontaneous and tariff-induced shifts of spending have different effects on tariff revenues and foreign earnings. If they are to have the same effect on national income, specific assumptions are required about the responses of the national government to changes in tax revenues and of foreign buyers to changes in dollar earnings. If such shifts involve equal increases in the value of imports after payment of duty, their effects on national income at factor cost are the same in the two cases if the difference between the combined government and foreign expenditures in this country is the same as the difference in revenue from taxes on domestic goods. The effects on national income at (current) market prices are the same in the two cases if, despite differences in the effects on revenues from taxes on domestic goods and on foreign earnings, the difference between the combined government and foreign expenditure in this country is the same as the difference in tariff revenues.

accompanied by an increase in total domestic spending at given levels of national income. To take account of these different possibilities, we shall consider five cases.

As Case 1 let us assume a highly artificial economy in which domestic buyers do not alter the amounts of their total purchases or their imports in response to changes in their incomes (although the level of imports is affected by changes in import barriers or in preferences between domestic and foreign goods), and in which exports do not respond to changes in imports. In such an economy, a shift of domestic buying from domestic to imported goods, if not accompanied by any change in total domestic buying, would cause a fall of national output just equal to the initial shift. This fall would result from the decrease in the output of the domestic goods and services from which demand had shifted. Because we have made the assumption, admittedly unrealistic, that there would be no income-induced changes of domestic expenditures and no changes of exports when imports change, no further income-induced changes of output, income, or imports would occur.

We must now consider more realistic cases, in which the amounts that buyers want to spend on goods from all sources vary with the level of output and income, and in which their spending on imports at given levels of import barriers varies with their total spending.[7] When incomes change, the resulting alterations in spending cause further changes in output, income, and imports, until previously specified relationships are restored.

How much output and income, when displaced by a shift of demand, will change before reaching a new stable level depends on two things: first, the amount of the initial displacement; and, second, the direction and amount that output, income, and imports have to change to restore desired relationships between total spending and income and between imports and total spending.

We may see the forces that cause further changes in output and

---

[7] With unforeseen changes in income, peoples' actual spending may remain unchanged temporarily and may thereby differ from the amounts they would have spent if the changes in their incomes had been foreseen, but they will soon take steps to bring their actual spending or saving into the desired relationship with the new levels of income.

imports and why these changes are limited by considering as Case 2 a situation that is only slightly more complicated than Case 1. In Case 2, we assume that total domestic spending (*i.e.,* spending by domestic residents on domestic and foreign goods combined) varies in the same direction as the level of national income or output but by a smaller amount. We also assume that, at any given level of import barriers, the amount spent on imports varies in the same direction as the total volume of goods and services purchased by domestic buyers, but by a smaller amount. To focus attention on the effects of these two relationships, however, we continue to assume that exports remain unchanged in the face of changes in imports.

In these circumstances, a shift in demand away from domestic goods to imports has the same *initial* effect on domestic output and income as in the first case: it reduces them. But the effects cannot stop there, for income has declined while the amount of total domestic spending has not. This is contrary to our assumption that a decline of income itself causes a decline of total domestic spending. Consequently, this spending declines and output and income fall further. The question is: How much further must they fall before relationships consistent with buyers' desires are restored and the process comes to an end?

To answer this question, let us suppose that a reduction of import barriers occurs and causes a change in the direction of domestic spending so as to raise imports and reduce spending on domestic goods and services, both by $12 million. This primary reduction of domestic output reduces domestic income by the same amount. Assume also that every decline of income reduces total domestic spending by half as much. Then, when income falls by $12 million, it reduces total spending by $6 million. Suppose further, that every decline of total domestic spending decreases imports by 2/10 as much, thereby reducing spending on domestic goods and services by 8/10 as much. The $6 million fall of spending then cuts back the import increase by $1.2 million and reduces spending on domestic goods by $4.8 million. Thus, spending on domestic goods has fallen by the original $12 million plus $4.8 million or $16.8 million, and output and income have also fallen by $16.8 million. Total spending, however, has fallen by only $6 million. This is less than half of the $16.8 million decline of income, so desired relationships are not satisfied and a further decline of total spending and income occurs.

Since income has fallen by $16.8 million, total spending must decline by $8.4 million, or an additional $2.4 million. Of this further decline, however, one fifth, or $480,000, will be on imports and only $1.92 million on domestic goods. This causes an equal additional fall of domestic output and income, bringing the total decline to $18.72 million. The decline of total spending has now reached $8.4 million, but, since this is still less than half of the $18.72 million decline of income, desired relationships are still unsatisfied. It should be noted, however, that the difference between the actual and the equilibrium relations of spending to income has diminished; while before it was equal to the difference between $8.4 million and $6.0 million, which is $2.4 million, now it is equal to the difference between $9.36 million and $8.4 million, which is only $960,000. Thus an equilibrium position is being approached.

It will be attained when the decline of income has reached $20 million and has induced a decline of $10 million in total domestic spending. This does satisfy the desired relationship between changes in total spending and in income. At this point, the other relationships are also satisfied. Imports are cut back by $2 million below their original increase of $12 million. Spending on domestic goods has fallen by $8 million because of the $10 million cut in spending, and this decline, when added to the $12 million decline due to the original shift to imports, brings the decline of spending on domestic goods to $20 million, which is just equal to the decline of income generated by its production. A $20 million decline of income is therefore sufficient to bring the changes to an end.

Thus, the result of the initial $12 million shift in the allocation of total domestic spending is to cause primary and secondary decreases of output of $20 million and to leave imports only $10 million, not $12 million above their pre-liberalization level.

It is important to note this offsetting income-induced effect on imports (as well as the multiplied effect on output) because it is so often assumed that a primary shift of demand to imports at given levels of income necessarily raises the final level of imports by the same amount. Actually, it is not likely to raise it that much if it is allowed to depress domestic income and expenditure.[8]

A similar type of analysis may be applied to more complicated cases. Thus, we may consider as Case 3 what happens in a situation differing from Case 2 only in that exports, instead of being constant, vary with the level of imports, but by a smaller amount, *i.e.,* an additional dollar of imports generates less than a dollar of additional exports. Then, when domestic buyers shift some of their spending from domestic to foreign goods, the initial decline in purchases of domestic goods and services by residents of this country is partially offset by an expansion of exports. Consequently, the final effect of such a shift of expenditure is still to reduce total output and income, but by a smaller amount than in Case 2, things other than exports being equal.

The effect of an initial change in imports on exports depends, of course, on the economic reactions of foreign countries as a group. The assumption that an increase of our imports is likely to cause a smaller increase of our exports is based on a judgment as to what the typical reactions actually are. It is worth noting, however, that if an increase of imports causes an equal rise of exports, an initial shift of expenditure by domestic citizens from domestic to foreign goods leaves total national output unchanged. The depressing influence of the loss of domestic markets is exactly offset by the stimulus resulting from the export reaction, and the net effect is to leave total output unchanged. If exports increase by more than imports, this stimulating effect exceeds the initial depressing effect of the shift in spending by domestic buyers, and demand for total output increases.

In all of the foregoing cases, we assumed that the initial change was only a shift in demand by domestic buyers from domestically produced to foreign goods and services within a given total of spending, *i.e.,* it was not accompanied by any increase in their total spending at given levels of income. As we have previously noted,

---

[8] Under the assumptions made in the above case, there is still a substantial increase of imports. The income-induced decreases do not entirely wipe out the initial increase caused by the original shift in demand because we assumed that changes of income cause desired total domestic expenditure to change by a smaller amount. If total domestic expenditure changes by an amount equal to any change in income, the initial increase in imports due to the shift at the original level of income is entirely, not just partially, wiped out by the induced effects on imports. Consequently, the final level of imports is no higher than the original level, despite the shift in the allocation of spending in favor of imports.

however, a reduction of barriers to imports may cause not only a shift in the allocation of buying but an increase in its total amount at given levels of income. This can happen if the reduction of import barriers results in the importation of goods that are not available here or are available only at higher prices than the imported products. It occurs, for example, if an increase of imports displaces less than an equal value of domestic output. Moreover, the mere fall in prices of imported goods or of the domestic goods that compete with them can cause an increase in the total quantity of goods purchased at given levels of total income, even if spending does not shift to imports. We must therefore consider what happens when a shift of domestic expenditure from domestic to foreign products is accompanied by an increase, at given levels of income, in the level of total spending by domestic buyers.[9]

In considering this situation, we assume that the initial increase in total expenditure is not greater than the initial increase in imports. We must consider the consequences of these simultaneous changes, first when exports do not vary with imports and then when they do.

Let us consider, as Case 4, what happens when a shift of domestic spending from domestic to imported products is accompanied by an increase in spending by domestic residents on foreign and domestic goods combined at given levels of income, but when exports remain constant.

When the increase in spending by domestic buyers is not greater than the initial shift from domestic to foreign goods and services, what happens to spending on domestic goods and services at the initial level of income? On the one hand, the shift to imports decreases it by the amount of that shift. An increase in spending by domestic buyers, on the other hand, increases it. Part of this increase, however, is directed toward imports, so only the remaining portion is directed toward domestic goods. Since the total increase in spending by domestic buyers is no greater than the shift to im-

---

[9] The possibility that a lowered tariff will lead to an increase in both imports and total spending by domestic buyers is discussed by several authors, including Wolfgang Stolper in "The Volume of Foreign Trade and the Level of Income," in *Quarterly Journal of Economics*, Vol. 61 (February 1947), pp. 294-300, and Thomas C. Schelling in *National Income Behavior*, pp. 181-84. Stolper's argument is commented on by Gottfried Haberler in the course of his discussion "The Foreign Trade Multiplier—Comment" in *American Economic Review*, Vol. 37 (December 1947), pp. 904-06.

ports, the portion of the total increase in spending that is directed toward domestic goods must be less than the shift. We can conclude, therefore, that the initial fall of expenditure on domestic goods caused by the shift to imports exceeds the initial rise caused by the expansion of domestic expenditure. Consequently, the combined initial effect is for domestic output to decline. Under the assumption of this case that exports remain constant, it will continue to decline until a stable level is reached.[10]

What is the effect on imports? Although the increase of spending and its shift toward imports have opposite effects on spending for domestic goods and therefore on output, they both stimulate imports initially. Since there is an induced decline of income, however, the ultimate rise in imports is less than the combined initial rise.

If we compare the results in this case with those in Case 2, where exports were also assumed to be constant and where the only difference was the initial increase in domestic spending, it is obvious that, if the shift to imports is equal in the two cases, both the initial and the final depressing effects on output are smaller in this case.

Finally, we need to consider, as Case 5, what happens to total output when, again, a shift of demand to imports is accompanied by an initial increase in domestic spending at given levels of income but when exports, instead of being unrelated to imports as in Case 4, vary with imports. This is the most complicated of the situations we have considered.

In Case 4, the initial impact on domestic output had two components: a decrease resulting from the shift to imports and equal to it, and an increase equal to the portion of the additional total domestic expenditure that was devoted to domestic goods. In the present case a third change occurs: an increase of exports caused by the initial rise of imports. It is clear that if the initial shift to

[10] There are conditions under which the two simultaneous changes would leave demand for output unchanged or would raise it. If the initial increase in domestic spending at given levels of income were so big that the portion of it spent on domestic goods were just equal to the initial shift of spending away from domestic goods to imports, total output would remain unchanged. If it were larger than the initial shift, demand for total output would increase, although total output itself could not do so if resources were already fully utilized. In these cases the ultimate rise of imports would equal or exceed the initial rise. However, these appear to be unlikely results of a reduction of import barriers.

imports and the initial addition to total expenditure are equal to those of Case 4, the initial decrease of output in this case will be smaller than in Case 4 because a portion of the increase in imports is reflected back, at the initial level of domestic income, in the form of increased exports. In fact, the addition of the export reaction may cause the demand for output to increase when, without this reaction, it would decrease.

These initial changes normally cause further changes of income in the same direction, and, as we have seen, these changes have a limit. In Case 4 exports were constant and therefore did not affect that limit. In the present case they do affect it. They make necessary a larger total change of output for any given initial change than was necessary in Case 4. Nevertheless, the final decrease of output is smaller in Case 5, where exports do respond to changes in imports, than in Case 4, where they do not.[11]

We may conclude that in the present case, where the shift to imports is accompanied both by a rise in domestic expenditure at given levels of income and by induced export reactions, total output may either rise or fall, depending on how much exports change in response to given changes in imports.

Relation of the Employment Estimates to All Employment Effects

Our consideration of the above cases has made it clear that when demand shifts from domestic to foreign goods, the initial or primary change of output—and therefore of employment—is by no means the total change. The primary change induces changes in some, perhaps all, of the components of expenditure, and these induced changes of expenditure cause further changes of output and income. We have seen that the relation between the initial change and the total change depends on the responses of the particular economy we are considering as well as on those of the rest of the

[11] This results from the fact that although the multiplier in Case 5 exceeds that in Case 4, it does so by a smaller percentage than the excess of the initial effect in Case 4 over the initial effect in Case 5.

world. These responses depend on how much corporate and consumer saving, private domestic investment, and government expenditures change as a result of changes in national income. The amounts of these changes, in turn, are influenced by the tax structure, corporate dividend policy, the structure of unemployment insurance benefits, the character of imports, how changes in total domestic spending are distributed among its various components, the effect of changes in domestic output and income on the relative prices of competing domestic and imported goods and services, and many other factors.

Some of these changes can be estimated with reasonable accuracy and others cannot. Still others depend on policy decisions. For example, a policy of changing public expenditure in a direction opposite to income-induced changes of tax revenue would diminish the induced effects on output of a given initial change, while a policy of changing expenditures in the same direction as tax revenues change so as to maintain an initial state of budget balance or imbalance would aggravate these induced effects. Such reactions were taken into account in the above cases, although only implicitly.

Even so, these cases are all highly simplified when compared with reality. They do not take into account, even implicitly, certain other effects that were mentioned in the first part of this chapter, such as the effects on the prices of economic resources.

This study does not attempt to estimate any of these domestic behavior reactions. Others have already made ambitious estimates of some or many of them and nothing would be added by an attempt to deal with them here.[12] In the remaining, quantitative part of this study, we shall confine our attention to the employment equivalents of (1) the initial shift in spending from domestic to foreign goods and (2) the increase in exports associated with this shift.

Estimates will be given of the employment changes accompanying both types of change. The effect of the first, which is considered in Part II, is the employment effect of the *primary* change

[12] The most ambitious effort to estimate these domestic reactions empirically is that made by Lawrence R. Klein and Arthur S. Goldberger in their study *An Econometric Model of the United States* (Amsterdam: North-Holland Publishing Company, 1955).

of output caused by a shift in domestic spending from protected domestic products to the corresponding imported products. The estimates of this effect, which are presented in the next chapter, include both direct and indirect (*i.e.,* output-induced) employ-ment effects but do not include employment effects induced either by changes of private income, government revenue, or exports (such as were considered in Cases 2 to 5) or by other secondary changes. They also allow for no initial expansion of total domes-tic spending, such as was considered in Cases 4 and 5. They would therefore be equivalent to the *total* changes of employment only in an economy that behaved in accordance with the assumptions of Case 1, *i.e.,* in an economy where changes of income induce no secondary changes of spending on domestic output, either by domestic or by foreign buyers. These estimates may also be con-sidered as corresponding to the *initial* effects of Case 2.

Part III gives estimates of the effects on domestic employment of the increase in exports arising from the assumed initial rise of imports and, in Chapter 9, combines the estimates of Parts II and III. The resulting net employment effects thus represent the net initial effects described more generally in this chapter as Case 3.

In Chapter 10 of Part IV it is pointed out that the estimates of Part II can be adjusted to take account of the possibility that, when import barriers are reduced, the displacement of domestic output is less than the initial increase in imports. This possibility implies that the shift of spending may be accompanied by an in-crease in the quantity of the liberalized product purchased. If this increase is not accompanied by a decrease in total spending on other products, it represents an example of an initial shift in the allocation of spending being accompanied by an initial increase in its total amount. It then represents one of the possibilities con-sidered in this chapter as Cases 4 and 5.

PART
11
Displacement of Domestic Output

CHAPTER 3

Primary Effects of Liberalization on Employment

THIS CHAPTER PRESENTS estimates of the primary short-term effects on domestic employment that occur when the domestic output of an industry declines because reductions of import barriers protecting it cause domestic buyers to shift their spending from domestic goods to imported goods by a specified amount. In this statement, the words "estimates," "primary," "short-term," and "shift . . . by a specified amount" imply many limitations that must be explained fully.

What the Estimates Measure

Some of the effects to be expected from reductions of import barriers were described in Chapter 2 in detail; others were referred to briefly. It is not feasible to make quantitative estimates of all these effects. Accordingly, it is necessary to make clear which of them are included in the estimates.

Inclusion of Primary Indirect Effects

The estimates are not confined to the direct effects on employment that are felt in the "liberalized" industry (*i.e.*, the industry making products similar to the liberalized imports); they include also the effects on employment in the industries that supply the liberalized industry, in those that supply these suppliers, and so on throughout the economy. They also tell us what groups of industries feel these employment effects and how great are the effects in each group—important questions in connection with any contemplated reductions of import barriers.

The fact that the estimates include employment effects in industries other than the one liberalized does not mean that they give us all the information we need to appraise fully the employment effects of reducing import barriers. The estimates have some limitations and rest on some assumptions that must also be explained before the estimates are presented.

Exclusion of Secondary Effects

When liberalization causes reductions of domestic output and employment, incomes decrease. As the preceding chapter explained, these decreases of income are likely to induce decreases of domestic spending and consequently some further reductions of output and employment. The estimates in this book do not include changes in employment associated with these income-induced changes in domestic spending, and the estimates in this chapter do not include the changes in employment associated with induced changes in exports.

Estimates as Ratios to Import Increases

The estimates refer to primary employment effects *per million dollars of increase in imports,* not to the *total* primary employment effect that would accompany some specified reduction of import barriers. The reasons for formulating the problem in this way and the implications of doing so require fuller explanation.

In order to know how domestic output and employment would be affected by a specified reduction of a tariff barrier, we would have to know how much of the total supply, both domestic and foreign, offered for sale in the United States would be purchased at various prices and how the total purchases would be distributed between the domestically produced and imported goods. The amount of the purchases depends on responses to price changes by both domestic and foreign producers and by both domestic and foreign buyers. Unfortunately, little is known about the amounts of these responses. Therefore, we have no reliable basis for estimating how large a shift of buying from domestic to foreign goods would occur under any specified import liberalization program.[1]

Furthermore, even if we could get or make reliable estimates of the shifts of buying associated with a specified import liberalization program, the estimates of the resulting employment effects would be valid only for that liberalization program, which would be only one of an infinite number of possible programs.

For these two reasons, no effort is made in this study to link the amount of the employment change to any specified program of liberalization. Instead, the estimates give the amount of primary employment change per million-dollar shift in buying from domestic to imported goods.

Domestic employment effects are of course directly related to changes in domestic output. By measuring employment effects in relation to increases in imports, we are implying a specific ratio of increases in imports to decreases in domestic output: viz., that they are of equal value in 1953 domestic prices. If one is willing to assume that this ratio of import increases to domestic output decreases is the same for all levels of import increases, the resulting estimates can readily be applied to any assumed import increases, irrespective of their amount.

Let us see what is implied by the assumption that an increase of a million dollars in imports is accompanied by a decrease of a million dollars in final purchases of the competing domestic product, when both changes are valued at prices in the United States market before the reduction of import barriers.

If we also assume that the imported and domestic products sell at the same price in domestic markets, the assumption of equal value substitution implies that the corresponding changes in physical quantities of imports and domestic output are also equal. Equal quantity changes, in turn, imply that the quantity of the product bought by domestic buyers from all sources, domestic and foreign combined, is unchanged. If prices have fallen, which is the

---

[1] Howard S. Piquet, in *Aid, Trade and the Tariff* (Thomas Y. Crowell Company, 1953), estimated some of these responses for a number of protected commodities after consultation with commodity experts. But, as Dr. Piquet himself says, his estimates are still guesses. While Dr. Piquet's book gives "guesstimates" of the amount of increase in imports, which is what he was chiefly interested in, it does not estimate the decrease in purchases of United States output that is associated with the import increases. Others have used econometric methods to make estimates of supply and demand responses to price changes for a few protected commodities, primarily agricultural.

typical result of liberalization, this constancy means that the domestic demand responses to price changes are zero. Since domestic demand responses are presumably not less than zero and are virtually certain to be greater in most cases, the assumption of equal value substitution adopted in this study, if coupled with the assumption that imports and domestic output sell at the same prices, would lead to an overestimate of employment decreases.

The assumption that imported and domestic goods sell at the same prices is not necessarily implied by equal value substitution, however, and is not implied in the present study. Imported products may sell for less than domestic products in the domestic market. In that case, substitution of equal values at the pre-liberalization prices implies that domestic buyers buy larger quantities when import barriers are reduced. If imports sell for more than domestic products, equal value substitution implies that they buy less. Whatever the relationship between prices of imported and domestic products, however, the assumption of equal value substitution does imply that imports are substituted for domestic goods in some fixed quantitative relationship, viz., the ratio that the price of domestic goods bears to the domestic price of imported goods.[2]

Composition of Assumed Import Increases

A given dollar value of shift between domestic output and imports can be associated with physical quantities, of course, only by specifying the prices at which these dollar values are measured. In this study the domestic output displaced represents a million dollars of output valued at 1953 factory prices. The import increases represent increases costing a million dollars in the United States at 1953 "domestic port values," *i.e.*, after payment of 1953 tariff duties and costs of international shipment.

Separate estimates are given for the effects of import competition with each of 72 industries that had significant protection in the form of barriers against imports in 1953 and that passed cer-

[2] If the reader rejects the assumption of equal value substitution at 1953 prices, he may adjust the estimates of this study to reflect whatever assumptions about value substitution he cares to make. How to make this adjustment is explained in Chapter 10 and Appendix G.

tain other tests designed to reduce the likelihood of error in the results. (These industries are listed in Table 3.1). Thus, there are separate estimates of the effects of one-million-dollar increases in imports of bicycles and motorcycles, of one-million-dollar increases in imports of watches and clocks, and so on.

This does not mean, however, that each of the 72 one-million-dollar increases of imports consists of imports of a single homogeneous commodity. It consists, rather, of products competing with those of one industry. These industries represent only a 200-fold division of the economy, and each one produces more than one commodity, usually a large number of commodities.[3]

The import increases in each of the 72 industry cases considered here consist, therefore, of a collection or "basket" of protected commodities similar to those produced by that domestic industry. For example, the million-dollar increase of imports of "watches and clocks," one of the most homogeneous of the 72 industries whose liberalization we consider, consists of watches, clocks, and watch cases. How the composition of each million-dollar industry basket was determined is indicated in Chapter 4.

To summarize these points, the estimates represent the primary direct and indirect employment change associated with a shift of buying from the output of a domestic industry to corresponding imports, when both the initial decrease in domestic output and the increase in competing imports have a value of a million dollars at 1953 domestic market prices. Thus, the estimates are not absolute numbers but coefficients, which represent employment effects per million dollars of import increases accompanied by domestic output decreases of equal value.[4]

[3] The data on interindustry relationships available for making the estimates divide total economic activity, except for construction, into 200 industries and show buying and selling relationships (in the base year) among them all. Each of these 200 industries can be regarded as consisting of several subindustries, but the data do not show the buying and selling relationships among these subindustries. Without knowledge of these subindustry interrelationships, there is no basis for estimating the primary effects of changes in one subindustry's output on all other subindustries. Therefore, it is not possible to estimate accurately the total primary effects of reducing the output of any grouping smaller than a 200-order industry. This makes it undesirable to try to estimate the total primary effects of import increases that compete with domestic output of only a limited portion of a 200-order industry. Their primary direct effects can be estimated, of course, since they do not involve interindustry relations.

[4] The portion of the estimates representing gross decreases of employment are equally valid for all reductions of domestic output having equal magnitude and similar composition, whatever their cause.

It follows from this characteristic of the estimates that, before they can be used to estimate the employment effects of any proposed program of import liberalization, an estimate of how much domestic output and imports would change must be obtained from other sources, and it must be assumed that the ratio of employment changes to output changes implied by these estimates is valid irrespective of the size of the output changes. This means that the information provided is not sufficient, although it is necessary, to answer questions about the primary employment effect of any specified United States import liberalization program.

It also follows from this characteristic of the estimates, however, that they are applicable to many different liberalization programs. This flexibility arises from the fact that the separate results of liberalizations in different industries can be combined in any way to get estimates of the employment effects of a specific liberalization program.

A General Warning About Assumptions

Finally, before presenting the estimates, it must be emphasized that they involve a number of assumptions other than those already mentioned. Assumptions are unavoidable in estimates such as these, and in some cases there is little choice about them.

For example, because the estimates in this study seek to identify the industries in which the employment effects occur, they have to be made by a technique that makes certain assumptions about interindustry relations. As generally applied, this technique assumes that when a domestic industry's output is reduced, it decreases its purchases of the raw materials and the other goods and services it uses in its current production in proportion to the reduction in its output. It also assumes that all the industries supplying these goods and services reduce their output by an amount equal to the decline in their sales, that these supplying industries in turn reduce purchases of their supplies when they reduce output, and so on.[5]

---

[5] This method of studying interindustry relations was first devised and was applied before World War II by W. W. Leontief of Harvard University. See *The Structure of*

This assumption does not have to be rigidly applied, however. Empirical evidence indicates that in six agricultural industries—farm dairy products, food grains and feed crops, cotton, tobacco, oil-bearing crops, and "all other agricultural products"—output is not likely to respond much in short periods to decreases in demand, although the industries that process their products, which are classified as manufacturing industries, do respond to such changes. Accordingly, the application of the technique was modified to incorporate the assumption that output and employment in these six industries do not readily respond to decreases in demand for their products and that they, in turn, do not buy less from their own suppliers.

It may be noted that a method of estimating that is based on observed data about interindustry relations, besides giving the distribution of primary employment effects among industries, can also give a more accurate estimate of the total effect than could be obtained by simply dividing the assumed output change in the liberalized industry by average value added per man in the whole economy.[6]

---

the American Economy, 1919–1939, 1st ed. (Harvard University Press, 1941); 2d. ed. (Oxford University Press, 1951). It was later applied in greater detail by the U. S. Bureau of Labor Statistics. The work of the Bureau is described by W. D. Evans and M. Hoffenberg in "The Interindustry Relations Study for 1947," *Review of Economics and Statistics,* Vol. 34 (May 1952), pp. 97-142. A simplified explanation of this method for nonprofessional readers is given by Leontief in "Input-Output Economics," *Scientific American,* Vol. 185 (October 1951), and by two articles, "Demand Under the Microscope" and "Facts for New Forecasts," in *The Economist* (London, Sept. 19, and 26, 1953). Appraisals of the method are to be found in Robert Dorfman's "The Nature and Significance of Input-Output," *Review of Economics and Statistics,* Vol. 36 (May 1954), pp. 121-33, and in *Input-Output Analysis: An Appraisal,* Studies in Income and Wealth, Vol. 18, by the Conference on Research in Income and Wealth, National Bureau of Economic Research (Princeton University Press, 1955). These are only a few references to the large literature on this subject that has developed since the war.

[6] Estimates obtained by using two variants of value added per man are given in Chapter 4 and are compared with those obtained by the method of this study. (See pp. 95-97.) The greater potential accuracy of the interindustry relations method arises from the fact that value added per man varies greatly from industry to industry. If one divides the value of output of a particular industry by the average value added per man for a group of industries, the estimate of employment will be accurate only if the average value added per man combines the different industries in proportion to their contribution to the particular industry's output. The average value added per man in the whole economy is far too crude an average to apply to the change in output of an individual industry. Estimates derived by this method give to the value added per man in each of the country's various industries a weight proportionate to the industry's contribution to total national production, not to its contribution to the product of any individual industry. Thus, an industry that contributes much to the national product, *e.g.,* food processing, has a weight in the

Where it was possible to choose among several assumptions, a considerable effort was made to base the choice on empirical evidence as to which was the most realistic. For example, it was regarded as reasonable to assume that changes of output are accompanied by proportionate changes of employment in commodity producing industries, but this could not be assumed for the service industries. Accordingly, a special study was made of the relations between output and employment changes in these industries to find the best relationship to use.[7]

Where there was no firm empirical basis for choosing between alternative assumptions and where the direction of the effects could be identified, the assumption that involves the greater decrease in employment was chosen. This choice was made so that any error in the estimates would tend to be in the direction of overstating rather than understating employment decreases and thereby enabling us to be as confident as possible that the results "tell the worst," from a short-run point of view .

The last point may be illustrated by the assumption already mentioned that an increase of imports valued at a million dollars in the United States after payment of duty is associated with a million-dollar decrease in domestic output. If the imported and domestic products sold at the same price before liberalization, this assumption of equal value substitution implies that the corresponding changes in quantities of imports and domestic output are also equal, which implies that the quantity of the product bought from all sources, domestic and foreign combined, remains unchanged when the import barriers are reduced. When buyers take larger rather than unchanged total quantities at lower prices, the decrease of domestic output is actually less, per million dollars of import increase, than the estimates assume, and the employment decrease is actually less than they indicate.

---

national average of value added per man that is likely to be wholly disproportionate to its contribution to the value of nonfood products such as textiles or watches, in whose liberalization we may be interested. There is, in fact, no accurate way of telling how much various industries contribute to the change of output of any one industry without using studies of interindustry relations such as underlie the present estimates.

[7] The evidence indicates that this assumption of proportionate changes is also not realistic for individual firms in some commodity producing industries, but considerations relating to the distribution of output decreases among firms made it seem a reasonable assumption to apply in the present study. These considerations are explained in Chapter 4.

Estimates of Primary Effects on Employment

The estimates of primary effects on employment, for each of the 72 industries whose liberalization is examined, are presented in Table 3.1. They represent the primary net decreases in domestic employment caused when domestic buying shifts from the protected domestic products of an industry to corresponding imported products. The decreases are *net* decreases because the process of importation involves some increases of domestic employment, and these increases have been subtracted from the decreases.[8]

The figures for employment in nonagricultural industries refer to the number of employees, rather than production workers, while those for agricultural industries include, in addition to employees in the strict sense, farmers and unpaid farm family workers. (All these workers will be referred to, however, by the term "employees.") The amount of employment effect in most industries represents the number of employees that would be required if the average number of hours worked per employee were the same in each industry as it was in 1953. The concept of full-time equivalent employment is used only in the case of agriculture.

We are now in a position to consider what the estimates show. It should be borne in mind that although they cover a wide range of protected industries, they do not cover all of them. The employment effects of liberalizing some protected industries could not be reliably estimated. Since the tests used to determine the probability of making reliable estimates may have introduced some bias into the choice of industries, the 72 industries analyzed may not be representative of all protected industries.

Total Primary Employment Effects

The median net primary decrease of employment in the 72 cases is 114 employees per million-dollar increase in imports. One

[8] The estimates shown in Table 3.1 differ slightly from those given by Walter S. Salant, with the collaboration of Beatrice N. Vaccara in "Primary Effects on Employment of Shifts in Demand from Domestic to Foreign Products," *The Review of Economics and Statistics*, Vol. 40, Pt. 2, Supplement (February 1958) because the latter do not take into account the employment increases in the ocean transportation and other industries participating in the process of importation.

Chart 3.1

Frequency Distribution of Total Net Primary Employment Effects

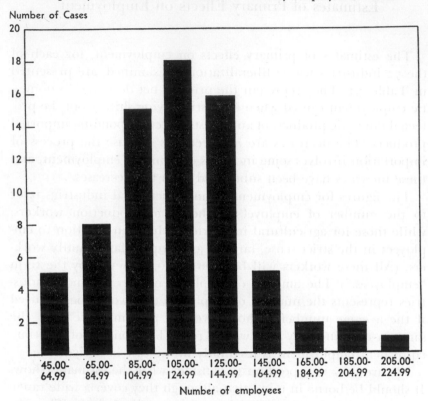

Source: Based on Column 1 of Table 3.1

of the most striking conclusions to be drawn from the estimates is the great variation around this median caused by the liberalizations of different industries. The primary decreases range from a minimum of 51 employees for liberalization of the grain mill products industry (industry #24) and an almost equally low figure of 53 employees in the case of the processed dairy products industry (#22) to a maximum of 214 employees in the case of the vegetables and fruits industry (#8). (The median, the extremes, and also the first and third quartiles and the range between them, are shown at the bottom of Table 3.1.)

The frequency with which different net decreases occur is

shown in Chart 3.1. As this chart shows, few cases are near the extremes. Out of the 72 cases examined, the total primary employment effect of liberalization in 49 cases, or nearly two thirds of those examined, is between 85 and 145 employees (using round numbers). Even this range, however, is quite large.

Reasons for Variation
in Total Primary Effects

Why do the total primary employment effects differ so much as we go from case to case? These effects, as presented in Table 3.1, are the net effects of gross decreases of employment, resulting from the decline of domestic output in the liberalized industry, partially offset by much smaller increases of employment associated with the process of importation. The total gross changes in each case are shown in the body of Table 3.2, and the characteristics of their distribution are shown at the end of the table. In all but one case the increases associated with importation are small relative to the gross decrease. We may therefore ignore them and concentrate on the difference in the gross decreases in seeking the reason for differences in the net decreases.

We may conceive of the value of domestic output of the liberalized industry as the sum of value added by many different industries—the liberalized industry, its suppliers, their suppliers and so on. The initial million-dollar decrease in domestic output of a liberalized industry in any case may thus be thought of as the sum of decreases in the value added by itself and by all these other industries. In each industry, moreover, a given change in value added is accompanied by a decrease of employment reflecting the ratio of change in employment to change in value added that characterizes the industry's production at the relevant scale of operations. The gross primary decrease of employment in all industries, per million dollars of initial decrease in output of any liberalized industry, is therefore merely a weighted average of these characteristic employment decreases in the affected industries per million-dollar decrease in their own values added, the weights being the values that each industry adds per dollar of initial change in output of the liberalized industry.

Table 3.1

Total Net Primary Employment Effects of Liberalization and Their
Distribution Between Liberalized and All Other Industries[a]

(Number of employees, farmers, and unpaid farm family workers)

	Liberalized Industry	Effect in All Industries	Effect in Liberalized Industry		Effect in Non-Liberalized Industries	
Code Number	Title	Number	Number	Per Cent of Total Effect	Number	Per Cent of Total Effect
		(1)	(2)	(3)	(4)	(5)
1	Meat animals and products.............	92.16	74.38	80.71	17.78	19.29
8	Vegetables and fruits..................	213.90	193.62	90.52	20.28	9.48
13	Lead and zinc mining..................	161.08	128.35	79.68	32.73	20.32
21	Meat packing and wholesale poultry.....	106.36	24.41	22.95	81.95	77.05
22	Processed dairy products..............	52.66	25.49	48.40	27.17	51.60
24	Grain mill products...................	50.77	16.90	33.29	33.87	66.71
27	Sugar................................	62.35	46.17	74.05	16.18	25.95
28	Alcoholic beverages...................	82.75	43.21	52.22	39.54	47.78
29	Tobacco manufactures.................	69.27	42.54	61.41	26.73	38.59
30	Spinning, weaving and dyeing..........	135.37	97.57	72.08	37.80	27.92
31	Special textile products................	105.54	73.57	69.71	31.97	30.29
34	Apparel..............................	194.18	133.87	68.94	60.31	31.06
35	House furnishings and other non-apparel..	132.20	47.74	36.11	84.46	63.89
38	Plywood..............................	139.08	80.93	58.19	58.15	41.81
40	Wood containers and cooperage........	159.33	93.87	58.91	65.46	41.09
41	Wood furniture.......................	169.90	102.76	60.48	67.14	39.52
45	Paper and board mills.................	83.60	39.98	47.82	43.62	52.18
46	Converted paper products.............	112.19	59.62	53.14	52.57	46.86
49	Industrial organic chemicals...........	75.01	35.19	46.91	39.82	53.09
51	Synthetic rubber.....................	62.56	19.25	30.77	43.31	69.23
52	Synthetic fiber.......................	90.20	55.10	61.09	35.10	38.91
54	Drugs and medicines..................	118.15	52.29	44.26	65.86	55.74
56	Paints and allied products.............	66.59	42.05	63.15	24.54	36.85
59	Vegetable oils........................	69.37	20.58	29.67	48.79	70.33
61	Miscellaneous chemical industries.......	103.97	35.77	34.40	68.20	65.60
65	Tires and inner tubes.................	91.60	44.68	48.78	46.92	51.22
66	Miscellaneous rubber products..........	116.86	76.62	65.57	40.24	34.43
67	Leather tanning and finishing..........	79.66	62.50	78.46	17.16	21.54
69	Footwear, except rubber...............	178.12	132.58	74.43	45.54	25.57
70	Glass................................	115.05	86.73	75.38	28.32	24.62
73	Pottery and related products...........	189.05	163.22	86.34	25.83	13.66
79.1	Carbon steel works and rolling mills.....	85.03	51.34	60.38	33.69	39.62
79.2	Alloy steel works and rolling mills, except stainless...........................	87.74	53.75	61.26	33.99	38.74
79.3	Stainless steel works and rolling mills....	90.85	72.82	80.15	18.03	19.85
85	Primary zinc.........................	94.60	36.29	38.36	58.31	61.64
88	Primary aluminum, including alumina....	62.32	29.95	48.06	32.37	51.94
89	Aluminum rolling and drawing.........	79.51	43.85	55.15	35.66	44.85
93	Tin cans and other tinware.............	105.88	42.11	39.77	63.77	60.23
94	Cutlery..............................	122.48	82.61	67.45	39.87	32.55
95	Tools and general hardware............	130.18	89.16	68.49	41.02	31.51
103	Lighting fixtures.....................	138.36	66.70	48.21	71.66	51.79
105	Metal barrels, drums, etc..............	103.93	42.89	41.27	61.04	58.73
106	Tubes and foils.......................	100.09	43.95	43.91	56.14	56.09
116	Machine tools and metalworking machinery..................................	108.36	62.90	58.05	45.46	41.95
118	Special industrial machinery...........	136.89	84.98	62.08	51.91	37.92
123	Industrial machinery n.e.c.............	123.09	55.66	45.22	67.43	54.78
127	Ball and roller bearings...............	125.39	94.46	75.33	30.93	24.67
131	Motors and generators.................	128.98	73.76	57.19	55.22	42.81
132	Transformers........................	112.85	60.50	53.61	52.35	46.39
133	Electrical control apparatus............	114.47	67.39	58.87	47.08	41.13
134	Electrical welding apparatus...........	101.92	31.10	30.51	70.82	69.49

Table 3.1 (*continued*)

Liberalized Industry		Effect in All Industries	Effect in Liberalized Industry		Effect in Non-liberalized Industries	
Code Number	Title	Number	Number	Per Cent of Total Effect	Number	Per Cent of Total Effect
		(1)	(2)	(3)	(4)	(5)
135	Electrical appliances..................	133.87	52.61	39.30	81.26	60.70
136	Insulated wire and cable..............	95.62	43.90	45.91	51.72	54.09
138	Electric lamps.......................	109.33	72.74	66.53	36.59	33.47
139	Radio and related products............	154.88	80.46	51.95	74.42	48.05
141	Communication equipment............	132.37	91.95	69.46	40.42	30.54
142	Storage batteries.....................	95.83	46.52	48.54	49.31	51.46
143	Primary batteries.....................	118.12	80.39	68.06	37.73	31.94
145.1	Passenger cars and light trucks..........	123.77	32.67	26.40	91.10	73.60
145.2	Heavy trucks and buses...............	113.20	32.90	29.06	80.30	70.94
145.3	Motor vehicle parts and accessories......	102.89	32.81	31.89	70.08	68.11
148	Aircraft and parts....................	118.44	76.31	64.43	42.13	35.57
152	Motorcycles and bicycles..............	128.06	67.66	52.83	60.40	47.17
154	Optical, ophthalmic and photo equipment.	127.91	83.92	65.61	43.99	34.39
156	Watches and clocks...................	136.49	94.82	69.47	41.67	30.53
157	Jewelry and silverware	136.46	90.95	66.65	45.51	33.35
158	Musical instruments and parts	135.01	97.42	72.16	37.59	27.84
159	Toys and sporting goods..............	157.48	100.12	63.58	57.36	36.42
160	Office supplies.......................	128.56	87.41	67.99	41.15	32.01
161	Plastic products......................	121.79	77.79	63.87	44.00	36.13
162	Cork products.......................	87.09	48.61	55.82	38.48	44.18
164	Miscellaneous manufactured products....	154.76	77.20	49.88	77.56	50.12
	Minimum...........................	50.77	16.90	22.95	16.18	9.48
	1st quartile..........................	91.22	43.05	46.41	35.38	31.98
	Median.............................	113.84	62.70	58.53	44.00	41.47
	3rd quartile.........................	133.12	84.45	68.02	60.36	53.59
	Maximum...........................	213.90	193.62	90.52	91.10	77.05
	Interquartile range...................	41.90	41.40	21.61	24.98	21.61

ᵃ Figures are estimated decreases of employment per million-dollar increase of imports after subtraction of increases associated with the process of importation.

It is obvious from this fact that if the change in an industry's employment, per million-dollar change in its own value added, were the same for all industries in the economy, it would make no difference how much any one industry contributed to the output of a liberalized industry; the total employment change per initial million-dollar change in the liberalized industry's output would always be the same, no matter what industry was liberalized. Differences in the total gross decreases among different cases of liberalization are possible only because the employment changes per million dollars of change in value added do in fact differ among industries. Since the employment change per million-dollar change in its value added remains the same for a given industry as we go from case to case, it follows that the difference among

Table 3.2

Gross and Net Primary Employment Effects of Liberalization[a]

(Number of employees, farmers, and unpaid farm family workers)

Liberalized Industry		Primary Gross Decrease Caused By Reduced Spending on Domestic Goods	Primary Increase Associated with Increased Importation of Liberalized Products[b]	Primary Net Decrease
Code Number	Title			
		(1)	(2)	(3)
1	Meat animals and products....................	95.84	3.68*	92.16*
8	Vegetables and fruits.........................	224.45	10.55*	213.90*
13	Lead and zinc mining.........................	164.85	3.77*	161.08*
21	Meat packing and wholesale poultry.............	107.99	1.63	106.36
22	Processed dairy products......................	54.27	1.61	52.66
24	Grain mill products...........................	51.15	.38	50.77
27	Sugar..	67.38	5.03*	62.35*
28	Alcoholic beverages..........................	85.39	2.64*	82.75*
29	Tobacco manufactures........................	69.99	.72	69.27
30	Spinning, weaving and dyeing..................	136.41	1.04	135.37
31	Special textile products.......................	106.85	1.31	105.54
34	Apparel......................................	195.41	1.23	194.18
35	House furnishings and other non-apparel.........	134.91	2.71*	132.20*
38	Plywood.....................................	139.24	.16	139.08
40	Wood containers and cooperage.................	166.64	7.31*	159.33*
41	Wood furniture...............................	170.72	.82	169.90
45	Paper and board mills.........................	84.29	.69	83.60
46	Converted paper products.....................	114.88	2.69*	112.19*
49	Industrial organic chemicals...................	79.41	4.40*	75.01*
51	Synthetic rubber.............................	65.20	2.64*	62.56*
52	Synthetic fiber...............................	91.32	1.12	90.20
54	Drugs and medicines..........................	118.58	.43	118.15
56	Paints and allied products.....................	90.55	23.96*c	66.59*c
59	Vegetable oils................................	71.12	1.75	69.37
61	Miscellaneous chemical industries...............	105.32	1.35	103.97
65	Tires and inner tubes.........................	92.07	.47	91.60
66	Miscellaneous rubber products..................	117.26	.40	116.86
67	Leather tanning and finishing..................	80.10	.44	79.66
69	Footwear, except rubber.......................	178.58	.46	178.12
70	Glass..	115.75	.70	115.05
73	Pottery and related products...................	189.43	.38	189.05
79.1	Carbon steel works and rolling mills.............	90.79	5.76*	85.03*
79.2	Alloy steel works and rolling mills, except stainless.	93.50	5.76*	87.74*
79.3	Stainless steel works and rolling mills...........	96.61	5.76*	90.85*
85	Primary zinc.................................	95.40	.80	94.60
88	Primary aluminum, including alumina...........	62.72	.40	62.32
89	Aluminum rolling and drawing.................	79.51	d	79.51
93	Tin cans and other tinware.....................	106.10	.22	105.88
94	Cutlery......................................	122.70	.22	122.48
95	Tools and general hardware....................	130.39	.21	130.18
103	Lighting fixtures.............................	138.36	d	138.36
105	Metal barrels, drums, etc.....................	103.93	d	103.93
106	Tubes and foils...............................	100.62	.53	100.09
116	Machine tools and metalworking machinery.......	109.05	.69	108.36
118	Special industrial machinery...................	137.54	.65	136.89
123	Industrial machinery n.e.c....................	123.42	.33	123.09
127	Ball and roller bearings.......................	125.86	.47	125.39
131	Motors and generators........................	129.23	.25	128.98
132	Transformers.................................	112.85	d	112.85
133	Electrical control apparatus...................	114.47	d	114.47
134	Electrical welding apparatus...................	102.03	.11	101.92
135	Electrical appliances..........................	134.30	.43	133.87
136	Insulated wire and cable......................	99.71	4.09*	95.62*
138	Electric lamps................................	109.48	.15	109.33
139	Radio and related products....................	155.15	.27	154.88

Table 3.2 (*continued*)

Liberalized Industry		Primary Gross Decrease Caused By Reduced Spending on Domestic Goods	Primary Increase Associated with Increased Importation of Liberalized Products[b]	Primary Net Decrease
Code Number	Title			
		(1)	(2)	(3)
141	Communication equipment....................	132.53	.16	132.37
142	Storage batteries...........................	96.09	.26	95.83
143	Primary batteries...........................	118.12	d	118.12
145.1	Passenger cars and light trucks................	124.48	.71	123.77
145.2	Heavy trucks and buses......................	113.90	.70	113.20
145.3	Motor vehicle parts and accessories............	103.59	.70	102.89
148	Aircraft and parts..........................	119.80	1.36	118.44
152	Motorcycles and bicycles.....................	129.43	1.37	128.06
154	Optical, ophthalmic and photo equipment........	128.26	.35	127.91
156	Watches and clocks..........................	137.54	1.05	136.49
157	Jewelry and silverware.......................	136.76	.30	136.46
158	Musical instruments and parts.................	135.38	.37	135.01
159	Toys and sporting goods......................	157.86	.38	157.48
160	Office supplies..............................	134.79	6.23*	128.56*
161	Plastic products............................	123.05	1.26	121.79
162	Cork products..............................	88.16	1.07	87.09
164	Miscellaneous manufactured products...........	157.31	2.55*	154.76*
	Minimum..................................	51.15	0	50.77
	1st quartile................................	94.45	.34	91.22
	Median....................................	114.68	.70	113.84
	3rd quartile................................	134.85	1.69	133.12
	Maximum..................................	224.45	23.96	213.90
	Interquartile range	40.40	1.35	41.90

* Increases and net decreases take account of indirect effects of direct increases in ocean freight and insurance industries.

a Figures state estimated changes of employment per million-dollar increase of imports.

b Except in cases marked with an asterisk, increases include only direct increases in ocean freight and insurance industries.

c Estimated increase due to process of importation is regarded as unreliable in this case.

d Less than .005.

the cases reflects the difference in the relative contributions that the various industries make, in terms of value added, to the initial changes of output of different liberalized industries.[9]

Thus, a large total gross decrease in employment from liberalization of a particular industry means that a large proportion of the change in the value of its output is added in industries that have large employment changes per million dollars of value added. It does not necessarily mean that the liberalized industry itself has

[9] The procedure actually used in these estimates requires a minor qualification of this statement. When an industry is the one liberalized, the effects on its output have been divided into direct and indirect components, and these output effects have been converted into employment effects separately. (See Chap. 4, pp. 89ff.) The implied ratio of employment change to change in value added may be different for these two components. As a result, the difference between cases is not entirely the result of differences in the relative contribution that each industry makes to a dollar of output of different liberalized industries.

a large employment change in relation to its change in value added, for other industries with that characteristic may contribute much to the change in the total value of its output.

Distribution of Primary Employment Effects
Between Liberalized and Other Industries

The second striking thing about the results is that the percentage of the total net primary effect that occurs in the liberalized industry varies greatly from case to case. This result is contrary to the common assumption that the employment effects of liberalization are highly concentrated, if not confined, to the liberalized industry. In fact, in many cases the percentage of the total net primary effect that occurs in the liberalized industry is very low. Although a low proportion of the total effects occurs in the liberalized industry in several cases where the total effects are high, it tends to occur more often in cases where the total effects are low. The coefficient of correlation between the amount of the total effect and the proportion of it that occurs in the liberalized industry is .41.

The percentage of the total net primary effect occurring in the liberalized industry is shown in Column 3 of Table 3.1.[10] The highest proportion, 90 per cent, results from liberalization of vegetables and fruits (#8). Liberalization of pottery and related products (#73) is a close second, with 86 per cent of the total effects of its own liberalization.

The other end of the range may be more surprising. The minimum percentage occurring in the liberalized industry, found in the case of liberalization of the meat packing and wholesale poultry industry (#21), is only 23 per cent; in other words, in that case 77 per cent of the total net primary effect occurs in other industries. For liberalization of passenger cars and light trucks (#145.1), only 26 per cent of the effect is felt in that industry, and in the case of heavy trucks and buses (#145.2) this "internal" effect is only 29 per cent.

[10] The percentage of the total gross decrease occurring in the liberalized industry is shown in the last line of Appendix Table F.1.

Chart 3.2

Frequency Distribution of Percentages of Total Net Primary Employment
Effects That Occur in Liberalized Industry

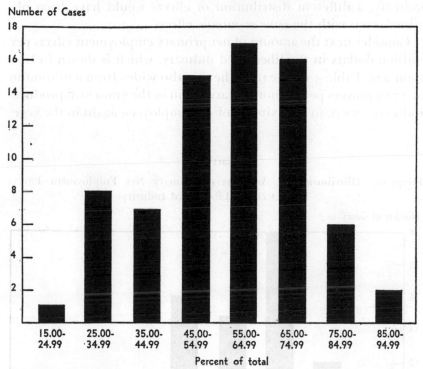

Source: Based on Column 3 of Table 3.1.

In fact, in 26 of the 72 cases, less than half of the effect is felt in
the liberalized industry and more than half in others, while in
48 out of the 72 cases the liberalized industry feels less than 65
per cent of the effect, more than 35 per cent being in other industries. The frequency with which various percentages occur is
shown in Chart 3.2.

The distribution of effects between the liberalized industry and
all others reflects the definition of an "industry," as well as economic facts. It is possible that some of the diversity (and also some
of the similarity) in the distribution of effects among different
cases reflects differences in the definition of an "industry" rather
than any significant economic phenomenon. For example, the

manufacture of components for Industry A may be included in
Industry A while that of components for Industry B may not be
included in Industry B. If other rules had been used to define an
industry, a different distribution of effects would have been obtained, even with the same economic effects.

Consider next the amount of net primary employment effects per
million dollars in the liberalized industry, which is shown in Column 2 of Table 3.1. The range here is also wide—from a minimum
of 17 employees per million dollars, again in the grain mill products
industry (#24), to a maximum of 194 employees, again in the vege-

Chart 3.3

Frequency Distribution of Amounts of Primary Net Employment Effects
That Occur in Liberalized Industry

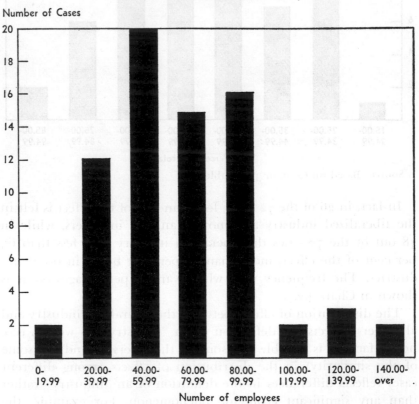

Source: Based on Column 2 of Table 3.1.

tables and fruits industry (#8). For 48 of the 72 cases, or two thirds of the total number, however, the effects felt in the liberalized industry itself are between 45 and 75 employees per million dollars. The frequency of various "internal" effects is shown in Chart 3.3.

The industries at the low end of the range, besides grain mill products, are synthetic rubber (#51), vegetable oils (#59), meat packing and wholesale poultry (#21), and processed dairy products (#22).

The industries feeling maximum effects of reduction of their own protection, besides vegetables and fruits, are pottery and related products (#73), apparel (#34), footwear other than rubber (#69), and lead and zinc mining (#13).

It may be noted that generally the industry liberalizations that cause the highest total net primary effects also cause the highest "internal" effects. The same relationship between total and internal effects also prevails at the low end of the range. A more systematic comparison of the figures in Columns 1 and 2 of Table 3.1 shows that this relationship prevails throughout the range of effects and not only at the extremes. The correlation coefficient between the total primary effects and the amount of the primary effects in the liberalized industry is .86.[11]

The effect on all industries other than the one for which protection is reduced is shown in Column 4 of Table 3.1. It also shows a wide range. The lowest of these "outside" effects, 16 employees, occurs in the case of liberalization of the sugar industry (#27). The highest, 91 employees, occurs in liberalization of "passenger cars and light trucks."

Among the liberalizations at the low end of the range are some which have small total effects, which is to be expected, but also two—liberalization of pottery and related products (#73) and of vegetables and fruits (#8)—which have total effects among the largest of all cases. Their small outside effects coexist with large total effects because these two industries have not only an unusually large employment per dollar of value added but also an unusually high ratio of value added to value of output, so that output

---

[11] A fairly high coefficient of correlation is to be expected because the two variables are not independent. The effect in the liberalized industry constitutes 58.5 per cent of the total effect in the median case.

and therefore employment effects in other industries are not a large part of the total.

An interesting contrast is offered by the liberalizations of five industries that have total net primary employment effects among the lowest of all the cases: those of sugar (#27), tobacco manufactures (#29), paints and allied products (#56), synthetic rubber (#51), and vegetable oils (#59). All five liberalizations cause total primary employment decreases of between 62 and 70 employees. The total effects of liberalizing the first three of these industries are small because the outside effects are small—among the smallest found in the 72 cases. In the case of liberalization of synthetic rubber and vegetable oils, however, the total effects are small because internal effects are small—only 19 and 21 employees, respectively; the effects in other industries—43 and 49 employees respectively—are close to the average for outside effects.

Distribution of Effects among Non-Liberalized Industries

So far, we have examined the distribution of total net primary employment effects only between the liberalized industry and all the non-liberalized industries combined. We may now turn to the distribution of the latter effects among the non-liberalized industries.

Estimates were obtained of the effects in each of the 200 industries, but to present them separately would require a table too large to read easily. The 200 industries have therefore been consolidated into 40 industry groups, and net primary effects outside the liberalized industry are shown for each of these 40 groups. This is done in Table 3.3, which appears at the end of this chapter. The main purpose of this table is to show, for each of the 72 cases of liberalization, the distribution of net primary effects among the 40 industry groups named at the left side of the table.[12]

In Table 3.3, each column represents one of the 72 cases of liberalization, the liberalized industries being identified in the

[12] A corresponding distribution of *gross* primary employment decreases among these industry groups is given in Appendix Table F.1. The industries in each of the 40 industry groups are indicated by the code numbers following the group titles at the left of both tables and are identified in Appendix A.

column headings by code numbers as well as by title. For convenience, the first three rows of figures repeat those in Columns 1, 2, and 4 of Table 3.1. It will be noted than one figure in each column bears an asterisk. This indicates that the industry group in that row contains the liberalized industry. The asterisk is intended to call attention to the fact that the estimate marked with an asterisk excludes the estimated effect on the liberalized industry.

Finally, it is to be noted that the figures in Table 3.3 represent net employment *de*creases, *i.e.*, gross decreases less the small increases associated with the process of importation. Because the shift in spending from domestic production to imports causes decreases in the output of the industry whose protection is reduced and, through its cuts in purchases of inputs, also causes decreases in the outputs of almost all industries, nearly all the net changes in this table are decreases. There are, however, some exceptions. Increases in imports *in*crease output and employment in the United States ocean shipping industry and in other industries that are involved in the process of getting shipments from abroad. Since the figures in the table refer generally to *de*creases of employment, these increases are shown in the table as negative figures.

Because a reduction of protection in one industry causes employment effects in nearly all industries of the economy, the effect on any single industry other than the one liberalized is usually quite small. In nearly every case, as Table 3.3 shows, a few outside industries feel a significant portion of the outside effects, but this effect is generally not large in relation to the total primary effect. In some cases, however, the outside effects are so concentrated on one or two industry groups that these groups are considerably affected.

The outstanding case of this kind is liberalization of products of the meat packing and wholesale poultry industry (#21). As might be expected, the effects are concentrated on the industries grouped under the heading "agriculture, forestry and fishing." Table 3.3 shows that the net decrease in this group is 58 employees per million dollar increase in imports. The more detailed unpublished data underlying Table 3.3 show that 54 of these employees are in the meat and livestock products industry. This effect is more than twice the effect on the meat packing and wholesale poultry industry itself, which is only 24 employees. The next largest outside effect occurs in wholesale and retail trade and is less than 7 employees.

A large effect on one non-liberalized industry also results from liberalization of house furnishings and other non-apparel products (#35). The effect in that industry itself is 48 employees. The number of employees affected in the spinning, weaving, and dyeing industry is almost as great—47. This reflects the fact that the "house furnishing and other non-apparel" industry includes so many textile products—floor coverings, coated fabrics, curtains and draperies, textile bags, and other fabricated textile products. The next most significant outside effect of liberalizing house furnishings and other non-apparel products, which in this case, too, is found in wholesale and retail trade, is less than 8 employees. The remaining 29 employees affected are distributed over the rest of the economy, with less than 4 employees to be found in any one of the other 38 industry groups.

Other cases in which liberalization has an impact on one outside industry group, or in two such groups combined, that is nearly as great as the effect in the liberalized industry are vegetable oils (#59), electrical welding apparatus (#134), passenger cars and light trucks (#145.1), heavy trucks and buses (#145.2), and motor vehicle parts and accessories (#145.3).

A substantial effect on one outside industry group also results from liberalization of plywood (#38), wood containers and cooperage products (#40), primary zinc (#85), and tin cans and other tinware (#93), although in these cases the effect on the most affected outside industry is much less than the effect on the liberalized industry.

In all but 2 of the 11 cases just discussed, in which there is a concentration of outside effects in 1 or 2 industry groups, the effect in all the non-liberalized industries is 60 per cent or more of the total effect in all industries. In 4 other cases 60 per cent or more of the total effect is in non-liberalized industries, but there is no such concentration of outside effects in one or two industries. Thus, for liberalization of grain mill products (#24), the total outside effect is 34 employees per million dollars of import increase, which is 67 per cent of the total effect, but in none of the 40 industry groups is the effect as great as 5 employees, or 10 per cent of the total effect. Similarly, for liberalization of synthetic rubber (#51), "miscellaneous chemicals" (#61), and electrical appliances (#135), the outside effect is at least 60 per cent of the total effect, but it is widely distributed.

We may now look at the distribution of net primary effects on the non-liberalized industries in another way. Instead of asking "What industry groups or industries are affected by liberalization of a given industry?" we may ask "Which liberalizations affect a given industry group or industry most, apart from liberalization of its own products?" Instead of examining selected columns of Table 3.3, we may examine selected rows.

Some industry groups are little affected by liberalization of the products of any of the 72 industries studied. Thus in 13 of the 40 industry groups, the outside effects of all of the 72 cases are less than 5 employees per million dollars of import increase of the liberalized products. Another 8 industry groups feel outside effects of 5 or more employees in only one of the 72 cases of liberalization. The groups most conspicuously immune from employment effects of liberalization in other industries are tobacco manufactures, apparel, and electric light and power and gas.

The reasons for this immunity are different in the first two of these three groups than in the last. The products of the tobacco manufacturing industry go almost entirely to final consumers. The amount that is an input in production of other commodities or services is almost negligible. Employment in tobacco manufacturing is not affected in 71 out of the 72 cases of liberalization. The only liberalization that decreases its employment is that of products of the "miscellaneous chemicals" industry. The reason for the decrease in this case is that nicotine produced by the tobacco manufacturing industry is used by the "miscellaneous chemical products" industry in producing insecticides. Even in this case the effect is practically zero.

Similarly, the apparel industry is rarely affected by liberalization elsewhere; it, too, is not a significant direct or indirect input into any of the liberalized products.

Employment effects on electric light and power and gas are also negligible in every case of liberalization, but the reason is quite different than in the case of tobacco manufactures and apparel. The output of this industry group is an input for almost every industry, so that its total contribution to the many industries directly and indirectly involved in any case of liberalization could add up to a significant total. Examination of the underlying data shows that this is in fact true; in some cases of liberalization the output effects on this industry group are high. The reason the employment effects are so low is that large changes in output are accompanied by very small changes in employment.

In 3 other industry groups, "instruments, optical and photographic equipment, watches and clocks," "auto and other repair services," and "other services," the effects of liberalizations elsewhere are in only one instance as high as 2 employees. In 5 other groups the effects of liberalization elsewhere are in every case less than 3 employees. In 2 others, they are in every case less than 5 employees. Thus there are 13 industry groups out of 40 that are affected by liberalization elsewhere to the extent of less than 5 employees in all of the 72 cases.

There are, of course, other industry groups in which employment is significantly or even greatly affected by liberalization in 1 or perhaps 2 of the 72 cases examined but very little affected by any of the other cases. This is true of "agriculture, forestry and fishing," which is affected to the extent of 58 employees by a shift of buying from domestic to imported products of the meat packing and wholesale poultry industry but is little affected by such a shift in any other of the 72 cases. Metal mining, too, is vulnerable to liberalization of primary zinc but to none of the other liberalizations examined.

On the other hand, some industry groups are vulnerable to liberalization of the products of many others. The industry group most often affected to the extent of 10 or more employees by liberalization elsewhere is "iron and steel and their primary products." It feels effects of that magnitude from liberalization in 11 of the 72 cases. Liberalization of tin cans and other tinware (#93) would have the largest effect on it—31 employees per million dollars of import increase. The next largest effect on it—25 employees per million dollars—comes from liberalization of "metal barrels, drums, etc." (#105). In both cases, the effects within the industry group are highly concentrated on carbon steel works and rolling mills. Liberalization of motor vehicle parts and accessories (#145.3) would affect this industry group to the extent of 20 employees, but in this case the major effect within the group is felt both in carbon steel works and rolling mills and in iron foundries, with more effect in the latter.

Employment Increases Associated with Importation of Liberalized Commodities

It has already been pointed out that the estimates given so far represent the net primary effect on employment of (1) the gross primary decrease associated with a million-dollar shift of buying away from the domestic production of the basket of liberalized commodities, and (2) the gross primary increase associated with a million-dollar increase in imports of the liberalized products. These two components of the net primary decrease were shown separately in Table 3.2.

The gross domestic employment increases associated with the process of importing the liberalized commodities amounted to a total of 5 or more employees in 8 of the 72 cases. Aside from paints and allied products, where the increase was 24 employees,[13] the industries whose liberalizations cause such employment increases are vegetables and fruits, sugar, wood containers and cooperage, carbon steel, alloy steel, stainless steel, and office supplies.

As might be expected, these employment increases associated with the process of importing the liberalized commodities occur mainly in the ocean transportation industry. Nearly all of the 72 cases of liberalization show increases in ocean freight activity. Where no increases are found in this industry, it is generally because the products are imported from Canada and do not require ocean transportation. Employment increases also occur frequently in the "communications, finance and business services" industry group, which supplies the insurance on ocean shipping, and in the "other transportation equipment" group, which supplies repair and maintenance services to ocean-going vessels. In almost every other industry group, the gross increase of employment associated with the process of importation is imperceptible.

In general, the estimates of the employment *increases* associated with the process of importation must be regarded as subject to

[13] There is no plausible apparent reason why the figure should be so high, and it probably should be disregarded as unreliable.

substantial percentage error. Nevertheless, a closer examination of the estimated effects on the ocean transportation industry is worthwhile because it reveals clearly some of the indirect effects of a shift in demand from domestic production to imports.

In eight cases of liberalization the ocean transportation industry experiences net *decreases* of employment. At first it may appear incredible that a reduction of import barriers, with its resulting increase of imports, could ever decrease employment in the ocean transportation industry. When we think about the wide ramifications of the initial decrease in domestic output, however, this result is less surprising. A decrease in the domestic production of a commodity whose protection is reduced decreases the use of products needed directly or indirectly in its current production. In some cases, a significant portion of these products is imported. If these output-induced decreases of imports are big enough, they may cause decreases of employment in ocean transportation that equal or even exceed the increases caused by the rise of imports of the liberalized product itself.

What is involved may be illustrated by liberalization of cork products (#162), which involves the only appreciable net decrease of employment in ocean transportation. A reduction of import barriers on cork products would cause a reduction in the domestic use of cork. Since the cork itself is obtained entirely from abroad, it would involve a large decrease of ocean transportation of cork. Moreover, it would also involve decreased use of paper and board mill products, carbon steel, primary copper and other primary metals, large amounts of metal stampings, and other products, which involve some imports. The form in which these materials are imported may be bulky and may involve larger quantities of ocean transportation services than the importation of cork products. This illustrates one factor that may make the employment decreases associated with the process of importation outweigh the employment increases associated with it, despite the rise in imports of the liberalized product itself.

In Chapter 4 we turn to the methods and major assumptions underlying these estimates.

Table 3.3

Distribution of Net Primary Employment Effects of Liberalization by Industry Groups[a]

(Number of employees, farmers, and unpaid farm family workers.)

Line Number	Industry Group Affected and Code Numbers of Industries in Group	Liberalized Industry	
		Meat Animals and Products (1)	Vegetables and Fruits (8)
1	Total, all industries...	92.16	213.90
2	Liberalized industry..	74.38	193.62
3	Other industries—total......................................	17.78	20.28
4	Agriculture, forestry, and fishing (1–10).........................	1.83*	.07*
5	Metal mining (11–15)..	.04	.05
6	Coal mining (16)..	.31	.51
7	Crude petroleum and natural gas (17).........................	.58	.47
8	Other nonmetallic minerals (18–20)..........................	.13	.43
9	Processed food and alcoholic beverages (21–28)................	.94	.24
10	Tobacco manufactures (29)...................................	—	—
11	Spinning, weaving, and dyeing (30)...........................	.24	.58
12	Apparel (34)...	—	—
13	All other textile products (31–33, 35).........................	.12	.50
14	Lumber, wood products, and furniture (36–43).................	.23	7.55
15	Pulp, paper, and paper products (44–46)......................	.34	.34
16	Printing and publishing (47).................................	.43	.28
17	Industrial chemicals (except synthetic rubber and fiber) (48–50, 53)....	.30	.89
18	Synthetic rubber and synthetic fiber (51, 52)..................	.04	.07
19	All other chemicals and allied products (54–61)................	.36	1.77
20	Products of petroleum and coal (62–64).......................	.20	.43
21	Tires, inner tubes, and misc. rubber products (65, 66)...........	.22	.37
22	Leather and products and footwear (excl. rubber) (67–69)........	.01	.02
23	Glass (70)...	.04	.05
24	Pottery and related products (73)............................		.01
25	Stone and clay products (71, 72, 74–77)......................	.05	.10
26	Iron and steel and their primary products (78–81, 92)...........	.53	.52
27	Nonferrous metals and their primary products (82–91)...........	.10	.10
28	Fabricated metal products (93–109)..........................	.23	.44
29	Machinery, except electrical (110–128).......................	.43	.42
30	Electrical machinery and products (129–138, 142–144).........	.11	.09
31	Communication equipment and products (139–141).............	.02	.01
32	Motor vehicles, parts and accessories (145–147)...............	.25	.38
33	Other transportation equipment (148–152)....................	−.13	−.50
34	Instruments, optical and photographic equip., watches and clocks (153–156)...	.04	.02
35	Miscellaneous manufactures (157–164).......................	.15	.06
36	Electric light and power, and gas (167, 168)..................	.04	.04
37	Railroad transportation (169)................................	1.93	1.74
38	Ocean transportation (172)..................................	−2.22	−6.21
39	Transportation (except railroad and ocean transportation) and allied services (170, 171, 173–175, 178).........................	1.31	.72
40	Wholesale and retail trade (176, 177)........................	5.70	6.23
41	Communication, finance, business services (179, 181, 186, 187)........	.92	.01
42	Auto and other repair services (188, 189).....................	.61	1.26
43	Other services (182–185, 190–192)...........................	1.35	.22

* Excludes employment effects in the liberalized industry, which is a part of this industry group. The employment effect in the liberalized industry is shown in Line 2.

[a] Figures are net decreases of employment per million-dollar increase of imports after subtraction of increases associated with the process of importation. Negative figures represent net increases. Dashes represent net effects of less than .005 employees, including some that are zero.

(*Table continued on following pages*)

Table 3.3 (continued)

Line Number	Lead and Zinc Mining (13)	Meat Packing and Wholesale Poultry (21)	Processed Dairy Products (22)	Grain Mill Products (24)	Sugar (27)	Alcoholic Beverages (28)	Tobacco Manufactures (29)
				Liberalized Industry			
1.....	161.08	106.36	52.66	50.77	62.35	82.75	69.27
2.....	128.35	24.41	25.49	16.90	46.17	43.21	42.54
3.....	32.73	81.95	27.17	33.87	16.18	39.54	26.73
4.....	.05	58.42	2.21	1.03	.08	4.24	.11
5.....	.18*	.06	.10	.08	.04	.11	.05
6.....	1.90	.54	1.06	.68	1.85	1.17	.58
7.....	.80	.56	.52	.66	.40	.32	.18
8.....	.09	.12	.12	.18	.20	.14	.14
9.....	.05	1.44*	2.58*	2.44*	.11*	1.43*	.41
10.....	—	—	—	—	—	—	—*
11.....	.09	.26	.30	1.93	.69	.17	.15
12.....	—	.08	—	.02	.01	—	—
13.....	.02	.13	.18	1.92	.67	.08	.08
14.....	6.50	.90	.81	.46	.22	2.73	2.06
15.....	.22	.50	2.83	1.99	1.40	2.56	4.09
16.....	.31	.80	1.10	2.36	1.16	4.14	3.95
17.....	4.36	.32	.35	.51	.32	.57	.72
18.....	.02	.15	.04	.17	.06	.06	.04
19.....	.56	.56	.59	.86	.22	.34	.42
20.....	.63	.24	.25	.25	.20	.22	.13
21.....	.50	.30	.26	.34	.08	.33	.18
22.....	.03	.02	.02	.12	.01	.02	.01
23.....	.04	.18	.23	.17	.03	4.30	.08
24.....	.01	—	—	—	—	.01	—
25.....	.30	.07	.10	.09	.11	.24	.05
26.....	3.79	.88	1.40	.96	.39	1.51	.43
27.....	.48	.14	.15	.20	.09	.19	.22
28.....	1.38	.81	1.50	.68	.17	2.53	.72
29.....	4.27	.75	.58	1.06	.39	.48	.35
30.....	.35	.18	.12	.22	.08	.10	.06
31.....	.02	.03	.03	.03	.02	.03	.02
32.....	.11	.24	.19	.19	.08	.11	.06
33.....	.31	.08	.09	.11	.11	−.04	.05
34.....	.03	.04	.05	.05	.03	.05	.04
35.....	.10	.21	.26	.29	.14	.47	.34
36.....	.62	.08	.12	.11	.19	.11	.04
37.....	1.58	2.39	1.99	4.74	2.49	2.56	1.69
38.....	−2.60	−1.30	−1.30	−.27	−2.98	−1.02	−.60
39.....	.46	1.42	.74	1.33	.51	.87	.58
40.....	2.84	6.52	3.77	3.31	2.25	2.33	3.34
41.....	1.61	1.85	2.24	3.39	3.59	4.74	5.04
42.....	.49	.72	.82	.51	.29	.49	.22
43.....	.23	1.26	.77	.70	.48	.85	.70

Table 3.3 (*continued*)

Line Number	Spinning, Weaving and Dyeing (30)	Special Textile Products (31)	Apparel (34)	House Furnishings and Other Non-apparel (35)	Plywood (38)	Wood Containers and Cooperage (40)	Wood Furniture (41)
				Liberalized Industry			
1.....	135.37	105.54	194.18	132.20	139.08	159.33	169.90
2.....	97.57	73.57	133.87	47.74	80.93	93.87	102.76
3.....	37.80	31.97	60.31	84.46	58.15	65.46	67.14
4.....	4.30	4.53	3.35	2.33	.10	.02	.33
5.....	.08	.02	.05	.12	.09	.13	.23
6.....	1.74	.90	.84	1.31	.70	.90	1.07
7.....	.49	.19	.23	.35	.40	.26	.26
8.....	.18	.06	.08	.15	.10	.06	.10
9.....	.58	.60	.25	.77	.18	.03	.11
10.....	—	—	—	—	—	—	—
11.....	—*	9.96	29.34	46.97	.16	.14	4.64
12.....	—	—*	.33		—	—	.37
13.....	.61	1.36*	1.06	1.24*	.06	.03	2.08
14.....	1.40	.35	.77	2.18	36.06*	48.79*	29.83*
15.....	1.32	1.34	1.58	1.98	.38	.42	.75
16.....	1.08	1.09	1.87	1.36	.76	.73	1.29
17.....	2.19	.61	.92	2.00	1.86	.16	.48
18.....	7.67	1.65	3.46	3.63	.04	.02	.40
19.....	.76	.24	.36	1.84	1.25	.22	1.33
20.....	.31	.14	.16	.24	.36	.38	.32
21.....	.20	.22	.48	1.15	.50	.43	.64
22.....	.04	.01	.39	.03	.13	.14	.17
23.....	.61	.20	.20	.36	.08	.08	1.09
24.....	—	—	—	.01	.01	.01	.02
25.....	.10	.04	.06	.12	.38	.51	.53
26.....	.07	.23	.38	.62	.88	2.19	2.33
27.....	.16	.05	.12	.18	.19	.20	.47
28.....	.29	.18	.33	.41	1.19	1.59	4.94
29.....	1.13	.26	.55	.87	1.29	1.07	1.04
30.....	.11	.05	.24	.10	.20	.22	.20
31.....	.02	.02	.02	.02	.02	.02	.02
32.....	.10	.06	.06	.09	.21	.21	.13
33.....	.07	.05	.10	−.08	.09	−.34	.07
34.....	.04	.02	.04	.04	.05	.05	.06
35.....	.37	.14	2.06	1.10	.20	.09	.48
36.....	.20	.09	.10	.15	.10	.09	.12
37.....	2.25	1.29	1.49	2.13	3.00	3.77	2.71
38.....	−.83	−.97	−1.00	−1.53	−.07	−4.60	−.67
39.....	.72	.44	.42	.56	1.76	1.97	1.08
40.....	4.78	3.72	6.10	7.65	1.72	2.69	3.80
41.....	2.75	1.84	2.65	2.41	2.39	1.31	2.97
42.....	.39	.34	.28	.42	.67	.91	.57
43.....	.92	.65	.92	.85	.66	.56	.78

Table 3.3 (*continued*)

Line Number	Liberalized Industry						
	Paper and Board Mills (45)	Converted Paper Products (46)	Industrial Organic Chemicals (49)	Synthetic Rubber (51)	Synthetic Fiber (52)	Drugs and Medicines (54)	Paints and Allied Products (56)
1.....	83.60	112.19	75.01	62.56	90.20	118.15	66.59
2.....	39.98	59.62	35.19	19.25	55.10	52.29	42.05
3.....	43.62	52.57	39.82	43.31	35.10	65.86	24.54
4.....	.13	.13	.87	.69	.30	1.41	.43
5.....	.07	.09	.71	.20	.21	.18	2.78
6.....	3.14	1.98	5.03	1.64	3.60	1.61	1.90
7.....	.54	.58	1.46	5.92	.56	.52	.76
8.....	.50	.31	.78	.34	.47	.30	.94
9.....	.40	.32	1.89	.74	.79	1.39	1.26
10.....	—	—	—	—	—	—	—
11.....	.64	.67	.22	.12	.12	.24	.22
12.....	—	—	—	—	—	.01	—
13.....	.51	.52	.08	.05	.04	.12	.04
14.....	8.46	4.92	2.78	.75	3.21	.99	.74
15.....	10.00*	24.10*	1.33	1.47	3.53	5.87	1.95
16.....	.62	1.35	.89	1.22	.86	11.41	1.06
17.....	.90	1.20	4.78*	7.93	8.11	4.89	7.59
18.....	.09	.08	.20	.06*	.01*	.20	.14
19.....	.53	.78	3.24	3.80	1.55	2.45*	3.03*
20.....	.38	.43	1.81	4.18	.54	.51	.81
21.....	.17	.49	.52	.35	.25	.58	.49
22.....	.06	.04	.03	.03	.02	.04	.03
23.....	.05	.07	.68	.23	.17	4.57	.24
24.....	.01	—	.01	.01	—	.02	.01
25.....	.25	.18	.25	.17	.18	.29	1.05
26.....	.75	.95	1.92	1.01	1.06	.97	2.61
27.....	.18	.25	.64	.36	.31	.44	1.30
28.....	.59	.58	1.20	.69	.43	1.06	2.47
29.....	1.31	1.06	1.06	1.54	.92	.88	2.00
30.....	.14	.11	.13	.10	.10	.11	.25
31.....	.02	.02	.02	.02	.02	.05	.02
32.....	.13	.09	.08	.05	.11	.12	.08
33.....	.15	−.05	−.05	.19	.13	.12	−1.27
34.....	.03	.19	.05	.10	.04	.13	.23
35.....	.14	.62	.16	.16	.50	1.01	.43
36.....	.20	.15	.37	.23	.13	.16	.17
37.....	3.66	4.21	4.00	2.91	3.17	2.70	2.89
38.....	−.53	−1.61	−2.59	−1.44	−.88	−.27	−15.06
39.....	1.32	1.12	.98	1.13	.86	.92	.63
40.....	5.46	4.07	1.77	3.03	.96	5.02	2.80
41.....	1.60	1.46	1.53	2.34	1.69	12.80	−1.12
42.....	.47	.44	.39	.35	.32	.44	.32
43.....	.55	.67	.60	.64	.71	1.60	.32

Table 3.3 (*continued*)

Line Number	Vegetable Oils (59)	Miscellaneous Chemical Industries (61)	Tires and Inner Tubes (65)	Miscellaneous Rubber Products (66)	Leather Tanning and Finishing (67)	Footwear (Except Rubber) (69)	Glass (70)
			Liberalized Industry				
1.....	69.37	103.97	91.60	116.86	79.66	178.12	115.05
2.....	20.58	35.77	44.68	76.62	62.50	132.58	86.73
3.....	48.79	68.20	46.92	40.24	17.16	45.54	28.32
4.....	1.37	2.20	.86	.48	.45	.31	.04
5.....	.11	.32	.10	.14	.06	.04	.12
6.....	1.05	2.05	1.41	1.22	1.24	.79	1.20
7.....	.87	1.26	.97	.65	.20	.16	.52
8.....	.91	1.04	.26	.23	.08	.07	1.27
9.....	11.01	1.96	.30	.23	.38	.21	.06
10.....	—	.02	—	—	—	—	—
11.....	.82	.48	14.91	6.92	.14	2.18	.26
12.....	.01	.01	—	—	—	.06	—
13.....	.68	.31	.12	.17	.06	.47	.05
14.....	.49	1.15	.52	1.47	.55	2.11	1.80
15.....	1.22	5.02	1.03	2.14	.25	2.76	4.99
16.....	1.49	8.28	1.42	1.15	.47	1.42	1.03
17.....	.80	6.49	2.10	1.84	1.29	.80	1.85
18.....	.15	.31	3.38	1.67	.03	.22	.03
19.....	.79*	5.37*	1.88	1.86	2.48	1.26	.29
20.....	.28	.75	.71	.50	.16	.13	.31
21.....	.46	.65	4.25*	5.18*	.28	2.60	.32
22.....	.10	.37	.02	.02	.32*	17.21*	.05
23.....	.52	1.77	.18	.34	.06	.08	—*
24.....	—	.02	—	.01	.01	—	.16
25.....	.13	.70	.15	.40	.16	.20	2.91
26.....	1.40	1.78	.78	1.42	.29	.37	1.04
27.....	.28	.74	.18	.32	.08	.11	.22
28.....	1.13	1.81	.36	1.58	.22	.40	.61
29.....	1.17	1.57	1.00	1.68	.20	.38	.90
30.....	.18	.16	.08	.18	.05	.06	.10
31.....	.05	.05	.02	.03	.01	.02	.02
32.....	.24	.09	.08	.26	.05	.05	.06
33.....	.16	.12	.09	.08	.04	.04	.07
34.....	.06	.77	.05	.06	.02	.04	.10
35.....	.33	.91	.18	.16	.10	.62	.17
36.....	.18	.20	.16	.16	.07	.08	.55
37.....	3.55	3.01	1.96	1.93	2.12	1.72	2.26
38.....	−1.11	−1.02	−.21	−.24	−.29	−.35	−.57
39.....	1.04	.80	.44	.40	.78	.45	.78
40.....	11.51	3.90	3.86	2.92	2.39	3.33	2.34
41.....	4.23	10.42	2.30	1.76	1.60	4.25	1.38
42.....	.75	.50	.33	.29	.24	.22	.38
43.....	1.08	1.20	.64	.63	.52	.68	.59

Table 3.3 (*continued*)

			Liberalized Industry				
Line Number	Pottery and Related Products (73)	Carbon Steel Works and Rolling Mills (79.1)	Alloy Steel Works and Rolling Mills Except Stainless)79.2)	Stainless Steel Works and Rolling Mills (79.3)	Primary Zinc (85)	Primary Aluminum Including Alumina (88)	Aluminum Rolling and Drawing (89)
1.....	189.05	85.03	87.74	90.85	94.60	62.32	79.51
2.....	163.22	51.34	53.75	72.82	36.29	29.95	43.85
3.....	25.83	33.69	33.99	18.03	58.31	32.37	35.66
4.....	.05	.01	.01	.01	.03	.02	.02
5.....	.21	3.28	3.45	1.43	27.52	3.04	1.66
6.....	1.03	6.05	6.00	2.68	3.07	1.90	1.59
7.....	.41	.63	.64	.27	.81	.78	.52
8.....	2.67	.51	.49	.18	.22	.34	.16
9.....	.08	.03	.03	.02	.03	.03	.02
10.....	—	—	—	—	—	—	—
11.....	.12	.03	.03	.02	.05	.04	.03
12.....	—	—	—	—	—	—	—
13.....	.04	—	—	—	.02	.02	.01
14.....	.81	.74	.51	.39	1.51	.23	.67
15.....	2.08	.16	.18	.12	.18	.17	.13
16.....	.71	.44	.38	.33	.49	.37	.42
17.....	.80	.40	.41	.26	1.11	1.42	.66
18.....	.02	.01	.01	.01	.01	.01	.01
19.....	1.94	.25	.27	.18	.27	.18	.17
20.....	.27	2.49	2.44	.87	.65	.69	.49
21.....	.22	.09	.08	.05	.26	.16	.16
22.....	.01	.02	.02	.01	.01	.01	.01
23.....	.17	.03	.03	.02	.03	.03	.02
24.....	—*	.02	.02	.01	.02	—	—
25.....	3.47	1.86	2.11	.79	1.84	.30	.17
26.....	.90	7.72*	5.87*	2.56*	1.40	1.60	1.12
27.....	.29	.81	.95	.73	4.40*	8.48*	18.15*
28.....	.39	.43	.34	.60	.52	.31	.27
29.....	.44	1.06	.65	.52	1.55	.94	.71
30.....	1.64	.33	.39	.47	.17	.12	.13
31.....	.05	.02	.02	.02	.02	.02	.02
32.....	.05	.06	.07	.05	.08	.08	.12
33.....	.06	−.02	−.02	−.17	.21	.17	.12
34.....	.04	.02	.04	.02	.03	.02	.02
35.....	.16	.09	.10	.08	.09	.08	.06
36.....	.33	.26	.30	.26	.68	.72	.44
37.....	2.08	4.53	5.58	4.26	5.21	3.32	2.30
38.....	−.27	−3.54	−3.48	−3.72	−.38	.27	.29
39.....	.59	1.12	1.26	.68	.52	.39	.29
40.....	1.38	2.52	3.61	2.94	3.58	4.42	2.97
41.....	1.60	.57	.56	.45	1.27	1.04	1.07
42.....	.34	.29	.30	.25	.37	.29	.23
43.....	.65	.37	.34	.38	.46	.36	.43

Table 3.3 (*continued*)

Line Number	Tin Cans and Other Tinware (93)	Cutlery (94)	Tools and General Hardware (95)	Lighting Fixtures (103)	Metal Barrels, Drums, etc. (105)	Tubes and Foils (106)	Machine Tools and Metal-working Machinery (116)
				Liberalized Industry			
1.....	105.88	122.48	130.18	138.36	103.93	100.09	108.36
2.....	42.11	82.61	89.16	66.70	42.89	43.95	62.90
3.....	63.77	39.87	41.02	71.66	61.04	56.14	45.46
4.....	.06	.09	.03	.07	.04	.04	.03
5.....	1.96	.52	.63	1.00	1.52	1.37	.49
6.....	3.48	.07	1.20	1.31	2.80	1.28	1.13
7.....	.50	.20	.25	.30	.39	.36	.21
8.....	.33	.10	.14	.19	.25	.12	.15
9.....	.09	.08	.03	.08	.06	.06	.03
10.....	—	—	—	—	—	—	—
11.....	.07	.26	.20	.32	.07	.08	.19
12.....	—	—	—	—	—	—	—
13.....	.04	.06	.03	.12	.03	.04	.05
14.....	1.66	1.54	2.72	2.09	.58	.76	.60
15.....	2.22	3.58	.62	2.83	.40	1.63	.31
16.....	.73	2.09	.44	1.03	.61	.71	.56
17.....	.55	.56	.20	.77	.36	.67	.17
18.....	.02	.03	.02	.06	.02	.02	.03
19.....	1.63	.38	.29	.64	1.00	.72	.21
20.....	1.41	.32	.45	.45	1.13	.37	.42
21.....	.14	.86	.34	.47	.24	.32	1.03
22.....	.02	.44	.02	.10	.02	.02	.11
23.....	.05	.06	.07	4.27	.04	.06	.05
24.....	.01	.01	.03	.23	.01	.01	.04
25.....	1.04	.65	1.38	.68	.91	.26	.77
26.....	30.71	7.32	9.59	7.30	25.15	2.64	13.12
27.....	.86	1.39	1.25	4.74	1.15	26.08	1.92
28.....	1.73*	6.62*	8.65*	11.98*	10.70*	6.82*	2.75
29.....	1.20	1.36	4.26	1.85	1.68	1.24	11.10*
30.....	.26	.31	.68	14.43	.37	.34	3.01
31.....	.04	.04	.05	.80	.09	.04	.10
32.....	.07	.06	.09	.11	.39	.11	.06
33.....	.20	.07	.10	.11	.17	.11	.13
34.....	.05	.07	.07	.32	.04	.07	.12
35.....	.16	2.14	.36	.90	.17	.13	.24
36.....	.23	.13	.16	.19	.20	.30	.12
37.....	4.46	1.48	1.67	2.31	3.62	2.87	1.50
38.....	−.06	−.15	−.14	.07	.13	−.29	−.58
39.....	.86	.34	.42	.56	.67	.44	.33
40.....	4.39	2.28	2.46	5.84	3.68	3.97	2.48
41.....	1.59	3.10	1.38	2.03	1.48	1.42	1.68
42.....	.43	.25	.26	.34	.33	.28	.22
43.....	.58	.76	.56	.77	.54	.65	.58

Table 3.3 (*continued*)

Line Num-ber	Special Industrial Machinery (118)	Industrial Machinery n.e.c. (123)	Ball and Roller Bearings (127)	Motors and Generators (131)	Trans-formers (132)	Electrical Control Apparatus (133)	Electrical Welding Apparatus (134)
				Liberalized Industry			
1.....	136.89	123.09	125.39	128.98	112.85	114.47	101.92
2.....	84.98	55.66	94.46	73.76	60.50	67.39	31.10
3.....	51.91	67.43	30.93	55.22	52.35	47.08	70.82
4.....	.06	.05	.03	.05	.10	.05	.09
5.....	.64	.91	.62	1.11	1.63	.89	1.08
6.....	1.26	1.40	1.43	1.58	1.34	.89	1.21
7.....	.19	.23	.30	.24	.43	.20	.28
8.....	.14	.18	.17	.29	.15	.18	.19
9.....	.04	.05	.02	.05	.07	.06	.10
10....	—	—	—	—	—	—	—
11....	.62	.31	.16	.40	1.30	.25	.28
12....	—	—	—	—	.01	.01	.01
13....	.05	.07	.03	.07	1.12	.07	.10
14....	1.52	1.05	.62	1.13	1.22	.79	1.56
15....	.70	.45	.26	.66	1.27	.93	1.62
16....	.50	.82	.48	.60	.58	.58	.96
17....	.28	.42	.15	.61	.42	1.21	.64
18....	.08	.06	.03	.05	.12	.04	.05
19....	.26	.53	.18	.41	.67	.51	1.55
20....	.44	.49	.55	.50	.54	.29	.44
21....	1.20	1.58	.35	.55	.53	.41	.74
22....	.10	.12	.20	.06	.02	.02	.04
23....	.10	.08	.03	.09	.07	.11	.21
24....	.02	.06	.02	.14	1.92	2.51	.55
25....	.50	1.20	1.26	1.88	.47	.53	.65
26....	13.42	13.78	11.40	12.03	7.68	5.03	8.72
27....	2.52	3.76	.84	4.34	5.76	4.09	3.85
28....	3.57	5.99	.80	3.92	4.09	4.24	4.04
29....	12.21*	20.49*	4.13*	5.08	1.51	1.98	3.54
30....	3.27	2.83	.34	5.82*	6.44*	9.24*	20.08*
31....	.11	.14	.03	2.03	2.18	2.13	6.62
32....	.06	.06	.04	.07	.06	.06	.08
33....	.12	.16	.09	.30	.11	.26	.14
34....	.26	1.03	.04	.22	.10	.19	.12
35....	.60	.28	.14	1.90	.54	1.50	.80
36....	.12	.14	.20	.14	.13	.10	.14
37....	1.82	2.10	1.89	2.20	2.22	1.47	2.12
38....	-.52	-.22	-.41	-.14	.08	.05	-.04
39....	.40	.43	.39	.48	.51	.34	.45
40....	2.92	3.46	2.19	3.50	4.41	3.29	4.63
41....	1.44	1.98	1.09	1.93	1.65	1.74	2.20
42....	.27	.30	.21	.25	.26	.21	.28
43....	.62	.66	.63	.68	.64	.63	.70

Table 3.3 (*continued*)

	Liberalized Industry						
Line Number	Electrical Appliances (135)	Insulated Wire and Cable (136)	Electric Lamps (138)	Radio and Related Products (139)	Communication Equipment (141)	Storage Batteries (142)	Primary Batteries (143)
1.....	133.87	95.62	109.33	154.88	132.37	95.83	118.12
2.....	52.61	43.90	72.74	80.46	91.95	46.52	80.39
3.....	81.26	51.72	36.59	74.42	40.42	49.31	37.73
4.....	.08	.08	.05	.10	.05	.12	.05
5.....	.88	4.91	.74	.62	.80	3.59	2.60
6.....	1.39	.09	.54	.90	.77	.96	1.07
7.....	.28	.32	.20	.26	.16	.37	.22
8.....	.19	.10	.19	.19	.07	.20	.17
9.....	.08	.06	.05	.08	.06	.21	.11
10.....	—	—	—	—	—	—	—
11.....	.50	1.07	.39	1.13	.45	.79	.15
12.....	.01	—	—	.04	.01	—	—
13.....	.09	.30	.04	.54	.09	.05	.04
14.....	3.09	3.61	.65	13.27	1.72	3.61	.61
15.....	1.36	.64	1.40	1.88	.69	.66	1.27
16.....	2.04	.42	1.57	2.56	.86	.78	.53
17.....	.80	1.18	.63	.88	.84	1.62	2.16
18.....	.11	.33	.13	.16	.09	.18	.10
19.....	.68	.59	.39	.48	.56	5.74	.46
20.....	.47	.30	.16	.29	.21	.36	.25
21.....	1.73	.57	.71	.97	.44	7.09	.81
22.....	.12	.07	.02	.10	.03	.01	.01
23.....	.19	.07	9.70	.74	.20	.10	.07
24.....	.15	.08	.04	.30	.06	.01	.10
25.....	1.21	.54	.54	.42	.22	.40	.31
26.....	9.01	2.45	1.20	3.21	3.24	1.00	1.55
27.....	6.07	19.01	1.96	2.84	3.34	7.00	8.51
28.....	12.10	2.84	2.56	7.83	3.24	.72	1.21
29.....	10.81	1.67	.85	2.14	1.18	1.05	.69
30.....	9.28*	3.46*	2.50*	7.54	5.50	.11*	6.91*
31.....	1.32	.20	1.20	8.02*	6.72*	.02	.40
32.....	.11	.14	.27	.16	.05	.11	.04
33.....	.55	—.14	.05	.08	.38	.08	.08
34.....	1.11	.03	.05	.30	.05	.05	.03
35.....	2.67	.17	1.20	2.92	.80	2.39	.34
36.....	.16	.16	.19	.13	.08	.18	.14
37.....	2.43	2.33	1.29	2.19	1.37	2.70	2.14
38.....	—.27	—2.52	—.10	—.18	—.12	—.14	.16
39.....	.55	.52	.32	.64	.34	.48	.31
40.....	4.77	3.71	1.78	5.24	3.02	3.03	2.09
41.....	3.07	.74	2.22	4.02	1.93	1.77	1.22
42.....	.34	.28	.23	.44	.26	.37	.24
43.....	.83	.44	.62	.99	.66	.58	.58

Table 3.3 (*continued*)

Line Number	Passenger Cars and Light Trucks (145.1)	Heavy Trucks and Buses (145.2)	Motor Vehicle Parts and Accessories (145.3)	Aircraft and Parts (148)	Motorcycles and Bicycles (152)	Optical, Ophthalmic and Photo Equipment (154)	Watches and Clocks (156)
				Liberalized Industry			
1.....	123.77	113.20	102.89	118.44	128.06	127.91	136.49
2.....	32.67	32.90	32.81	76.31	67.66	83.92	94.82
3.....	91.10	80.30	70.08	42.13	60.40	43.99	41.67
4.....	.23	.13	.06	.06	.07	.12	.07
5.....	.94	.82	1.18	.49	.80	.34	.65
6.....	1.82	1.61	1.95	.83	1.72	1.08	.58
7.....	.45	.39	.32	.28	.30	.24	.15
8.....	.26	.22	.23	.08	.17	.24	.23
9.....	.10	.09	.06	.05	.05	.14	.06
10....	—	—	—	—	—	—	—
11....	3.04	1.66	.70	.30	.83	.69	.34
12....	.57	.01	.01	.04	—	—	—
13....	1.09	.29	.53	.11	.06	.23	.16
14....	1.07	2.96	.98	1.46	1.19	1.50	1.04
15....	.92	.77	.82	1.10	1.30	2.94	1.61
16....	1.32	1.35	1.14	1.36	.71	1.79	3.31
17....	.67	.60	.45	.28	.33	3.28	.54
18....	.43	.37	.16	.05	.18	.08	.04
19....	1.10	1.11	.64	.48	.53	.99	.35
20....	.67	.59	.72	.33	.65	.26	.15
21....	4.30	5.37	1.58	.71	2.85	.51	.24
22....	.14	.14	.26	.03	.17	.18	.51
23....	1.96	1.04	.15	.09	.09	2.48	1.42
24....	.08	.08	.05	.02	.03	.03	.01
25....	1.58	1.25	1.18	.47	.65	.57	.50
26....	13.23	12.16	20.38	7.71	15.95	1.81	1.42
27....	2.88	2.58	4.11	3.66	1.52	1.36	3.67
28....	12.66	8.28	6.57	4.78	4.29	4.75	3.54
29....	6.98	6.15	10.27	4.54	9.57	1.59	1.48
30....	5.15	5.28	4.86	2.20	2.21	2.60	.62
31....	.44	.12	.13	.64	.06	.39	.08
32....	14.05*	14.15*	.02*	.79	3.52	.05	.05
33....	.98	.37	.32	.46*	2.62*	.07	.07
34....	.98	.57	.54	2.30	.12	1.21*	1.87*
35....	.80	.53	.31	.30	.16	2.49	5.07
36....	.19	.13	.16	.14	.14	.14	.09
37....	3.72	3.25	3.46	1.51	2.53	1.78	1.43
38....	—.54	—.54	—.53	—1.16	—1.04	—.25	—.68
39....	.76	.67	.71	.34	.54	.44	.34
40....	3.11	2.67	2.64	2.34	3.15	3.57	5.52
41....	1.95	2.04	1.93	2.38	1.47	3.23	3.98
42....	.35	.35	.35	.22	.29	.26	.26
43....	.67	.69	.68	.36	.62	.81	.90

Table 3.3 (*continued*)

	Liberalized Industry						
Line Number	Jewelry and Silverware (157)	Musical Instruments and Parts (158)	Toys and Sporting Goods (159)	Office Supplies (160)	Plastic Products (161)	Cork Products (162)	Miscellaneous Manufactured Products (164)
1.....	136.46	135.01	157.48	128.56	121.79	87.09	154.76
2.....	90.95	97.42	100.12	87.41	77.79	48.61	77.20
3.....	45.51	37.59	57.36	41.15	44.00	38.48	77.56
4.....	.18	.11	.16	.24	.41	.12	.91
5.....	1.58	.23	.54	.20	.12	.24	.39
6.....	.59	1.01	.92	.72	1.16	.84	1.02
7.....	.26	.14	.25	.18	.28	.36	.29
8.....	3.71	.08	.13	.16	.17	.08	.16
9.....	.04	.06	.12	.22	.32	.62	.45
10.....	—	—	—	—	—	—	—
11.....	.19	1.38	1.73	1.41	5.68	.18	1.80
12.....	—	—	—	—	—	—	.01
13.....	.05	.06	1.15	.08	.18	.07	.50
14.....	1.82	7.06	6.38	9.47	2.25	.82	6.61
15.....	1.34	.87	4.01	3.08	2.93	.64	7.47
16.....	3.44	3.55	2.47	2.63	1.40	1.30	21.67
17.....	.42	.48	1.49	1.27	7.57	.25	1.44
18.....	.03	.12	.24	.17	.49	.03	.38
19.....	.22	.47	1.09	1.67	1.11	.22	1.15
20.....	.21	.19	.26	.18	.27	.32	.28
21.....	.41	.42	4.02	2.49	1.12	.18	.42
22.....	.08	.05	1.11	.05	.04	.03	.22
23.....	.18	.05	.35	.16	.13	.07	.42
24.....	.01	.01	.02	.01	.01	.01	.03
25.....	.40	.25	.48	.50	4.08	.29	.34
26.....	.83	2.24	2.44	.89	.74	9.75	2.14
27.....	9.44	.54	1.05	.81	.27	.82	1.46
28.....	2.84	1.52	3.33	1.83	.44	12.90	3.52
29.....	.92	.74	1.95	.89	.79	.97	2.20
30.....	.12	.14	.70	.19	.12	.27	1.23
31.....	.03	.02	.05	.03	.02	.13	.07
32.....	.07	.05	.32	.37	.12	.09	.11
33.....	.09	.05	.53	-.28	.07	.37	-.06
34.....	.04	.05	.21	.05	.04	.04	.17
35.....	3.42*	6.53*	9.78*	7.07*	4.90*	5.87*	7.13*
36.....	.14	.10	.14	.11	.14	.13	.13
37.....	2.01	1.41	1.71	1.47	1.66	.93	2.26
38.....	-.08	-.26	-.26	-3.67	-1.09	1.75	-1.55
39.....	.33	.44	.49	.57	.45	.24	.64
40.....	4.48	2.11	2.93	2.97	2.91	1.34	8.52
41.....	4.53	4.26	3.08	1.95	1.77	2.53	2.24
42.....	.27	.25	.30	.30	.27	.17	.48
43.....	.87	.81	.76	.71	.66	.51	.91

Methods and Major Assumptions of Estimates of Primary Employment Effects*

I T HAS ALREADY been pointed out that the estimates presented in the preceding chapter are, unavoidably, based on a number of assumptions, some implicit in the method used, others expressly chosen either for lack of alternatives or in preference to available alternatives. Some of these assumptions have already been identified. It is now necessary to state the major assumptions more completely, to appraise their validity wherever possible, and to indicate the direction of any bias they may have, where its direction is known. (The "bias" of an assumption refers to any error in it that tends to make the estimates deviate systematically from what they would have been had we been able to base them on data that accurately represent the relevant relationships instead of on approximations of these relationships or on assumptions about them.) The best way to make these assumptions clear is to outline the general method of making the estimates, to point out the assumptions involved in each stage of the estimating process, and, where a choice could be made between alternative assumptions, to explain the reasons for the choice that was made.

The estimating process will be described in terms of its five major steps. The first step was to select the industries the employment effects of whose liberalization could be reliably estimated. The second step was to estimate the gross primary decreases of domestic output in every industry resulting from the liberalization of each of these selected industries. The third was to estimate the employment decreases associated with these output decreases. Fourth, it was necessary to estimate, in each case of liberalization,

---

* This chapter may be omitted by readers who are not interested in the estimating methods.

the gross *increases* of employment associated with the process of importation. The final step was the simple arithmetic one of subtracting the gross employment increases from the gross decreases to get the net decreases.

It is not the main purpose of this chapter to describe the method for its own sake. In fact many technical details of the procedure and some major problems that had to be faced will be referred to only briefly or not at all. The main purpose is to enable the reader to understand the relevance and significance of the assumptions underlying the estimates, to enable him to appreciate both the limitations and the flexibility of the estimates, and to help him understand them well enough to use them correctly.

Selection of Industries Whose Liberalization Is to Be Studied

The first step, preliminary to the estimating process, was to select the industries the employment effects of whose liberalization was to be estimated. Of course, tariffs and other protective measures are not applied to "industries," which after all are only more or less arbitrarily defined groupings, but to commodities—and often to very precisely defined commodities. Employment effects and their industry distribution, however, cannot be estimated on a commodity basis. The employment-output relationships required to estimate the employment effects of changes in output are rarely available for such narrowly defined commodity classifications. Although Tariff Commission studies provide employment and output data for many individual protected commodities, they do not provide them for all such commodities. Moreover, estimates of the industry distribution of employment effects require comparable data for the entire economy, and such data are not available on a basis comparable with those of the Tariff Commission.[1] Since the most detailed categories for which comparable

[1] The requirements imposed by the purposes and methods of the study may be listed as follows: (1) Employment and output data are needed for every industry in the economy, including unprotected commodity-producing industries and industries

employment and output data are available are subindustries, it was not feasible to examine the effects of liberalizing individual protected commodities. The subindustries were therefore the smallest economic sectors for which the employment effects of *direct* changes in output could be accurately estimated.[2] The employment effects of total changes in output, however, could not be accurately estimated for subindustries, for reasons explained below, and that is why employment effects are estimated on an industry basis.

In selecting the industries the employment effects of whose liberalization was to be estimated, the objective was to select those for which affirmative answers could be given to the following four questions: (1) Does the industry include commodities that have significant tariff or other government protection from import competition? (2) Is it likely that we can reliably estimate the direct employment effects of a change in output of the protected commodities in the industry? (3) For agricultural industries that pass the preceding tests, is their protected output sufficiently flexible so that a reduction in demand for it would cause a significant reduction of output within a period of one year? (4) Is it likely that we can reliably estimate the output effects in all industries of a direct change in the output of the industry's protected commodities?

The first three tests were applied to every subindustry, without regard to what industry it was in. Then the subindustries that passed these tests were grouped into industries and the fourth test was applied to these industries.

---

producing services, because indirect as well as direct employment effects are to be estimated and the data for direct and indirect effects must be comparable. (2) Employment and output data for each industry must cover identical firms in the industry if the employment-output relationships derived from them are to be significant. (3) The concepts of employment must be the same from one industry to another, and so must the concepts of output. (4) The definition of an industry had to be convertible into the definitions used in the interindustry relations data used in estimating indirect output effects.

[2] For manufacturing, the term "subindustry" is used to refer to an industry in the four-digit classification of the Census of Manufactures, which is generally the same as that of the Standard Industrial Classification. In agriculture and extractive industries, the term refers to an industry in the 450-order classification used by the Bureau of Labor Statistics in its 1947 interindustry relations study. See "Industry Classification Manual for the 1947 Interindustry Relations Study," prepared June 6, 1952, and revised March 20, 1953, by the Division of Interindustry Economics, U. S. Bureau of Labor Statistics (mimeo).

The Criterion of Significant Protection

To determine whether a subindustry has significant protection requires determining what commodities have significant protection and then determining the subindustry to which each commodity belongs.

In general a commodity was regarded as having a significant degree of protection if the duty or its ad valorem equivalent was 5 per cent or more in 1953.[3] This criterion was subject to the qualification that if the ad valorem equivalent of the duty in 1953 did not exceed 10 per cent, the value of imports in 1953 had to be a million dollars or more. Where protection took the form of an import quota, it was regarded as significant wherever there was some evidence that in a normal year the quota had some effect in restricting imports.[4]

A special problem arose in connection with agricultural commodities that are protected against imports only because their prices are supported by government programs. It appeared pointless to consider the effects of reducing protection of commodities subject to price support programs unless prices were above support levels. If market prices are at or near the support levels, a reduction of import barriers without a reduction of support levels would force an increase of government purchases of domestic output as private purchases of it declined. There would be no primary output and employment effects; the primary effect would be merely an increase in the amounts going into government stocks through purchase or loan operations under the price-support program.[5]

[3] The mere presence of a duty would not constitute protection if domestic output were subject to an equal excise tax from which imports were exempt. All United States excise taxes in effect in 1953 except those on lubricating oils, however, applied to imports as well as domestic output. The year 1953 was used as a reference year for this and most other purposes in the study because it was the latest year for which relevant data were available at the time the study was begun. It was also a year of "full" employment and relatively stable prices.

[4] Global absolute quotas that are subdivided into country quotas and tariff quotas both required further refinement of these criteria.

[5] There might be some output increases but they would be secondary changes resulting from the expansion of exports. Apart from this export effect, domestic output would be unchanged because the contractive effect of the shift in private domestic spending toward imports would be exactly offset by the rise in government spending on domestic output. It may also be noted that if the government reduced protection but not support levels for such commodities, it would, in effect, be sup-

A reduction of barriers against imports of such commodities needs be considered, therefore, only in conjunction with a reduction of support prices. A substantial reduction of support prices for some commodities, however, would reduce them to levels at which the corresponding foreign products would not be competitive. In these cases, there would be no tendency for domestic demand to shift from the domestic to the foreign product, even if import barriers were eliminated. The only price-supported commodities whose liberalization seemed worth considering, therefore, were those for which unrestricted imports would be competitive if domestic prices were lowered substantially.

On these grounds, it was decided to exclude from the category of significantly protected commodities all agricultural commodities whose prices were actually being supported in 1953 and whose support prices, if cut 25 per cent, would be below the landed prices of corresponding foreign goods in the United States market. This test was applied by estimating the 1953 landed price of imports of their corresponding foreign commodities and comparing it with a hypothetical domestic price 25 per cent below the level of 1953 supports. If the landed price of the foreign commodity was above this level, the domestic commodity was rejected.

According to this test, the commodities with which imports would not have been competitive under reduced price supports, even in the absence of import restrictions, were wheat, rye, barley, corn, oats, flaxseed, soybeans, tobacco, and peanuts. The only significantly protected commodity that passed this test was cotton.[6]

Significantly protected commodities that passed these tests, hereafter referred to as "accepted" commodities, were assigned to subindustries that produced the most nearly similar commodity. Of the 551 subindustries in the economy, 336 contained some commodities accepted under these tests.

---

porting the price of foreign as well as domestic output. The fact that present law seeks to avoid this consequence indicates that this alternative is unrealistic as well as devoid of primary effects.

[6] It may be noted that some experts in the Department of Agriculture expressed the personal opinion that, given 1953 conditions and the absence of any price support and import barriers, imports of cotton, as well as other major export crops, would not be likely to increase. See also J. K. Galbraith, "Economic Preconceptions and the Farm Policy," *American Economic Review*, Vol. 44 (March 1954), p. 49.

Representativeness of Subindustry
Employment-Output Relationships

The second criterion is whether the relation between employment and output of accepted commodities in a subindustry can be reliably estimated from available data on the relationship between employment and output of the entire subindustry. This problem involves two questions: (1) How well do the employment-output relations for the subindustry represent those of the accepted commodities it contains? and (2) Are the available data for the subindustry reliable?

Obviously if the relationship between total employment and total output prevailing in a subindustry at a given time is not representative of the relationship that would apply to changes in the output of a basket of its accepted commodities, we cannot assume that it will give an accurate estimate of the direct employment effects of such a change. To test this representativeness directly would require comparing the employment-output ratio of the subindustry with the ratio of changes in employment to changes in output for the basket of its accepted commodities. The data needed for such a test are not available. The a priori probability that a subindustry represents its accepted commodities accurately in this respect is obviously greater, however, the greater the extent to which it consists of such commodities, because then the ratio of changes in the subindustry's employment to changes in its output is more likely to be similar to that of the basket of its accepted commodities. Of course, mere representativeness provides no guaranty that the relationship of total employment to total output of a subindustry is an accurate measure of the relationship between changes in its employment and changes in its output, and therefore of the relationship between such changes for its accepted commodities. That question, which relates to the economic behavior of a subindustry rather than to how well the subindustry represents the basket of its accepted commodities, is considered on page 87 and in Appendix D. Nevertheless, representativeness of its accepted commodities is one test that a subindustry must meet if data concerning it are to provide accurate estimates of the corresponding characteristics of its accepted commodities. Since the representativeness of a subindustry could not be tested directly, it could best be judged by testing this a priori probability.

This probability could best be tested by measuring the importance of the output of a subindustry's accepted commodities in its total output. If the output of the accepted commodities produced by a subindustry was 75 per cent or more of its total output, the employment-output relationships in the subindustry were regarded as representing satisfactorily the corresponding relationships of its accepted component.[7] They were also regarded as representative in a few cases where this fraction was between 50 and 75 per cent, so long as the employment-output relationships for the accepted commodities and for the whole subindustry appeared likely to be approximately the same. Of the 336 subindustries that contained accepted commodities, 134 were rejected because they did not pass this test, leaving 202 subindustries accepted on this criterion.

It is to be noted that we are assuming that if the total domestic output of a subindustry in 1953 consisted largely of accepted commodities, the employment-output relationship for that subindustry is equal to an average of the employment-output relationships of the collection of accepted commodities that it contains.

The second question in deciding whether available data for a subindustry's employment-output relationship reliably represent those of its collection of accepted commodities was whether these data reliably represent the actual relationship for the subindustry

[7] The available data do not permit making precisely this test, either. For most commodities, the bulk of output is produced in one subindustry but some output may be produced in other subindustries as "secondary" production. The proportion of the total output of all commodities "primary" to a subindustry that is produced in that subindustry can be determined from available data. For individual commodities, however, the only available output data are for total output wherever it is produced; no data are available for only that portion of the output of an individual commodity that is produced by the establishments in the manufacturing subindustry which produces it as a "primary" product. Therefore it is not possible to find the value of output of accepted commodities produced in a single subindustry. This would not constitute a problem if data were also available for total employment in producing a commodity and for input-output relations between commodities, since then we would not have to be concerned with subindustries. But employment data are available only for total establishments, which are classified according to their primary production, and input-output relations are available only for industry aggregates of establishments. Therefore, the test had to be carried out by measuring the ratio of the total output of accepted commodities primary to a subindustry, in whatever subindustry they were produced, to the total output, wherever produced, of all the commodities produced primarily in that subindustry.

itself. This problem arises only because the available data were based on a sample rather than a census; it is a technical question that need not be explored here. It is sufficient to note that of the 202 subindustries that were accepted up to this point, 25 were rejected because the available data on their employment-output ratios were regarded as not reliable for sampling reasons. Five more were rejected because of other deficiencies in the data, leaving 172 subindustries that were accepted for estimation of employment effects.

Short-Period Variability of Agricultural Output

It was also necessary to consider whether the output of subindustries producing accepted unprocessed agricultural commodities would be likely to respond significantly in a short period to decreases of demand, for if there were no output response there would be no employment response. While there appears to be no clear agreement among agricultural economists about how responsive agricultural outputs or inputs are to changes in demand or about the time required before there is any response at all, there does appear to be agreement that output of few agricultural commodities responds much within a year, even when prices decline substantially. The literature concerning the responsiveness of particular agricultural commodities was reviewed, and subindustries that consist mainly of commodities whose output appears to be relatively unresponsive to changes of demand within a year, even with substantial price decreases, were rejected for analysis of employment changes. The subindustries rejected on this ground were cotton, tree nuts, legumes and grass seeds, and sugar and sirup crops. Elimination of these four subindustries reduced the number of accepted subindustries to 168.

Applicability of Interindustry Relationships

Although it was believed that direct employment decreases could be reliably estimated for the 168 subindustries, it does not follow that the total employment effects of liberalization can be reliably estimated for all of them. Total employment effects have to be estimated from total output effects, and estimates of total output effects require a pattern of interindustry relations between all the sectors of the economy to tell us the change in the output of every sector resulting from an initial change in the output of any one sector. Such a pattern of relationships is not available for subindustries. The most detailed available pattern of inter-sectoral buying and selling relationships divides production of the economy (other than construction) into 200 industries. The total output effects can therefore be estimated only for liberalization of those accepted subindustries whose buying and selling relations are reliably represented by those of the 200-order industry of which they are a part.

The 168 accepted subindustries fall in 89 of these 200 industries. It was possible that the accepted subindustries in a single one of these 89 industries accounted for only a small part of that industry's total output. Where that was the case, we could not safely assume that the interindustry buying and selling relations of the entire industry, which the available pattern of interindustry relations reflects, were representative of those of its accepted sub-industries, in whose initial changes of output we were interested. (More strictly, the question is whether we could safely assume that an industry's buying and selling relations represent well those of the accepted *commodities* in accepted subindustries—for we must remember that output of the accepted subindustries may consist, up to 25 per cent —or in a few cases up to 50 per cent—of output of rejected commodities.) Since accurate estimates could be made only on the assumption of representativeness, the question therefore became: What is required for an industry's buying and selling relations to be representative of the basket of commodities we wish to examine? The requirement is two-fold. First, the industry should not contain too large a portion of commodities that are excluded from the basket and are likely to have different buying and selling relations. Second, the commodities that are in the basket should be included in the industry and in the basket in the same relative proportions.

Let us first consider the second of these two requirements. We could not control the relative proportions of subindustries in the whole industry, for that was determined by the actual composition of the industry that was reflected in the basic data underlying the interindustry buying and selling relations. But we could control the composition of the basket we were considering, for that was of our own making. Accordingly, our million-dollar industry basket of import increases had to combine accepted subindustries in the proportions that were reflected in the basic data, namely, their relative importance in domestic output, not their relative importance in some other respect, such as imports. This assumption about the composition of the million-dollar basket was imposed on us by the interindustry relations data and the fact that we wanted to frame our question in a way that gave us the greatest possible assurance that the answer would be correct.[8]

The other requirement that had to be met before we could assume that an industry's buying and selling relations are representative of those of its accepted subindustries was that it should not contain too large a portion of commodities that are not in the basket and that are likely to have buying and selling relations different from those of commodities in the basket. To meet this requirement, it was necessary to examine the composition of each of the 89 industries containing accepted subindustries. It was assumed that the relevant purchase patterns of the industry as a whole would represent well those of such accepted commodities if shipments of accepted commodities primary to accepted subindustries constituted at least 33 per cent of the total 1947 shipments of all products primary to the industry. This percentage appeared to be sufficiently high for a test because, in classifying subindustries into industries, the Bureau of Labor Statistics had already sought to avoid putting into the same industry subindustries that had greatly

[8] Even though there was no choice about the composition of the basket of import increases, it may nevertheless be asked whether it is plausible to assume or imply that protection for the different commodities in an industry would ever be reduced in a manner that caused their imports to increase in proportion to their domestic output. Would it not be more reasonable to consider reductions of barriers that permit imports to increase in proportion to the pre-liberalization pattern of imports? A politically realistic answer probably is "No, it would not be." Since the ratio of imports to domestic production varies greatly from one commodity to another, such a pattern of import increases would imply that the direct effects on domestic output for different commodities would be very unequal percentages of their total domestic output. Since it is politically more realistic to suppose that the percentage effects on domestic output would be regarded as the important factor in determining the amount of reduction in import barriers, a pattern of equal percentage increases in imports appears less plausible than a pattern of import increases that is proportional to competing domestic output.

different patterns of purchases of goods and services for current production.

Of the 89 industries containing accepted subindustries, 17 were rejected on the ground that they failed to pass this test, and 72 industries, containing 151 accepted subindustries, were accepted. It may be noted that for 64 of the 72 industries accepted, shipments of accepted commodities primary to accepted subindustries were 50 per cent or more of total shipments of all products primary to the industry, for 41 of the 72 accepted industries they were 75 per cent or more, and for 19 industries, shipments of products primary to the industry consisted entirely of accepted commodities primary to accepted subindustries. (These percentages for each accepted industry are shown in Appendix Table B.1, Column 1.

Estimation of Gross Primary Decreases of Domestic Output

Having described selection of the industries whose interindustry relations could be expected to represent well those of their accepted components, we turn to the process of estimating the gross primary decreases of domestic output in all industries resulting from an initial decrease in the output of each of the 72 accepted industries.

The estimates were made in the following steps: (1) The decreases in supplies from each industry, including both domestic output and imports competing with it, that would result from the assumed initial million-dollar decrease in domestic output of each accepted industry were estimated from the pattern of interindustry relations.[9] These decreases included decreases in the agricultural

[9] Data on the pattern of interindustry relations are available in several forms. Some were designed to answer the question, How much domestic output of every industry is required by an initial requirement for the domestic output of an industry, if all requirements are supplied by domestic output and none are supplied by imports? Others were designed to answer the question, How much total supply of the products of every industry, including not only its domestic output but also imports competing with it, is required by an initial requirement for the output of both the domestic and imported supplies of any industry, assuming that the domestic output of each industry and the imports competing with this output always maintain the

output that is assumed in this study *not* to change in the short-period, as well as decreases in output used directly or indirectly in producing this agricultural output. These portions therefore, had to be regarded as fictitious for purposes of this study. (2) The second step, accordingly, was to eliminate the fictitious decreases of output from the total gross decrease in output. The figures resulting from this process, however, still included decreases in the imports competing with each domestic supplying industry. (3) Accordingly, the third step was to eliminate these decreases in imports in order to get the decreases in the domestic output of every industry.

Combined Decreases of Domestic Output and Competing Imports

The combined decreases in domestic output and competing imports of every industry that would result from the assumed initial million-dollar decreases in domestic output of accepted industries were estimated from a pattern of interindustry buying and selling relations that had been prepared by the Bureau of Labor Statistics. Although this pattern had been modified to take into account certain later data, it was based primarily on data for the year 1947.[10]

Use of this pattern of interindustry relationships involves the major assumption that the structure of relationships between an industry's purchases of current inputs and its sale of outputs, as incorporated in the available interindustry relations data, correctly portrays the relationships between *changes* in such purchases and *changes* in its sales at the time to which the estimates

---

same relative shares that are implied in the data on which the interindustry pattern is based? The form of interindustry patterns chosen was one that answered the latter question. The reasons for this choice and a discussion of the problems involved in applying this form of interindustry relations to the present problem may be found in Appendix C.

[10] Since these interindustry relationships were expressed in 1947 prices while the assumed million-dollar direct decreases of output of the liberalized industries represented domestic values expressed in 1953 prices, it was necessary to convert these stipulated decreases into equivalent 1947 values before the interindustry relationships could be applied. The industry price indices used to make this conversion were calculated by averaging the price indices for the accepted component subindustries, using 1953 domestic output as weights. The price indices for the accepted subindustries were obtained from the U. S. Bureau of Labor Statistics. The industry and subindustry price indices are shown in Appendix Table D.1.

arc assumed to apply. This assumption raises two distinct questions: First, how much have these relationships changed since the basic data were collected? Second, is the ratio of the *changes* in an industry's purchases from another industry to the *changes* in its sales the same as the ratio of its *total* purchases from that industry to its *total* sales, even at a given time?

Two kinds of change over time are relevant. First are changes in technology or relative prices which alter the proportions of purchased materials and services used to produce a given output and may even result in the substitution of materials purchased from one industry for those purchased from another. Second are changes in the composition of an industry's output, which may involve substantial changes in its sources of supply. Both types of change could alter the structure of interindustry relationships significantly.

Some of these changes have been allowed for in the structure of relationships used.[11] Despite these changes, it may be taken for granted that many other changes have also occurred since 1947 and that the relationships used are, to that extent, out of date. Unfortunately, this difficulty could not be avoided, since no network of interindustry relationships based on a more recent year was available when the estimates were made. It therefore had to be assumed that the 1947 relationships, as modified, give an accurate approximation of 1953 relationships. There is no basis for judging the direction or the size of the error involved in this assumption.

The assumption that the ratio of the *changes* in purchases from each industry for current production would bear the same ratio to *changes* in sales as the *total of* such purchases bears to *total* sales may also be questioned. Purchases for current production do not always expand and contract proportionally to output. Advertising is one "input" of services that provides an obvious, although perhaps extreme, illustration of this point. When output

---

[11] The distribution of the output of eighteen industries was revised to incorporate 1951 or later distributions. Of these revisions, the most important was the substitution of the 1953 distribution of fuels and electrical energy for that of 1947. In addition, selected revisions were made to reflect changes since 1947 in the inputs of seven industries. See "The Mobilization Model Matrix," a Working Document dated March 15, 1954, prepared by Jack G. Faucett of the Division of Interindustry Economics, U. S. Bureau of Labor Statistics.

of a commodity decreases, advertising of it does not necessarily or even usually diminish by the same proportion; indeed, it may even increase. Unfortunately, there is also little basis for judging the direction or size of error introduced by this consideration.

Elimination of Effects of Fictitious Decreases in Agricultural Output

These estimates of output changes imply that all changes in demand for an industry's product (at the initial prices) cause equal declines of its output. This assumption, if applied to a period long enough to permit inventories to be adjusted to sales, appears reasonable enough for most industries but not for all agricultural industries. For three such industries—meat animals and their products, poultry and eggs, and fruits and vegetables— it was accepted as a reasonable approximation of what would happen. It probably exaggerates the short-period responsiveness of production in all of them, however, and certainly exaggerates it for parts of the meat animals and products industry, such as beef cattle. Insofar as it does exaggerate their decreases of output, it necessarily also exaggerates the cut in their purchases from their suppliers and thus in the output of these suppliers, and similarly in the output of the suppliers' suppliers, etc., further overstating the output and employment decreases.

For the other 6 agricultural industries—farm dairy products, food grains and feed crops, cotton, tobacco, oil-bearing crops, and "all other agricultural products"—the assumption of full responsiveness of output was rejected. Studies of the responsiveness of agricultural production appeared to indicate that for these industries it would be more realistic to assume that domestic output does not respond to decreases of market demand in periods as short as one year, either because of characteristics inherent in their production or because large portions of their outputs are price-supported. An adjustment was therefore made in the estimates of output decreases that were obtained from the pattern of interindustry relations, in order to eliminate the component that was being treated as fictitious. This adjustment, which was made in 12 of the 72 cases, involved eliminating both the decreases of output of these 6 agricultural industries and any further significant decreases of output that are generated by these decreases.[12] If error is introduced into the final estimates by this adjustment, it is in the direction of understating the output decrease, but the available evidence suggests that any error that does exist is very slight for periods of a year and is probably not large for periods of two years. In any event, none of these agricultural industries is among the 72 industries whose liberalization is examined, so the error can arise only in connection with their participation in the effects of liberalization in other industries, a participation which is in most cases small.

Estimation of Domestic Output Decreases

The estimate obtained after this adjustment had been made still included decreases in imports along with decreases of domestic output. Since, for the purpose of estimating the gross decreases of domestic employment, we are interested in the decreases only of domestic output, it was necessary to eliminate the component that represented decreases of imports. The pattern of interindustry relations that was used to get the estimates divides the total supply of products of each industry between domestic production and imports in the ratio that existed in 1952.[13] In using it to allocate the decrease of supplies between domestic output and imports, we thus assume implicitly that the ratio of total domestic output of each of the 200 industries to total imports of similar goods in 1952 correctly represents the ratio of the *change* in its domestic output to the *change* in imports of similar goods. We must consider whether this is a reasonable assumption.

Many economists have expressed the opinion that, for commodities obtained both from domestic production and abroad,

[12] The decision as to whether to assume a full output response or none at all for each agricultural industry, was based on a review of the literature concerning output responses in agriculture. The cases in which the adjustment was made, the criteria for deciding whether to make it, and the procedure used to make it will be found in Appendix C. It may be noted that output also does not respond to changes in demand for by-products, but adjustments to allow for this fact were not made.

[13] One of the ways in which the U. S. Bureau of Labor Statistics adjusted the 1947 interindustry relations data was to substitute 1952 relationships between imports and total output for those of 1947.

the proportion of a *change* in domestic use that comes from imports is higher than the proportion of the *total* amount that comes from imports, *i.e.,* that imports change by a larger percentage than domestic output. If this view is correct, it means that the proportion of any change that comes from domestic production is lower than is assumed by these estimates and that the change in domestic production and employment tends, on this account, to be overstated. It is also possible that changes in domestic production may play a smaller role in changes of total supply now and in the future than in 1952, as our dependence on foreign sources for some goods increases. This, if true, would also tend to make these estimates overstate the domestic effects of future changes.

Although either or both of these points may be valid for some industries, it is far from certain that they are valid for all, and it seems quite likely that contrary statements could be correctly made about some industries.[14] Thus, it may well be that domestic production provides a higher, not a lower, proportion of the increments in supply of products of some industries than of their total supply. It is undoubtedly true, also, that while our dependence on foreign supplies is now and will in the future be higher than in 1952 for some goods, it probably will be lower for others, as the past history of synthetic substitutes for imports suggests. The net effect of such changes for the economy as a whole is uncertain. Thus, if any error is involved in our assumption about this point, its direction is conjectural.

The estimates of this study also assume that when the ratio of domestic production to imports in one industry is decreased by its liberalization, the corresponding ratios for other industries remain unaffected. In some cases, this is unrealistic because imports of the products of one industry may compete, directly or indirectly, with those of another. For example, a reduction of barriers against imports of raw wool, while reducing domestic production of wool, would reduce the cost of wool to domestic woolen goods manufacturers and permit them to compete more effectively with imports. Therefore, it would probably raise the proportion of the total supply of woolen goods that comes from domestic production and reduce the proportion that comes from abroad. The estimates

---

[14] For a fuller discussion of this point, see Appendix C.

make no allowance for any shift to domestic production from competing imports that may occur in one industry when liberalization in another makes its raw materials or other costs cheaper. Insofar as such shifts do occur, the estimates overstate adverse effects on output and employment.[15]

The figures obtained after the import component of the estimates was eliminated represented estimates of the total gross primary decreases in domestic output, direct and indirect, resulting from the assumed million-dollar initial reductions in output of the liberalized industries. The next step was to estimate, in each case, the employment decreases associated with these output decreases in each industry.

Estimating Employment Decreases Associated with Gross Primary Output Decreases

At this stage of the estimating process, we had, for each of 72 cases, the total (combined direct and indirect) gross decrease of domestic output in each industry resulting from an initial million-dollar reduction in the domestic output of a basket of commodities in a liberalized industry. The next problem was to convert these decreases of output in each industry into the associated decreases of employment.

General Problems of Converting Output Changes into Associated Employment Changes

In estimating employment changes from output changes, three general questions arise. The first problem—a very important one in its effect on the results—is to determine the relationship be-

---

[15] The user can allow for these shifts toward domestic production, however, by stipulating whatever increases he thinks would occur in the output of these industries. See Chapter 10 and Appendix G. As was noted in Chapter 2, such shifts may also result less directly through competition between the liberalized industry and another industry for productive resources. Changes in production that require shifts in the use of resources are not taken into account in these estimates, which relate to short-period changes.

tween changes in output and changes in employment. The second is whether to estimate changes in the number of production workers or in the number of total employees (which includes executives, office employees, custodial workers, etc.). The third is whether to use a man-year or a man-hour concept of employment.

What does the empirical evidence indicate about the relationship between changes in employment and changes in output? Published studies of this relationship suggest that ratios of employment to output are generally higher, the lower the level of output, and that this is true of industries as well as of individual firms. This implies that industry-wide changes in employment are less than proportional to industry-wide changes in output. These studies, however, do not provide a conclusive answer to the question whether the use of a proportional relationship between total employment in an industry and its total output causes overstatement or understatement of the employment decreases associated with output decreases caused by liberalization. Some of these studies relate to industries in other countries. Their findings are also affected by changes in the commodity composition of the output of individual industries, an effect that would have to be eliminated to obtain an answer that would be conclusive for our purposes. Moreover, to find any other more valid single relationship would have required a statistical investigation amounting to another major study. Therefore, in determining the relationship between changes in output and changes in employment for subindustries and industries that produce commodities, the best general assumption to make appeared to be that the ratios of change in employment to change in output are equal to their ratios of total employment to total output in 1953.[16]

Although the assumption of proportionality appeared to be a valid one for commodity-producing industries, it was not regarded as a safe one to apply to non-commodity-producing industries. It is well known that in many of these industries—electric power, railroads, wholesale and retail trade, to mention only a few— changes of employment are far from proportional to changes of

---

[16] Considerations bearing on the validity of this assumption are discussed in the text below. The empirical evidence referred to in the text is summarized in Appendix D.

output. Special studies of postwar data were therefore made to find the best relationships to use for these industries.[17]

The answer to the second question—whether to convert output changes into changes in employment of total employees or of production workers only—depended in part on the decision that was made concerning the relationship between changes in employment and changes in output. Since this relationship was assumed to be equal to the ratio between *total* employment and *total* output, the choice between estimating changes in employment of all employees or changes in employment only of production workers depended on whether the number of total employees or the number of production workers is more likely, in economic behavior, to bear the more constant ratio to total industry output when the level of output changes.

Two considerations appeared relevant to this question. First, in any individual firm, some of the employees, such as office personnel, constitute overhead labor whose number changes less than proportionately to output if it changes at all. Consequently, if output declines, the total number of employees changes less than proportionately. On this ground, the use of a constant ratio of total employees to output therefore seemed undesirable; to apply it to decreases in output would result in overstating decreases of employment. It is true that when output declines, there is some decline in employment of nonproduction workers, so that some understatement would probably result from using ratios of production workers to output. Nevertheless, since the number of production workers changes more nearly in proportion to output than does the number of employees, it would be more accurate, so far as this consideration alone is concerned, to use a ratio of production workers to value of output.

The second consideration, however, works in the opposite direction. A fall in output is not likely to reduce the output of all domestic firms in the same proportion, but is likely to fall more heavily on those with the highest variable costs. These are likely to be the firms that use a larger number of employees per unit of output than does the industry as a whole. If we translate the

---

[17] See Appendix D for an explanation of how the incremental employment-output relationships for these industries were derived. The analytical work on this problem was done by Mrs. Eva Jacobs.

output change into the change in employment by applying to it a ratio applicable to the industry as a whole, the resulting employment change will on this account be understated. Thus, if we had used industry ratios of production workers to output, we would almost certainly have understated the employment effects of given output changes. With the use of ratios of total employees to output, the tendency toward overstatement resulting from the less-than-proportionate changes in employment of nonproduction workers is at least partially and perhaps wholly or more than wholly offset by the tendency toward understatement resulting from the fact that decreases of output and therefore of employment in an industry are probably concentrated on the firms with the highest employment-output ratios.

For the answer to the third question—whether to define employment in man-years or man-hours—there was little choice. It would have been preferable to estimate the employment effects of given changes in output in terms of man-hours worked, because this would have permitted taking into account the fact that changes of output are sometimes reflected in changes in the number of hours worked per week rather than in changes in the number of people employed. However, the available industry data on all employees are in the form of man-years rather than man-hours.

We may now turn to the specific problem of converting the decreases in the domestic output of the various industries into the associated decreases of employment. To do this most accurately, it was necessary to apply to each industry's decrease in output a relationship between changes of employment and changes of output that would most accurately reflect the commodity composition of the changes in output.

The changes of output in an industry may have two components, direct changes, which are confined to the protected commodities whose output is assumed to be displaced, and indirect changes, which occur when the industry supplies goods or services to the liberalized industry or to its direct or indirect suppliers. Although in all cases most of the direct change of output occurs in the liberalized industry, some of it occurs in other industries.[18]

[18] As indicated in footnote 7, above, not all the output of a commodity is produced by the industry to which the commodity is primary; some of its output, usually a small portion, is produced by other industries as a secondary product. In

The commodity composition of the direct change in output in any case is known because its composition has been stipulated. Attainment of maximum accuracy in the employment estimates requires using this information by computing employment-output relationships appropriate to the direct portion of the output changes.

We are able to say how much of the total output decrease is the direct decrease because we have stipulated that the direct decrease is a million dollars in 1953 prices. Since we also have data that enable us to estimate the proportion of this direct decrease that occurs in the liberalized industry, and since we are in a position to compute the average employment-output ratio that is most appropriate to the direct decrease of output, it is desirable to estimate separately the employment changes associated with the direct and the indirect output changes in the liberalized industry.

For a non-liberalized industry, however, there is no way of determining how its total ouput decrease is distributed between the indirect component and any direct component that may exist. Therefore the total output change in a non-liberalized industry must be treated as a whole.

Thus the translation of the total output changes into employment changes in each case was accomplished in three steps. First, the direct output of the liberalized industry was isolated and converted into the associated employment decrease by use of an employment-output ratio appropriate to its accepted subindustries; second, the indirect decrease of employment in the liberalized industry was estimated; and, third, the total decrease of output in each of the 199 non-liberalized industries was converted into associated employment decreases.[19]

---

the pattern of interindustry relations used in this study, the "output" of an industry is defined as the total output of the products primary to that industry, wherever they are produced, plus its output of secondary products. This means that the output of a secondary product is counted twice, once in the output of the industries that actually produce it and again in the output of the industry to which it is primary. Thus, the coal produced as a secondary product by the steel industry is counted in the output of both the steel and coal industries. Because of this type of duplication, output results obtained from this pattern of interindustry relations must be adjusted in estimating the associated employment effects. How this adjustment was made is described in Appendix D.

[19] Since the output changes of an industry, as obtained from the pattern of interindustry relationships, were expressed in 1947 prices, they had to be converted into 1953 prices before their employment equivalents were estimated. In the case of a liberalized industry, the total output decrease had to be apportioned between its

Employment Decreases Associated with Direct
Output Decreases in Liberalized Industries

To estimate the employment decrease associated with the direct decrease in output of the liberalized industry, it was necessary in each case (1) to compute average employment-output ratios for its accepted subindustries; (2) from these ratios to compute an average employment-output ratio applicable to the direct changes in the industry's output; (3) to estimate the portion of the industry's total output decrease that was direct; and (4) to apply the average ratio to the direct portion of its output decrease.

The first step in obtaining employment-output ratios applicable to the direct changes in output was to obtain 1953 ratios of employment to output for the accepted subindustries of the liberalized industries. The problems involved in obtaining them were mainly of a technical character and need not be described here.[20]

For manufacturing, the only available employment and output data for a subindustry include the total employment and output of the business establishments in that subindustry. Of course, the major share of the output of an establishment in a subindustry consists of the commodities that are produced primarily in that particular subindustry; that is why the establishment is classified in it. But many of these establishments also produce commodities that are produced primarily in another subindustry, and of course some portion of their employees' efforts is devoted to such "sec-

direct and indirect components before being converted into 1953 prices, because these two portions were to be converted into their employment equivalents separately and the indices appropriate to converting them into 1953 prices are different. The direct portion of the output change was converted to 1953 prices by using the price indices applicable to its accepted subindustries, described in footnote 10, above, and shown in Appendix Table D.1. Conversion of the indirect portion required price indices for the liberalized industries that reflected the ratio of 1953 to 1947 prices for their entire domestic output, not just that of their accepted subindustries. In the non-liberalized industries, the total output decreases, like the indirect portion of the decrease in the liberalized industries, were converted into equivalent 1953 money values by averaging the price indices for all their component subindustries, combining them with 1953 domestic output weights. The resulting industry price indices are shown in Appendix Table D.2.

[20] *E.g.*, output data were not available for many subindustries and had to be estimated from data on shipments, book value of inventories at the beginning and end of 1953, and relevant price indexes. The basic data used to derive employment-output relationships were those of the U. S. Bureau of the Census for manufactured products, the U. S. Bureau of Mines for minerals, and the U. S. Department of Agriculture for agricultural products.

ondary" production. For this reason and because the employment-output ratios are based on data for entire establishments, the ratios for some industries are affected by the presence of this secondary production and the employment on it, and therefore may not represent accurately the employment-output ratios of their "primary" products alone. In general, the smaller the share of a subindustry's total output that is devoted to such secondary output, the more confident we can be that its employment-output ratio represents accurately that of its "primary" products.[21]

For agriculture, the employment data were not available in terms of employee man-years, the concept used for other areas of the economy. The available information for subindustries represented the annual full-time-equivalent number of hours worked by all persons engaged in producing the subindustry's primary commodities—hired workers, unpaid family workers, and the farmer himself. To obtain greater comparability with the concept of employment used for other industries, these data were converted into man-year data by the use of an estimated average work week. Employment figures for agriculture still differ from those for other areas, however, in not being confined to employees.

The second step in obtaining employment-output ratios applicable to the direct changes in output of a liberalized industry was to obtain an average of the corresponding ratios for its accepted subindustries, weighted in proportion to the importance of these subindustries in the direct change of the industry's 1953 output.

The composition of this direct output decrease is known. It consists only of accepted commodities in accepted subindustries. For reasons given on pages 78 and 79, accepted subindustries must be combined in their domestic output proportions. The appropriate employment-output ratio to apply to the direct decrease in output of a liberalized industry, therefore, is an average of the ratios for its accepted subindustries, weighted in proportion to their 1953 outputs.

The employment-output ratios for the accepted subindustries in these 72 industries, the weights used in averaging them, and the

---

[21] The problem of secondary output does not arise in agricultural and mineral production because the ratios were based on data for employment on, and production of commodities, not on data for establishments.

resulting direct employment-output ratios for the 72 accepted industries are shown in Appendix Table D.1.[22]

The third step was to determine the portion of the total output decrease in the liberalized industry that was direct and to which the employment-output ratio just described should be applied.

Although the direct output decrease in the economy as a whole is, by assumption, equal to the million-dollar increase in imports that was stipulated, this does not mean that the direct output decrease occurring in the liberalized industry is a million dollars. Since the commodities primary to an industry are not all produced in it, some—generally a small portion—being produced as secondary products elsewhere, it cannot be assumed that the direct output decreases occur entirely in the liberalized industry. This fact made it necessary to estimate the portion of this whole million-dollar direct decrease that occurs in the liberalized industry. In estimating the proportion of direct decrease occurring in the liberalized industry, it was assumed that a liberalized industry's share of the direct output decrease is the same as its 1947 share in the whole economy's production of all the commodities primary to it.

The process of obtaining the direct employment decrease in each liberalized industry was completed simply by applying its direct employment-output ratio to the estimated direct decrease of its output.

Employment Decreases Associated with Indirect Output Decreases in Liberalized Industries

It was pointed out earlier that the output decreases derived by the application of an interindustry pattern of relationships represent *total* output decreases in an industry and that even in the

[22] The total direct decrease of employment resulting from a million-dollar decrease in domestic output of a basket of commodities may be estimated by multiplying by 1,000 the figure for employment per $1,000 of direct output in the appropriate liberalized subindustry or industry, shown in Appendix Table D.1. It should be noted, however, that although part of this million-dollar decrease of output occurs in subindustries which produce these commodities as secondary products, the employment-output ratios were derived solely from data relating to the subindustry that produces them as primary products. An estimate of direct employment decreases based on these ratios therefore implies that the relation of employment to output in the subindustry is representative of the ratio for all production of this basket of commodities, wherever it occurs.

case of the liberalized industry these effects are not necessarily only direct output effects. Although the major portion of this decrease in the liberalized industry will be the direct decrease resulting from the shift to imports away from domestic production, some of it may result from the fact that products of this industry may be required, directly or indirectly, to produce the liberalized commodities. Since the direct portion of the total output decrease in the liberalized industry had been determined, the amount of the indirect decrease in its output was estimated simply as the difference between its estimated total output decrease and its estimated share of the million-dollar decrease of output.

This indirect output decrease can, and probably often does, include decreases in the output of commodities produced by rejected subindustries within the liberalized industry. It would not have been appropriate, therefore, to estimate the employment effect of the indirect output decrease in the liberalized industry by using the same employment-output ratio that was used to estimate its direct employment decrease, because that ratio reflected employment-output relationships in accepted subindustries only. The employment-output ratio appropriate to the indirect decrease of output in the liberalized industry is in most cases probably one that reflects employment-output relationships for *all* its subindustries, combined in 1953 domestic output proportions.[23]

Employment Decreases Associated with Total
Output Decreases in Non-Liberalized Industries

The final step in estimating the employment decreases associated with the gross primary decreases of domestic output was to estimate the decreases of employment that would be associated in each of the 72 cases with the total decreases in domestic output in each of the 199 non-liberalized industries. In these industries there is no means of determining the distribution of the total decrease in output between the indirect component and any direct component that may exist, so there is no way of identifying the subindustries

[23] In a good many of the 72 liberalization cases, all subindustries within an industry were accepted for analysis. In such cases the direct and indirect employment-output coefficients are the same.

in which the total decreases occur. Just as in the case of the indirect decrease in the liberalized industry, the best employment-output relationship we can apply is one for the industry as a whole. This procedure implied that the various parts of each industry would contribute to the output decrease of their industry in the same proportions that they contributed to its total output in the period from which its employment-output relationship was derived.

The ratios of changes in employment to changes in output that were used to translate total output changes in non-liberalized industries and indirect output changes in liberalized industries into the employment changes associated with them are shown in Appendix Tables D.2 and D.3. There are 200 such relationships, one for each industry in the economy.

The resulting employment decreases in the non-liberalized industries, when added to the decreases in the liberalized industry, give the total *gross* primary employment decreases resulting from the assumed initial decrease of domestic purchases of the liberalized products. These gross decreases in each case for all industries combined were presented in Column 1 of Table 3.2. Their distribution among the 40 industry groups and the liberalized industry is shown in Appendix Table F.1.

Estimates of Gross Primary Employment Decreases by Short-Cut Methods

It was pointed out in Chapter 3 that gross primary employment decreases can be crudely estimated by applying to the stipulated million-dollar decrease of domestic output the average gross value added to production per worker in the economy as a whole, or its reciprocal, the average number of workers per dollar of gross value added to production. While an estimate made by this method cannot take into account the different employment requirements of different kinds of domestic output having equal value and cannot identify the industries in which the employment decreases occur, it has the advantage of simplicity; it can be calculated for any year directly from published data relating to national income and output. It is therefore of some practical interest to know how estimates of gross primary employment decreases in all industries obtained by this simplified method compare with the estimates based on interindustry relationships.

To answer this question, the crude estimate for 1953 may be compared with the estimate for the median of the 72 cases, which is 114.7 employees per million-dollar decrease of domestic output. Dividing the average number of full-time and part-time employees in 1953 (57.9 million) by total gross national product for that year ($365.4 billion) gives an average employment per million dollars of gross national product of 158.5 employees. This figure, besides being much higher than the median estimate in the 72 cases here analyzed, is higher than the estimates for all but 7 of them, as may be verified by inspecting Column 1 of Table 3.2.

This crude estimate differs conceptually from the estimates based on interindustry relations not only in giving different weights to the outputs of industries that are included in both methods but in three other respects. Although both methods give weighted averages of the number of employees required per dollar of gross value added to production in different industry sectors, the crude method includes in this average the number of employees required per dollar of gross value added in government and in such private nonbusiness sectors as households, private nonprofit institutions, and the rest of the world.

The ratios of employment to gross value added in these sectors of the economy are not reflected in the estimates based on interindustry relationships. The number of employees per dollar of gross value added in these economic sectors is substantially higher than in private nonagricultural business as a whole, so their inclusion in the crude estimate raises the weighted average.

The crude method also implies that changes of employment are proportional to changes of output in the service industries as well as in the commodity-producing industries, while the present study uses much lower ratios of change in employment to change in output for the service industries. This difference also tends to make the crude estimates of employment effects higher than those of this study.

Another difference is that the crude estimate implies a measurement of employment effects in agriculture based on the number of hired employees only, while the estimates of the present study treat the farm owner and unpaid farm family workers as employees. This difference tends to make the crude estimates of employment

effects lower than those of the present study. This influence, however, is clearly not a very strong one, partly because changes in
agricultural output are excluded from 12 cases of the present study,
but mainly because gross value added to output in agriculture had
a weight of only about 6 per cent in 1953 gross national product.

The crude method can be slightly refined and made more comparable to the concept implicit in the estimates of this study by
eliminating government and private nonbusiness employment and
output from the computation and by including in farm employment the non-employees engaged in farming. Thus refined, the
crude estimate becomes 153.0 men required per million dollars of
output.[24] This is not much closer to the median estimate of this
study than was obtained by the unrefined version of the crude
method and is higher than the estimates of this study for all but
10 of the 72 cases. Apparently the crude method yields estimates
substantially greater than those obtained in this study, whether it
is applied with or without adjustments for these two conceptual
differences. It may nevertheless be a useful method of establishing
quickly an upper limit for the gross primary employment decreases
caused by a liberalization program covering a number of industries.

The estimates of decreases of employment with which the crude
estimates have just been compared represent the gross, not the net
primary employment decreases resulting from the assumed shift of
purchases from domestic products to imports, because they do not
include the increases in domestic employment resulting from shipment of the additional imports. How these increases are estimated
is explained in the following section of this chapter.

Estimation of Employment Increases Associated with Increases of Imports

Increases in the importation of the liberalized commodities require additional ocean shipping and insurance services, which are
provided partly by the United States. They thereby give rise to

[24] The derivation of both versions of the crude estimate is shown in Appendix
Table G.1.

some increases in domestic employment.[25] To estimate these domestic employment increases, it is necessary first to estimate how
much the demand for the output of the domestic industries providing these services will increase in each case of liberalization as
a direct result of the stipulated million-dollar increase of imports.
Second, since increases in the output of these industries will generate increases in the output of their immediate and remote
suppliers, it is necessary to take into account the effects of these
direct increases on the output of all industries and to convert the
output effects into corresponding employment effects.

*Direct Effect on Output of Ocean Freight
and Insurance Industries*

To determine the amount of the transportation and insurance
services provided by the United States, it was necessary to estimate
the amount of each million-dollar basket of liberalized imports
that was absorbed by payments to all suppliers of these services
and then to distribute these payments between their foreign and
American recipients.

Unfortunately, there was no satisfactory basis for estimating the
total ocean freight and insurance costs per million-dollar industry
basket of imports in the year 1953. The only data available were
those obtained from the study of interindustry relations by the
Bureau of Labor Statistics, which related to 1947, and to all the
imports of an industry, not just its accepted imports. Accordingly,
it had to be assumed that both ocean freight and insurance costs
on the accepted imports of an industry in 1953 bore the same
relationship to foreign port values of these imports as did the ocean
freight and insurance costs on all the imports of an industry in
1947.

No satisfactory way of appraising the validity of this assumption
was found.[26] The assumption may introduce an error into the

---

[25] Output-induced decreases of imports of course give rise to decreases of ocean
shipping and insurance services and therefore of domestic employment in the industries providing these services. These decreases are automatically included in the
gross decreases discussed in the preceding section, because they are taken into account in the pattern of interindustry relations that was used.

[26] Total ocean freight earned on imports was 8.5 per cent of the adjusted total
value of merchandise imports in 1947 and 7.2 per cent in 1953. The fact that the

estimates of increases in domestic employment resulting from the process of importation, but if it does, the error must be small in relation to the gross employment decreases resulting from liberali zation. Even a substantial error in this assumption would affect the estimates significantly in very few of the 72 cases, because the frac tion of the $1 million that is absorbed by these charges exceeds 10 per cent of the domestic port value in only a few of the 72 cases and only the estimated American share affects domestic employment.

In most cases, this method of estimating the ocean freight and insurance costs gave plausible results. Ocean freight costs were generally less than 10 per cent of foreign port value. Only in the case of paints and allied products (#56) did they exceed 28 per cent. Similarly, insurance costs were generally less than one per cent of foreign port value and exceeded 5 per cent in only one case— also paints and allied products.[27]

Ocean freight on imports could not be allocated between domestic and foreign sources in proportions appropriate to each industry basket of imports because adequate data were not available, so the same allocation was made for all 72 cases of liberalization. It was based on the distribution of these earnings from transportation of all United States merchandise imports in recent years, which

---

total ratio changed between 1947 and 1953 is not necessarily inconsistent with the assumption that the ratios for imports of individual industries remained the same, because the relative importance of imports in individual industries—the weights in the weighted average ratio—changed considerably between the two years. For the same reason, however, the fact that the change in the total ratios was very small does not confirm the assumption; changes in individual industry ratios might have been offset by changes in the relative importance of different industries in total imports. Ocean freight earnings are given in Table 3 of "Developments in Overseas Transportation," *Survey of Current Business* (March 1956), p. 17, and the value of adjusted merchandise imports is given in the July 1954 and March 1956 issues of the *Survey*.

[27] In the case of paints and allied products, the source data indicated that ocean freight costs were 93 per cent of foreign value and that insurance costs were nearly 16 per cent of foreign port value. Estimates of both costs for paints and allied products are so far out of the range of other cases and are so implausible on their face that they must be presumed either to be incorrect or (since imports of paints and allied products in 1947 were extremely small) to reflect some unusual kind of shipment. In either case, they are bound to introduce error when applied generally to imports of paints and allied products. It must be concluded, therefore, that the employment increases associated with importation of paints and allied products are seriously overestimated. Since these estimated increases are substantial in relation to the estimated gross employment decreases in this case, the *net* employment decreases are probably seriously underestimated.

averaged 48 per cent to American shipping and 52 per cent to foreign countries.[28]

No information was available on the American and foreign shares of the insurance earnings on the carriage of American imports. Since these charges are relatively small, they were arbitrarily allocated in the same proportions as the ocean freight charges.

Effects on Output and Employment in All Industries

These methods provided estimates of the direct increases in output of the ocean freight and insurance industries resulting from the stipulated increases in imports. In order to determine the total domestic employment effects of these direct output increases, it was necessary to estimate their direct and indirect domestic output effects and to convert these output changes into the associated changes of employment.

In principle, the total output effects were estimated in the same way as were the total output effects of the decreases in domestic output of the liberalized industries (described on pages 80 to 86). In many cases of liberalization, however, the combined direct increases in output of the ocean freight and insurance industries were small in relation to the million-dollar direct decreases in output of the liberalized industries. It was clear, from inspection of the pattern of interindustry relations, that in such cases the indirect effects would be so small as to be not worth computing. It was therefore decided to ignore indirect output effects in all cases where the direct increases in the combined outputs of the ocean freight and insurance industries amounted to less than $25,000 per million dollars, *i.e.*, less than 2½ per cent of the direct decrease in domestic output of the liberalized industry. Of the 72 cases, 55 had direct increases in output small enough, on this criterion, to permit neglect of their indirect effects. For the other 17 cases, total output effects were estimated from the pattern of interindustry re-

[28] These percentages are averages of percentages for 1952, 1953, and 1954. The percentages of the total earned by American shipping in these three years were 49.1, 46.3, and 48.5, respectively. They were calculated from data published in *Survey of Current Business* (September 1953), Table 4, p. 23, and (March 1956), Table 3, p. 20.

lations described earlier in this chapter.[29]

Having estimated, in all 72 cases, the effects of the process of importation on the output of every industry that was perceptibly affected, the associated employment effects were estimated by applying to the output effects in every industry the employment-output ratios appropriate to it, shown in Appendix Tables D.2 and D.3. The resulting increases of employment in all industries were shown in Column 2 of Table 3.2.

To obtain the net effects on employment, it was necessary only to subtract the estimated employment increases caused by the addition to imports from the estimated decreases caused by the decrease in buying of domestic products. The gross decreases, the increases, and the net decreases for the whole economy were shown in Table 3.2. The net decreases for each industry group were discussed in Chapter 3 and shown in Table 3.3.

It should be noted that these increases have nothing to do with any effect that liberalization may have on exports. Such effects are considered quantitatively in the next chapters of this study.

[29] Since these relations were expressed in 1947 prices and the estimates of the direct increases in the output of the ocean freight and insurance industries were expressed in 1953 prices, it was first necessary to deflate the direct increases in output of both industries. For output of the ocean freight industry, a deflator was constructed from data on average freight revenue earned per ton of imports transported by ocean liners or tramp vessels, depending on the type of import carried. An index based on tramp rates was used to deflate the increase in ocean shipping resulting from increased imports of lead and zinc mining (#13), imports of the three baskets of steel products (#79.1, 79.2, and 79.3), and primary aluminum (#88). Liner rates were used to construct the deflator in the other cases. The basic data were obtained from the Balance of Payments Division of the Office of Business Economics, U. S. Department of Commerce. The output of the insurance industry was deflated by an index of domestic prices of the accepted subindustries in an industry, on the assumption that the insurance charges on a given basket of imports changed between 1947 and 1953 in proportion to the change in its value.

PART
III | *Export Increases*

CHAPTER 5

Employment Effects of Export Increases Associated with Liberalization

CHAPTER 3 PRESENTED estimates of the primary effect on employment of 72 baskets of import increases, each of which consisted of counterparts of protected commodities produced by one domestic industry. Those estimates, if considered alone, convey an unbalanced impression of the effects of liberalization on employment. Increases in imports are bound to have some stimulating effect on exports and therefore on employment, and this effect on employment offsets, at least partly, the employment decreases caused by the shifts of buying from domestic to imported products.

To estimate the employment effects of the liberalization-caused export increases, however, involves many difficulties. It requires making assumptions not only about most of the questions involved in estimating the primary employment effects of liberalization but about other questions as well—such as how foreign countries use the additional dollars they earn when the United States buys more of their goods. The range of possible answers to these additional questions is very wide; a solution based on any single set of answers is consequently more hazardous than it was when the primary effects were being estimated. Nevertheless, it seemed preferable to estimate these effects on one possible set of assumptions rather than to leave an unbalanced impression by not estimating export effects at all. Estimates of these effects are presented in this chapter, and the methods and assumptions used in making them are described fully in Chapters 6, 7, and 8.

What Is Estimated and Assumed

The estimates presented in this chapter represent the employment effects of 72 baskets of additional exports, each of which is assumed to result from one of the baskets of import increases that were the subject of Chapters 3 and 4. These employment effects include those in the industries directly affected and also those in their direct and indirect supplying industries, just as the estimates of primary effects did. But they exclude, as did the earlier estimates, the effects on employment of any changes in consumption, investment, and government expenditure or taxation that are caused by changes in output and income or in tariff revenues.

The export changes whose employment effects are being estimated must also be defined. An increase of foreign earnings gives rise to successive "waves" of export increases that can be distinguished conceptually, if not from actual statistical data. The export effects here taken into account are intended to include the direct spending in the United States of additional earnings by the countries that supply our additional imports, and also all the additional spending in the United States by other countries whose earnings are directly or indirectly increased when the supplying countries increase their spending in the rest of the world.

This additional spending by foreign countries results mainly from the effects that increases in their foreign earnings have on their domestic incomes.[1] Thus, the estimates of the employment effects of United States exports reflect the effects of income changes abroad. It will be recalled that the estimated employment effects of decreases in American buying of domestic output are confined to primary changes, *i.e.*, they exclude the effects of decreases in buying that result from income changes in the United States. It may at first appear inconsistent with this treatment to include the effects of any foreign income changes. Both the domestic and foreign income changes are logical economic consequences of a primary change in spending in the United States. There is a difference, however. The domestic income changes caused by liberalization can be offset by appropriate policy measures and need not be regarded as unavoidable, while the foreign income changes are a consequence about which the United States can do nothing. From the point of view of United States policy, they are an unalterable fact, and they must be included if our measure of employment

---

[1] Mainly but not entirely, because changes in a country's foreign earnings may affect its imports independently of secondary effects on its domestic income.

effects is not to be misleading. Inconsistency would occur only if we took into account the secondary increases in domestic income caused by the increases in United States exports or the further series of foreign income changes that would result from any of the secondary changes of income and imports in the United States.[2]

The question may also be raised whether all the waves of foreign income and import changes due to the primary changes of United States imports can occur in a period of time short enough to be taken into account in a study of short-period effects. It is true, of course, that ordinarily time is required for such changes to work themselves out fully, but the effects that occur within a relatively short period of time can and often do account for a large portion of the total effects. The time horizon of this study has been considered in determining how much a foreign country's imports change per dollar of change in its export earnings, and the assigned relationship, consequently, is lower than it would have been had a longer time period been contemplated.

The additional employment associated with these increases of exports depends on the amount and composition of the exports generated by the assumed million-dollar increases in imports as well as on the employment generated by a dollar of additional exports of each industry. The additional assumptions required by the estimates presented in this chapter relate to the amount and composition of these export changes rather than to the employment changes that are equivalent to given export changes. The specific nature of these assumptions is described in Chapters 6 and 7. Their general character may best be indicated by describing the procedure used to make the estimates. Underlying this procedure is the general assumption that increases in exports by foreign countries that result directly or indirectly from reductions of import barriers by the United States are not made at the expense of their other exports or of their domestic use of goods and services.

To estimate the total effect on United States exports, the 1953 million-dollar increases in the domestic value of liberalized imports were distributed between the United States share and the foreign share. (The foreign share consists of the foreign port value

---

[2] Our thinking on the question of what foreign repercussions to take into account was greatly clarified by discussions with Professor Thomas C. Schelling. He is of course not responsible for the decisions we made.

of the increase in imports and the foreign share of the cost of shipping these imports.) This gross increase in the dollar earnings of all foreign countries was then distributed among individual foreign countries. The distribution was based on the assumption that the increase in imports, and also the foreign share of the associated shipping costs, would be supplied entirely by the countries that were the *major* suppliers of accepted commodities in 1953 and by each one in proportion to its 1953 contribution to their combined total.

The next step was to estimate how each major supplier would use the addition to its foreign dollar earnings. In the light of its known past behavior and its probable future behavior and policies, a judgment was formed as to how much a country would increase its spending on merchandise imports and on their shipment as a direct and indirect result of a one-dollar increase in its export earnings. (This proportion is called its "merchandise reflection ratio.") The resulting increases in its imports are assumed to come from the United States and from the rest of the world in the same proportions as its total merchandise imports in 1953. The portion bought outside the United States gives rise to increases in the earnings of other countries and thus to increases in their incomes and imports, including their imports from the United States. (These indirect increases in United States exports, *i.e.*, those not directly attributable to major suppliers, are called "multilateral" increases in exports, while the increases in United States exports that are directly attributable to major suppliers are called "bilateral" increases.)

To estimate total multilateral increases in United States exports, foreign countries were divided into four world trade groups, according to whether the merchandise reflection ratios assigned to them were above or below a selected ratio, and whether the percentage of their total imports that came from the United States was "high" or "low" in 1953. Each major supplier is assumed to obtain the increase in its merchandise imports from these four groups of countries in the same proportions as it obtained its total merchandise imports from them in 1953. When the major suppliers increase their imports from these four world trade groups, the groups experience gross increases in their export incomes.

These gross increases are partially offset, however, by the loss of export earnings resulting from the output-induced decreases in United States imports. This decrease in the dollar earnings of each world trade group was therefore deducted from the gross increase in its earnings from major suppliers to get the initial net increase in its export earnings.

The net increase in the earnings of each world trade group is assumed to give rise to increases in its total current spending abroad in an amount determined by its reflection ratio, which is a weighted average of the reflection ratios of its constituent countries. Increases in the imports of a given group are assumed to be distributed among the four groups and the United States in the same proportions as its total imports in 1953. The increases in the exports of all groups (but not those of the United States) are assumed to give rise to a series of further, although diminishing, increases in trade with each other and in imports from the United States. Thus there is a succession of increases in their imports from the United States. The sum of these successive import increases for all four groups constitutes the multilateral increase in United States exports of merchandise and associated shipping services.[3]

The value of the total export increase in each case was then distributed between shipping services and merchandise on the basis of the ratio of United States ocean freight earnings to total United States exports in 1953. The merchandise portion, in turn, was distributed among United States industries, this being done separately for its bilateral and multilateral components. For bilateral exports, each major supplier is assumed to distribute its purchases from the United States among various industries in the same proportions as it did in 1953, except that some countries are assumed not to increase their purchases from several United States agricultural and food processing industries. For multilateral exports, the merchandise component is distributed among United States industries in proportion to the assumed industry distribution of United States exports to all the major suppliers.[4] In this way an estimate was obtained of the increase in foreign spending on the products of each United States industry resulting from a million-

[3] These successive increases occur largely because of income increases in foreign countries generated by their export increases, but they are all generated by the primary net increase in United States imports.

[4] In 1953, exports to the major suppliers constituted nearly three quarters of the value of all United States exports. The distribution among industry groups of exports to each major supplier and to the world as a whole is shown in Appendix Table E.6.

dollar shift of American spending from domestic to foreign products.

The effects of these increases in the exports of each industry on domestic output and thence on employment in every United States industry were estimated in the same way that the primary employment effects of liberalization were estimated, although the procedure used deviated in a few points of detail.

The assumptions made in converting given export effects into direct and indirect employment effects are also largely the same as those made in estimating primary employment effects, as described in Chapter 4; mere mention of them here is sufficient. It is assumed (1) that current output of every industry changes proportionately with changes in demand for its products, except in the case of six agricultural industries, whose output is assumed not to respond to changes in demand; (2) that when the physical quantity of an industry's exports increases, its purchases of domestic and imported supplies increase by an amount that bears the same ratio to the export increase as the entire industry's purchases of such supplies bore to its total output in 1947;[5] (3) that the ratio of changes in imports to changes in domestic output of each industry other than the liberalized one is the same as the ratio of the industry's total imports to its total domestic output in 1952; and (4) that employment changes proportionately to output in commodity-producing industries, although not necessarily in service industries.

Although all these assumptions were also made in estimating primary employment effects, the second one must be regarded as riskier here, because it had to be applied to all industries producing affected exports, without subjecting them to the tests of reliability that were imposed in estimating primary employment effects. It was not possible to avoid estimating the employment effects of changes in a given industry's exports merely because output of its exported products constituted a small portion of its total output and the observed employment-output and input-output relationships of the industry might therefore be unrepresentative of its exports. Unfortunately for the reliability of the estimates, foreign buyers do not take this statistical test into account in deciding

---

[5] In several industries, 1951 or later relationships were used. See Chap. 4, footnote 11.

what they will buy, and the coverage of the estimates had to be governed by their assumed purchases.

As this outline makes clear, the procedure requires making specific assumptions about how great an addition to earnings would accrue to the major supplying countries from a million-dollar increase of imports (valued at domestic ports after payment of duty); how much of their additional earnings the countries that are the major suppliers in each case would spend in the United States and how much they would spend in other countries; how much of their own additional earnings these other countries would spend in the United States and elsewhere; and how the total increase in United States exports would be distributed among different industries. In all cases, the increases in exports are assumed to consist of products of a wide range of American industries, but the composition of the total increases differs from case to case, depending on which countries are the customers.

Estimated Employment Effects of Exports

We may now consider the estimates of employment associated with the exports induced by the various cases of liberalization, the major factors determining them, and the distribution of this employment among industry groups.

Total Effects

The estimated total employment associated with the exports generated in each of the 72 cases of liberalization, including the employment associated with their shipment, is shown in the first column of Table 5.1. It ranges from a minimum of 8 employees per million-dollar increase in imports of cork and cork products (Industry #162) to a maximum of 70 employees per million-dollar increase in imports of wood containers and cooperage (Industry #40). The median effect of 26 employees is well below the midpoint of this range. (The median, the extremes, and also the first

Table 5.1

Employment Increases from Exports Associated with Liberalization of Selected Industries and Factors Determining Them[a]

	Liberalized Industry	Employment Increase per Million-Dollar Increase of Imports (Number of Employees[b])	Net Increase in Foreign Dollar Earnings per Million-Dollar Increase of Imports (In Thousands of 1953 Dollars)	Export Increase per Dollar of Net Increase in Foreign Earnings	Employment Increase per Thousand Dollars of Export Increase
Code Number	Title	(1)	(2)	(3)	(4)
1	Meat animals and products	68.53	846.1	.722	.1122
8	Vegetables and fruits	64.93	744.8	.775	.1124
13	Lead and zinc mining	66.93	850.4	.701	.1123
21	Meat packing and wholesale poultry	54.32	825.7	.599	.1098
22	Processed dairy products	31.28	830.5	.363	.1038
24	Grain mill products	55.80	853.9	.597	.1094
27	Sugar	65.30	806.6	.749	.1081
28	Alcoholic beverages	47.58	837.1	.510	.1113
29	Tobacco manufactures	34.39	736.7	.436	.1070
30	Spinning, weaving, and dyeing	19.37	758.4	.271	.0941
31	Special textile products	20.11	727.3	.268	.1032
34	Apparel	19.55	722.4	.291	.0930
35	House furnishings and other non-apparel	20.86	721.5	.300	.0964
38	Plywood	39.65	820.1	.469	.1031
40	Wood containers and cooperage	70.47	770.7	.814	.1124
41	Wood furniture	28.17	817.7	.331	.1041
45	Paper and board mills	48.28	841.4	.520	.1103
46	Converted paper products	20.53	754.3	.267	.1018
49	Industrial organic chemicals	16.25	675.1	.220	.1094
51	Synthetic rubber	61.44	822.2	.665	.1124
52	Synthetic fiber	18.52	819.0	.212	.1066
54	Drugs and medicines	18.52	836.5	.221	.1001
56	Paints and allied products	36.28	627.8	.520	.1112
59	Vegetable oils	63.82	789.6	.723	.1119
61	Miscellaneous chemical industries	15.36	767.9	.194	.1032
65	Tires and inner tubes	10.03	791.6	.132	.0953
66	Miscellaneous rubber products	25.75	758.8	.349	.0973
67	Leather tanning and finishing	40.66	866.5	.435	.1079
69	Footwear (excluding rubber)	24.01	839.3	.284	.1009
70	Glass	17.48	735.5	.237	.1006
73	Pottery and related products	17.32	684.7	.269	.0942
79.1	Carbon steel works and rolling mills	18.77	813.0	.216	.1069
79.2	Alloy steel works and rolling mills, except stainless	18.21	802.3	.212	.1070
79.3	Stainless steel works and rolling mills	18.92	816.7	.217	.1067
85	Primary zinc	60.48	804.0	.674	.1115
88	Primary aluminum, including alumina	57.66	836.5	.613	.1124
89	Aluminum rolling and drawing	37.49	826.8	.417	.1090
93	Tin cans and other tinware	38.71	847.7	.415	.1099
94	Cutlery	19.67	739.5	.251	.1059
95	Tools and general hardware	19.20	810.9	.232	.1021

Table 5.1 (continued)

Code Number	Liberalized Industry Title	Employment Increase per Million-Dollar Increase of Imports (Number of Employees[b]) (1)	Net Increase in Foreign Dollar Earnings per Million-Dollar Increase of Imports (In Thousands of 1953 Dollars) (2)	Export Increase per Dollar of Net Increase in Foreign Earnings (3)	Employment Increase per Thousand Dollars of Export Increase (4)
103	Lighting fixtures	20.30	732.4	.261	.1066
105	Metal barrels, drums, etc.	16.71	710.5	.228	.1034
106	Tubes and foils	14.62	766.4	.180	.1060
116	Machine tools and metalworking machinery	28.53	870.9	.298	.1102
118	Special industrial machinery	26.38	841.5	.290	.1079
123	Industrial machinery n.e.c.	39.53	859.9	.416	.1105
127	Ball and roller bearings	35.37	810.5	.390	.1104
131	Motors and generators	56.70	843.8	.602	.1116
132	Transformers	22.23	847.1	.248	.1058
133	Electrical control apparatus	21.35	827.0	.239	.1080
134	Electrical welding apparatus	42.96	888.9	.439	.1100
135	Electrical appliances	23.34	822.4	.278	.1020
136	Insulated wire and cable	44.96	722.7	.572	.1088
138	Electric lamps	19.54	808.8	.298	.0809
139	Radio and related products	51.21	900.3	.513	.1109
141	Communication equipment	58.69	861.0	.610	.1119
142	Storage batteries	15.15	738.8	.197	.1038
143	Primary batteries	53.59	785.7	.610	.1118
145.1	Passenger cars and light trucks	25.82	861.4	.286	.1047
145.2	Heavy trucks and buses	57.07	851.1	.606	.1118
145.3	Motor vehicle parts and accessories	51.38	849.7	.545	.1109
148	Aircraft and parts	52.16	837.1	.561	.1109
152	Motorcycles and bicycles	24.42	848.4	.274	.1054
154	Optical, ophthalmic and photo equipment	26.33	825.0	.297	.1077
156	Watches and clocks	18.93	703.5	.242	.1113
157	Jewelry and silverware	13.88	672.0	.220	.0938
158	Musical instruments and parts	31.11	813.1	.355	.1079
159	Toys and sporting goods	16.23	712.0	.254	.0894
160	Office supplies	17.45	700.3	.252	.0989
161	Plastic products	34.36	766.8	.426	.1050
162	Cork products	7.99	365.3	.230	.0952
164	Miscellaneous manufactured products	22.69	736.5	.296	.1042
	Minimum	7.99	365.3	.132	.0809
	1st quartile	19.06	739.2	.250	.1031
	Median	26.36	812.0	.299	.1070
	3rd quartile	49.74	840.4	.532	.1106
	Maximum	70.47	900.3	.814	.1124
	Interquartile range	30.68	101.2	.282	.0075
	Mean	33.65	788.3	.392	.1056
	Average per cent deviation from mean	45.27	7.17	39.01	3.48

[a] The first column of this table is equal to the product of the other three columns, except for discrepancies resulting from rounding of figures.
[b] Also includes farmers and unpaid farm family workers.

113

and third quartiles and the range between them, are shown at the end of Table 5.1.) The frequency of different increases, shown in Chart 5.1, confirms what the low median suggests: the cases tend to be concentrated at the low end of the range; relatively few are at its upper end.

Compared with the median employment decrease of 114 employees resulting from the primary effect of liberalization, this median increase of 26 employees associated with exports may appear to be surprisingly small. The main reason for the relatively low employment increases is to be found in the low proportion of the net increases in its export earnings that the rest of the world is assumed to spend in the United States on commodities and on the shipping services associated with them. (The basis for this assumption is explained in Chapter 7.) As Column 3 of Table 5.1 shows, these United States exports range from 13 to 81 per cent of the net increases in foreign earnings that induce them, but in half of the 72 cases they are 30 per cent or less of the total net increases in such earnings, and in three quarters of the cases they are 53 per cent or less. For the rest of the world as a whole, all increases in earnings from the United States must be matched either by increases in expenditures in the United States or by increases in net holdings of financial assets. These figures therefore imply that in half of the 72 cases 70 per cent or more of the net increase in the rest of the world's dollar earnings is used either to pay the United States for services other than shipping services on commodities, including investment income, or to increase net holdings of financial assets, and that in three quarters of the cases 47 per cent or more of the net increase in dollar earnings is so used.

It should be noted that this is a high proportion devoted to such uses, compared to what is commonly assumed. A common assumption is that additional dollar earnings made available to the rest of the world by an expansion of United States imports will result in a nearly equal expansion of purchases of American commodities and associated shipping services. Indeed, several experts recommended that this assumption be made in estimating the most probable effect upon exports in this study. The fact that the assumptions actually chosen yielded estimates of United States commodity exports considerably lower than the net additions to dollar earnings reflects the use of reflection ratios judged relevant

Chart 5.1

Frequency Distribution of Total Employment Effects of Exports

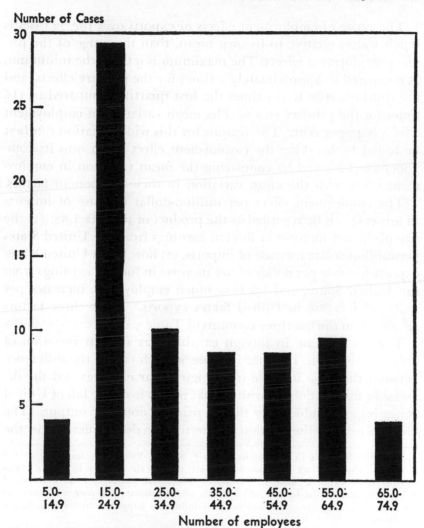

Source: Based on Column 1 of Table 5.1

to the short run. For some countries the ratios used are probably lower than those relevant to the long run.[6] They may even be low for the short run. If so, the export estimates are conservative and the estimates of associated employment tend also to be conservative.

[6] For all foreign countries combined, the increases in imports could not fall far

Range of Employment Effects
and Its Major Determinants

The range of employment effects of exports over the 72 cases is much wider, relative to its own mean, than the range of the primary employment effects. The maximum is 9 times the minimum, as compared to approximately 4 times for the primary effects, and the third quartile is 2½ times the first quartile, compared to 1½ times for the primary effects. The mean variation in employment effects is 45 per cent.[7] The reasons for this wide variation can best be found by breaking the employment effect down into its component factors, and by comparing the mean variation in employment effect with the mean variation in these component factors.

The employment effect per million-dollar increase of imports in any case can be regarded as the product of three factors: (1) the size of the net increase in foreign earnings from the United States per million-dollar increase of imports, (2) how much United States exports increase per dollar of net increase in foreign earnings from the United States, and (3) how much employment increases per dollar of increase in United States exports.[8] These three factors are shown in the last three columns of Table 5.1.

The net increase in foreign earnings has a mean variation of only 7.2 per cent. This net increase in each case is the difference between the gross increase in foreign dollar earnings and the decrease in foreign dollar earnings that results from the fall of United States imports induced by the decrease in domestic output. (The gross increase is the portion of the million-dollar increase in the

---

short of the increases in exports indefinitely. Such a discrepancy implies that the increase in United States payments for imports exceeds the increase in United States receipts from exports. Such an excess, if substantial, could not be maintained indefinitely because the balance of payments would ultimately impose a restraint on the increase of imports unless independent influences happened to compensate for the excess.

[7] Mean variation is measured by finding the deviation in each case from the average amount in all 72 cases, averaging these deviations, and expressing the average deviation as a percentage of the average amount.

[8] Although each of these factors itself consists of several components, it is sufficient for the present discussion to consider only these three. The determinants of the net increases in foreign earnings, the increases in United States exports, and the associated increases in employment, as well as the method of estimating their amounts per million dollars of increase in United States imports, are described in Chapters 6, 7, and 8, respectively.

domestic port value of imports that is left after payment of duties at the 1953 rates and of ocean freight and insurance services provided by American firms.) The main factor accounting for the variation of the net increases in foreign earnings is the variation in the gross increases; the output-induced decreases of earnings vary relatively little and, except in the case of liberalization of cork and cork products, are also relatively small.[9]

The mean variation in export increases per dollar of net increase in foreign earnings is 39.0 per cent, by far the largest variation shown by any of the three factors. These increases are determined by several elements—which countries are the major suppliers of the liberalized United States imports and how much their imports are stimulated by increases in their export earnings, what proportion of their additional imports they obtain from the United States and what proportion from other areas of the world, and from which other areas of the world these imports come. The most important causes of the variation, however, are the variations in two characteristics of the major suppliers of the liberalized United States imports: the percentage of additional earnings that they spend on imports and the percentage of these additional imports that they obtain from the United States.[10]

Average employment per dollar of increase in aggregate exports varies less from case to case than does either of the other two factors, its mean variation being only 3.5 per cent. In view of the considerable differences between industries in employment per dollar of increase in their own output, this low variation may

[9] It may be noted that liberalization in nearly all other countries would cause much larger output-induced effects on imports than does liberalization in the United States because in most other countries domestic production has a larger import content.

[10] In fact it is possible to approximate fairly closely the present estimates of export increases per dollar of net increase in foreign dollar earnings from these two percentages alone. (See Chap. 7, pp. 176-78.) This result illustrates the general proposition that the effect of a change in a country's imports on its exports "will be greater, the greater are the marginal propensities to import and the multipliers of the countries from which it imports" and the theorem underlying the proposition (stated for trade decreases) that "If A reduces its imports from B, the reaction on its own exports will be greater if B buys mainly from A than if B's imports are obtained from C, D, and E." See "Foreign Trade Policy in the Business Cycle" by William A. Salant, first published in *Public Policy*, Vol. 2, C. J. Friedrich and E. S. Mason, eds. (Harvard University Press, 1941) and reprinted in *Readings in The Theory of International Trade* (The Blakiston Co., 1949).

appear surprising. It is explained by the facts that the outputs of many industries are involved in producing the exports of any one industry and that increases in the exports of many industries are involved in all cases of liberalization, so that these differences tend to cancel.[11]

Of the three factors determining total employment, exports per dollar of net addition to foreign earnings has by far the greatest average variation: 39 per cent. Total employment, however, has a variation of 45 per cent, which is slightly larger than the variation of its most variable component. This fact implies that the components are positively correlated, high values of one tending to be associated with high values of one or both of the others.

These observations suggest that the total employment effect in a given case of liberalization is highly correlated with the exports per dollar of net increase in foreign earnings in that case. That turns out to be true. If we correlate the total employment increases with the exports per dollar of net increase in foreign earnings, we find a correlation coefficient of over .98. Consequently, similar estimates of the employment effects of exports could be obtained in most cases of liberalization by determining the volume of exports that would be generated per dollar of net addition to foreign earnings and applying to it the probable relationship of employment increase to export increase. Because, as was noted above, two characteristics of the major supplying country are the main determinants of the volume of exports per dollar of net increase in foreign earnings, the employment estimates can be approximated even more directly from these characteristics of the major supplying countries.[12]

---

[11] The main reason for such variation as there is, in fact, is the difference among the cases in the percentage of their total additional exports that consists of products of the six unresponsive agricultural industries. Since additional exports of these products have no employment effects, they bring down the average employment effect per dollar of increase in exports, and they do so approximately in proportion to their relative importance in the additional exports induced in that case. The coefficient of correlation between employment per dollar of additional exports and the percentage of additional exports coming from these six agricultural industries is —.98. Its square, the coefficient of determination, is .96, indicating that 96 per cent of the variation in employment per dollar of additional exports is "explained" (in the statistical sense) by the relative importance of these agricultural products in the additional exports.

[12] The equation for the regression of employment effects on the important characteristics of the major suppliers is given in Chap. 8, footnote 13.

Distribution of Effects
Among Industry Groups

How the employment effects of the export increases are distributed in each case among the forty industry groups into which the economy has been divided is shown in Table 5.3, which appears at the end of this chapter. Inspection of the individual columns of that table shows that in every case of liberalization the bulk of the employment effect of exports is concentrated in a few industry groups. In fact, if we take the five industry groups most affected in each case and calculate their share of the total of these employment effects, we find that their share is in no case less than 41 per cent of the total employment effect. Moreover, the combined share of the five leading industry groups in the total effect varies very little from case to case; in all 72 cases of liberalization, it is between 41 and 48 per cent.

Inspection of the rows of Table 5.3 shows that the identity of the most affected groups is substantially the same, no matter what industry's liberalization gives rise to the export increases. "Machinery other than electrical" is the most affected industry group in every liberalization case except that of sugar—where it is the fourth most affected group. "Wholesale and retail trade" is the second most affected group in 54 of the 72 cases and is the third most affected in the other cases. "Iron and steel and their primary products" is the second or third most affected group in all but one case, and this case is also the liberalization of sugar. Thus, in all but one case, the same group is most affected and the same two groups are either the second or third most affected. This fact is brought out clearly in the upper part of Table 5.2, which shows the number of cases in which specified industry groups are among the five having the largest employment effects.

As Table 5.2 also shows, coal mining is the fourth most affected "group" in 48 of the 72 cases, and railroad transportation is fourth most affected in 13 other cases. In the remaining 11 cases, the fourth rank is occupied by 7 other industry groups. Railroad transportation, besides being the fourth most affected group in 13 cases, is the fifth most affected in 41 other cases.

Why do the employment effects of exports tend to be concentrated in the same few industry groups in most cases of liberaliza-

Table 5.2

Number of Cases in Which Specified Industry Groups Rank Among Five Having Greatest Increases in Liberalization-Induced Exports and Associated Output and Employment

Industry Group Affected[a]	Number of Cases in Which Industry Group Had Indicated Rank					
	1st	2nd	3rd	4th	5th	1st through 5th
A. Ranked by Domestic Employment Effects of Exports						
Machinery except electrical (110–128)..	71	—	—	1	—	72
Wholesale and retail trade (176, 177)...	—	54	18	—	—	72
Iron and steel and their primary products (78–81, 92)......................	—	18	53	—	—	71
Railroad transportation (169).........	—	—	—	13	41	54
Coal mining (16).....................	—	—	—	48	3	51
Fabricated metal products (93–109)....	—	—	—	3	21	24
Spinning, weaving and dyeing (30)....	1	—	—	2	6	9
Agriculture, forestry and fishing (1–10).	—	—	1	1	—	2
Electrical machinery and products (129–138, 142–144)......................	—	—	—	2	—	2
Apparel (34).........................	—	—	—	1	—	1
Motor vehicles, parts and accessories (145–147).......................	—	—	—	1	—	1
Processed food and alcoholic beverages (21–28).........................	—	—	—	—	1	1
All other chemicals and allied products (54–61)..........................	—	—	—	—	—	—
Products of petroleum and coal (62–64).	—	—	—	—	—	—
Total.........................	72	72	72	72	72	360
B. Ranked by Domestic Output Effect of Exports[b]						
Machinery except electrical (110–128)..	71	—	—	—	1	72
Wholesale and retail trade (176, 177)...	—	—	—	17	5	22
Iron and steel and their primary products (78–81, 92)......................	—	51	13	4	3	71
Railroad transportation (169).........	—	—	—	—	—	—
Coal mining (16)	—	—	—	—	—	—
Fabricated metal products (93–109)....	—	—	—	—	2	2
Spinning, weaving and dyeing (30)....	—	—	1	—	—	1
Agriculture, forestry and fishing (1–10).	—	1	8	25	19	53
Electrical machinery and products (129–138, 142–144)......................	—	—	—	1	—	1
Apparel (34).........................	—	—	—	—	—	—
Motor vehicles, parts and accessories (145–147).......................	—	1	28	7	17	53
Processed food and alcoholic beverages (21–28).........................	1	1	1	2	12	17
All other chemicals and allied products (54–61)..........................	—	18	21	16	12	67
Products of petroleum and coal (62–64).	—	—	—	—	1	1
Total......................	72	72	72	72	72	360

Table 5.2 *(continued)*

Industry Group Affected[a]	Number of Cases in Which Industry Group Had Indicated Rank					
	1st	2nd	3rd	4th	5th	1st through 5th
C. Ranked by Liberalization-Induced Exports[b]						
Machinery except electrical (110–128)..	61	9½	1½	—	—	72
Wholesale and retail trade (176, 177)...	—	—	13	19	29½	61½
Iron and steel and their primary products (78–81, 92).....................	—	—	—	1	—	1
Railroad transportation (169).........	—	—	—	—	2	2
Coal mining (16).....................	—	—	—	—	—	—
Fabricated metal products (93–109)....	—	—	—	—	—	—
Spinning, weaving and dyeing (30)....	—	1	—	1	—	2
Agriculture, forestry and fishing (1–10).	9	31	10	16	3	60
Electrical machinery and products (129–138, 142–144).....................	—	—	—	—	1	1
Apparel (34).........................	—	—	—	—	—	—
Motor vehicles, parts and accessories (145–147)........................	—	26½	10½	16	9	62
Processed food and alcoholic beverages (21–28).........................	2	—	—	11	4½	17½
All other chemicals and allied products (54–61)...........................	—	4	37	8	22	71
Products of petroleum and coal (62–64).	—	—	—	—	1	1
Total........................	72	72	72	72	72	360

[a] Numbers in parentheses are code numbers of component industries. For titles corresponding to code numbers, see Appendix A.
[b] Rank based on measurement in 1947 prices.

tion? Is it because the same products tend to be exported in most cases? Or do exports differ in composition but still affect outputs of the same industries in different cases because these industries are direct or indirect suppliers of materials for so many different kinds of exports? Or is the explanation that, although output effects are differently distributed in most cases, a few industry groups have very large employment effects per unit of output change so that they experience the greatest employment effects even though they may not experience the greatest output effects?

Table 5.2 suggests answers to some of these questions. It indicates that no single answer will explain the high employment effects in all the industry groups that feel such effects.

The export section of the table shows that nonelectrical machinery is the leading export industry group in 61 of the 72 cases. This is the main explanation of why it is so often a locus of large

employment effects. Its importance in exports evidently is rein-
forced by its high indirect contribution to the production of other
industries' exports; the domestic output section of the table shows
that it is the leading group in total output effects in 71 of the 72
cases. The relation between changes in its employment and output
is sufficiently high to leave it the most affected group in terms of
employment in all 71 cases.

The group next most important as the object of employment
effects is wholesale and retail trade, which is either the second or
third most affected in every case. The export section of Table 5.2
indicates that it is among the five most important exporting groups
in 61 of the cases and is tied for fifth rank in another case.[13] (It is
also the sixth or seventh most important exporting group in all the
other cases, although this cannot be learned from Table 5.2.) This
fact is an important element in explaining why it so persistently
feels large employment effects. But it is not enough to explain why
trade always ranks second or third in employment effects. Its indirect participation in the output of a wide range of exported
commodities must be less than that of several other industry
groups, for it is among the five leading groups in output effects in
only 22 cases and is among the three leading groups in none. The
rest of the explanation for its position as the second or third most
important group in employment effects in every case must therefore be that its employment per unit of added output is considerably higher than that of the other groups which experience important output effects from exports.

The group whose employment is third most affected is "iron
and steel and their primary products," which ranks second or third
in employment effects in all but one of the 72 cases. The explanation for its importance in employment effects is very different from
that of nonelectrical machinery or wholesale and retail trade. In
only one case is it among the five most important exporting groups.
The main reason it ranks high in employment effects is that its
output is greatly affected, although indirectly, by production of
other exported products; it ranks among the five most important

[13] The distributive services sold by wholesale trade and embodied in the export
value of commodities are regarded as sold directly to the foreign buyers rather than
to the producers of these exports. Trade is therefore an exporting group. This way
of looking at trade does not affect the estimates of total output or employment or of
their distribution among industries. Its effect is confined to their division between
direct and indirect effects.

groups in output effects in 71 of the 72 cases. The relation between its employment and output changes is evidently high enough to permit it to maintain its rank as compared with all other industry groups except wholesale and retail trade.

Railroad transportation, which in 54 cases ranks fourth or fifth in employment effects, is similar to the wholesale and retail trade group in that the services it renders in connection with exported products are treated as sold to the buyers of these products; it therefore is an exporting industry. As an exporting industry, it ranks as high as fifth in only 2 of the 72 cases, but it ranks eighth or higher in 59 cases. In output effects its rank was generally lower than in export effects. This indicates that it experiences employment effects relatively greater than its export effects mainly because the relation between its employment and output changes is relatively high.

Similarly, in 51 of the 72 cases, coal mining is among the industry groups having the fourth or fifth most important employment effects. In no case, however, is it among the 5 most important groups as an exporter and in only 3 cases is it among the 10 most important. Apparently it also does not play a large role as an intermediate product required in producing exports, for in no case does it rank among the first 10 groups in total output effects. It is an important locus of employment effects because it has a relatively high ratio of employment change to output change.

Thus far, we have found that, of the five industry groups most often among the five whose employment is most affected, only two, nonelectrical machinery and wholesale and retail trade, are generally or even often among the five which are most important as exporters. High rank as an exporter accounts for the frequency of important employment effects in the nonelectrical machinery group. The frequency of large employment effects in wholesale and retail trade, although attributable partly to the frequency of its importance as an exporter, also results partly from the high ratio of its employment to its output changes. In railroad transportation it results mainly, and in coal mining almost entirely, from a high ratio of employment to output changes. In iron and steel and their primary products the explanation is to be found in the high indirect participation of these products in producing the exports of other industries.

We may get further light on what determines which industry

groups often feel high employment effects by considering why some industry groups which often have large exports nevertheless do not often experience high employment effects.

The most conspicuous of these groups is agriculture, forestry, and fishing. In only 2 cases is this group among the 5 most important in employment response. Yet, as Table 5.2 shows, it is the largest or second largest exporter in 40 of the 72 cases of liberalization and is among the 5 largest in 69 cases. The main reason for its low employment response is that, for 6 of the 10 industries in this group, output was assumed to remain unchanged in the face of changes in demand, and these are the industries that make the group a leading exporter. The short period effect of exports on this industry group is largely on the prices of government-held stocks of its products, not on its employment.

"All other chemicals and allied products" (*i.e.,* chemical products other than industrial chemicals and synthetic rubber and fibers) and "motor vehicles, parts and accessories" also rank high as exporters in nearly all cases, but the first of these two groups ranks among the five with the most important employment effects in no case and the second does so in only one case. The reason that employment effects in the "all other chemicals and allied products" group are never high enough to put it in the five most affected groups is that changes in its output involve relatively small changes in employment. In the motor vehicles, parts, and accessories group, additions to output also require relatively little additional employment, so that it is among the five most affected groups in only one case, although it is very often among the ten most affected groups.

While most cases conform to a general pattern in the location of the employment effects of their export increases, liberalization of sugar appears to be atypical. It has already been noted that this is the only case in which nonelectrical machinery is not the group whose employment is most affected by liberalization-induced exports and that it is the only case in which iron and steel and their primary products is neither the second nor the third most affected group. Most affected in this case is the spinning, weaving, and dyeing industry and second most affected is wholesale and retail trade. Third is agriculture, forestry, and fishing, which, as Table 5.2 shows, is among the five most affected industry groups in only two cases. The reason for the unusual distribution of effects in the case of sugar liberalization is that the main suppliers of sugar in 1953, Cuba and the Philippines, normally spend large portions of their additional earnings in the United States and, as a result, are the main purchasers of the additional exports induced by liberalization of sugar imports. Both of these countries, and especially the Philippines, allocate a much larger portion of their total American spending than do other countries to products of the spinning, weaving and dyeing industry.

Since the largest decrease of employment in any one industry resulting from any single liberalization is to be expected in the liberalized industry itself, it is of interest to note that employment in the liberalized industry is not much stimulated by exports in any of the cases. This conclusion is apparent from Table 5.3, line 2 of which shows the employment effects in the liberalized industry alone, separated from the effects on the other industries of its group. The largest *absolute* employment increase in an industry resulting from exports induced by its own liberalization occurs in the vegetables and fruits industry (#8), where the increase is 1.6 employees per million-dollar increase in its imports. The largest *proportion* of the total export-induced employment increases occurring in the liberalized industry results from liberalization of the spinning, weaving, and dyeing industry (#30); even here, the increase is less than 5 per cent of the total employment increase associated with exports. The estimates in this line of Table 5.3 point quite clearly to the conclusion that any employment decrease in an industry caused by reduction of its own protection is not likely to be significantly offset by increases associated with the exports which that reduction stimulates.

It should also be noted, however, that many protected industries experience employment increases because of export increases induced by liberalization of other industries. Consequently, for some industries that are themselves liberalized, a program of liberalization that reduces protection over a broad range of industries might cause employment increases from exports that are significant in relation to the employment decreases that it causes.

(Table 5.3 follows on succeeding pages)

Table 5.3

Distribution of Employment Effects of Export Increases, by Industry Groups[a]

(Number of employees, farmers, and unpaid farm family workers)

Line Number	Industry Group Affected and Code Numbers of Industries in Group	Liberalized Industry	
		Meat Animals and Products (1)	Vegetables and Fruits (8)
1	Total all industries...	68.53	64.93
2	Liberalized industry...	.60	1.63
3	Other industries—total......................................	67.93	63.30
4	Agriculture, forestry, and fishing (1–10).........................	2.48*	1.45*
5	Metal mining (11–15)..	.56	.50
6	Coal mining (16)..	2.76	1.73
7	Crude petroleum and natural gas (17)..........................	1.09	1.05
8	Other nonmetallic minerals (18–20)............................	.40	.35
9	Processed food and alcoholic beverages (21–28).................	.92	.87
10	Tobacco manufactures (29)...................................	.06	.08
11	Spinning, weaving, and dyeing (30)............................	1.83	1.60
12	Apparel (34)...	.65	.67
13	All other textile products (31–33, 35)..........................	.35	.32
14	Lumber, wood products, and furniture (36–43)...................	1.87	1.83
15	Pulp, paper, and paper products (44–46).......................	1.21	1.19
16	Printing and publishing (47)..................................	1.43	1.28
17	Industrial chemicals (except synthetic rubber and fiber) (48–50, 53)....	1.30	1.34
18	Synthetic rubber and synthetic fiber (51, 52)...................	.22	.21
19	All other chemicals and allied products (54–61).................	1.84	2.01
20	Products of petroleum and coal (62–64)........................	.85	.84
21	Tires, inner tubes, and miscellaneous rubber products (65, 66)........	.88	.88
22	Leather and products and footwear (excluding rubber) (67–69)........	.31	.26
23	Glass (70)...	.58	.53
24	Pottery and related products (73).............................	.14	.10
25	Stone and clay products (71, 72, 74–77)........................	1.02	1.00
26	Iron and steel and their primary products (78–81, 92).............	6.29	5.99
27	Nonferrous metals and their primary products (82–91).............	1.14	1.09
28	Fabricated metal products (93–109)............................	3.50	3.31
29	Machinery, except electrical (110–128).........................	10.67	9.94
30	Electrical machinery and products (129–138, 142–144).............	2.62	2.59
31	Communication equipment and products (139–141)................	1.24	1.19
32	Motor vehicles, parts and accessories (145–147).................	2.98	3.14
33	Other transportation equipment (148–152)......................	.95	.96
34	Instruments, optical and photographic equipment, watches and clocks (153–156)..	1.00	.95
35	Miscellaneous manufactures (157–164).........................	1.02	.98
36	Electric light and power, and gas (167, 168)....................	.09	.09
37	Railroad transportation (169).................................	3.35	3.15
38	Ocean transportation (172)...................................	1.13	1.06
39	Transportation (except railroad and ocean transportation) and allied services (170, 171, 173–175, 178).............................	.79	.76
40	Wholesale and retail trade (176, 177).........................	6.01	5.66
41	Communication, finance, business services (179, 181, 186, 187)........	1.62	1.59
42	Auto and other repair services (188, 189)......................	.32	.31
43	Other services (182–185, 190–192)............................	.46	.45

* Excludes employment effects in the liberalized industry, which is a part of this industry group. The employment effect in the liberalized industry is shown in line 2.

[a] Figures are increases of employment associated with the export increases stimulated by million-dollar increases in imports of liberalized products. Dashes represent effects that are less than .005 employees, including some that are zero.

Table 5.3 (continued)

Line Number	Lead and Zinc Mining (13)	Meat Packing and Wholesale Poultry (21)	Processed Dairy Products (22)	Grain Mill Products (24)	Sugar (27)	Alcoholic Beverages (28)	Tobacco Manufactures (29)
1.....	66.93	54.32	31.28	55.80	65.30	47.58	34.39
2.....	.08	.11	.05	.10	.04	.03	.02
3.....	66.85	54.21	31.23	55.70	65.26	47.55	34.37
4.....	2.94	1.87	1.06	2.29	5.18	2.00	2.06
5.....	.57*	.58	.32	.61	.28	.54	.31
6.....	3.53	3.52	1.35	3.86	1.03	3.16	.92
7.....	1.06	.83	.53	.86	.95	.73	.57
8.....	.43	.44	.35	.44	.23	.36	.17
9.....	.91	.63*	.53*	.73*	4.04	.70*	1.38
10.....	.04	.03	.04	.02	.01	.03	—*
11.....	1.93	1.74	1.19	1.79	6.42	1.59	1.74
12.....	.60	.43	.53	.45	.79	.39	.40
13.....	.36	.29	.13	.30	.70	.26	.25
14.....	1.78	1.42	.69	1.41	1.65	1.19	.91
15.....	1.15	.86	.51	.91	2.04	.78	.80
16.....	1.50	1.26	.60	1.32	1.38	1.12	.66
17.....	1.17	.83	.50	.87	.95	.76	.52
18.....	.23	.19	.13	.20	.55	.17	.18
19.....	1.52	1.01	1.02	1.07	2.04	.95	.98
20.....	.80	.61	.41	.63	.54	.53	.38
21.....	.83	.63	.34	.64	.83	.54	.43
22.....	.31	.24	.12	.24	.78	.21	.27
23.....	.59	.48	.22	.52	.90	.42	.36
24.....	.15	.14	.05	.14	.24	.12	.08
25.....	.99	.75	.31	.80	.56	.64	.35
26.....	6.06	4.98	2.73	4.94	3.39	4.17	2.46
27.....	1.13	.94	.54	.94	.74	.84	.56
28.....	3.43	2.76	1.32	2.80	2.73	2.34	1.51
29.....	10.34	8.87	5.30	8.61	5.12	7.40	4.63
30.....	2.48	1.94	1.07	1.96	1.95	1.66	1.20
31.....	1.22	.94	.50	.98	.95	.79	.57
32.....	2.55	1.78	.92	1.78	1.64	1.52	1.03
33.....	.85	.66	.65	.62	.58	.58	.45
34.....	.95	.76	.40	.79	.66	.66	.37
35.....	1.00	.80	.39	.83	1.15	.69	.50
36.....	.09	.07	.04	.07	.08	.06	.04
37.....	3.28	2.70	1.54	2.77	3.42	2.35	1.75
38.....	1.10	.92	.55	.96	1.09	.79	.59
39.....	.77	.92	.37	.64	.86	.55	.44
40.....	5.92	4.88	2.84	4.99	6.13	4.28	3.21
41.....	1.53	1.20	.77	1.23	1.84	1.05	.89
42.....	.32	.26	.16	.27	.34	.23	.20
43.....	.44	.35	.21	.36	.50	.31	.25

Table 5.3 (*continued*)

Line Number	Liberalized Industry						
	Spinning, Weaving and Dyeing (30)	Special Textile Products (31)	Apparel (34)	House Furnishings and Other Non-Apparel (35)	Plywood (38)	Wood Containers and Cooperage (40)	Wood Furniture (41)
1.....	19.37	20.11	19.55	20.86	39.65	70.47	28.17
2.....	.91	.02	.39	.06	.02	.25	.04
3.....	18.46	20.09	19.16	20.80	39.63	70.22	28.13
4.....	.64	.64	.63	.80	1.53	3.46	1.11
5.....	.24	.19	.25	.27	.42	.47	.32
6.....	.90	.80	.94	1.06	2.54	1.20	1.27
7.....	.33	.27	.32	.35	.61	1.18	.39
8.....	.13	.11	.12	.14	.27	.32	.17
9.....	.45	.39	.46	.50	.72	.94	.58
10.....	.02	.02	.02	.03	.02	.09	.09
11.....	—*	.98	.86	.81	1.42	1.65	1.31
12.....	.39	.27	—*	.22	.36	.74	.43
13.....	.09	.09*	.09	.04*	.22	.33	.13
14.....	.51	.43	.46	.52	.96*	1.79*	.61*
15.....	.34	.34	.33	.34	.65	1.33	.49
16.....	.38	.39	.39	.38	.89	1.34	.55
17.....	.36	.35	.36	.38	.64	1.54	.47
18.....	.10	.11	.10	.10	.16	.22	.14
19.....	.61	.73	.61	.70	.89	2.39	.85
20.....	.25	.22	.25	.26	.45	.96	.31
21.....	.21	.38	.21	.22	.45	.98	.30
22.....	.09	.08	.08	.08	.19	.27	.14
23.....	.13	.18	.13	.13	.34	.57	.21
24.....	.02	.03	.02	.02	.08	.11	.05
25.....	.19	.20	.19	.20	.50	1.11	.30
26.....	1.49	1.61	1.52	1.65	3.42	6.55	2.26
27.....	.34	.33	.35	.39	.67	1.17	.50
28.....	.76	.85	.79	.83	1.94	3.60	1.17
29.....	3.12	2.91	3.21	3.47	6.18	10.75	4.45
30.....	.60	.73	.61	.68	1.36	2.84	1.02
31.....	.26	.35	.28	.31	.67	1.27	.43
32.....	.59	.94	.58	.57	1.30	3.70	.78
33.....	.35	.44	.36	.41	.55	1.10	.52
34.....	.24	.27	.25	.27	.56	1.04	.42
35.....	.26	.24	.24	.24	.55	1.02	.42
36.....	.03	.03	.03	.03	.05	.10	.04
37.....	.95	1.00	.97	1.04	1.97	3.42	1.42
38.....	.38	.36	.39	.41	.71	1.14	.49
39.....	.24	.24	.24	.26	.46	.83	.34
40.....	1.75	1.83	1.79	1.92	3.57	6.10	2.62
41.....	.49	.52	.49	.52	.91	1.77	.70
42.....	.10	.10	.10	.11	.19	.34	.14
43.....	.13	.14	.14	.14	.26	.49	.19

Table 5.3 (*continued*)

Line Number	Liberalized Industry						
	Paper and Board Mills (45)	Converted Paper Products (46)	Industrial Organic Chemicals (49)	Synthetic Rubber (51)	Synthetic Fiber (52)	Drugs and Medicines (54)	Paints and Allied Products (56)
1.....	48.28	20.53	16.25	61.44	18.52	18.52	36.28
2.....	.30	.14	.13	.03	.07	.18	.15
3.....	47.98	20.39	16.12	61.41	18.45	18.34	36.13
4.....	1.90	.92	.70	2.56	.87	.56	1.46
5.....	.53	.29	.24	.69	.22	.23	.44
6.....	3.01	1.23	.84	4.30	1.00	.76	2.33
7.....	.72	.34	.22	.94	.25	.25	.58
8.....	.33	.15	.11	.46	.11	.13	.28
9.....	.71	.51	.39	.82	.47	.34	.50
10.....	.04	.02	.02	.02	.02	.03	.02
11.....	1.66	.73	.64	2.02	.76	.92	1.15
12.....	.42	.19	.53	.47	.23	.68	.29
13.....	.25	.09	.07	.35	.09	.09	.20
14.....	1.16	.51	.36	1.53	.40	.41	.90
15.....	.46*	.20*	.27	.99	.30	.32	.59
16.....	1.10	.42	.30	1.47	.33	.35	.84
17.....	.74	.37	.17*	.94	.32	.32	.58
18.....	.18	.09	.08	.19*	.02*	.10	.13
19.....	.95	.04	.52	1.06	.62	.86*	.53*
20.....	.53	.25	.18	.68	.21	.20	.42
21.....	.56	.22	.18	.72	.23	.23	.42
22.....	.23	.09	.10	.30	.08	.11	.16
23.....	.43	.14	.11	.57	.13	.14	.32
24.....	.12	.02	.02	.14	.02	.02	.08
25.....	.05	.21	.15	.88	.18	.18	.50
26.....	4.32	1.62	1.21	5.53	1.41	1.45	3.23
27.....	.88	.38	.32	1.05	.34	.34	.65
28.....	2.48	.86	.64	3.16	.74	.73	1.84
29.....	7.66	3.21	2.40	9.56	2.68	2.00	5.86
30.....	1.71	.65	.49	2.12	.61	.62	1.28
31.....	.80	.27	.19	1.09	.27	.26	.62
32.....	1.62	.62	.46	2.00	.71	.58	1.15
33.....	.75	.30	.30	.65	.41	.42	.42
34.....	.68	.25	.23	.87	.26	.26	.51
35.....	.68	.26	.29	.94	.24	.33	.55
36.....	.06	.03	.02	.08	.02	.02	.05
37.....	2.38	1.03	.80	3.03	.93	.80	1.79
38.....	.82	.38	.28	1.03	.32	.34	.61
39.....	.55	.25	.20	.70	.23	.21	.42
40.....	4.30	1.90	1.50	5.48	1.73	1.67	3.23
41.....	1.07	.50	.40	1.33	.46	.46	.80
42.....	.23	.11	.08	.29	.10	.09	.17
43.....	.31	.14	.11	.39	.13	.13	.23

129

Table 5.3 (*continued*)

Line Number	Liberalized Industry						
	Vegetable Oils (59)	Misc. Chemical Industries (61)	Tires and Inner Tubes (65)	Misc. Rubber Products (66)	Leather Tanning and Finishing (67)	Footwear (except rubber) (69)	Glass (70)
1.....	63.82	15.36	10.03	25.75	40.66	24.01	17.48
2.....	.06	.08	.03	.20	.06	.04	.12
3.....	63.76	15.28	10.00	25.55	40.60	23.97	17.36
4.....	2.79	.60	.28	.98	1.23	.77	.73
5.....	.53	.18	.14	.31	.55	.33	.23
6.....	2.55	.52	.36	1.52	1.98	.97	.91
7.....	1.06	.19	.13	.43	.63	.41	.26
8.....	.38	.09	.08	.17	.30	.18	.11
9.....	.83	.31	.15	.58	.55	.46	.43
10.....	.06	.04	.02	.02	.03	.03	.02
11.....	1.70	.56	.38	.92	1.25	.95	.75
12.....	.59	.26	.11	.23	.36	.54	.20
13.....	.33	.07	.03	.13	.18	.11	.08
14.....	1.68	.48	.23	.65	.91	.62	.39
15.....	1.11	.26	.16	.44	.67	.43	.29
16.....	1.35	.26	.19	.56	.84	.48	.32
17.....	1.21	.22	.17	.45	.68	.45	.30
18.....	.21	.06	.04	.11	.15	.11	.09
19.....	1.69*	.32*	.29	.70	1.01	.71	.58
20.....	.81	.15	.10	.33	.49	.31	.21
21.....	.80	.16	.08*	.09*	.46	.27	.19
22.....	.26	.10	.04	.12	.11*	.08*	.07
23.....	.54	.11	.07	.19	.31	.16	—*
24.....	.13	.02	.02	.04	.07	.04	.02
25.....	.92	.15	.10	.32	.50	.26	.16
26.....	5.89	1.15	.83	2.09	3.69	1.93	1.36
27.....	1.07	.36	.21	.44	.86	.48	.32
28.....	3.25	.68	.43	1.13	1.97	1.02	.71
29.....	10.01	2.39	1.86	4.10	7.00	4.02	2.71
30.....	2.46	.76	.39	.81	1.68	.80	.57
31.....	1.14	.64	.18	.41	.63	.33	.24
32.....	2.81	.39	.28	.84	1.40	.73	.63
33.....	.91	.33	.32	.37	.81	.44	.36
34.....	.94	.18	.13	.35	.57	.30	.21
35.....	.92	.18	.12	.35	.56	.35	.19
36.....	.08	.02	.01	.03	.06	.03	.02
37.....	3.12	.73	.49	1.29	1.98	1.16	.88
38.....	1.05	.28	.19	.50	.70	.44	.32
39.....	.74	.18	.12	.31	.47	.28	.21
40.....	5.59	1.36	.91	2.32	3.56	2.12	1.64
41.....	1.52	.36	.24	.62	.94	.59	.44
42.....	.30	.08	.05	.13	.19	.12	.09
43.....	.43	.10	.07	.17	.27	.16	.12

Table 5.3 (continued)

Line Number	Pottery and Related Products (73)	Carbon Steel Works and Rolling Mills (79.1)	Alloy Steel Works and Rolling Mills Except Stainless (79.2)	Stainless Steel Works and Rolling Mills (79.3)	Primary Zinc (85)	Primary Aluminum Including Alumina (88)	Aluminum Rolling and Drawing (89)
			Liberalized Industry				
1	17.32	18.77	18.21	18.92	60.48	57.66	37.49
2	.02	.64	.08	.05	.04	.04	.04
3	17.30	18.13	18.13	18.87	60.44	57.62	37.45
4	.67	.83	.81	.84	2.64	2.47	1.40
5	.25	.20	.19	.20	.02	.66	.47
6	.99	.97	.94	.98	3.50	4.12	2.13
7	.30	.26	.25	.26	.95	.88	.63
8	.11	.13	.13	.14	.41	.42	.28
9	.50	.43	.41	.43	.81	.82	.56
10	.02	.03	.03	.03	.04	.02	.03
11	.67	.67	.65	.67	1.73	1.84	1.33
12	.19	.27	.26	.27	.42	.43	.34
13	.09	.08	.08	.08	.31	.33	.20
14	.45	.42	.41	.42	1.57	1.41	.98
15	.31	.30	.29	.30	1.00	.91	.65
16	.34	.34	.33	.34	1.37	1.38	.86
17	.33	.32	.31	.32	1.03	.89	.64
18	.08	.08	.06	.08	.21	.21	.15
19	.59	.63	.61	.63	1.33	1.03	.80
20	.22	.21	.20	.21	.71	.64	.46
21	.18	.22	.22	.23	.72	.66	.44
22	.07	.06	.06	.06	.27	.26	.17
23	.12	.12	.12	.12	.54	.53	.31
24	—*	.03	.03	.03	.14	.13	.07
25	.17	.19	.18	.19	.88	.80	.48
26	1.29	.81*	1.33*	1.41*	5.46	5.15	3.27
27	.31	.35	.34	.35	.98*	.95*	.66*
28	.66	.80	.77	.80	3.05	2.93	1.73
29	2.68	2.82	2.73	2.84	9.46	8.97	6.25
30	.54	.66	.64	.67	2.22	2.00	1.30
31	.23	.25	.25	.26	1.11	1.02	.59
32	.50	.77	.75	.78	2.22	1.86	1.17
33	.29	.48	.47	.49	.74	.63	.50
34	.21	.26	.26	.27	.86	.80	.50
35	.20	.21	.20	.21	.91	.86	.52
36	.02	.02	.02	.02	.08	.08	.05
37	.88	.94	.91	.94	2.98	2.86	1.84
38	.35	.32	.31	.33	1.01	.97	.64
39	.22	.23	.22	.23	.70	.65	.44
40	1.62	1.73	1.68	1.74	5.40	5.16	3.33
41	.44	.46	.45	.47	1.37	1.25	.85
42	.09	.10	.09	.10	.29	.27	.18
43	.12	.13	.12	.13	.40	.37	.25

Table 5.3 (*continued*)

Line Number	Tin Cans and Other Tinware (93)	Cutlery (94)	Tools and General Hardware (95)	Lighting Fixtures (103)	Metal Barrels, Drums, etc. (105)	Tubes and Foils (106)	Machine Tools and Metalworking Machinery (116)
			Liberalized Industry				
1.....	38.71	19.67	19.20	20.39	16.71	14.62	28.53
2.....	.06	.01	.08	.03	.02	—	.51
3.....	38.65	19.66	19.12	20.36	16.69	14.62	28.02
4.....	1.76	.93	.92	.97	.59	.61	1.23
5.....	.45	.28	.25	.19	.20	.19	.34
6.....	2.32	1.14	1.15	.83	.83	.78	1.70
7.....	.62	.29	.28	.26	.24	.18	.40
8.....	.28	.12	.11	.10	.12	.16	.19
9.....	.71	.52	.56	.50	.26	.34	.58
10.....	.03	.02	.03	.12	.02	.02	.02
11.....	1.31	.64	.81	1.25	.65	.62	1.14
12.....	.38	.22	.30	.44	.18	.43	.65
13.....	.20	.09	.09	.10	.08	.06	.15
14.....	.98	.52	.46	.46	.40	.32	.67
15.....	.62	.32	.31	.38	.27	.23	.47
16.....	.84	.37	.35	.41	.34	.26	.59
17.....	.63	.37	.34	.34	.26	.24	.49
18.....	.15	.09	.10	.12	.06	.07	.14
19.....	.93	.66	.65	.62	.40	.48	.78
20.....	.46	.23	.22	.21	.18	.15	.31
21.....	.43	.21	.20	.23	.19	.15	.33
22.....	.17	.08	.08	.12	.06	.07	.15
23.....	.26	.15	.14	.16	.12	.10	.22
24.....	.07	.02	.02	.02	.04	.02	.04
25.....	.48	.21	.19	.20	.20	.13	.31
26.....	3.32	1.50	1.44	1.55	1.44	1.10	2.27
27.....	.69	.38	.34	.32	.31	.28	.51
28.....	1.73*	.78*	.65*	.82*	.74*	.54*	1.24
29.....	6.06	3.05	2.80	2.76	2.79	2.16	3.72*
30.....	1.31	.61	.58	.67	.63	.47	.89
31.....	.61	.26	.24	.26	.31	.21	.40
32.....	1.21	.54	.56	.61	.53	.42	.89
33.....	.73	.36	.39	.34	.37	.33	.45
34.....	.52	.24	.21	.30	.24	.20	.39
35.....	.54	.26	.22	.37	.22	.21	.47
36.....	.05	.03	.02	.03	.02	.02	.04
37.....	1.90	1.00	.98	1.03	.83	.73	1.42
38.....	.66	.35	.35	.35	.30	.26	.47
39.....	.44	.24	.24	.24	.19	.17	.34
40.....	3.47	1.86	1.83	1.92	1.50	1.37	2.62
41.....	.88	.48	.48	.52	.39	.36	.67
42.....	.19	.10	.10	.10	.08	.08	.14
43.....	.26	.14	.13	.14	.11	.10	.19

Table 5.3 (*continued*)

Line Number	Special Industrial Machinery (118)	Industrial Machinery n.e.c. (123)	Ball and Roller Bearings (127)	Motors and Generators (131)	Transformers (132)	Electrical Control Apparatus (133)	Electrical Welding Apparatus (134)
			Liberalized Industry				
1.....	26.38	39.53	35.37	56.70	22.23	21.35	42.96
2.....	.59	.17	.20	.55	.03	.07	.06
3.....	25.79	39.36	35.17	56.15	22.20	21.28	42.90
4.....	1.12	1.88	1.51	2.31	.71	.64	1.89
5.....	.37	.46	.36	.64	.27	.26	.50
6.....	1.45	2.29	2.24	3.81	.84	.78	2.53
7.....	.43	.59	.54	.88	.30	.27	.66
8.....	.16	.28	.25	.44	.15	.14	.31
9.....	.56	.77	.62	.78	.36	.32	.76
10.....	.03	.03	.05	.02	.03	.02	.03
11.....	.94	1.30	1.27	1.84	.99	.99	1.40
12.....	.27	.38	.31	.46	.92	.99	.39
13.....	.12	.20	.19	.30	.08	.11	.23
14.....	.67	.97	.86	1.44	.46	.45	1.08
15.....	.46	.64	.58	.93	.38	.38	.71
16.....	.55	.86	.70	1.34	.42	.41	.95
17	.47	.63	.55	.88	.38	.36	.70
18.....	.11	.15	.14	.20	.12	.12	.16
19.....	.75	.97	.76	1.03	.62	.61	1.00
20.....	.32	.44	.39	.64	.24	.22	.49
21.....	.20	.44	.41	.66	.27	.25	.49
22.....	.10	.18	.14	.25	.14	.17	.19
23.....	.19	.33	.31	.52	.16	.16	.37
24.....	.04	.07	.07	.14	.03	.02	.09
25.....	.30	.49	.44	.80	.23	.24	.55
26.....	2.14	3.38	3.08	5.07	1.79	1.68	3.74
27.....	.50	.70	.61	.99	.42	.40	.76
28.....	1.14	1.82	1.71	2.90	.92	.89	2.05
29.....	3.70*	5.91*	5.21*	8.94	3.51	3.18	6.77
30.....	.89	1.34	1.25	1.40*	.69*	.62*	1.41*
31.....	.38	.63	.57	.99	.25	.29	.69
32.....	.77	1.21	1.20	1.80	.70	.71	1.36
33.....	.42	.82	.50	.65	.45	.47	.70
34.....	.34	.58	.50	.81	.36	.32	.58
35.....	.34	.56	.48	.84	.49	.50	.61
36.....	.04	.05	.05	.07	.03	.03	.06
37.....	1.31	1.95	1.76	2.80	1.08	1.02	2.13
38.....	.46	.67	.59	.95	.39	.37	.73
39.....	.32	.46	.42	.65	.25	.24	.50
40.....	2.41	3.56	3.20	5.05	1.98	1.89	3.86
41.....	.62	.91	.80	1.24	.54	.52	.98
42.....	.13	.20	.17	.27	.10	.10	.21
43.....	.18	.26	.23	.36	.15	.14	.28

Table 5.3 (*continued*)

Line Number	Electrical Appliances (135)	Insulated Wire and Cable (136)	Electric Lamps (138)	Radio and Related Products (139)	Communication Equipment (141)	Storage Batteries (142)	Primary Batteries (143)
				Liberalized Industry			
1.....	23.34	44.96	19.54	51.21	58.69	15.15	53.59
2.....	.09	.07	.02	.43	.25	.03	.01
3.....	23.25	44.89	19.52	50.78	58.44	15.12	53.58
4.....	.83	1.79	.64	2.24	2.41	.55	2.21
5.....	.33	.49	.22	.58	.65	.20	.62
6.....	1.02	2.95	1.22	3.23	3.96	.55	3.65
7.....	.42	.70	.35	.78	.90	.26	.84
8.....	.19	.34	.12	.38	.43	.09	.40
9.....	.48	.62	.67	.83	.81	.30	.72
10.....	.03	.05	.02	.03	.02	.07	.02
11.....	.81	1.43	.84	1.70	1.93	.62	1.67
12.....	.25	.38	.20	.44	.51	.15	.42
13.....	.10	.23	.10	.27	.32	.07	.29
14.....	.60	1.09	.49	1.28	1.42	.33	1.36
15.....	.42	.73	.33	.82	.94	.26	.86
16.....	.46	1.05	.38	1.16	1.38	.29	1.27
17.....	.43	.70	.36	.80	.90	.26	.83
18.....	.10	.16	.10	.19	.21	.08	.19
19.....	.71	.89	.72	1.07	1.08	.39	.95
20.....	.32	.52	.26	.57	.65	.20	.61
21.....	.26	.52	.21	.59	.69	.18	.63
22.....	.10	.20	.08	.24	.26	.07	.24
23.....	.16	.40	.14	.46	.54	.11	.50
24.....	.06	.10	.02	.11	.13	.02	.12
25.....	.25	.62	.23	.68	.82	.16	.76
26.....	1.89	4.04	1.38	4.50	5.28	1.31	4.82
27.....	.47	.79	.30	.90	1.01	.27	.95
28.....	1.01	2.28	.75	2.52	3.02	.68	2.74
29.....	3.99	7.18	2.86	8.02	9.10	2.42	8.47
30.....	.71*	1.60*	.56*	1.80	2.05	.51*	1.89*
31.....	.32	.79	.29	.43*	.78*	.20	.94
32.....	.69	1.45	.61	1.62	2.02	.58	1.71
33.....	.42	.52	.31	.73	.68	.46	.58
34.....	.29	.63	.23	.72	.86	.22	.74
35.....	.30	.66	.25	.75	.87	.17	.80
36.....	.03	.06	.03	.07	.08	.02	.07
37.....	1.15	2.20	.99	2.52	2.90	.74	2.65
38.....	.42	.77	.44	.86	.98	.27	.90
39.....	.28	.51	.25	.59	.66	.18	.61
40.....	2.10	3.95	1.80	4.58	5.24	1.34	4.79
41.....	.57	1.00	.52	1.14	1.29	.37	1.17
42.....	.12	.21	.11	.25	.28	.07	.25
43.....	.16	.29	.14	.33	.38	.10	.34

Table 5.3 (continued)

Line Number	Passenger Cars and Light Trucks (145.1)	Heavy Trucks and Buses (145.2)	Motor Vehicle Parts and Accessories (145.3)	Aircraft and Parts (148)	Motorcycles and Bicycles (152)	Optical, Ophthalmic and Photo Equipment (154)	Watches and Clocks (156)
			Liberalized Industry				
1	25.82	57.67	51.38	52.16	24.42	26.33	18.93
2	.17	.15	1.18	.14	.01	.12	.02
3	25.65	57.52	50.20	52.02	24.41	26.21	18.91
4	.85	2.36	2.06	2.09	.92	1.28	.55
5	.39	.67	.57	.59	.36	.30	.24
6	.97	3.86	3.30	3.40	1.03	1.74	.69
7	.47	.89	.81	.82	.43	.38	.21
8	.20	.44	.39	.38	.19	.16	.11
9	.44	.79	.72	.73	.48	.63	.27
10	.03	.02	.03	.03	.03	.02	.02
11	.94	1.85	1.69	1.72	.84	.86	.98
12	.28	.47	.42	.43	.27	.26	1.06
13	.11	.31	.28	.29	.11	.12	.10
14	.72	1.46	1.30	1.30	.65	.06	.37
15	.49	.94	.85	.86	.45	.42	.32
16	.54	1.36	1.21	1.22	.48	.54	.35
17	.48	.89	.82	.83	.45	.44	.32
18	.11	.20	.19	.19	.10	.11	.11
19	.71	1.04	.98	.98	.72	.77	.53
20	.36	.65	.59	.59	.33	.29	.18
21	.28	.68	.60	.60	.27	.30	.24
22	.11	.26	.23	.23	.10	.12	.19
23	.18	.53	.47	.47	.18	.22	.15
24	.06	.13	.11	.11	.06	.04	.02
25	.30	.81	.71	.70	.25	.31	.20
26	2.15	5.19	4.58	4.67	1.98	2.10	1.48
27	.54	1.01	.90	.91	.49	.46	.37
28	1.12	2.93	2.59	2.61	1.04	1.15	.77
29	4.59	9.09	8.25	8.33	4.23	3.84	2.69
30	.91	2.02	1.80	1.83	.85	.84	.58
31	.35	1.01	.86	.88	.34	.40	.22
32	.59*	1.73*	.47*	1.74	.71	.92	.64
33	.45	.64	.61	.47*	.41*	.42	.41
34	.32	.82	.72	.73	.31	.22*	.28*
35	.36	.86	.76	.76	.31	.35	.50
36	.04	.08	.07	.07	.03	.03	.02
37	1.26	2.85	2.53	2.58	1.21	1.33	.89
38	.47	.97	.86	.87	.43	.46	.31
39	.30	.66	.59	.60	.29	.32	.21
40	2.27	5.15	4.58	4.67	2.20	2.45	1.65
41	.62	1.20	1.13	1.15	.59	.63	.46
42	.12	.27	.24	.25	.12	.14	.09
43	.17	.37	.33	.34	.17	.18	.13

Table 5.3 (*continued*)

Line Number	Jewelry and Silverware (157)	Musical Instruments and Parts (158)	Toys and Sporting Goods (159)	Office Supplies (160)	Plastic Products (161)	Cork Products (162)	Miscellaneous Manufactured Products (164)
				Liberalized Industry			
1	13.88	31.11	16.23	17.45	34.36	7.99	22.69
2	.02	.02	.03	.03	.12	—	.08
3	13.86	31.09	16.20	17.42	34.24	7.99	22.61
4	.54	1.22	.59	.74	1.30	.08	.91
5	.18	.40	.21	.25	.40	.06	.29
6	.73	1.67	.91	.99	2.05	.23	1.20
7	.23	.52	.27	.29	.57	.12	.40
8	.09	.21	.10	.11	.24	.02	.15
9	.36	.55	.47	.49	.58	.07	.47
10	.02	.03	.02	.02	.03	.11	.02
11	.59	1.06	.68	.66	1.17	.23	.85
12	.15	.30	.15	.19	.30	.07	.23
13	.06	.15	.07	.08	.18	.02	.11
14	.34	.80	.40	.42	.91	.16	.55
15	.24	.54	.28	.30	.58	.11	.40
16	.25	.67	.31	.33	.77	.15	.46
17	.26	.54	.29	.32	.57	.12	.41
18	.06	.13	.08	.08	.13	.03	.10
19	.47	.79	.57	.59	.78	.30	.65
20	.18	.38	.21	.22	.42	.12	.28
21	.14	.36	.18	.18	.39	.09	.26
22	.05	.15	.07	.07	.17	.01	.10
23	.10	.24	.11	.12	.29	.05	.17
24	.02	.05	.02	.02	.07	.01	.04
25	.14	.39	.17	.18	.45	.07	.24
26	1.07	2.64	1.20	1.33	2.95	.90	1.88
27	.26	.59	.29	.32	.61	.14	.42
28	.52	1.43	.64	.67	1.63	.32	.98
29	2.32	5.17	2.53	2.79	5.59	1.43	3.65
30	.42	1.07	.50	.54	1.19	.50	.74
31	.17	.46	.24	.20	.53	.35	.30
32	.40	.94	.49	.50	1.08	.20	.79
33	.27	.46	.30	.30	.46	.12	.37
34	.15	.41	.20	.22	.49	.15	.28
35	.14*	.42*	.15*	.18*	.38*	.10*	.19*
36	.02	.04	.02	.02	.04	.01	.03
37	.69	1.54	.82	.88	1.69	.36	1.14
38	.27	.54	.34	.33	.60	.16	.40
39	.17	.36	.20	.21	.40	.09	.27
40	1.27	2.79	1.50	1.63	3.06	.62	2.07
41	.35	.72	.42	.44	.79	.22	.54
42	.07	.15	.09	.09	.17	.03	.12
43	.10	.21	.11	.12	.23	.06	.15

Methods and Assumptions: Effects of Liberalization on Dollar Earnings of Foreign Countries*

IT WAS POINTED OUT in Chapter 5 that estimates of the employment effects associated with the changes of exports induced by liberalization involve shakier assumptions than do the estimates of primary employment effects. The reason is that to estimate the employment effects of exports involves not only all the empirical questions that were involved in the estimates of primary employment effects but also other questions, including some that are even more problematical, such as how foreign countries would respond to increases in their dollar earnings. Since the effort to estimate import-induced changes in exports introduced additional conceptual and empirical questions, further assumptions were, of course, required to answer them. These problems and the methods of dealing with them are described in this and the two following chapters.

It should be noted at the outset of this description that the effect on United States exports with which we are here concerned is the effect of an initial increase of United States imports of an amount that would have been valued at a million dollars in 1953 *after payment of 1953 shipping costs and United States duty.* The effect of such an increase on our exports depends partly on how much of the million dollars is absorbed, at this valuation, by the duties and the American share in the shipping costs; only the balance is earned by foreign countries. It also depends on which countries supply the additional imports and how they use their additional dollar earnings. Since the duties, the shipping costs, and the identity of the supplying countries may differ among the different cases of liberalization, and since different supplying countries may use their additional earnings in different ways, it was not possible to assume that a million-dollar increase of imports would have the

* This chapter may be omitted by readers who are not interested in the estimating methods.

same effect on United States exports in every case of liberalization. In each of the 72 cases, therefore, the effect on exports had to be estimated separately, although by the same method.

The effect of liberalization on the volume of exports was estimated in three broad steps. First, it was necessary to estimate the initial impact of the changes in United States imports on the dollar earnings of the various foreign countries that supply our merchandise imports and the services associated with their importation. Second, it was necessary to estimate how these additional dollar earnings would be likely to affect foreign spending in the United States. In this connection, the composition as well as the total volume of this change in United States exports had to be determined, because the employment effects per dollar of exports depend partly on the products exported. Finally, these estimated effects on exports had to be translated into effects on employment. The first of these steps is described in this chapter and the other two are described in the two following chapters.

To determine how the dollar earnings of foreign countries would be affected by increases in imports of the liberalized products valued at a million dollars at domestic ports after payment of duty, it was necessary, first, to see how much of the million dollars represents duties and shipping costs paid to Americans and how much represents payments to the rest of the world, both for the imported commodity itself and for the foreign share of its shipping costs. Second, these increases in the rest of the world's dollar earnings had to be allocated to individual countries for reasons already indicated.

This is not the end of the process, however, for it will be recalled that liberalization involves a shift of domestic spending from American to foreign output and that the reduction in domestic output induces a decrease in a wide variety of imports used directly and indirectly in producing it. Because of these output-induced decreases of imports (and the foreign share of the shipping costs associated with them), some deduction must be made from the gross increase of foreign earnings on the sale and shipping of the liberalized commodities in order to get the net increase in foreign earnings resulting from liberalization. Estimation of the total amount of this offsetting decrease and its allocation is the third step required in estimating the net increase in dollar earnings of foreign countries.

Effect on Foreign Dollar Earnings of Increased Imports of Liberalized Products

The gross increase in foreign export earnings resulting from the increase in United States imports of the liberalized products consists of the foreign port value of the goods plus the foreign share of the shipping costs (freight and insurance charges). This is equal to a million dollars less the duty and the American share of these charges. Since the import increases are stipulated as being valued at a million dollars in 1953 prices and consist of accepted commodities only, the duties that had to be deducted to get the 1953 foreign port value of these imports were those prevailing in 1953.

Fortunately, data compiled for the Bureau of Labor Statistics gave duties and foreign port values of imports of individual commodities in 1953, grouped and totaled by subindustries. From these data an average ratio of duties to foreign port values was obtained for the accepted commodities in each accepted subindustry. These ratios for the accepted subindustries in a liberalized industry were then averaged, using 1953 domestic output as weights, to obtain a ratio to foreign port values that would reflect the average rate of duty in 1953 on accepted imports in the accepted subindustries of a liberalized industry. (Domestic output weights were used in combining the subindustry ratios because this was the ratio in which imports are combined in each million-dollar basket of import increases.)

Before obtaining the American and foreign shares of the shipping costs (freight and insurance) on the stipulated import increases, it was necessary to estimate in each case the total amount of these expenses in 1953. The method of doing so was explained on pages 98-99 and need not be repeated here.

The division between domestic and foreign sources of the freight and insurance earnings on imports was based on the distribution of earnings from the transportation of all United States merchandise imports in 1952 to 1954, which averaged 48 per cent to American shippers and 52 per cent to foreign shippers. (See page 99.) The assumptions involved in estimating the freight and

Table 6.1

Derivation of Foreign Shares of Million-Dollar Increases of Imports of
Liberalized Industries

(In thousands of dollars at 1953 prices)

Liberalized Industry		Total Domestic Port Value	Duty[a]	Freight	Insurance	Foreign Port Value[b]	U. S. Share[c]	Foreign Share[d]
Code Number	Title							
		(1)	(2)	(3)	(4)	(5)	(6)	(7)
1	Meat animals and products........	1000.0	101.4	63.8	10.6	824.2	137.1	862.9
8	Vegetables and fruits............	1000.0	136.5	179.9	30.0	653.6	237.2	762.8
13	Lead and zinc mining............	1000.0	81.9	71.5	0	846.6	116.2	883.8
21	Meat packing and wholesale poultry	1000.0	111.7	41.5	6.9	839.9	134.9	865.1
22	Processed dairy products..........	1000.0	114.0	41.5	7.0	837.5	137.3	862.7
24	Grain mill products..............	1000.0	104.6	9.7	1.4	884.3	109.9	890.1
27	Sugar.........................	1000.0	64.5	89.1	12.5	833.8	113.3	886.7
28	Alcoholic beverages.............	1000.0	112.9	31.1	27.4	828.6	140.9	859.1
29	Tobacco manufactures...........	1000.0	213.6	19.0	3.1	764.3	224.2	775.8
30	Spinning, weaving and dyeing......	1000.0	196.9	26.4	4.4	772.3	211.7	788.3
31	Special textile products..........	1000.0	187.2	34.7	5.8	772.3	206.6	793.4
34	Apparel.......................	1000.0	229.2	31.4	5.2	734.2	246.8	753.2
35	House furnishings and other non-apparel.....................	1000.0	139.0	48.0	7.9	805.2	165.8	834.2
38	Plywood.......................	1000.0	146.6	4.2	0.8	848.5	149.0	851.0
40	Wood containers and cooperage....	1000.0	121.1	130.6	21.8	726.5	194.3	805.7
41	Wood furniture.................	1000.0	138.4	21.8	3.4	836.3	150.5	849.5
45	Paper and board mills...........	1000.0	85.1	20.5	0.1	894.3	95.0	905.0
46	Converted paper products.........	1000.0	126.0	47.5	8.8	817.7	153.0	847.0
49	Industrial organic chemicals.......	1000.0	220.5	77.4	12.9	689.2	263.9	736.1
51	Synthetic rubber................	1000.0	85.8	47.9	8.0	858.4	112.6	887.4
52	Synthetic fiber.................	1000.0	127.5	29.1	4.9	838.6	143.8	856.2
54	Drugs and medicines.............	1000.0	119.0	10.7	1.8	868.5	125.0	875.0
56	Paints and allied products........	1000.0	52.0	422.6	70.8	454.6	288.9	711.1
59	Vegetable oils..................	1000.0	73.6	42.7	7.1	876.7	97.5	902.5
61	Miscellaneous chemical industries...	1000.0	154.8	35.2	5.9	804.1	174.5	825.5
65	Tires and inner tubes...........	1000.0	89.5	12.0	3.0	895.5	96.7	903.3
66	Miscellaneous rubber products......	1000.0	172.0	10.4	2.1	815.4	178.1	821.9
67	Leather tanning and finishing......	1000.0	101.7	10.8	1.8	885.7	107.7	892.3
69	Footwear, except rubber..........	1000.0	125.5	12.0	2.1	860.4	132.3	867.7
70	Glass.........................	1000.0	235.9	18.6	3.3	742.1	246.5	753.5
73	Pottery and related products......	1000.0	293.7	10.0	1.7	694.6	299.3	700.7
79.1	Carbon steel works and rolling mills.	1000.0	91.3	100.5	16.3	791.9	147.4	852.6
79.2	Alloy steel works and rolling mills, except stainless...............	1000.0	91.3	100.5	16.3	791.9	147.4	852.6
79.3	Stainless steel works and rolling mills	1000.0	91.3	100.5	16.3	791.9	147.4	852.6
85	Primary zinc...................	1000.0	53.0	19.8	3.3	923.9	64.1	935.9
88	Primary aluminum, including alumina	1000.0	58.7	10.2	1.8	929.3	64.5	935.5
89	Aluminum rolling and drawing.....	1000.0	91.4	e	e	908.6	91.4	908.6
93	Tin cans and other tinware........	1000.0	107.2	6.6	e	886.2	110.4	889.6
94	Cutlery.......................	1000.0	238.9	5.9	1.0	754.2	242.2	757.8
95	Tools and general hardware........	1000.0	169.0	5.7	0.7	824.6	172.1	827.9
103	Lighting fixtures................	1000.0	238.5	e	e	761.5	238.5	761.5
105	Metal barrels, drums, etc..........	1000.0	259.3	e	e	740.7	259.3	740.7
106	Tubes and foils..................	1000.0	164.4	12.9	4.3	818.5	172.6	827.4
116	Machine tools and metalworking machinery....................	1000.0	105.6	18.8	2.8	872.8	116.0	884.0
118	Special industrial machinery.......	1000.0	129.9	17.4	3.1	849.6	139.7	860.3
123	Industrial machinery n.e.c.........	1000.0	112.3	8.5	1.4	877.8	117.0	883.0
127	Ball and roller bearings..........	1000.0	165.2	14.0	e	820.7	172.0	828.0
131	Motors and generators...........	1000.0	125.4	6.2	1.6	866.8	129.2	870.8
132	Transformers...................	1000.0	111.2	f	f	888.8	111.2	888.8
133	Electrical control apparatus........	1000.0	149.3	e	e	850.7	149.3	850.7
134	Electrical welding apparatus.......	1000.0	79.4	3.3	e	917.3	81.0	919.0
135	Electrical appliances.............	1000.0	142.7	10.3	2.6	844.4	148.9	851.1
136	Insulated wire and cable..........	1000.0	132.7	74.0	10.6	782.7	173.4	826.6
138	Electric lamps..................	1000.0	166.2	4.6	e	829.3	168.4	831.6
139	Radio and related products........	1000.0	67.6	7.0	1.4	924.0	71.7	928.3
141	Communication equipment........	1000.0	112.7	4.6	e	882.7	114.9	885.1
142	Storage batteries................	1000.0	161.3	7.6	e	831.1	165.0	835.0
143	Primary batteries...............	1000.0	148.9	f	f	851.1	148.9	851.1
145.1	Passenger cars and light trucks.....	1000.0	88.9	18.7	3.2	889.2	99.4	900.6
145.2	Heavy trucks and buses..........	1000.0	105.1	18.3	3.1	873.4	115.4	884.6
145.3	Motor vehicle parts and accessories.	1000.0	108.2	18.3	3.1	870.4	118.5	881.5
148	Aircraft and parts...............	1000.0	124.9	35.7	6.6	832.8	145.2	854.8
152	Motorcycles and bicycles..........	1000.0	103.3	36.6	6.1	854.0	123.8	876.2

Table 6.1 (*continued*)

Code Number	Liberalized Industry Title	Total Domestic Port Value (1)	Duty[a] (2)	Freight (3)	Insurance (4)	Foreign Port Value[b] (5)	U. S. Share[c] (6)	Foreign Share[d] (7)
154	Optical, ophthalmic and photo equipment....................	1000.0	143.1	9.3	1.5	846.0	148.3	851.7
156	Watches and clocks..............	1000.0	246.3	27.4	4.5	721.8	261.6	738.4
157	Jewelry and silverware..........	1000.0	242.4	7.9	1.3	748.4	246.8	753.2
158	Musical instruments and parts.....	1000.0	164.7	9.6	1.6	824.1	170.0	830.0
159	Toys and sporting goods..........	1000.0	247.2	9.9	1.8	741.1	252.8	747.2
160	Office supplies...................	1000.0	208.2	108.4	18.2	665.2	208.9	731.1
161	Plastic products..................	1000.0	189.0	34.0	4.9	772.1	207.7	792.3
162	Cork products...................	1000.0	218.1	28.0	4.8	749.1	233.9	766.1
164	Miscellaneous manufactured products	1000.0	196.5	46.1	7.7	749.7	222.3	777.7

[a] It should be noted that the customs duty shown in the second column of this table represents the revenue on such imports at the 1953 rates, not the revenue that would be collected if imports increased by the stipulated amount as a result of a reduction of duties.
[b] Column 5 is equal to Column 1 less Columns 2, 3, and 4. except for differences due to rounding.
[c] Sum of Column 2 and 48 per cent of Columns 3 and 4.
[d] Sum of Column 5 and 52 per cent of Columns 3 and 4.
[e] Not available. The absolute value of this charge in 1947 was less than $500. The value of imports was sufficiently high to indicate that, as a percentage of the value of imports, it could not be sufficiently different from zero to affect the employment results.
[f] Not available. The absolute value of this charge in 1947 was less than $500. but the value of imports was not sufficiently high to permit any inference as to its percentage relation to value of imports. It was treated as zero.

insurance costs of imports and the foreign share of these costs may introduce an error into the estimates of foreign earnings, but any such error must be small because the fraction of the million dollars that is absorbed by freight and insurance charges exceeds 10 per cent of the foreign port value in few of the 72 cases and only the American share of these charges reduces the estimate of foreign earnings.[1]

Given the ratios to foreign port values of the customs duties and of the American and foreign shares of the freight and insurance expenses, it was a simple matter to determine the portion of the million-dollar increase that was earned by foreign countries, both from sales of the imported products and from the portion of the associated freight and insurance service that they provided. The resulting distribution of the million-dollar increases is shown in Table 6.1.

[1] With a duty of 20 per cent of foreign port value, with freight and insurance charges assumed to be 15 per cent of foreign port value, and with 52 per cent of these charges earned by foreigners, foreign earnings would be 79.8 per cent of the million dollars. If the ratio of freight and insurance to foreign port value were actually 50 per cent higher than assumed (*i.e.*, 22½ per cent instead of 15 per cent), the foreign earnings would be reduced only to 78.4 per cent of the million dollars, so the error in estimating foreign earnings would be only 1.8 per cent.

Allocation of Gross Increase in Dollar Earnings to Supplying Countries

How much more is spent in the United States when foreign dollar earnings increase depends in great part on which countries earn the additional dollars. An increase in earnings of one country may not give the same stimulus to its total imports as an equal increase of earnings gives to imports in another country. Also, as we shall see later, the proportion of a given increase in a country's total imports that comes from the United States differs greatly among countries. Moreover, the effect on employment of increases in foreign purchases from the United States depends on what commodities are bought as well as on the total amount bought, and this commodity composition depends on which countries do the buying. For these reasons, it was necessary to allocate the increases in the foreign dollar earnings that we have just estimated to individual countries.

One obvious way of making this allocation would have been to assume that the increases in foreign dollar earnings from additions to United States imports are distributed among foreign countries in proportion to the 1953 origin of these imports. Many of the imports accepted for study, however, were supplied by fifteen to twenty countries, some of which supplied trivial amounts. Adoption of this procedure would thus have involved a large amount of computation that would have had imperceptible effects on the estimates. It was therefore assumed that the additional earnings from sale of the imported commodities would accrue entirely to the countries that were the *major* suppliers of these commodities to the United States in 1953, and would accrue to them in the same proportions that each contributed to the combined sum of these imports in 1953.

Allocation of the foreign earnings from freight and insurance was less realistic. Freight and insurance services would be provided by the relatively few countries that have substantial merchant shipping fleets or financial centers. There was no basis for apportioning these earnings from importation of the products of individual industries to individual countries, however. For the sake of simplicity, therefore, it was assumed that such earnings accrue to the countries supplying the additional imports and accrue to them in proportion to their share of the increase in total imports. Although this assumption is unrealistic, the error involved is unimportant because these earnings are generally a minor share of the total foreign earnings. Moreover, errors in the allocation of these earnings do not affect the result insofar as the countries to which they are allocated respond to additional dollar earnings in the same way as the countries that would actually earn them.

Each of the 72 industry baskets of additional imports contained more than one, generally many, accepted commodities, which were often in more than one accepted subindustry. These commodities generally had different major suppliers. To determine what countries would be major suppliers from the point of view of the entire industry basket required taking into account both the share of each accepted commodity in the imports of its subindustry and the relative importance of each accepted subindustry in an industry basket. The process was carried out in the steps described below.

Major Suppliers of Imports of
Accepted Subindustries

For each accepted commodity[2] in an accepted subindustry, the value of imports in 1953 from each of the four main supplying countries was listed. The commodities were grouped into subindustries and the contributions of each main supplier to all the accepted imports of the subindustry were then added to get its total contribution to the increase in imports of the subindustry.

Since four main supplying countries had been selected for each individual commodity, and these suppliers often differed for different commodities in the same subindustry, many countries appeared as suppliers to a single subindustry. The three most important were selected, and the percentage contributions of each to the sum of their contributions was then calculated. This procedure involved the assumptions that all additional supplies of im-

[2] As defined in U. S. Bureau of the Census, *Schedule A, Statistical Classification of Commodities Imported into the United States.*

ports in an accepted subindustry would come from the countries that were the three major suppliers of the subindustry in 1953, and that they would do so in the same proportion that these countries contributed to its imports in 1953.[3]

Major Suppliers of Industry Baskets of Imports

The resulting percentage contribution of each of the three suppliers of a subindustry was then multiplied by the percentage share of that subindustry in the combined 1953 domestic output of all the accepted subindustries in the same industry. Since, in many cases, a country appeared as a major supplier of more than one accepted subindustry in an industry, the weighted percentage contributions of a country to imports of all the accepted subindustries in an industry had to be added to get its percentage contribution to the additional imports of the entire industry basket.

These estimates of the percentage contribution of each country to additional imports had to be modified before being used, however. Because in many cases accepted subindustries in the same industry had different major suppliers, more than three countries—in at least two cases as many as twelve countries—often appeared as suppliers of additional imports in a single industry basket. To treat all these countries as recipients of additional dollar earnings would have involved an enormous amount of computation later, when it came to calculating the effects of additional foreign earnings on exports. To keep down the number of countries to which additional earnings were attributed, the preliminary figure for each country's percentage share in the industry basket of additional imports was reviewed. If it was less than 10 per cent and if this contribution to the additional imports of the whole industry

[3] Since the contribution of each country to a subindustry's 1953 imports was estimated as the sum of its contribution to the imports of the subindustry's accepted individual commodities in 1953, this method also implies that additional imports of these commodities enter into those of a subindustry in accordance with 1953 import proportions. For reasons explained on pages 78-79, it is generally assumed in this study that the composition of an industry basket of import increases is proportional to the composition of the industry's 1953 domestic output, not its 1953 imports. Strict adherence to this assumption therefore would have required combining the individual commodities in a subindustry, as well as the subindustries in an industry, in proportion to their importance in 1953 domestic output. It was not feasible to combine individual commodities in this way, however, because there are no data for domestic outputs of individual commodities that accord with the definitions of commodities in Schedule A.

basket arose entirely from contributions to the imports of sub-industries in which the country was a third (or, in some cases, a second) supplier, the country was eliminated as a supplier in all the subindustries in which it appeared. The imports that had been allocated to it were re-allocated proportionately to the remaining suppliers of the subindustry, whose percentage contributions were then recalculated. In no case, however, was a country eliminated as a contributor to an industry's imports if another country with a smaller contribution to the whole industry's imports could not also be eliminated because it was a first or close second supplier of imports to a subindustry. By these eliminations, the number of countries, and therefore the burden of computation, was reduced to more easily manageable proportions, while the sources to which additional imports in each industry were attributed remained broadly representative of the source distribution in 1953.[4]

The percentage contributions of the surviving main suppliers were used to allocate to individual countries the increases of total gross foreign dollar earnings. (See Column 1 of Appendix Table E.4.)

Effect on Foreign Dollar Earnings of Output-Induced Decreases of Imports

The gross increases in foreign dollar earnings are partially offset by decreases in foreign dollar earnings that result from the decreases of imports caused by the reductions of domestic output associated with liberalization. It was necessary to estimate the amount of these decreases in earnings and to find some method of allocating them to individual countries. These decreases arise mainly from the reduction of sales to the United States of goods, some competitive and some not competitive, that enter directly or indirectly into domestic output, but they also include some reduction in earnings from shipping and other services that foreign

---

[4] This process of elimination was also applied in some cases where there was only one accepted subindustry in an industry and where, therefore, only three countries were originally listed as suppliers. If, in such cases, the third country contributed less than 10 per cent, it was eliminated to ease the computing burden.

countries provide in connection with United States importation of these goods.

Estimating Output-Induced Decreases of Imports

The portion of the total output-induced decrease of imports that consisted of imports of competitive commodities was already known in industry detail. It had emerged as a by-product when the decrease of domestic requirements for total output, domestic and foreign combined, was adjusted to get the decrease of requirements for domestic output alone. (This adjustment was described on pages 84-86.)

The portion that consisted of noncompetitive imports did not emerge from the calculation of the domestic output effects of liberalization because these imports are not incorporated in the structure of interindustry relations. The 1947 input of noncompetitive imports of each industry was known from the basic interindustry data, however. The inputs of these imports per 1947 dollar of output of each industry was computed, and this ratio was applied to the change of output of each industry caused by the assumed liberalization to get output-induced decreases of noncompetitive imports.

The foreign shares of the output-induced changes in transportation, insurance, and other shipping services, whether associated with the decreases of competitive or of noncompetitive merchandise imports, are competitive imports of services. Because they are competitive imports, they emerged as a by-product of the computation of domestic output changes, just as did the output-induced decreases of competitive merchandise imports.

Effect on Foreign Dollar Earnings

Although the output-induced decreases of noncompetitive imports obtained by this process were expressed in foreign port values, those of competitive goods and services were expressed in domestic values. All these decreases of imports, moreover, were expressed in 1947 prices. In order to estimate the declines in foreign dollar earnings associated with them, they all had to be expressed in foreign port values and 1953 prices.

The output-induced decreases of competitive merchandise imports generally consisted of small decreases distributed over a wide range of industries. To have applied a separate conversion factor to the imports competing with each industry in each of the 72 cases of liberalization would have required far more computation than their dollar importance justified. In each case of liberalization, therefore, the average percentage relationship between foreign and domestic port values of all United States imports of competitive merchandise was applied to the sum of the decreases in these imports, measured at domestic port values, in order to get their sum in terms of foreign port values.[5]

Converting the decreases in imports of shipping services from domestic values into foreign port values presented no problem; since no duties or significant payments to Americans are associated with imports of these services, the two valuations may be regarded as equal.

In order to convert the output-induced decreases of foreign earnings from 1947 to 1953 prices, an average price index for merchandise imports was used.[6] The same price index was used in all 72 cases of liberalization, even though the composition of the output-induced decrease of imports presumably differed in different cases. The crudity of this price adjustment could not significantly affect the *net increase* in foreign earnings from liberalization in many cases, however, because the decreases being considered would in nearly all cases have been a small fraction of the gross increase in foreign earnings, no matter what price index had been used to adjust them from a 1947 to a 1953 price basis.

The resulting estimates gave the output-induced decreases of

[5] This percentage was obtained from the 1947 interindustry relations study and reflected an average of ratios of values in 1947, weighted by the relative importance of each industry's imports in 1947. An average of ratios at 1947 values was appropriate because the import changes in domestic port values obtained from the matrix of interindustry relations were in 1947 port values, but it should, of course, have been based on the relative importance in each case of each industry's import decline rather than on 1947 weights.

[6] The index used for this purpose was the U. S. Department of Commerce index of the average unit value of merchandise imports. Only after this computation was made was it learned that the department has an index of the price of imported goods and services. This index is unpublished and is used in deflating the current value of net foreign investment in obtaining gross national product in 1947 prices. Since the output-induced decreases of imports include some services as well as merchandise, this index might have been the more appropriate one to use. In any event, since the service component of these import decreases is small, the omission of services from the index used is not serious.

dollar earnings of all foreign countries combined. (See Appendix Table F.3.) It was not feasible to allocate these decreases to individual countries, both because they were spread over a large number of industries in each case and because their detailed commodity composition was not known. Some allocation had to be made, however, if the effects of these decreases on United States exports were to be taken into account. How this problem was treated can best be explained in the next chapter.

CHAPTER 7

Methods and Assumptions: Effects of Changes in Foreign Dollar Earnings on United States Exports*

THE PRECEDING CHAPTER explained the method of estimating the effects of import liberalizations on dollar earnings of foreign countries. The present chapter explains the methods used to estimate the effects of these changes in dollar earnings on United States exports and the assumptions underlying them.

The effort to determine a realistic quantitative relation between changes in foreign earnings and foreign buying from the United States required greater exercise of judgment in choosing between possible economic responses than any other portion of the study. It also involved new problems of translating these judgments into concrete estimates. The problems involved can be understood best after a summary description of how increases in dollar earnings of other countries may be expected to cause changes in United States exports.

The General Problem of Estimating Export Effects

An expansion of United States imports increases the dollar earnings of the countries that supply them. In countries that exercise direct control over imports from the United States and have an unsatisfied demand for United States goods, the mere increase of dollar earnings may permit a relaxation of the import or exchange

* This chapter may be omitted by readers who are not interested in the estimating methods.

control and result in an expansion of imports from the United States. In countries whose exports use imported raw materials, the increase in exports will also cause some output-induced increase in imports. Apart from these direct effects, purchase of goods by the United States from the supplying country tends to expand the level of that country's national income. If this expansive force is not offset by a reduction of other demands on that country's output, it raises the country's national income to a higher level. The rise in national income results in a rise of the exporting country's imports.

The total increase in imports of a supplying country is likely to come from many countries, including the United States. The additional demand for the goods of these countries, if not offset, will result in an expansion of *their* imports, some portion of which is likely to come from the United States, giving rise to a further increase of United States exports. Similarly, the increase in imports from other countries may be expected to give rise to increases in income and imports in other countries. At each stage, the United States may be expected to participate in supplying the goods for the further import expansion, so that there are successive rounds of increases in United States exports.

International Effects
Included in the Estimates

Except in the countries where purchases of United States goods are still restricted by direct controls, increases of exports to the United States raise the effective demand of the supplying country for United States goods mainly, if not wholly, by increasing the level of its money incomes. Similarly, the indirect, or "multilateral," increases of United States exports depend mainly on the further increases of income generated in other countries by the additional purchases of supplying countries and their suppliers.

As Chapter 5 has already stated, all the United States exports generated directly and indirectly by the increases in foreign earnings are included in the exports whose employment effects are estimated in this study. Thus the estimates include the effects on United States employment of the foreign income changes generated by the changes in United States imports, even though they exclude those of income changes in the United States. As was explained in Chapter 5, inclusion of the effects of foreign income changes follows from the objective of the estimates. This objective implies that the estimates should include all indirect effects on United States exports arising from the primary changes in United States imports but none of the effects of changes in United States exports on United States incomes and thereby on United States spending, either on domestic goods or on imports.

The implications of this objective for the estimating procedure are twofold: (1) the estimates must take into account the effect of export increases on imports, not only for foreign countries that supply the United States but for countries that supply these United States suppliers, and for countries that in turn supply these countries, and (2) the cumulative expansion of world trade generated by the initial rise of United States imports must be treated as ceasing when it hits the United States.

Relationships that Determine the Employment
Effects of Increases in United States Exports

Having determined what export effects are to be estimated, we must next consider what determines their employment effects. These employment effects depend on both the size of the total export effects and their distribution among various industries. If all foreign countries increased their total imports by the same amount per dollar of additional export earnings and also obtained the same percentages of their additional imports from each United States industry, then both the total amount and the composition of our additional exports would be unaffected by which foreign country bought them. Under these conditions, a given increase of dollar earnings by foreign countries would always have the same effect on United States employment, no matter what country received the initial addition to earnings. The estimating problem would then be relatively simple.

Countries are not the same in these respects, however. Some of them may not spend all of an addition to earnings on increased imports. They also differ in the percentage of their total imports that they obtain from individual supplying countries and in the industry distribution of their purchases in the United States. Consequently, the effect of increases in foreign earnings on United States employment depends on which countries receive these additional earnings.

If the additional export earnings of United States suppliers induce small additions to their imports, the initial impetus to expansion of world trade will be less than if they induce large additional imports. Moreover, if these suppliers spend a given amount on imports from countries which, in turn, use little of their increased export earnings for imports, the further expansion of world trade will obviously be less than if our suppliers spend the same amount on imports from countries that spend much of the addition to their earnings. The distribution of the additional imports by these countries, in turn, is important in determining the next round of repercussions. Similarly, if the countries supplying the United States, or their suppliers, increase their imports of American automobiles, the effect on employment in the United States may be different than if they increase their imports from the United States by an equal amount but buy coal instead of automobiles. The total effect on the exports of each American industry per dollar of addition to foreign earnings therefore depends on how the additional foreign earnings are distributed among the major suppliers, which was estimated in Chapter 6, and on the percentages of its additional earnings that a country spends on additional imports from each foreign country and from each United States industry. The percentage it spends in each foreign country, in turn, is the product of the percentage of its additional earnings that it spends on additional imports from all sources, which we shall call its "reflection ratio," and the percentage distribution of its total additional imports among all foreign countries.[1] The percentage it spends on the output of each United States industry is

[1] The concept of "reflection ratio" relevant to the present estimates is more clearly explained below. The term is used by J. J. Polak in *An International Economic System* (University of Chicago Press, 1953), especially pp. 41-44, and "Conceptual Problems Involved in Projections of the International Sector of Gross National Product," in *Long Range Economic Projections*, Studies in Income and Wealth, Vol. 16, by the Conference on Research in Income and Wealth (Princeton University Press, 1954), pp. 398-401. An algebraic analysis of the effects of changes in exports on income and thereby on imports may be found in Thomas C. Schelling's *National Income Behavior* (McGraw-Hill Book Company, 1951), Chap. 13. See also Fritz Machlup's *International Trade and the National Income Multiplier* (The Blakiston Company, 1943) and L. A. Metzler's "The Transfer Problem Reconsidered," *Journal of Political Economy*, Vol. 50, pp. 397 ff., reprinted in *Readings in the Theory of International Trade* (The Blakiston Company, 1949).

the product of its reflection ratio, the percentage of its imports it obtains in the United States, and the percentage of its imports from the United States that comes from each United States industry.

Independence of These Relationships

The question immediately arises whether, for a given country, these relationships can be estimated independently of each other. Can the increase in a country's total imports of all goods from all sources be regarded as determined independently of what products it buys and where it buys them? If there were no general pressure for a country to import, so that it would not tend to buy more from one country when it buys less from another, its reflection ratio would not tend to be stable. General pressures to import do exist, however, so that the concept of an over-all reflection ratio as a stable phenomenon has some validity.

Assuming that the reflection ratio of a country can be independently determined, the question then arises whether the distribution of its imports among various countries is stable and can be estimated independently. Clearly, the actual values of the percentages are not entirely independent of each other. At least some economic forces affect simultaneously both the amount of total imports per dollar of additional earnings and their percentage distribution. There is nevertheless some reason to believe that the percentage distribution of a country's additional imports among different sources is at least fairly stable. This is especially true of the percentage of imports bought from the United States by countries that restrict dollar purchases and have unsatisfied demands for United States products. A reduction in their spending on the goods of one United States industry often results in an increase of their purchases from another. The distribution of additional imports among different sources of supply was therefore independently estimated.

The next question is whether the industry distribution of a country's additional imports from the United States can be reliably estimated independently of its total additional purchases from the United States. The evidence needed to answer this question is not available, but there is evidence about the distribution of purchases of individual countries among specific United States products. As would be expected, the composition of purchases by some countries varies considerably from year to year, but for most countries it does not fluctuate widely, especially among nonagricultural commodities. In any case, no alternative to the assumption that the industry compositions of purchases by individual countries could be independently estimated was any more satisfactory.

On the basis of these assumptions, the procedure used was to estimate the merchandise reflection ratio of each country (the ratio of the total export-induced change in its imports of merchandise and shipping services to the change in its export earnings) independently of the composition of such imports. Then, as an independent step, the additional imports were allocated among the various countries, including the United States. Finally, the additional purchases in the United States, derived from the first two steps, were distributed among the different United States industries that export goods and shipping services.

Estimation of Merchandise Reflection Ratios

The assignment of realistic merchandise reflection ratios required exercising judgment about the probable economic behavior of the countries concerned. It also required considering a number of technical matters in order to adapt the concept as precisely as possible to the requirements of our problem. '

The General Problem

There is a question as to precisely what the reflection ratio is to measure. The ratio of a country's increment in imports to its increment in earnings is to be used in estimating the effect on United States employment of increases in the rest of the world's imports from the United States. This ratio therefore should include all the additions to imports from the United States that require current production in the United States, and only such additions. Interest and dividends paid to investors in the United States do not constitute a direct demand for United States output; if they affect United States employment, they do so only through their effects on income and income-induced expenditure, effects that are excluded from the estimates in this study. Changes in interest and dividends paid to American investors, therefore, should be excluded from the reflection ratios to be estimated. However, these reflection ratios should include *all* the additions to foreign payments that given rise to additional earnings in countries other than the United States, including income on foreign investments paid to them, because such income enters into the earnings to which their own reflection ratios are to be applied. In short, it should include induced changes in imports of all goods and all services, including income on foreign investments paid to all countries other than the United States.

The ratio of the change in these imports of a country to the change in its exports may be considered as having two main parts: (1) the imports of these goods and services that are required to produce the increment of exports; and (2) the imports of these goods and services induced by the changes in national income and spending generated by the expansion of exports. The latter component can be regarded as the product of three factors: (a) The percentage of the total increase in foreign earnings that gets into the domestic income stream. (This percentage discounts the portion of the change in export earnings that does not enter the domestic income stream because it is used to make foreign payments associated directly with export production.) (b) The ratio of the earnings-induced increase in national income to this portion of the increase of foreign earnings (often called "the export multiplier"); and (c) the ratio of income-induced increases of all imports of goods and services, except income on United States investments, to the increase of income that induces them (a modified version of what is called "the marginal propensity to import" or "the marginal import : income ratio").

This reflection ratio includes, in (1) and (2c), all services except income paid on United States investments. It will be recalled that the purpose of getting a reflection ratio for each country is to find the relevant total of induced foreign payments made by each country, which is then to be distributed among the various countries that receive them. Although it was feasible to obtain the country distribution of each country's merchandise imports and, for most countries, the total imports of services, it was unfortunately not feasible to obtain the country distribution of imports of services or payments of investment income to foreign investors. Moreover, it did not seem reasonable to assume that these services and income payments are distributed among countries in the same ratio as merchandise imports. Since statistical sources made it possible to distribute only merchandise imports (at valuations that included shipping costs) and since they constitute the bulk of additional imports, it was decided to include only these imports in the reflection ratio for each country.

The merchandise reflection ratio consists of the same four components that make up the more comprehensive reflection ratio except that it excludes services other than shipping from the components designated in the second preceding paragraph as (1) and (2c). Omission of these services has the effect of understating the effects of liberalization on United States exports and therefore the employment-stimulating effect of liberalization. The omitted items, however, are in most cases small relative to the theoretically correct total, probably less than 10 per cent.[2]

It was not feasible to estimate the merchandise reflection ratios for each country by estimating their four components separately. To do so would have required determining what portion of the marginal imports of merchandise and shipping of every foreign country results directly from changes in export production and what portion results from changes in national income. The reflection ratios used were obtained by the much simpler method described below. These ratios are believed to be a reasonable approximation for most countries of the ratios desired.[3]

Assigning Values to the Merchandise Reflection Ratios

The whole range of factors determining a country's response to changes in export earnings is relevant to determination of its

---

[2] See last paragraph of Appendix E. Export-induced changes in payments of income on foreign investments have been regarded as confined to dividend payments, since interest payments are more or less fixed.

[3] Appendix E explains the relationship of the merchandise reflection ratios actually obtained to the theoretically correct ratios, which include services and income on non-United States investment, and the conditions under which they are identical.

merchandise reflection ratio. For some countries, familiarity with their economic history and policies over a period of time made it possible to assign values to their merchandise reflection ratios without estimating more than one component of the ratio from statistical data. In other cases, it was necessary to estimate as many of the components as possible.

1. In some cases, the economic history and policies of a country and the role of foreign capital in its current export production led to the conclusion that increases in export earnings would give rise to an at least equal increase in imports of all goods and services within a short period (say, a year or two). This implied that its *total* reflection ratio (its ratio of changes in *all* current foreign payments, including investment income paid to all countries) was equal to one. In general, a total reflection ratio of one was assigned to all constitutionally independent countries that are pursuing development programs or that, for other reasons, have shown a persistent tendency to spend abroad within one or two years all increases of their foreign earnings. These are countries that, since the war, have shown a chronic inability or lack of desire to build up their international assets out of their international earnings and, at the time the judgments were made, showed no signs of changing their economic behavior in this respect. While some of these countries have increased their net international assets over a period of a year, they have lost the gains in the following year. Total reflection ratios of one were assigned to 67 countries.[4]

The balances of payments of these countries were next examined to see how important increments of income paid on foreign investments were likely to be in increments of their total receipts. If dividends paid to foreign countries were less than 5 per cent of export earnings in 1953, it was assumed that increments of such payments could be neglected. For these countries, of which there were 41, the merchandise reflection ratio was also assumed to be one.

In the remaining 26 countries whose total reflection ratios were judged to be one, it was found that income paid to foreign investors in 1953 was a significant proportion of export earnings. In-

[4] The major suppliers to whom a total reflection ratio of unity was assigned are Argentina, Australia, Brazil, Cuba, Finland, India, Iran, Italy, Mexico, New Zealand, Norway, Spain, Turkey, and the Philippines. There is some doubt as to whether the same total reflection ratios would have been assigned if the decision had been made a year or two later.

sofar as this income arises directly from the additional exports, it should be deducted from the export earnings that generate domestic income. To allow for this factor, the percentage of increments in exports that would not enter the domestic income stream was estimated from the ratio of dividends to export earnings in 1952, 1953, and 1954, although this ratio was modified in some cases to take account of known changes in the position of foreign capital. When the resulting ratio was 5 per cent or more, it was deducted from the total reflection ratio to get the estimated merchandise reflection ratio.

Although the procedure used to obtain the merchandise reflection ratios of these countries is not theoretically correct, it gives a result identical with that of the theoretically correct procedure if increments of exports do in fact generate equal increments of imports and these imports consist solely of goods, shipping costs, and income paid on foreign investments. Probably these conditions are approximately, although not fully, realized in the countries to which this procedure was applied.

2. There were, of course, many countries that could not be assumed to have total reflection ratios of one, either because there was insufficient knowledge of its payments histories and policies or because knowledge of the country indicated that their total reflection ratio is less than one. In general, independent countries that have retained or were expected in the next few years to retain a significant part of increments in their foreign earnings, whether because of structural characteristics of their economies or because of deliberate policy measures, were regarded as having total reflection ratios significantly below one. Underdeveloped countries that are colonies of countries having total reflection ratios of less than one were assumed to be controlled by their mother countries in the policies affecting their international payments and were also assumed to have total reflection ratios of less than one. Altogether, there were 34 countries that were not assumed to have total reflection ratios of one. To determine a merchandise reflection ratio for each of these countries, it was necessary to make explicit estimates of as many as possible of its components.

Since it was not possible to distinguish between increments of merchandise imports required to produce increments of a country's exports and increments generated by changes in its domestic spending, all merchandise imports were treated as generated by domestic spending. In terms of the components of the ratio described earlier in this section, as modified to exclude the omitted services, this means that the component designated as (1) was treated as zero and all merchandise imports were included in (2c).

It was also not possible to distinguish between the increments of payments of investment income generated by additional export production and those generated by changes in income from domestic sales. In countries where additional payments of income to foreign investors are substantial in relation to the additional export earnings, the additional payments usually come almost entirely from investments in export industries. For the countries whose income payments on foreign investments were large enough to be taken into account, all such payments were treated as being generated in export industries and were deducted from the additional export earnings in estimating the portion that enters the domestic income stream. No other payments for foreign services were treated as generated by exports. Since no merchandise imports were treated as required for additional export production, total additional payments of investment income were the only part of additional export earnings that were deducted in estimating component (2a), the portion of additional exports that gets into the domestic income stream.

The third component of the reflection ratio is the export multiplier, earlier designated as (2b). The size of this component depends on the sum of all the uses of additional domestic income that do not generate further income inside the country. These "leakages" from the income stream consist of a "domestic leakage," made up of increments of domestic income that are not spent on any goods and services, and a "foreign leakage," made up of increments spent on goods and services obtained from outside the country, including payments of income on foreign investments to all countries.

The size of the domestic leakage was determined on the basis of a general, more or less arbitrary judgment about the increases in spending that may be expected to result from additional foreign earnings. This judgment sought to allow roughly for all such increases in spending, including not only those induced directly by changes of income but also those resulting from the effects of changed foreign earnings on monetary policy, the wage level, etc., where these net effects could be predicted from the recent history of the country's international payments. For independent countries that were not judged to have an international reflection ratio of one, a value of .15 was assigned to the domestic leakage, except in the case of Canada and the United Kingdom, where values of .05 and .10, respectively, were given.

The foreign leakage, consisting of all increments of domestic income that are spent abroad, could be estimated from statistical data, making plausible assumptions. It will be recalled that, because there is no way of distinguishing how much of the addition to merchandise imports is required by additions to export production and how much is generated by additions to domestic income, it was assumed, in estimating the export-generated portion of the merchandise reflection ratio of these countries, that no merchandise imports are necessary for their export production. This implies that all the additional merchandise imports of these countries are generated by increases in their domestic incomes. All expenditures on merchandise imports, therefore, were included in the foreign leakage from additions to their domestic incomes. Since it had also been assumed that all additional payments of investment income by these countries arise directly from additional export sales, it was assumed that no such payments are generated by additions to their domestic incomes. Accordingly, no such payments were included in the foreign leakage from additions to their domestic incomes. Imports of other services (except for shipping) were also excluded because data on gross payments were lacking for many countries. Thus the foreign leakage was conceived, for purposes of making the estimates, as consisting only of additions to merchandise imports, but as including all such additions.

On these assumptions, the foreign leakages were estimated from data on international payments and national income for 1952, 1953, and 1954, interpreted in the light of what was known about the forces affecting them in those years.[5]

---

[5] The main sources of data for these years were the *Balance of Payments Yearbook* of the International Monetary Fund and *Statistics of National Income and Expenditure,* published by the United Nations.

The fourth component of the merchandise reflection ratio, the ratio of income-induced increases of merchandise imports to the increases of income that induce them, does not contain increments of domestic income spent on imported services. Because these services had been omitted, perforce, from the foreign leakages in estimating the leakages from domestic income, the marginal merchandise import:income ratio could be taken as equal to the foreign leakage.

Since it was assumed that no additions to merchandise imports were required to produce additional exports, the desired merchandise reflection ratio was obtained as the product of the second, third, and fourth ratios (components (2a), (2b), and (2c)).[6]

Distribution of Additional Imports of Foreign Countries

The next step in estimating the effects of liberalization on United States exports was to estimate the distribution of foreign countries' additional imports. Ideally, this step requires that we determine for each country of the world the pattern of its marginal spending in every country of the world other than the United States, and the pattern of its marginal spending on the products of each of 200 specific United States industries. Even if the mass of basic material needed to estimate these factors could have been compiled, its use to obtain the effects on the exports of individual United States industries would have required constructing and working with a pattern of trade relations linking each of about 100 foreign countries to every other country and to almost 200 United States export industries. The amount of computation required by such a procedure would have been far greater than could be justified, considering the elements of judgment and the consequent possibility of error that would still have been unavoidable. Means of avoiding these difficulties therefore had to be found.

[6] It may be noted that this method of estimating the merchandise reflection ratio, besides being conceptually correct when the assumptions stated above are realized, is also correct under some other conditions.

The most obvious simplification of the problem presented by the large number of countries would have been to group all countries into a few groups, each of which was fairly homogeneous with respect to the relevant characteristics (*i.e.*, reflection ratios, percentage distribution of imports among countries, and industry distribution of imports from the United States), and from this grouping to estimate the total effect on United States exports. This procedure would have implied that, in the relevant characteristics, all countries in a group were the same.

Therein lies the objection to it. We know that such an assumption has only limited validity. The various merchandise reflection ratios, which are important in determining the export effects, cover a wide range of values that do not fall readily into a few groups. Furthermore, information about the industry distribution of foreign purchases from the United States that is available for 32 countries indicates that countries differ greatly with respect to these distributions.[7] This information is not available for all countries, and we have no basis for classifying all countries into groups that are homogeneous with respect to this characteristic. Failure to take these differences into account in making the groupings could introduce substantial error into the estimates of employment effects.

For the 32 countries the industry composition of whose purchases in the United States is known, it was possible to estimate the amount and industry composition of the additional United States exports that they would buy as a result of increases in their earnings. In view of this possibility, lack of such data for other countries could not justify estimating total export effects by grouping all countries, for that method of estimating would have failed to make use of the information for the 32 countries that was avail-

[7] The Congressional Joint Committee on the Economic Report, now known as the Joint Economic Committee, obtained a tabulation of these data from the U. S. Bureau of the Census in connection with the hearings of its Subcommittee on Foreign Economic Policy. See *Foreign Economic Policy*, Hearings, 84 Cong. 1 sess. (1955). The table on pages 253-57 of that volume shows the percentage distribution of United States exports in 1953, by industry, to 32 selected countries that were major suppliers of protected United States imports in 1953. These data were tabulated in connection with the testimony given before the subcommittee by Walter S. Salant on "Short-Term Domestic Economic Effects of Reducing Import Barriers." The tables are also shown in a reprint of this testimony, published under that title as Brookings Institution Reprint No. 10.

able. These countries were major suppliers of protected imports in 1953. Obviously, the estimates of total export effects would be more reliable if these "bilateral" exports, *i.e.,* those resulting *directly* from increases in sales of liberalized imports to the United States, were estimated by using the available data for major supplying countries and the cruder grouping procedure were confined to the estimates of the indirect or "multilateral" export effects. For this reason, bilateral and multilateral effects were estimated separately.

To estimate the bilateral effects, it was necessary to divide the additional imports of each major supplying country between the United States and the rest of the world and then to distribute their additional imports from the United States among the various industries. To estimate the multilateral effects, it was necessary to classify all countries into world trade groups, to determine how the additional imports that each major supplier would obtain from outside the United States would be distributed among these groups, and to determine the trading relationships of these groups with each other and the United States. The grouping of countries is basic to the process of estimating the multilateral effects. Moreover, one of the characteristics of countries on which the grouping is based is also essential for estimating the bilateral effects. It is therefore desirable to explain next the process by which foreign countries were combined into world trade groups.

Basis for Grouping of Countries

In combining countries into groups, it was necessary to classify them according to the characteristics that are most important in determining the employment effects of additional United States exports. As was pointed out earlier, the relevant characteristics are the percentage of its additional earnings that a country spends on imports from all sources, the percentage distribution of these additional imports among countries, and the percentage of its imports from the United States that it spends on the products of each United States industry. Since it was impracticable to estimate all these characteristics, they could not be used as the basis for grouping countries. It was necessary, therefore, to group countries in accordance with the most relevant characteristics that could be estimated.

The percentage of its additional export earnings that a country spends on merchandise imports, measured by its merchandise reflection ratio, was estimated by the methods described in the preceding section. Since the reflection ratio of the United States was treated as zero while the reflection ratios of all other countries were considerably above zero and differed much less from each other than they did from that of the United States, the size of the multilateral effect would always depend more on the distribution of a country's imports between the United States and all other countries combined than on their distribution among foreign countries. For this reason, it was possible to avoid considering the percentage of its additional imports that a country spends on imports from every other country. Consideration was given only to the division of its additional imports between the United States and all other countries combined.

Since information regarding the industry distribution of purchases in the United States was available for only 32 countries and could not be estimated for other countries, this characteristic was ignored in classifying countries into groups.[8] Judging from the available data, countries do not confine their purchases to a few industries; they spread them over a large number of industries. It was assumed, therefore, that there would not be great differences between the employment effects per dollar of *aggregate* purchases by different countries. For this reason it is believed that the reliability of the estimates is little impaired by neglect of this factor.

Thus, the characteristics taken into account in grouping countries were reduced to two: their merchandise reflection ratios, the assignment of which has already been described, and the

[8] At first it was hoped that it might be possible to use the data for the 32 countries to construct patterns of purchases from each United States industry for the 60 or more other countries. Although the patterns of industry purchases for the 32 countries showed considerable variation, if these differences had been related to the differences in their reflection ratios and in the percentages of their total imports that they purchased from the United States, it would have been possible to form some general judgments about the relationships between industry purchase patterns on the one hand and reflection ratios and channels of trade on the other. Unfortunately no such correlation was evident in the data for the 32 countries. It was therefore decided that there was no basis for estimating industry distribution of purchases in the United States for the other countries.

distribution of their total merchandise imports between the United States and all other countries combined, which must be considered next.

Percentage of Foreign Imports
Obtained from the United States

The percentage of total merchandise imports coming from the United States was computed for every country for 1952, 1953, and 1954.[9] It was found that for most countries this percentage remained remarkably constant during these three years. Its range over the three years exceeded 7 percentage points for only 15 of the 91 countries for which data were available for all three years. The 1953 percentages appeared to provide as reasonable a basis for estimating the portion of a country's increase in imports that would come from the United States as any other that could be found. Some confidence in them as indicators of marginal ratios was derived from the fact that, for the countries that seemed likely to be most important in export effects, the United States share of their annual *changes* in imports between 1952 and 1954 was close to the United States share of their total 1953 imports.

For most countries, the data used to measure the percentages of their imports that come from the United States include cost of shipping services. Since it was not feasible to distinguish these costs, it was assumed that the portion of its total purchases of foreign shipping services that an importing country obtains from the United States is approximately the same as the United States portion of its merchandise imports. This assumption appeared to be a reasonable one in the cases of the few countries for which its correctness could be examined.[10]

[9] Data for individual countries, which are shown in Appendix Table E.3a, were obtained from *Direction of International Trade, 1938, 1948 and 1951-1954*, published jointly by the United Nations, the International Monetary Fund, and the International Bank for Reconstruction and Development (Statistical Papers, Series T, Vol. 6, No. 10).

[10] According to the *Balance of Payments Yearbook* of the International Monetary Fund, Canada obtained from the United States between 70 and 73 per cent of its merchandise imports in the years 1953 to 1955 and between 69 and 81 per cent of its imported services for "transportation," and "insurance and miscellaneous." For Australia, Austria, Brazil, United Kingdom, and West Germany, data were available only for the combined United States and Canadian share. The percentages of their total shipping obtained from these countries were generally very close to the corresponding percentages of their total merchandise imports.

Estimating Bilateral Effects on Exports

The percentage of additional earnings that each major supplier would spend on United States merchandise was estimated by multiplying its merchandise reflection ratio by the estimated percentage of its merchandise imports coming from the United States. Since both factors are assumed to include payments for shipping services obtained abroad, the resulting percentages could be used to estimate the supplying country's additional imports from the United States of merchandise and shipping services combined, per dollar of its additional export earnings.

These amounts, being percentages of additional export earnings, are the same, for a given supplier, in all cases of liberalization. The percentage for each supplier was applied to the dollar amount of its share of the gross increase in foreign earnings in each case of liberalization, estimated as described in Chapter 6, to get the bilateral increase in United States exports to each major supplier in each case.[11] These exports are shown in Column 2 of Table 7.3.

Estimating Multilateral Effects on Exports

It was pointed out earlier in this chapter that increases in the dollar earnings of suppliers of American imports may affect United States exports to every country of the world and that, to estimate these effects, it was necessary to classify foreign countries into a few homogeneous groups. The classification of foreign countries into such groups was the first step in estimating multilateral effects on exports.

The next step was to estimate the direct trade relationships between each pair of country groups, including the United States

[11] In one case, that of cork products, the decrease in major suppliers' earnings resulting from their share of the output-induced decrease of exports was subtracted from the gross increase in their earnings and the percentage for each supplier was applied to its share of the *net* change in earnings. The reason for this deviation from the normal procedure is explained in footnote 18 of this chapter.

as one group, and from this network of direct world trade relationships to calculate the total (direct and indirect) effect of an initial change in the exports of any group on the exports of every group, including the United States. This step makes it possible to calculate the total effect of a dollar of additional exports of each group on the exports of the United States.

The third step was to estimate the initial net change in the exports of each group of foreign countries that would result in each case of liberalization from the increases in its exports to the major suppliers and the decrease in its exports to the United States caused by the total output-induced decline of United States imports. These initial net changes in the exports of each group of foreign countries could then be multiplied by the relevant ratios obtained in the second step to get the absolute amount of the multilateral effects on United States exports.

Grouping of Countries

As has already been explained, the characteristics taken into account in classifying foreign countries were reduced to two: their merchandise reflection ratios and the distribution of their total merchandise imports between the United States and all other countries combined.

The merchandise reflection ratios ranged from a low of .46 (for France) to a high of 1.00. Of the 89 countries for which such ratios were calculated, 55 had ratios of .85 or higher. Of the remaining countries, 22 had ratios of between .65 and .84 and 12 had ratios between .46 and .64. (See Appendix Tables E.1 and E.3.) It was decided to divide the foreign countries into two groups, those with merchandise reflection ratios of .85 or more and those with ratios under .85.

The estimated shares of additional merchandise imports supplied by the United States ranged between 9.3 and 83.1 per cent. Despite this wide range, it was found that when foreign countries (or dependent areas) were arrayed according to the percentages of total merchandise imports that they obtained in the United States during 1953, they fell into two fairly distinct groups. Of the 95 countries or dependent areas for which 1953 percentages could be computed, 66 obtained 20 per cent or less of their merchandise imports from the United States. Of the remaining 29 countries, 14 obtained 60 per cent or more from the United States.[12] It was therefore decided to subdivide both groups of countries (*i.e.*, those having high and low merchandise reflection ratios) into those that normally obtain one third or less and those that normally obtain more than one third of their merchandise imports from the United States.

The Network of Trade Relations

Once the number of foreign entities engaged in world trade had been reduced to four by the process of grouping countries, it became possible to construct a network of direct trade relationships between each country group and every other group. The United States had to be included in this network of trading relationships because the effect on its exports was to be estimated, and it had to be treated as a separate group so that its identity would not be lost.

These direct trade relationships were expressed as a set of ratios, or coefficients, each of which relates a group's imports from another group to its own export earnings. The method of obtaining these ratios was to calculate group merchandise reflection ratios by averaging the reflection ratios for the countries in a group, weighting the ratio for each country by its share in the group's exports, and then to multiply these group reflection ratios by the percentage of the group's total imports that came from each group in 1953.[13]

[12] Geographical position was clearly the dominant factor determining the general level of this percentage, with political relations next. In 1953 all independent countries in the Western Hemisphere obtained 50 per cent or more of their imports from the United States, except Argentina, Bolivia, Brazil, Paraguay, and Uruguay, which are the countries in the Hemisphere most distant (except for Chile) from the United States, Moreover, the only country outside the Western Hemisphere that obtained more than 50 per cent of its imports from the United States was the Philippine Republic, a former territory of the United States. The only other ones that obtained over 35 per cent of their imports from the United States were South Korea and Formosa, which receive large quantities of aid from the United States, and Saudi Arabia. All Western Hemisphere dependencies of other countries obtained less than 17 per cent of their imports from the United States, except the Bahama Islands. These conclusions also apply, with hardly any modification, to foreign countries' imports in 1954. These percentages are shown in Appendix Tables E.2, E.3, and E.3a.

[13] The percentage of its total imports that a group obtained from each group of foreign countries in 1953 was computed from data on imports of individual countries obtained from *Direction of International Trade, 1938, 1948 and 1951-54.*

Thus, a network of direct trading relationships among all the country groups and the United States was obtained. It took the form of Table 7.1, in which the columns represent importing country groups, including the United States, and the rows represent the same groups as exporters. The numbers in this table were used to represent the estimated portion of an addition to its own

Table 7.1

Direct Trade Relationships Between Merchandise Imports and Exports of Country Groups[a]

Exporting Groups	Increase in Merchandise Imports per Dollar Increase of Its Own Export Earnings by				
	Group 1	Group 2	Group 3	Group 4	United States
Group 1................	$.0275	$.0130	$.0144	$.0184	0
Group 2................	.0518	.2357	.0337	.1607	0
Group 3................	.0282	.0451	.0293	.0414	0
Group 4................	.2049	.5611	.1306	.3324	0
United States...........	.5976	.1351	.5520	.0671	0
Total (merchandise reflection ratio)......	$.9100	$.9900	$.7600	$.6200	0

[a] Group 1 contains countries with merchandise reflection ratios of 85 per cent or more which obtain more than one third of their imports from the United States.

Group 2 contains countries with merchandise reflection ratios of 85 per cent or more which obtain one third or less of their imports from the United States.

Group 3 contains countries with merchandise reflection ratios of less than 85 per cent which obtain more than one third of their imports from the United States.

Group 4 contains countries with merchandise reflection ratios of less than 85 per cent which obtain one third or less of their imports from the United States.

export earnings that the importer named in the column heading would spend on merchandise imports (including imports of shipping services) from the exporter named in the row.

As was to be expected, Table 7.1 shows that Group 1, characterized by a high merchandise reflection ratio and a high percentage of imports from the United States, purchases the most in the United States per dollar of its own exports and that Group 4, with a low merchandise reflection ratio and a low percentage of imports from the United States, purchases the least. It may also be noted that, although Group 2 has a higher reflection ratio than Group 3 (*i.e.*, it spends more on imports from all sources per dollar of its exports), it nevertheless spends much less, per dollar of its exports, on United States goods than does Group 3. This results from the fact that the percentage of its total imports obtained from the United States is lower than that of Group 3 by so much that it far more than offsets the higher reflection ratio of Group 2.[14]

Although this table shows how much United States exports to a given group will change as a direct effect of a given change in that group's exports, it does not show the total effect on United States exports of such an initial change. An initial rise in any group's exports will cause it to import more not only from the United States but from all other groups as well, including itself. The exporting

Table 7.2

Effects on United States Exports of One Dollar Increase in Export
Earnings of Foreign Country Groups

World Trade Group Receiving Increase of Earnings	Effect on U. S. Exports		
	Total[a]	Direct[b]	Indirect[c]
Group 1..............	$.7095	$.5976	$.1119
Group 2..............	.4162	.1351	.2811
Group 3..............	.6285	.5520	.0765
Group 4..............	.2592	.0671	.1921

[a] Direct and indirect effects, from Appendix Table E.5.
[b] From Table 7.1.
[c] Total effect less direct effect.

groups would then also buy more from the United States. Moreover, they, in turn, would also buy more from all groups, including the first one. All would buy more from the United States and each other, and so on, in an infinite but diminishing series of repercussions. Although the *total* effect on United States exports, per dollar of addition to a group's earnings, is not shown by the network or matrix of direct relationships given in Table 7.1, it is implied in that table and can be obtained from it.[15] These implied total effects appear in the first column of Table 7.2.

It will be noted from this table that, in their total effects on

[14] Additional imports by the United States from all exporters are entered in the table as zero, because the estimates to be based on it exclude income-induced changes in United States imports and because additional imports induced directly by export changes were assumed to be negligible.

[15] This is done by "inverting the matrix," the essence of which can be explained as follows: For each importing group we can write an equation stating that the change in its total imports is the sum of the changes in its imports from each group. Each term of this equation that represents the change in imports from a single group consists of a constant, representing the change in imports from that group per dollar of change in the importing group's exports, multiplied by an unknown representing the change in the importing group's exports. The numbers in each column of Table

United States exports, additions to the earnings of Groups 2 and 4 are more important than Table 7.1 might have made them appear. Their additional earnings have much larger indirect effects on United States exports, both absolutely and in proportion to direct effects, than do those of Groups 1 and 3.

Initial Changes in Earnings of
World Trade Groups and Their Effects
on United States Exports

In order to know the absolute amount of the multilateral effects on United States exports, it was of course not enough to know how much they would change for every dollar of initial change in the exports of each group of foreign countries. It was necessary also to estimate the absolute amount of the net changes in the export earnings of each group in every case of liberalization.

It will be recalled that, in the process of estimating bilateral export effects, the amount of each major supplying country's additional purchase of merchandise and shipping services was divided between the amount bought in the United States and the amount bought in all other countries combined. It was necessary to allocate the latter portion among the four groups of foreign countries. This allocation was made by assuming that each major supplier's additional imports from outside the United States would be distributed among the four foreign country groups in the same way as its total imports from them were in 1953.[16]

7.1 are the constants of these terms in the equation for the change in the total imports of the group named in the column heading. The whole table thus represents the constants in a set of such simultaneous equations. "Inverting the matrix" simply means solving this system of simultaneous equations to get the ratios between certain pairs of unknowns, in this case between the total (direct and indirect) change in the exports of a group and a direct change in the exports of any group. The resulting inverse matrix is shown as Appendix Table E.5. Each of the ratios obtained in the solution and shown in the inverse matrix depends on all the constants in the original set of simultaneous equations.

The principle of using the interrelations among economic sectors to estimate the total effects of changes in individual sectors has been applied to world trade by Timothy Sweeney of the Research Department of the International Monetary Fund in an unpublished study and by W. Beckerman in "The World Trade Multiplier and the Stability of World Trade, 1938 to 1953," *Econometrica*, Vol. 24, No. 3 (July 1956).

[16] The 1953 distribution of imports of the major suppliers was computed from data obtained from *Direction of International Trade, 1938, 1948 and 1951-54.* The results are shown in Appendix Table E.2.

Table 7.3

Estimated Increases in United States Exports Associated with Million-Dollar Increases in Imports[a]

Liberalized Industry		Export Increase per $1,000,000 of Import Increase (In thousands of dollars in 1953 prices)			Percentage Distribution of Total Export Increase		Total Export Increase as a Percentage of Increase in:	
Code Number	Title	Total	Bilateral	Multilateral	Bilateral	Multilateral	Gross Foreign Dollar Earnings	Net Foreign Dollar Earnings
		(1)	(2)	(3)	(4)	(5)	(6)	(7)
1	Meat animals and products.........	611.0	559.6	51.4	91.6	8.4	70.8	72.2
8	Vegetables and fruits..............	577.5	543.9	33.6	94.2	5.8	75.7	77.5
13	Lead and zinc mining..............	596.0	551.2	44.8	92.5	7.5	67.4	70.1
21	Meat packing and wholesale poultry.	494.5	410.3	84.2	83.0	17.0	57.2	59.9
22	Processed dairy products...........	301.3	82.0	219.3	27.2	72.8	34.9	36.3
24	Grain mill products................	510.0	448.1	61.9	87.9	12.1	57.3	59.7
27	Sugar............................	604.2	578.2	26.0	95.7	4.3	68.1	74.9
28	Alcoholic beverages...............	427.6	336.0	91.6	78.6	21.4	49.8	51.0
29	Tobacco manufactures............	321.4	180.5	140.9	56.2	43.8	41.4	43.6
30	Spinning, weaving and dyeing.......	205.8	72.9	132.9	35.4	64.6	26.1	27.1
31	Special textile products...........	194.8	76.3	118.5	39.2	60.8	24.6	26.8
34	Apparel..........................	210.2	75.6	134.6	36.0	64.0	27.9	29.1
35	House furnishings and other non-apparel......................	216.4	82.4	134.0	38.1	61.9	29.5	30.0
38	Plywood..........................	384.7	275.3	109.4	71.6	28.4	45.2	46.9
40	Wood containers and cooperage.....	627.1	604.3	22.8	96.4	3.6	77.8	81.4
41	Wood furniture....................	270.7	66.8	203.9	24.7	75.3	31.9	33.1
45	Paper and board mills..............	437.8	323.8	114.0	74.0	26.0	48.4	52.0
46	Converted paper products..........	201.6	95.8	105.8	47.5	52.5	23.8	26.7
49	Industrial organic chemicals........	148.5	44.1	104.4	29.7	70.3	20.2	22.0
51	Synthetic rubber..................	546.8	510.9	35.9	93.4	6.6	61.6	66.5
52	Synthetic fiber...................	173.8	49.4	124.4	28.4	71.6	20.3	21.2
54	Drugs and medicines...............	185.1	61.0	124.1	33.0	67.0	21.2	22.1
56	Paints and allied products.........	326.3	268.4	57.9	82.3	17.7	45.9	52.0
59	Vegetable oils....................	570.4	546.1	24.3	95.7	4.3	63.2	72.3
61	Miscellaneous chemical industries....	148.9	60.7	88.2	40.8	59.2	18.0	19.4
65	Tires and inner tubes..............	105.2	40.7	64.5	38.7	61.3	11.6	13.2
66	Miscellaneous rubber products.......	264.7	155.3	109.4	58.7	41.3	32.2	34.9
67	Leather tanning and finishing.......	377.0	202.9	174.1	53.8	46.2	42.3	43.5
69	Footwear, except rubber............	237.9	64.4	173.5	27.1	72.9	27.4	28.4
70	Glass............................	173.7	50.5	123.2	29.1	70.9	23.1	23.7
73	Pottery and related products........	183.9	66.2	117.7	36.0	64.0	26.2	26.9
79.1	Carbon steel works and rolling mills..	175.6	50.6	125.0	28.8	71.2	20.6	21.6
79.2	Alloy steel works and rolling mills, except stainless...................	170.2	50.6	119.6	29.7	70.3	20.0	21.2
79.3	Stainless steel works and rolling mills.	177.4	50.6	126.8	28.5	71.5	20.8	21.7
85	Primary zinc......................	542.3	513.8	28.5	94.7	5.3	57.9	67.4
88	Primary aluminum, including alumina	513.1	481.3	31.8	93.8	6.2	54.8	61.3
89	Aluminum rolling and drawing......	344.1	218.7	125.4	63.6	36.4	37.9	41.7
93	Tin cans and other tin ware........	352.2	215.7	136.5	61.2	38.8	39.6	41.5
94	Cutlery..........................	185.7	46.6	139.1	25.1	74.9	24.5	25.1
95	Tools and general hardware.........	188.0	54.8	133.2	29.1	70.9	22.7	23.2
103	Lighting fixtures..................	191.3	33.3	158.0	17.4	82.6	25.1	26.1
105	Metal barrels, drums, etc...........	161.6	83.6	78.0	51.7	48.3	21.8	22.8
106	Tubes and foils...................	137.9	43.9	94.0	31.8	68.2	16.7	18.0
116	Machine tools and metalworking machinery......................	259.0	124.4	134.6	48.0	52.0	29.3	29.8
118	Special industrial machinery.......	244.4	88.7	155.7	36.3	63.7	28.4	29.0
123	Industrial machinery n.e.c.........	357.8	215.7	142.1	60.3	39.7	40.5	41.6
127	Ball and roller bearings...........	320.5	222.7	97.8	69.5	30.5	38.7	39.6
131	Motors and generators.............	508.0	432.9	75.1	85.2	14.8	58.3	60.2
132	Transformers.....................	210.1	62.3	147.8	29.7	70.3	23.6	24.8
133	Electrical control apparatus.........	197.6	57.7	139.9	29.2	70.8	23.2	23.9
134	Electrical welding apparatus........	390.5	250.9	139.6	64.3	35.7	42.5	43.9
135	Electrical appliances..............	228.9	53.7	175.2	23.5	76.5	26.9	27.8
136	Insulated wire and cable...........	413.3	343.2	70.1	83.0	17.0	50.0	57.2
138	Electric lamps....................	241.5	125.7	115.8	52.0	48.0	29.2	29.8
139	Radio and related products.........	461.7	348.9	112.8	75.6	24.4	49.7	51.3
141	Communication equipment.........	524.7	455.2	69.5	86.8	13.2	59.3	61.0
142	Storage batteries.................	145.9	40.8	105.1	28.0	72.0	17.5	19.7
143	Primary batteries.................	479.5	426.5	53.0	88.9	11.1	56.3	61.0
145.1	Passenger cars and light trucks......	246.7	48.5	198.2	19.7	80.3	27.4	28.6
145.2	Heavy trucks and buses...........	515.9	444.1	71.8	86.1	13.9	58.3	60.6
145.3	Motor vehicle parts and accessories..	463.5	367.2	96.3	79.2	20.8	52.6	54.5
148	Aircraft and parts.................	470.2	376.9	93.3	80.2	19.8	55.0	56.1
152	Motorcycles and bicycles..........	231.7	46.9	184.8	20.2	79.8	26.4	27.4

Table 7.3 (*continued*)

Liberalized Industry		Export Increase per $1,000,000 of Import Increase (In thousands of dollars in 1953 prices)			Percentage Distribution of Total Export Increase		Total Export Increase as a Percentage of Increase in:	
Code Number	Title	Total	Bi-lateral	Multi-lateral	Bi-lateral	Multi-lateral	Gross Foreign Dollar Earnings	Net Foreign Dollar Earnings
		(1)	(2)	(3)	(4)	(5)	(6)	(7)
154	Optical, ophthalmic and photo equipment	244.4	129.2	115.2	52.9	47.1	28.7	29.7
156	Watches and clocks	170.1	55.4	114.7	32.6	67.4	23.0	24.2
157	Jewelry and silverware	147.9	56.1	91.8	37.9	62.1	19.6	22.0
158	Musical instruments and parts	288.4	136.7	151.7	47.4	52.6	34.7	35.5
159	Toys and sporting goods	181.5	75.1	106.4	41.4	58.6	24.3	25.4
160	Office supplies	176.4	55.1	121.3	31.2	68.8	24.1	25.2
161	Plastic products	327.1	212.0	115.1	64.8	35.2	41.3	42.6
162	Cork products	83.9	34.7	49.2	41.4	58.6	11.0	23.0
164	Miscellaneous manufactured products	217.8	88.8	129.0	40.8	59.2	28.0	29.6
	Minimum	83.9	33.3	24.3	17.4	3.6	11.0	13.2
	1st quartile	165.0	55.8	76.6	30.4	20.3	23.7	25.0
	Median	252.9	110.1	114.9	47.8	52.2	29.2	29.9
	3rd quartile	449.8	346.1	134.6	79.7	69.6	49.9	53.2
	Maximum	627.1	604.3	219.3	96.4	82.6	77.8	81.4
	Interquartile range	283.9	290.3	58.0	49.3	49.3	26.2	28.2

ᵃ Imports valued in 1953 prices at domestic ports.

The additional imports of a supplying country from a given foreign country group bear the same ratio to its additional earnings in every case of liberalization. Their dollar amounts, however, differ among the different cases in which the country appears as a supplier because the amount of its additional earnings is different in every case. The sum of the imports obtained from a given group by all the major suppliers in each case constitutes the initial gross increase in the earnings of that group.

It was still necessary, however, to take into account the loss of earnings that each group would suffer because of the output-induced decreases of United States imports. The impact of this decrease on total foreign earnings had already been estimated for each case of liberalization. (See end of Chapter 6.) The estimated decrease in total foreign earnings now had to be allocated among the four groups of foreign countries.

It was observed earlier that in almost every case of liberalization these output-induced decreases of imports are distributed among imports attributed to a large number of United States industries. Because of the broad range of commodities affected, it was believed that the decreases could also be assumed to affect a broad range of foreign countries. Consequently, it was assumed that they are distributed among the four groups of foreign countries in the proportions that these countries contributed to total United States merchandise imports in 1953.[17]

This assumption is a very crude one, but its importance in the final estimates is small. It was used to allocate a component of the change in foreign export earnings that is in almost every case of liberalization very small compared to the increases of earnings that the rest of the world receives from increased United States imports of the liberalized commodities.[18]

The decreases in earnings of each foreign group resulting from the decreases in its exports to the United States were subtracted from the increase resulting from its additional exports to the major suppliers. The resulting estimated net increases in earnings represent the initial effects that work through the network of world trade. They were then multiplied by the coefficients representing each group's ratio of direct and indirect additional imports from the United States per dollar of additional export earnings. The results were the estimated multilateral effects on United States exports in each case of liberalization, shown in Column 3 of Table 7.3.

Summary and Appraisal of Estimates of Total Effects on United States Exports

Considering the whole procedure for estimating export effects, it appears far more likely that employment-creating exports are underestimated than that they are overestimated. The reasons for this judgment are, first, that the use of merchandise reflection

[17] The distribution of United States imports among the four groups was obtained from *Direction of International Trade, 1938, 1948 and 1951-54.*

[18] The only case of liberalization in which the output-induced decrease of foreign dollar earnings was more than 15 per cent of the initial gross increase was that of cork products. (See Appendix Table F.3.) As was pointed out at the end of Chap. 3, liberalization of cork products causes a very large output-induced decrease of imports. Moreover, this decrease consists very largely of one product, raw cork, which comes from three countries (Spain, Portugal, and Algeria). In this combination of circumstances, allocation of the output-induced decrease of earnings in accordance with that of 1953 total imports would introduce an error that might be large into a component of the change in foreign earnings that was certainly large. In this

ratios to estimate the import reactions of foreign countries excludes from the effects on United States exports all services other than the shipping associated with merchandise purchases. This exclusion has a double effect on the export estimates. It causes underestimation of a country's non-merchandise purchases from the United States per dollar of increase in its earnings. In addition, it causes underestimation of a country's purchases from other foreign countries and thereby of the increases in the earnings of all countries through multilateral channels. This effect causes both the merchandise and non-merchandise exports of the United States to be underestimated.

Second, the total reflection ratios of some countries may in fact exceed 1.0, which is the maximum value assumed in the procedure, and some of those that are much less than 1.0 perhaps should be higher than they are, because international reserves of some of these countries have improved sufficiently, since the estimates were made, to reduce pressure for their further replenishment.[19] It is true that the omission of non-merchandise imports from the foreign leakages makes for an overestimate of the income multiplier and therefore of the reflection ratios of some foreign countries, but it is believed that this influence is greatly outweighed by those making for underestimation.

As the above conclusion suggests, the relation between the estimated effects on United States exports and the net increases in foreign earnings, shown in the third column of Table 5.1, is in most cases probably a great deal lower than many experts would have predicted. Although United States exports are estimated to be 81 per cent of the net increase in foreign earnings in the case of liberalization of wood containers and cooperage (#40), the median export increase is only 30 per cent of the net increase in foreign earnings. In only 15 of the 72 cases of liberalization is the

case, therefore, the general procedure for allocating the output-induced decreases of earnings was not followed. Since the major share of the decreases falls on the countries that are major suppliers of cork products, their share in the output-induced decrease of imports was subtracted from their earnings in determining the bilateral export effects in this case and only the remainder of the output-induced decrease of earnings was distributed to the four world trade groups.

[19] Some economists who were consulted about the choice of procedures advocated treating total reflection ratios for all countries as equal to one. In the article cited in footnote 15, above, Beckerman implies merchandise reflection ratios (which he calls "propensities to import") higher than those used in the present estimates.

estimated increase of United States exports 60 per cent or more of the net increase in foreign earnings; in 21 cases, it is 25 per cent or less, reaching a low of 13 per cent in the case of tires and inner tubes (#65).

Further inspection of the results reveals another interesting conclusion. Although the procedure for estimating the export increases from the gross increases of foreign earnings takes into account many factors—the reflection ratios of the major suppliers, the percentage of their imports that comes from the United States, the distribution among the four foreign country groups of their other imports, the offsetting decreases in foreign earnings resulting

	Number of Industry Liberalizations That Cause Increases in Exports per Dollar of Gross Increase in Earnings of:		
	30 per cent or more (rounded)	Less than 30 per cent (rounded)	Total
Number in which major suppliers include one or more of the four named countries..........	33	6	39
Number in which major suppliers include none of the four named countries...............	2	31	33
Total...............................	35	37	72

from the output-induced decreases of United States imports and its distribution among the four foreign country groups, and the reflection ratios and sources of imports of the countries that make up these groups—the estimated increases in exports per dollar of gross increase in foreign earnings are dominated by only two characteristics, the reflection ratios of the major suppliers and the percentages of their imports that come from the United States. In 17 of the 20 cases in which the increases of exports were 50 per cent or more of the gross increases in foreign earnings, the major supplier was Canada, a country with a high reflection ratio that obtains a high percentage of its imports from the United States. In 2 of the other 3 cases Mexico was the major supplier, and in the other Cuba and the Philippines were the major suppliers. All 4 of these countries obtain 74 per cent or more of their merchandise imports from the United States and have reflection ratios of 78 per cent or more. One or more of them is a major supplier in all but 2 of the 35 liberalizations in which exports increase by 30 per cent or more of the gross increase in foreign earnings. Among the 37 liber-alizations in which exports increase by less than 30 per cent, how-ever, 1 of these 4 countries is a major supplier in only 6. This corre-lation is readily seen from the grouping of the cases on page 176. Although many of the other major suppliers have equally high or even higher reflection ratios, none buys as large a proportion of its imports from the United States as these four countries. Only one, Brazil, buys as much as 28 per cent of its imports from the United States; the others buy 17 per cent or less here. Thus, it appears that where none of these four countries is a major sup-plier, increases in exports are a relatively small percentage of gross increases in foreign earnings.

The conclusion that the increases in exports per dollar of gross increase in foreign earnings are dominated by the reflection ratios of the major suppliers and the percentages of their imports ob-tained in the United States is supported by a more formal analysis. If we correlate the export increases per dollar of gross increase in foreign earnings in each case with the average reflection ratios of the major suppliers in that case and the average percentage of their imports obtained from the United States, weighting both averages by the individual supplier's share in the gross increase of earnings, we find that more than 97 per cent of the variation in the export increases per dollar of gross increase in earnings is "explained" (in the statistical sense) by variation in these two characteristics of the major suppliers. The second of these two characteristics, moreover, is found to be almost three times as important as the first in explaining variation in the result.[20]

The fact that the estimates of total exports per dollar of gross increase in foreign earnings can be predicted in each case from two characteristics of the major suppliers and from their shares in the gross increase of earnings could indicate either that the other factors have only a trivial effect on the estimated export

[20] The regression equation is:

$$X_{0.12} = -8.84 + 41.76 X_1 + 54.20 X_2$$

where X_0 is the estimated increase of United States exports per dollar of gross in-crease in foreign earnings, X_1 is the weighted average of the major suppliers' merchan-dise reflection ratios, and X_2 is the weighted average of the percentages of their im-ports obtained in the United States (expressed as a ratio). The coefficient of determina-tion is .975. The beta coefficients $B_{01.2}$ and $B_{02.1}$ are .284 and .767 respectively.

increases or that they are highly correlated with these two characteristics. It happens that both things are true. The total increases in spending by major suppliers in the four world trade groups combined are positively correlated with the reflection ratios of the major suppliers and negatively correlated with the percentage of their imports obtained from the United States, so the gross increases in earnings of the four world trade groups are accounted for by these two characteristics. The decreases in their earnings resulting from output-induced decreases of United States imports are generally small in relation to these increases of earnings, being 15 per cent or less in 50 out of 72 cases. Consequently, the net increases in the total earnings of the four groups are also highly correlated with the two characteristics of the major suppliers.

These increases are often quite high, because major suppliers are in many cases countries that obtain most of their imports outside the United States. It might be expected, therefore, that a third factor, the distribution of the spending of the major suppliers among the four world trade groups, would show up as an important variable, especially since the effect on United States exports of a given expenditure in a single one of these groups varies from 26 cents to 71 cents per dollar (see Table 7.2). This factor turns out to be unimportant, however. One reason is that a dollar's worth of spending by major suppliers in the four world trade groups stimulates United States exports by much less than a dollar's worth of their spending in the United States. In only one case do United States exports increase by more than 40 cents per dollar of additional spending by major suppliers outside the United States. The average effect is only 33 cents per dollar of such spending, as contrasted with an effect of $1.00 for $1.00 of major suppliers' spending in the United States. This low multilateral effect on United States exports results from the concentration of world trade in the group whose increases in earnings have the smallest total effect on United States exports.

Moreover, the multilateral effect per dollar of major suppliers' spending outside the United States, besides being low, does not vary much from case to case. The distribution of this spending among the four world trade groups does not vary much from case to case while the distribution of the output-induced decreases of earnings is, by assumption, the same in all cases (except in that of cork and cork products, which received special treatment). Consequently, the distribution among the four world trade groups of the *net* changes in their earnings does not differ much among the cases. As a result, the effect on United States exports of a dollar of net increase in combined earnings of all four trade groups varies only between 21.1 and 46.2 cents, and in 56 of the 72 cases it is between 30 and 37 cents.[21] Therefore, when the net increase in the combined earnings of these four groups, which is correlated with the two main characteristics of the major suppliers, is multiplied by the average of 33 cents per dollar, the resulting figure, which represents multilateral effects on United States exports, is also correlated with these two characteristics.

Thus, given the equation in footnote 20, one can estimate the effects on United States exports of gross increases in foreign earnings without troubling to determine the reflection ratios of countries that are not major suppliers, the percentages of their imports that they obtain from the United States, or a world trade matrix. Of course, it was necessary to go through the detailed estimating procedure and analyze its results to reach this conclusion. The conclusion is nevertheless useful because it suggests that total export effects in cases not here considered can be estimated from the regression equation, so long as one knows the reflection ratios of countries that are major suppliers, the percentage of their imports coming from the United States, and their relative importance as suppliers. It also means that an estimator may substitute, in any of the present cases, his own ideas of the appropriate reflection ratios of the major suppliers and of the percentages of the change in their imports that they obtain from the United States and still use the coefficients of the regression equation to approximate the results of the more detailed procedure, so long as the countries for which he makes the substitutions do not, together, account for a substantial portion of world trade.

[21] The occurrence of an average export increase of 21 cents per dollar of net increase in earnings of all four trade groups when the lowest increase per dollar earned by any single group is 26 cents results from the fact that some groups suffer net decreases in earnings, so that the average increase is an average of positive and negative changes.

CHAPTER 8

Methods and Assumptions: Effects of Changes in Exports on Employment*

THE TWO PRECEDING CHAPTERS described the method of estimating the effects of increases in United States imports on the total volume of United States exports. The present chapter explains how the employment effects of these changes in exports were estimated. The two broad steps required were to allocate the increase of total exports among the various United States industries and to estimate their total (direct and indirect) primary effects on domestic output and employment.

Distribution of Increases in Exports Among United States Industries

The estimates of the bilateral and multilateral increases in United States exports include spending by foreign countries both on United States merchandise and on shipping costs incurred in the United States. Before the employment effects of such changes could be estimated, this expenditure in the United States had to be distributed between these two elements, and the portion spent on merchandise had to be allocated to the various industries incorporated in the structure of interindustry relations. Since the foreign expenditures on goods and services were expressed in 1953 prices, they also had to be converted into 1947 prices before they could be used in conjunction with the pattern of interindustry

* This chapter may be omitted by readers who are not interested in the estimating methods.

relations. Finally, the expenditures on merchandise had to be further divided into the parts going to pay for the merchandise itself, for its domestic transportation, for trade margins, and for excise taxes.

Distribution of Foreign Spending
Between Shipping and Merchandise

The distribution of foreign expenditures between ocean freight costs and merchandise was based on the fact that, in 1953, ocean freight earnings on United States merchandise exports amounted to 6.7 per cent of the value of exports, and United States vessels received 42 per cent of these freight earnings.[1] No information about insurance earnings on United States exports was available, but since these earnings are undoubtedly a much smaller percentage of exports than the freight earnings, they were ignored. Thus, it was assumed that all foreign spending in the United States would be divided between merchandise and shipping in the ratio implied by the above percentages, which works out at 97.3 and 2.7 per cent, respectively.[2]

This 1953 distribution of total foreign spending between merchandise and the United States share in the cost of shipping it abroad was applied to the combined spending on multilateral and bilateral exports. Since there is some presumption that the cost of shipping merchandise is related to the distance of the buyers from the United States and to the composition of the goods they buy, it could be argued that the estimates should have taken these factors into account. In the case of the multilateral expenditures, however, a distribution based on an average relationship for all United States customers, although it does not take these factors into account explicitly, is justifiable because the multilateral expenditures involve almost all United States customers. In the case of bilateral expenditures, use of such a distribution is, admittedly, less justifiable; use of the average may introduce error because fewer countries are involved. Moreover, since the buying countries can be identified, it might have been possible to take these factors

---

[1] Based on data in tables on pages 6 and 20, respectively, of the *Survey of Current Business* (March 1956).

[2] The merchandise portion is $1.00 \div [1.00 + (.42 \times .067)] = 1.00 \div 1.028 = .973$.

explicitly into account. There are several major suppliers in every case of liberalization, however, and the purchases of most of them are widely distributed over the range of United States exports. For these reasons, it was regarded as justifiable to allocate all parts of foreign spending in a given case in accordance with the world pattern and to do so in all 72 cases.

Distribution of Foreign Spending on Merchandise Among United States Industries

After allocating foreign expenditure in the United States between international shipping services and merchandise, it was necessary to determine the probable distribution of the merchandise expenditures among the various United States industries that produce for export. Thanks to the Joint Committee on the Economic Report, as it was formerly called, the distribution by industries of United States exports to major suppliers in 1953 had been tabulated from unpublished export statistics.[3] This tabulation provided the only information about the past distribution of expenditures of individual countries that was on an industry basis, and it provided the main basis for estimating the industry distribution of additional bilateral exports to each major supplier and of total multilateral exports.

Although the distribution of *total* purchases in 1953 does not necessarily indicate what the distribution of *changes* in purchases would be, even under 1953 conditions, the pattern of a country's total purchases provides the only basis for estimating the probable pattern of its additional purchases. Some adjustments were made in the 1953 patterns, however, before they were applied to the bilateral and multilateral increases in exports. One of the more obvious reasons the incremental pattern of foreign purchases might differ from its total pattern is that a country's requirements for food are likely to have a high priority in its total purchases, and are likely to be filled as fully as possible with the amount of dollar exchange available. Once these needs are satisfied, the portion of additional expenditures devoted to them is likely to be smaller.

[3] See footnote 7, Chap. 7 above.

The pattern of additional foreign purchases in the United States may also differ from the 1953 pattern because the 1953 pattern, like that of any single year, may have been greatly influenced by special conditions, either in the buying country or in the United States. Special grants of United States aid, harvest failures, or other unusual factors may have made the 1953 pattern of a country's total purchases seriously different from the pattern of its additional purchases to be expected at the present time or in the near future. Such factors are likely to be particularly important for agricultural commodities. To take account of such considerations, each major supplier's purchases of the products of the twenty industries producing unprocessed or processed agricultural commodities were examined separately to see if the proportion of its additional merchandise expenditure that it is likely to spend on the products of each of those industries is the same as the proportion it spent on each of them in 1953.

It was not possible to select one most probable percentage for a hypothetical future period. To simplify the question, therefore, a decision was made as to whether the percentage of total additional expenditure in the United States that each major supplier would spend on the products of each of these twenty industries was likely to be closer to the 1953 percentage or to zero.[4] In cases where one or more of these industries did not share in a country's estimated additional purchases from the United States, the total of the country's additional purchases in the United States was nevertheless assumed to be unaffected. Accordingly, this total was redistributed among the remaining industries by raising their 1953 shares in equal proportions. (The resulting percentage industry distributions of each major supplier's additional purchases are shown in Appendix Table E.6, together with the corresponding 1953 distributions.)

The assumption that a major supplier would buy from the United States an unchanged proportion of its total additional imports, even when it spends a smaller proportion on American processed or unprocessed agricultural products, is plausible for coun-

---

[4] These decisions were made with heavy reliance on advice generously given by experts in the government who had special knowledge of the conditions of supply and requirements and of the trade policies and regulations in the foreign countries concerned.

tries that have an unsatisfied demand for American products. In other cases, it is admittedly not plausible on *a priori* grounds. However, it would also have been implausible to assume that none of the "saving" on 1953 agricultural purchases from the United States would be spent on products of other United States industries. In any event, the countries without substantial unsatisfied demand for American products whose import patterns were most altered by the adjustment of their 1953 patterns either were relatively unimportant buyers of additional imports or did not appear at all as major suppliers in the vast majority of cases of liberalization.[5] For this reason, any error involved in the procedure had a small effect on the estimates of export effects.

The merchandise component of multilateral exports had to be allocated to different United States industries without knowledge of the industry pattern of purchases of the many countries that were not major suppliers. Fortunately, the countries whose patterns of additional exports had been estimated were important in world trade. They accounted for 72.7 per cent of the value of United States exports in 1953.[6] Therefore, the share of each industry in additional exports to the world could be estimated with reasonable safety as the average of its shares in the additional exports of these countries. The resulting estimated industry distribution of United States exports to the world in 1953 was used to allocate the multilateral increases in exports.

This procedure, with its implicit assumption that the industry pattern of the multilateral increases in United States exports would be similar to that of 1953 exports to the major suppliers, could introduce error only into the multilateral portion of the export effects. This portion is less than 20 per cent of the total export effects in 18 of the 72 cases of liberalization and less than 53 per cent in half of them, as may be seen from Column 5 of Table 7.3.

[5] In 62 out of the 72 cases, these countries purchased less than 20 per cent of the additional exports. In only one case, that of cork and cork products (#162), did they purchase more than one third of the additional exports. It will be recalled that this is the case with the smallest additional exports.

[6] The 72.7 per cent refers to the share of these countries in United States exports of domestic merchandise other than "special category," which are excluded from the basic data on exports to individual countries because of security regulations.

Conversion of Exports from 1953 Purchaser
Values to 1947 Producer Values

The steps just described provided estimates of the sales of each United States industry, including the ocean shipping industry, to each major supplier and to the multilateral purchasers. For each case, the sales of a given industry were then added to obtain the total addition to its exports.

These additional exports were expressed in 1953 prices. They had to be converted into 1947 prices because the pattern of inter-industry relations that was used to estimate effects on total output was expressed in 1947 prices. To accomplish this price deflation, it was necessary to deflate the estimated expenditure on each industry by a price index appropriate to its exports.[7]

The expenditures on merchandise were expressed in United States export, or purchaser, values, *i.e.*, in prices paid by the purchaser. This basis of valuation includes not only the amounts paid to industries producing merchandise but the value of services that the purchaser obtains from five domestic transportation industries and from wholesale trade, and his payments of excise taxes. (These are referred to as "spread items," since they represent the "spread" between producer and purchaser values.) The expenditures at purchaser values had to be distributed among producer values and the various spread items because the pattern of interindustry relations used to estimate effects on total output assumes that the purchaser rather than the producer of the goods buys the transportation and the distribution services and pays the taxes.

The component consisting of producer value was estimated by applying to the deflated purchaser value of expenditure on the products of each industry a ratio of 1947 producer value to 1947

---

[7] Such price indices had to be specially constructed. Unfortunately, the only price indices for merchandise that were available represented movements of wholesale prices, not export prices. Wholesale price indices for subindustries were obtained from unpublished tabulations of the Bureau of Labor Statistics. The price index for each industry was obtained by combining the indices for its subindustries in accordance with the relative importance of each subindustry's exports in the 1953 exports of the industry. These weights were obtained from an unpublished tabulation of 1953 export data.

No price index was available for deflating ocean freight expenditures. An index

purchaser value appropriate to the exports of an industry.[8] The remaining portion of the purchaser value, consisting of the spread items, was split among its various components according to the distribution of these components in total United States exports in 1947. To apply to the exports of every individual industry a distribution appropriate to total exports was of course a cruder procedure than to apply distributions appropriate to their own exports. The errors, however, affect only the distribution among the spread items rather than the total amount of spread, and are probably not large.

Estimation of Output and Employment Effects of Export Increases

The foregoing steps yielded estimates of the direct increases in output of each United States industry in each of the 72 cases of liberalization. To estimate their primary direct and indirect effects on employment, it was necessary first to estimate these effects on the domestic output of every industry and then to convert these output effects into employment effects.

Estimation of Direct and Indirect Effects on Domestic Output

The procedure for estimating the effects on domestic output of additions to exports paralleled that used in estimating the gross

---

was constructed from 1947 and 1953 data on United States freight revenues per ton of exports carried by tramp, liner, and tanker, respectively, obtained from the *Survey of Current Business,* March 1956, Tables 2 and 3, pages 19-20, and unpublished data obtained from the U. S. Department of Commerce.

[8] Industry ratios were based on subindustry ratios obtained from Table II, pages 3-40 to 3-58, of the statistical appendix of "Foreign Trade," by Murray Weitzman and Philip Ritz of the Division of Interindustry Economics, U. S. Bureau of Labor Statistics, which appears as Chapter 3 of *Input-Output Analysis: Technical Supplement* (National Bureau of Economic Research, 1955, multilithed). These subindustry ratios were combined in accordance with their relative importance in the 1953 exports of their industry.

decreases that accompanied the originally stipulated shifts of spending from domestic to imported products. It was necessary, however, to re-examine one of the assumptions of that procedure to see if it would be appropriate to apply it in estimating the output effects of export increases. It will be recalled that when we were dealing with decreases in the demand for the products of six agricultural industries, changes in their output and, therefore, in the output of industries supplying them were treated as fictitious. The reason for this treatment was that it was believed that the output of these six industries would in fact be unresponsive to decreases in demand in the short period, either because of inherent characteristics of their production or because large proportions of their output are price supported.[9] It could not be assumed, merely on the ground of symmetry, that output of these industries should be regarded as equally unresponsive to increases of demand. The question had to be asked and answered anew.

For industries producing mainly price-supported commodities, the effect of an increase in demand depends on whether the government holds substantial stocks and on the policies governing their release. If an increase in demand will result in the release of stocks and these stocks are sufficiently large to satisfy the increase, it may reasonably be assumed that output will not be increased in response to the rise of demand. Output of commodities for which this is not true may also fail to rise, however, because of technical characteristics of their production. Generally speaking, output of agricultural commodities is probably more likely to rise in response to increases of demand than to decline in response to decreases, but the differences in probable responsiveness did not appear sufficiently great to justify a change in the method of treating any of these six industries.

The steps required to estimate the domestic output effects of export increases were the same as those performed earlier to estimate the primary effect of the shift of spending from domestic output to imports. Since these steps were fully described in Chapter 4, they need merely be summarized.

1. The total effects on output of the direct increases in output were obtained in each of the 72 cases of liberalization from the

[9] See Chap. 4, especially pp. 83-84.

pattern of interindustry relations.

2. These total increases were adjusted to eliminate the effects on every industry of those increases in agricultural output of six industries that were regarded in this study as fictitious, *i.e.*, output of farm dairy products, food grains and feed crops, tobacco, oil-bearing crops, cotton, and "all other agricultural commodities."[10]

3. The resulting adjusted changes of total output included increases in competitive imports of goods and of the ocean shipping and other services associated with their importation because, as will be recalled from Chapter 4, the pattern of interindustry relations used gives the effects of direct changes on domestic and imported supply combined. The increases in competitive imports therefore had to be subtracted to get the total increases in domestic output alone.[11]

*Estimation of Employment Effects
of Domestic Output Increases*

The steps just described provided estimates of the changes in domestic output resulting from liberalization-caused increases in exports. The employment effects of these export increases were estimated by converting the domestic output effects in each industry into their employment equivalents.

For this purpose, no distinction was made between direct and indirect output effects. The total output effect in each industry was multiplied by the estimated ratio of the change in employment to the change in output for the industry as a whole. Use of this ratio implies that the increase in the output of an industry is dis-

---

[10] See Appendix C for the criteria and procedure used to make the adjustment. Under the criteria used in estimating the output effect of exports, the fictitious output was large enough to warrant elimination only in the case of sugar.

[11] When we estimated the primary effects of liberalization, the initial shift of domestic spending in each of the 72 cases occurred only in the demand for the products of the liberalized industry. It was therefore necessary to estimate the effects on 200 industries of an initial change in the output of only one industry. The additional merchandise exports resulting from each single-industry liberalization, however, directly affect nearly all the 200 industries in the economy, and each of these direct effects has an output effect on 200 industries. The computation of these effects therefore involved nearly 200 times as great a burden and required use of electronic equipment.

tributed among its subindustries in proportion to their domestic output in 1953.[12]

The foregoing procedure yielded the estimates of employment effects of the exports induced by a million-dollar increase in imports. It was noted in Chapter 5 that these estimates are highly correlated with the increases in exports per dollar of net increase in foreign dollar earnings and that there is relatively little difference between net and gross increases in foreign dollar earnings. Thus, these estimates are also highly correlated with the increases in exports per dollar of gross increase in foreign dollar earnings. In Chapter 7 it was noted that gross increases in foreign dollar earnings are highly correlated with the average reflection ratios of the major supplying countries and the average percentage of their imports that they obtain from the United States, weighted by the relative importance of these countries as major suppliers in each case. It is therefore to be expected that the estimates of the total employment effects of export increases in most cases of liberalization could be closely approximated directly from the characteristics of the major suppliers and their relative contributions to the increase of imports of the liberalized products. This proves to be the case. The coefficient of correlation between the employment effects of exports on the one hand and the weighted averages of the major suppliers' reflection ratios and of the percentages of their imports that they obtain from the United States is .98.[13] This find-

[12] The ratios used were the employment-output ratios that were used to estimate the employment effects of total output decreases in nonliberalized industries and the indirect portion of output decreases in liberalized industries when we were estimating the employment effects associated with the shift of buying from domestic goods to imports. See Appendix Tables D.2 and D.3. The alternative would have been to use separate employment-output ratios to convert direct and indirect output effects into employment. This alternative would have required deriving direct employment-output ratios in which the subindustry ratios were weighted by their export importance. Such ratios would have been required for nearly all industries, because nearly all industries had direct as well as indirect output effects.

[13] The regression equation is:

$$X_{0.12} = -15.54 + 46.56X_1 + 54.73X_2$$

where X_0 is the estimated employment increase per million dollars of import increase, X_1 is the weighted average of the merchandise reflection ratios of the major suppliers, and X_2 is the weighted average of the ratios of their imports from the United States to their imports from all sources. The coefficient of determination is .962, indicating that 96 per cent of the variation in the employment increase is ing indicates that in most cases of liberalization similar estimates of the employment effects of additional exports can be obtained directly from knowledge of the merchandise reflection ratios of the major suppliers of the liberalized imports, the percentages of their imports that they obtain from the United States, and their relative shares in the gross increase of foreign dollar earnings.

"explained" by variations in the weighted averages of these two characteristics of the major suppliers.

Net Employment Effects

CHAPTER 9

Comparison of Decreases and Increases of Employment

IN CHAPTER 3 the estimated net primary effects of liberalization on employment were presented. These effects are the differences between the decreases in employment resulting from the reductions in buying of domestic goods and services and the much smaller, often negligible, increases resulting from increased importation of the liberalized products. Chapter 5 presented estimates of the increases in employment resulting from the increases in exports that the same liberalizations cause if foreign countries use the proceeds of these additional imports in the way specified. The assumptions underlying the specified use of these proceeds is only one of a large number of assumptions that can reasonably be made. For this reason, great stress should not be placed on estimates of the *net* employment effects that result from comparing these estimated employment increases with the estimated net primary decreases of employment. Nevertheless, the temptation to make the comparison is too strong to be resisted entirely. This chapter, therefore, presents the direction and size of the total net effects on employment and the distribution of these net effects among industry groups in each case of liberalization. It also examines the proportions of the gross decreases that are offset by the *total* gross increases that result from transportation of the liberalized imports and from the additions to exports.

In considering the results to be presented, the reader should recall several things about the estimates. First, they assume that increased imports displace domestic production of equal value; they do not take into account the possible effects of lower import barriers in stimulating total domestic expenditure on consumption or investment, and thereby in stimulating employment.

Second, the estimates do not include the employment effects of changes in spending for personal consumption and fixed capital that result from the changes in domestic income induced by liberalization. The estimated primary employment effects may be expected, therefore, to occur within a relatively short period—a few months—so long as domestic industries adjust their output rapidly to changes in their sales instead of letting such changes be offset by inventory changes. The employment increases due to stimulation of exports, however, do include increases that are induced by income changes abroad. A portion of these induced increases probably takes longer to materialize. Therefore, the time required for realization of all the employment increases due to exports is likely to be greater than that required for realization of the primary net decreases.

Within the framework of these broad assumptions, furthermore, the employment increases resulting from exports are probably more likely to be underestimated than are the primary employment decreases. For this reason, the total net employment decreases appear, in general, more likely to be overstated than understated.

Comparison of Gross Employment Decreases and Increases

The gross decreases and increases in employment in all industries and the net changes per million-dollar increase in imports valued at 1953 prices are shown in Table 9.1. The first three columns show, respectively, the gross primary decrease resulting from the cut in buying of the domestic products of the liberalized industry, the increase resulting from the process of transporting the additional imports to which buying has shifted, and the increase resulting from the assumed rise in exports (including the process of transporting them) that is caused by the increase in imports. The sum of these two increases is shown in the fourth column, and the net employment change is shown in the fifth column. The ratio of the total gross increase to the gross decrease is shown in the last column.

The most important conclusion to be drawn from the table is clear from a scanning of the direction of the net changes shown in the fifth column: In 70 of the 72 cases of liberalization, the net change in employment is a decrease. The two exceptions are liberalization of grain mill products (#24) and of sugar (#27), which result in net increases of five and three employees, respectively, per million-dollar increase of imports. The net decrease in employment is largest for liberalization of apparel (#34), where it is 175 employees, but it is nearly as large—172 employees—for liberalization of pottery and related products (#73). Other cases in which it exceeds 140 employees are liberalization of vegetables and fruits (#8), wood furniture (#41), footwear other than rubber (#69), and toys and sporting goods (#159).[1] In 65 of the 72 cases, the net decreases exceed 30 employees. This is shown in Chart 9.1, which is a frequency distribution summarizing the number of cases causing various amounts of net change in employment.

Liberalization of grain mill products and of sugar cause net increases of employment, partly because the gross increases are large —especially in the case of sugar—but also because in both cases the gross decreases are small; large percentages of supplies are obtained from agricultural industries whose output and employment do not change much in short periods. (The gross decrease in the case of grain mill products, in fact, is the smallest found in any of the cases.)

As Column 6 of Table 9.1 shows, the increases in these 2 cases exceed the decreases by 10 per cent and 4 per cent, respectively. In only 3 other cases (liberalization of synthetic rubber (#51), of vegetable oils (#59), and of primary aluminum (#88)) are increases as much as 90 per cent of decreases. In all cases other than these 5, the gross increase in employment is 75 per cent or less of the gross decrease, and in most cases it is much less. This is clear

---

[1] It may be recalled that vegetables and fruits were found to be the industry whose liberalization causes by far the largest gross decrease of employment—224 employees. The net decrease in that case, although large—149 employees—is nevertheless well below the largest. The offsetting increases of 75 employees are the second highest found. They reflect not only the fact that the imports are supplied almost entirely by Mexico and Canada, which spend large proportions of their additional dollar earnings in the United States and thus create substantial exports, but the additional fact that the process of importing them results in larger employment increases than does importation of the products of most other industries.

Table 9.1

Gross and Net Employment Effects of Liberalization[a]

Code Number	Liberalized Industry Title	Gross Primary Decrease (1)	Gross Increase Primary (2)	Gross Increase Export (3)	Gross Increase Total (4)	Total Net Effect (5)	Total Gross Increase as Percentage of Gross Decrease (6)
		(Number of employees, farmers, and unpaid farm family workers)					
1	Meat animals and products....	95.84	3.68	68.53	72.21	−23.63	75.3
8	Vegetables and fruits.........	224.45	10.55	64.93	75.48	−148.97	33.6
13	Lead and zinc mining........	164.85	3.77	66.93	70.70	−94.15	42.9
21	Meat packing and wholesale poultry....................	107.99	1.63	54.32	55.95	−52.04	51.8
22	Processed dairy products......	54.27	1.61	31.28	32.89	−21.38	60.6
24	Grain mill products...........	51.15	0.38	55.80	56.18	5.03	109.8
27	Sugar......................	67.38	5.03	65.30	70.33	2.95	104.4
28	Alcoholic beverages..........	85.39	2.64	47.58	50.22	−35.17	58.8
29	Tobacco manufactures........	69.99	0.72	34.39	35.11	−34.88	50.2
30	Spinning, weaving and dyeing..	136.41	1.04	19.37	20.41	−116.00	15.0
31	Special textile products.......	106.85	1.31	20.11	21.42	−85.43	20.0
34	Apparel....................	195.41	1.23	19.55	20.78	−174.63	10.6
35	House furnishings and other non-apparel................	134.91	2.71	20.86	23.57	−111.34	17.5
38	Plywood....................	139.24	0.16	39.65	39.81	−99.43	28.6
40	Wood containers and cooperage.	166.64	7.31	70.47	77.78	−88.86	46.7
41	Wood furniture..............	170.72	0.82	28.17	28.99	−141.73	17.0
45	Paper and board mills.........	84.29	0.69	48.28	48.97	−35.32	58.1
46	Converted paper products.....	114.88	2.69	20.53	23.22	−91.66	20.2
49	Industrial organic chemicals...	79.41	4.40	16.25	20.65	−58.76	26.0
51	Synthetic rubber.............	65.20	2.64	61.44	64.08	−1.12	98.3
52	Synthetic fiber..............	91.32	1.12	18.52	19.64	−71.68	21.5
54	Drugs and medicines..........	118.58	0.43	18.52	18.95	−99.63	16.0
56	Paints and allied products.....	90.55	23.96	36.28	60.24	−30.31	66.5
59	Vegetable oils...............	71.12	1.75	63.82	65.57	−5.55	92.2
61	Miscellaneous chemical industries...................	105.32	1.35	15.36	16.71	−88.61	15.9
65	Tires and inner tubes.........	92.07	0.47	10.03	10.50	−81.57	11.4
66	Miscellaneous rubber products.	117.26	0.40	25.75	26.15	−91.11	22.3
67	Leather tanning and finishing...	80.10	0.44	40.66	41.10	−39.00	51.3
69	Footwear, except rubber.......	178.58	0.46	24.01	24.47	−154.11	13.7
70	Glass......................	115.75	0.70	17.48	18.18	−97.57	15.7
73	Pottery and related products...	189.43	0.38	17.32	17.70	−171.73	9.3
79.1	Carbon steel works and rolling mills....................	90.79	5.76	18.77	24.53	−66.26	27.0
79.2	Alloy steel works and rolling mills, except stainless.......	93.50	5.76	18.21	23.97	−69.53	25.6
79.3	Stainless steel works and rolling mills....................	96.61	5.76	18.92	24.68	−71.93	25.6
85	Primary zinc................	95.40	0.80	60.48	61.28	−34.12	64.2
88	Primary aluminum, including alumina...................	62.72	0.40	57.66	58.06	−4.66	92.6
89	Aluminum rolling and drawing.	79.51	0	37.49	37.49	−42.02	47.1

[a] Sources: Columns 1 and 2 from Table 3.2; Column 3 from Table 5.1; Column 4 = Sum of Columns 2 and 3; Column 5 = Column 4 less Column 1; Column 6 = Column 4 divided by Column 1.

Table 9.1 (*Continued*)

Code Number	Title	Gross Primary Decrease	Gross Increase			Total Net Effect	Total Gross Increase as Percentage of Gross Decrease
			Primary	Export	Total		
		(Number of employees, farmers and unpaid farm family workers)					
		(1)	(2)	(3)	(4)	(5)	(6)
93	Tin cans and other tinware.....	106.10	0.22	38.71	38.93	−67.17	36.7
94	Cutlery....................	122.70	0.22	19.67	19.89	−102.81	16.2
95	Tools and general hardware....	130.39	0.21	19.20	19.41	−110.98	14.9
103	Lighting fixtures............	138.36	0	20.39	20.39	−117.97	14.7
105	Metal barrels, drums, etc......	103.93	0	16.71	16.71	−87.22	16.1
106	Tubes and foils..............	100.62	0.53	14.62	15.15	−85.47	15.1
116	Machine tools and metalworking machinery.............	109.05	0.69	28.53	29.22	−79.83	26.8
118	Special industrial machinery...	137.54	0.65	26.38	27.03	−110.51	19.7
123	Industrial machinery n.e.c.....	123.42	0.33	39.53	39.86	−83.56	32.3
127	Ball and roller bearings.......	125.86	0.47	35.37	35.84	−90.02	28.5
131	Motors and generators.......	129.23	0.25	56.70	56.95	−72.28	44.1
132	Transformers................	112.85	0	22.23	22.23	−00.62	19.7
133	Electrical control apparatus ...	114.47	0	21.35	21.35	−93.12	18.7
134	Electrical welding apparatus...	102.03	0.11	42.96	43.07	−58.96	42.2
135	Electrical appliances..........	134.30	0.43	23.34	23.77	−110.53	17.7
136	Insulated wire and cable......	99.71	4.09	44.96	49.05	−50.66	49.2
138	Electric lamps...............	109.48	0.15	19.54	19.69	−89.79	18.0
139	Radio and related products....	155.15	0.27	51.21	51.48	−103.67	33.2
141	Communication equipment....	132.53	0.16	58.69	58.85	−73.68	44.4
142	Storage batteries............	06.09	0.26	15.15	15.41	−80.68	16.0
143	Primary batteries............	118.12	0	53.59	53.59	−64.53	45.4
145.1	Passenger cars and light trucks.	124.48	0.71	25.82	26.53	−97.95	21.3
145.2	Heavy trucks and buses.......	113.90	0.70	57.67	58.37	−55.53	51.2
145.3	Motor vehicle parts and accessories...................	103.59	0.70	51.38	52.08	−51.51	50.3
148	Aircraft and parts	119.80	1.36	52.16	53.52	−66.28	44.7
152	Motorcycles and bicycles......	129.43	1.37	24.42	25.79	−103.64	19.9
154	Optical, ophthalmic and photo equipment.................	128.26	0.35	26.33	26.68	−101.58	20.8
156	Watches and clocks..........	137.54	1.05	18.93	19.98	−117.56	14.5
157	Jewelry and silverware.......	136.76	0.30	13.88	14.18	−122.58	10.4
158	Musical instruments and parts.	135.38	0.37	31.11	31.48	−103.90	23.3
159	Toys and sporting goods......	157.86	0.38	16.23	16.61	−141.25	10.5
160	Office supplies..............	134.79	6.23	17.45	23.68	−111.11	17.6
161	Plastic products.............	123.05	1.26	34.36	35.62	−87.43	28.9
162	Cork products..............	88.16	1.07	7.99	9.06	−79.10	10.3
164	Miscellaneous manufactured products..................	157.31	2.55	22.69	25.24	−132.07	16.1
	Minimum..................	51.15	0	7.99	9.06	5.03[b]	9.3
	1st quartile................	94.45	.34	19.06	20.53	−57.14	16.2
	Median...................	114.68	.70	26.36	26.86	−86.36	25.6
	3rd quartile................	134.85	1.69	49.74	51.78	−103.66	47.0
	Maximum.................	224.45	23.96	70.47	77.78	−174.63[b]	109.8
	Inter-quartile range..........	40.40	1.35	30.68	31.25	46.52	30.8

[b] For net effects, "minimum" is maximum net increase and "maximum" is maximum net decrease.

from Chart 9.2, which shows the frequency of different ratios of gross increase to gross decrease. This chart shows that in 46 of the 72 cases the gross increase of employment is less than 35 per cent of the gross decrease.

The total gross increase is smallest in relation to the gross decrease—only 9 per cent—in the case of liberalization of pottery and related products (#73), but it is almost as small—approximately 10 per cent—in liberalization of apparel (#34), tires and inner tubes (#65), jewelry and silverware (#157), toys and sporting goods (#159), and cork products (#162).

Distribution of Net Employment Effects Between Liberalized and All Non-Liberalized Industries

For some purposes, it is of more interest to know how the estimated net employment changes are distributed among the various industries of the economy than to know the net effect in the economy as a whole. We may approach this question by considering first how the net effects are divided between the liberalized industry and all other industries combined. This division is shown in Table 9.2.

We have already noted that, for the economy as a whole, net increases in employment occur in only two cases of liberalization. In no case does a net increase occur in the liberalized industry itself. (See Column 2 of Table 9.2.) This result is to be expected, of course, because the liberalized industries always experience a substantial part of the gross decreases of employment, while their share of the increases in employment resulting from additional exports is small (always less than two employees) and their participation in employment increases resulting from the shipping of additional imports is infinitesimal. It is clear, in fact, that no significant offsets to gross decreases of employment can be expected to occur in an industry as a result of its own liberalization. In no case was the total increase of employment in the liberalized industry as high as 4 per cent of its gross decrease, and in only two cases was it as high as 1 per cent. Even if the estimated amounts of additional exports underlying the present estimates of employment increases are greatly understated and were to be multiplied many times, this conclusion would remain valid, so long as the composition of these additional exports was not altered drastically in favor of products exported by the liberalized industry.

Chart 9.1

Number of Cases with Specified Net Effects on Employment

No. of cases

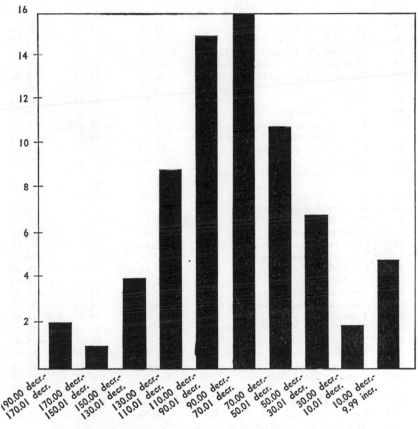

Source: Column 5 of Table 9.1

As was noted at the end of Chapter 5, this conclusion, of course, does not imply that a simultaneous reduction of barriers against imports competing with several industries cannot cause net increases of employment in one or more of them. It merely means that if such increases do occur in a liberalized industry, they result from the liberalizations of other industries and not from its own liberalization.

Table 9.2

Net Employment Effects and Their Distribution Between Liberalized and All Other Industries

(Number of employees, farmers, and unpaid farm family workers)

Liberalized Industry		In All Industries	In Liberalized Industry	In Non-Liberalized Industries
Code Number	Title			
		(1)	(2)	(3)
1	Meat animals and products.........	−23.63	−73.78	50.15
8	Vegetables and fruits..............	−148.97	−191.99	43.02
13	Lead and zinc mining.............	−94.15	−128.27	34.12
21	Meat packing and wholesale poultry.	−52.04	−24.30	−27.74
22	Processed dairy products...........	−21.38	−25.44	4.06
24	Grain mill products...............	5.03	−16.80	21.83
27	Sugar...........................	2.95	−46.13	49.08
28	Alcoholic beverages...............	−35.17	−43.18	8.01
29	Tobacco manufactures.............	−34.88	−42.52	7.64
30	Spinning, weaving and dyeing.......	−116.00	−96.66	−19.34
31	Special textile products............	−85.43	−73.55	−11.88
34	Apparel.........................	−174.63	−133.48	−41.15
35	House furnishings and other non-apparel.........................	−111.34	−47.68	−63.66
38	Plywood........................	−99.43	−80.91	−18.52
40	Wood containers and cooperage.....	−88.86	−93.62	4.76
41	Wood furniture..................	−141.73	−102.72	−39.01
45	Paper and board mills.............	−35.32	−39.68	4.36
46	Converted paper products..........	−91.66	−59.48	−32.18
49	Industrial organic chemicals........	−58.76	−35.06	−23.70
51	Synthetic rubber.................	−1.12	−19.22	18.10
52	Synthetic fiber...................	−71.68	−55.03	−16.65
54	Drugs and medicines..............	−99.63	−52.11	−47.52
56	Paints and allied products.........	−30.31	−41.82	11.51
59	Vegetable oils	−5.55	−20.52	14.97
61	Miscellaneous chemical industries....	−88.61	−35.69	−52.92
65	Tires and inner tubes.............	−81.57	−44.65	−36.92
66	Miscellaneous rubber products......	−91.11	−76.42	−14.69
67	Leather tanning and finishing.......	−39.00	−62.44	23.44
69	Footwear, except rubber...........	−154.11	−132.54	−21.57
70	Glass...........................	−97.57	−86.61	−10.96
73	Pottery and related products.......	−171.73	−163.20	−8.53
79.1	Carbon steel works and rolling mills..	−66.26	−50.70	−15.56
79.2	Alloy steel works and rolling mills, except stainless...................	−69.53	−53.67	−15.86
79.3	Stainless steel works and rolling mills.	−71.93	−72.77	.84
85	Primary zinc.....................	−34.12	−36.25	2.13
88	Primary aluminum, including alumina	−4.66	−29.91	25.25
89	Aluminum rolling and drawing......	−42.02	−43.81	1.79
93	Tin cans and other tinware........	−67.17	−42.05	−25.12
94	Cutlery.........................	−102.81	−82.60	−20.21

Table 9.2 (continued)

Liberalized Industry		In All Industries	In Liberalized Industry	In Non-Liberalized Industries
Code Number	Title			
		(1)	(2)	(3)
95	Tools and general hardware.........	−110.98	−89.08	−21.90
103	Lighting fixtures..................	−117.97	−66.67	−51.30
105	Metal barrels, drums, etc..........	−87.22	−42.87	−44.35
106	Tubes and foils....................	−85.47	−43.95	−41.52
116	Machine tools and metalworking machinery......................	−79.83	−62.39	−17.44
118	Special industrial machinery........	−110.51	−84.39	−26.12
123	Industrial machinery n.e.c..........	−83.56	−55.49	−28.07
127	Ball and roller bearings............	−90.02	−94.26	4.24
131	Motors and generators.............	−72.28	−73.21	.93
132	Transformers.....................	−90.62	−60.47	−30.15
133	Electrical control apparatus.........	−93.12	−67.32	−25.80
134	Electrical welding apparatus........	−58.96	−31.04	−27.92
135	Electrical appliances...............	−110.53	−52.52	−58.01
136	Insulated wire and cable...........	−50.66	−43.83	−6.83
138	Electric lamps....................	−89.79	−72.72	−17.07
139	Radio and related products.........	−103.67	−80.03	−23.64
141	Communication equipment.........	−73.68	−91.70	18.02
142	Storage batteries..................	−80.68	−46.49	−34.19
143	Primary batteries..................	−64.53	−80.38	15.85
145.1	Passenger cars and light trucks....	97.95	−32.50	−65.45
145.2	Heavy trucks and buses............	−55.53	−32.75	−22.78
145.3	Motor vehicle parts and accessories..	−51.51	−31.63	−19.88
148	Aircraft and parts.................	−66.28	−76.17	9.89
152	Motorcycles and bicycles...........	−103.64	−67.65	−35.99
154	Optical, ophthalmic and photo equipment.........................	−101.58	−83.80	−17.78
156	Watches and clocks................	−117.56	−94.80	−22.76
157	Jewelry and silverware.............	−122.58	−90.93	−31.65
158	Musical instruments and parts......	−103.90	−97.40	−6.50
159	Toys and sporting goods...........	−141.25	−100.09	−41.16
160	Office supplies....................	−111.11	−87.38	−23.73
161	Plastic products...................	−87.43	−77.67	−9.76
162	Cork products.....................	−79.10	−48.61	−30.49
164	Miscellaneous manufactured products	−132.07	−77.12	−54.95
	Maximum increase (or min. decr.)...	5.03	−16.80	50.15
	1st quartile......................	−57.14	−43.02	4.15
	Median...........................	−86.34	−62.42	−18.15
	3rd quartile......................	−103.66	−84.10	−30.32
	Maximum decrease................	−174.63	−191.99	−65.45
	Inter-quartile range...............	46.52	41.08	34.47

Although employment in the whole economy decreases on balance in all but 2 of the 72 cases analyzed, this is not true of the net effects in all industries other than the one liberalized. Employment outside the liberalized industry decreases on balance in 49 of the 72 cases and increases in 23 cases, although in a few of these 23 cases the estimated increases are too small to be regarded as significant.

A visual impression of how many cases have net effects of specific direction and amount is given by Chart 9.3. The net changes in non-liberalized industries range from a decrease of 65 employees to an increase of 50 employees. The largest net decrease of employment in non-liberalized industries results from liberalization of passenger cars and light trucks (#145.1). The largest net increase results from liberalization of meat animals and their products (#1).

Distribution of Net Employment Effects Among Non-Liberalized Industries

To obtain some idea of the economic significance of the net changes in employment outside the liberalized industry, it is desirable to consider their dispersions among the various groups of non-liberalized industries. The economic significance of net changes of a given size depends partly on the size of the gross increases and decreases and on whether they are similarly distributed among industries.[2] If they are, the location of job opportunities is not shifted much among industries, even if the gross changes are large. If the distributions of gross increases and decreases among industries differ, however, the effect of a given net change on the industrial location of jobs depends on whether the gross changes are small or large.

Information regarding the dispersion of net changes and the

[2] The size of the gross changes also has significance from a statistical point of view. Where a gross change is large, a given percentage error in it will cause a bigger absolute change in the net effect than it will where the gross change is small. Where, in addition, the net effect is small, a given percentage error in the estimate of a gross change is also more likely to change the direction of the net effect.

size of gross changes is provided in Table 9.3. Its first column repeats the estimates of net effects in the non-liberalized industries that were presented in Column 3 of Table 9.2. Its second and third columns show, respectively, the gross increases and decreases

Chart 9.2

Number of Cases with Specified Ratios of Gross Increases to Gross Decreases of Employment

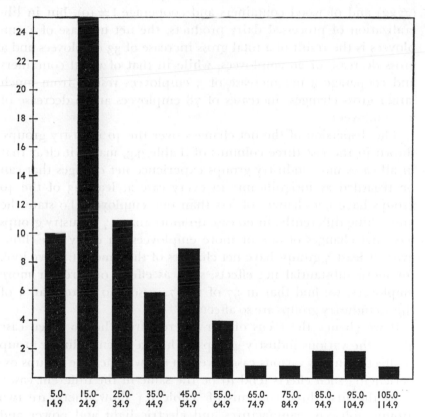

Source: Column 6 of Table 9.1.

that result in these net effects. The last three columns show how many of the 40 industry groups into which the economy has been divided experience net increases of at least one employee per million dollars of increase in imports, how many have estimated net changes of less than one employee in either direction and may therefore be regarded as experiencing virtually no change, and how many experience net decreases of at least one employee. (These three columns are based on the more detailed Appendix Table F.2, which shows the amount of the net change in every industry group in every case of liberalization.)

A comparison of the gross increases and decreases shows that liberalizations having similar net effects sometimes have very different gross effects. Thus, small and approximately equal net increases result from liberalization of processed dairy products (#22) and of wood containers and cooperage (#40), but in liberalization of processed dairy products, the net increase of 4 employees is the result of a total gross increase of 33 employees and a gross decrease of 29 employees, while in that of wood containers and cooperage a net increase of 5 employees results from much larger gross changes—increases of 78 employees and a decrease of 73 employees.

The dispersion of the net changes over the 40 industry groups, shown in the last three columns of Table 9.3, makes it clear that in all cases most industry groups experience net changes that can be regarded as insignificant; in every case at least 23 of the 40 groups have net changes of less than one employee. To state the same thing differently, in no case do more than 17 industry groups have net changes of one or more employees. In every case, however, at least 5 groups have net changes of this amount. If we look for more substantial net effects, such as effects of three or more employees, we find that in 57 of the 72 cases, no more than 4 of the 40 industry groups are so affected.

If we change the focus of our interest from how a given case affects the various industry groups to how a given industry group is affected in the various cases, we can see whether the groups experiencing such effects tend to be the same in the different cases.

As the first three columns of Table 9.4 show, there are two groups, tobacco manufactures and electric light and power and gas, whose employment is not affected, even to the extent of one employee, in any of the 72 cases.[3] Five other groups experience net effects of one employee or more in only one or two cases, and

---

[3] Why these two groups are invulnerable to primary employment decreases was explained earlier (see Chap. 3, pp. 55-56). These reasons apply also to increases resulting from exports.

only nine groups are affected this much in as many as half of the
72 cases. The industry group most frequently affected is non-electrical machinery, which experiences such employment changes in
66 cases.

Chart 9.3

Number of Cases with Specified Net Effects on Employment in
Non-Liberalized Industries

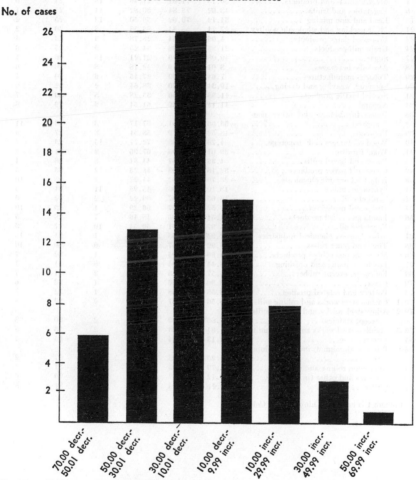

No. of cases

Source: Column 3 of Table 9.2.

As the last three columns of Table 9.4 show, far fewer groups
experience changes of three or more employees in many cases.
Only non-electrical machinery has such changes in as many as half
of the cases and only one other group, iron and steel and their pri-

Table 9.3

Net and Gross Employment Effects in Non-Liberalized Industries

Code Number	Title	Net Effects[a]	Gross Increases	Gross Decreases	Increase of 1.0 or More	Effect of Less Than 1.0	Decrease of 1.0 or More
	Liberalized Industry				Number of Industry Groups Having Indicated Net Effects		
		(Number of employees, farmers, and unpaid family workers)					
		(1)	(2)	(3)	(4)	(5)	(6)
1	Meat animals and products........	50.15	71.61	21.46	16	24	0
8	Vegetables and fruits.............	43.02	73.84	30.82	14	25	1
13	Lead and zinc mining.............	34.12	70.62	36.50	13	25	2
21	Meat packing and wholesale poultry	−27.74	55.84	83.58	8	30	2
22	Processed dairy products..........	4.06	32.84	28.78	3	33	4
24	Grain mill products...............	21.83	56.08	34.25	9	25	6
27	Sugar...........................	49.08	70.29	21.21	13	26	1
28	Alcoholic beverages...............	8.01	50.19	42.18	8	26	6
29	Tobacco manufactures...........	7.64	35.09	27.45	6	30	4
30	Spinning, weaving and dyeing.....	−19.34	19.50	38.84	2	32	6
31	Special textile products............	−11.88	21.40	33.28	3	30	7
34	Apparel.........................	−41.15	20.39	61.54	3	29	8
35	House furnishings and other non-apparel.......................	−63.66	23.51	87.17	3	26	11
38	Plywood.........................	−18.52	39.79	58.31	8	27	5
40	Wood containers and cooperage....	4.76	77.53	72.77	15	23	2
41	Wood furniture...................	−39.01	28.95	67.96	2	31	7
45	Paper and board mills.............	4.36	48.67	44.31	8	28	4
46	Converted paper products.........	−32.18	23.08	55.26	2	33	5
49	Industrial organic chemicals.......	−23.70	20.52	44.22	2	28	10
51	Synthetic rubber.................	18.10	64.05	45.95	11	24	5
52	Synthetic fiber..................	−16.65	19.57	36.22	2	32	6
54	Drugs and medicines..............	−47.52	18.77	66.29	1	29	10
56	Paints and allied products.........	11.51	60.05	48.46	7	28	5
59	Vegetable oils....................	14.97	65.51	50.54	10	27	3
61	Miscellaneous chemical industries..	−52.92	16.63	69.55	1	24	15
65	Tires and inner tubes.............	−36.92	10.47	47.39	0	30	10
66	Miscellaneous rubber products.....	−14.69	25.95	40.64	1	32	7
67	Leather tanning and finishing......	23.44	41.04	17.60	8	31	1
69	Footwear, except rubber..........	−21.57	24.43	46.00	2	31	7
70	Glass...........................	−10.96	18.06	29.02	1	33	6
73	Pottery and related products.......	−8.53	17.68	26.21	1	32	7
79.1	Carbon steel works and rolling mills.	−15.56	23.87	39.43	2	32	6
79.2	Alloy steel works and rolling mills, except stainless.................	−15.86	23.89	39.75	2	30	8
79.3	Stainless steel works and rolling mills	.84	24.63	23.79	2	33	5
85	Primary zinc.....................	2.13	61.24	59.11	11	25	4
88	Primary aluminum, including alumina.......................	25.25	58.02	32.77	11	27	2
89	Aluminum rolling and drawing.....	1.79	37.45	35.66	7	31	2
93	Tin cans and other tin ware.......	−25.12	38.87	63.99	5	29	6
94	Cutlery.........................	−20.21	19.88	40.09	1	31	8

[a] Column 1 is equal to Column 2 less Column 3.

Table 9.3 (*continued*)

	Liberalized Industry	Net Effects[a]	Gross Increases	Gross Decreases	Number of Industry Groups Having Indicated Net Effects		
Code Number	Title	(Number of employees, farmers and unpaid family workers)			Increase of 1.0 or More	Effect of Less Than 1.0	Decrease of 1.0 or More
		(1)	(2)	(3)	(4)	(5)	(6)
95	Tools and general hardware........	−21.90	19.33	41.23	0	35	5
103	Lighting fixtures................	−51.30	20.36	71.66	0	30	10
105	Metal barrels, drums, etc.........	−44.35	16.69	61.04	1	31	8
106	Tubes and foils..................	−41.52	15.15	56.67	0	32	8
116	Machine tools and metal working machinery................	−17.44	28.71	46.15	3	31	6
110	Special industrial machinery......	−26.12	26.44	52.56	2	33	5
123	Industrial machinery n.e.c.........	−28.07	39.69	67.76	3	30	7
127	Ball and roller bearings..........	4.24	35.64	31.40	6	33	1
131	Motors and generators...........	.93	56.40	55.47	7	26	7
132	Transformers....................	−30.15	22.20	52.35	1	28	11
133	Electrical control apparatus.......	−25.80	21.28	47.08	2	29	9
134	Electrical welding apparatus.......	−27.92	43.01	70.93	5	29	6
135	Electrical appliances..............	−58.01	23.68	81.69	0	26	14
136	Insulated wire and cable..........	−6.83	48.98	55.81	6	30	4
138	Electric lamps...................	−17.07	19.67	36.74	1	31	8
139	Radio and related products........	−23.64	51.05	74.69	6	25	9
141	Communication equipment........	18.02	58.60	40.58	9	28	3
142	Storage batteries................	−34.19	15.38	49.57	1	29	10
143	Primary batteries................	15.85	53.58	37.73	8	28	4
145.1	Passenger cars and light trucks.....	−65.45	20.36	91.81	1	26	13
145.2	Heavy trucks and buses..........	−22.78	58.22	81.00	5	28	7
145.3	Motor vehicle parts and accessories.	−19.88	50.90	70.78	5	29	6
148	Aircraft and parts...............	9.89	53.38	43.49	8	27	5
152	Motorcycles and bicycles..........	−35.90	25.78	61.77	1	29	10
154	Optical, ophthalmic and photo equipment........................	−17.78	26.56	44.34	2	28	10
156	Watches and clocks..............	−22.76	19.96	42.72	3	28	9
157	Jewelry and silverware...........	−31.65	14.16	45.81	1	28	11
158	Musical instruments and parts.....	−6.50	31.46	37.96	2	34	4
159	Toys and sporting goods..........	−41.16	16.58	57.74	0	26	14
160	Office supplies...................	−23.73	23.65	47.38	2	28	10
161	Plastic products.................	−9.76	35.50	45.26	6	27	7
162	Cork products...................	−30.49	9.06	39.55	0	34	6
164	Miscellaneous manufactured products........................	−54.95	25.15	80.10	2	27	11
	Minimum......................	50.15[b]	9.06	17.60			
	1st quartile....................	4.15	20.38	37.84			
	Median.......................	−18.15	26.50	45.98			
	3rd quartile....................	−30.32	50.98	61.29			
	Maximum......................	−65.45[b]	77.53	91.81			
	Inter-quartile range..............	34.47	30.60	23.45			

[b] For net effects, "minimum" is maximum net increase and "maximum" is maximum net decrease.

mary products, has them in more than one quarter of the cases. At the other extreme, ten groups have such changes in either direction in none of the cases and seven others have them in only one or two cases.

Non-electrical machinery, the industry group in which net changes of 3 or more employees occur most often, has net increases of 3 or more employees in 31 cases and has net decreases in 5 other cases. The frequency of net increases in non-electrical machinery is not surprising because, as we found in Chapter 5, it is the industry group that, in all but one case, has the largest increase of employment from liberalization-induced exports. The gross decreases of employment in non-electrical machinery resulting indirectly from reductions in the domestic output of liberalized industries are too small in most cases of liberalization to offset the stimulating effects of exports on its employment.

Iron and steel and their primary products, the group which experiences net changes in employment next most frequently, experiences substantial net decreases of employment more frequently than any other group, having net decreases of 3 or more employees in 21 of the 72 cases. It also has net increases in 13 cases, which makes it second to non-electrical machinery in frequency of net increases.

It will be recalled from the discussion in Chapter 5 that there are several groups besides non-electrical machinery and iron and steel and their primary products whose employment is substantially affected by export increases in many cases of liberalization—specifically, wholesale and retail trade, railroad transportation, and coal mining. Why do these industry groups have substantial net increases of employment in few or no cases? The reason is that the reduction in domestic output of the liberalized products decreases their employment enough to bring the net increases of employment down to less than three employees in all but three cases. In wholesale and retail trade, in fact, these decreases cause net employment reductions of three or more employees in ten cases of liberalization.

Table 9.4

Frequency of Net Employment Effects on Industry Groups[a]

Affected Industry Group	Number of Liberalizations Having Specified Net Effects					
	Increase of 1.0 or More	Effect of Less Than 1.0	Decrease of 1.0 or More	Increase of 3.0 or More	Effect of Less Than 3.0	Decrease of 3.0 or More
	(1)	(2)	(3)	(4)	(5)	(6)
Agriculture, forestry, and fishing (1–10)	30	34	8	2	67	3
Metal mining (11–15)	0	57	15	0	67	5
Coal mining (16)	19	44	9	3	66	3
Crude petroleum and natural gas (17)	0	69	3	0	71	1
Other nonmetallic minerals (18–20)	0	68	4	0	71	1
Processed food and alcoholic beverages (21–28)	2	64	6	1	70	1
Tobacco manufactures (29)	0	72	0	0	72	0
Spinning, weaving, and dyeing (30)	25	36	11	1	64	7
Apparel (34)	2	70	0	0	72	0
All other textile products (31–33, 35)	0	64	8	0	72	0
Lumber, wood products, and furniture (36–43)	5	30	28	0	59	13
Pulp, paper, and paper products (44–46)	0	40	32	0	62	10
Printing and publishing (47)	4	48	20	0	65	7
Industrial chemicals (except synthetic rubber and fiber) (48–50, 53)	2	50	20	0	64	8
Synthetic rubber and synthetic fiber (51, 52) ..	0	66	6	0	68	4
All other chemicals and allied products (54–61)	5	55	12	0	70	2
Products of petroleum and coal (62–64)	0	66	6	0	71	1
Tires, inner tubes, and miscellaneous rubber products (65, 66)	0	60	12	0	66	6
Leather and products and footwear (excluding rubber) (67–69)	0	70	2	0	71	1
Glass (70)	0	64	8	0	68	4
Pottery and related products (73)	0	70	2	0	72	0
Stone and clay products (71, 72, 74–77)	1	61	10	0	70	2
Iron and steel and their primary products (78–81, 92)	27	20	25	13	38	21
Nonferrous metals and their primary products (82–91)	3	40	29	0	55	17
Fabricated metal products (93–109)	16	27	29	1	54	17
Machinery, except electrical (110–128)	58	6	8	31	36	5
Electrical machinery and products (129–138, 142–144)	21	31	20	0	60	12
Communication equipment and products (139–141)	9	56	7	0	69	3
Motor vehicles, parts and accessories (145–147)	29	40	3	0	69	2
Other transportation equipment (148–152)....	4	67	1	0	72	0
Instruments, optical and photographic equipment, watches and clocks (153–156)	2	67	3	0	72	0
Miscellaneous manufactures (157–164)	1	54	17	0	64	8
Electric light and power, and gas (167, 168)...	0	72	0	0	72	0
Railroad transportation (169)	5	37	30	0	67	5
Ocean transportation (172)	44	27	1	11	61	0
Transportation (except railroad and ocean transportation) and allied services (170, 171, 173–175, 178)	0	69	3	0	72	0
Wholesale and retail trade (176, 177)	16	27	29	3	59	10
Communication, finance, business services (179, 181, 186, 187)	2	24	46	0	64	8
Auto and other repair services (188, 189)	0	71	1	0	72	0
Other services (182–185, 190–192)	0	70	2	0	72	0

[a] Net employment effects exclude those in liberalized industries.

Summary

The comparisons of the gross increases and decreases of employment presented in this chapter make clear that the increases of employment due to exports, as here estimated, and the increases due to increased transportation of imports are insufficient in all but two cases to offset the decreases caused by the assumed shifts of buying from domestic to foreign production. Even in the non-liberalized industries, the combined net change of employment is in most cases a decrease rather than an increase, although net increases do occur in many of the 72 cases.

These conclusions, it should be remembered, are based on estimates of the gross decreases of employment, which assume, among other things, that for every increase of imports that is worth $1 million at 1953 domestic prices and is due to a reduction of import barriers, there is an initial reduction in purchases of domestic goods by United States buyers of equal 1953 dollar value. At the same time, the estimates of gross increases of employment due to exports assume that the exports induced by these additional imports are substantially less in dollar amount than the net addition to dollar earnings of foreign counties—in fact less than 53 cents per dollar of such earnings in three quarters of the cases. They also assume that these exports have the commodity composition specified in Chapter 8. The estimating method that was described in earlier chapters, however, is flexible enough to permit making estimates based on different assumptions concerning both domestic displacement and the volume of liberalization-induced exports. How such alternative estimates may be made is explained in Chapter 10.

PART
V

*Summary of Findings and
Their Significance*

Principal Findings and Their Current Validity

T HE ESTIMATES PRESENTED in the preceding chapters provide some of the information that would be needed to appraise the short-period domestic employment effects of specific liberalization programs. They also suggest significant conclusions concerning the employment and other aspects of liberalization programs in general. In this chapter, the principal findings that have already been mentioned are brought together, and some that were implicit are made explicit.

Since the estimates are based primarily on economic relationships that prevailed in 1953, or in some cases in earlier years, this chapter also considers how they are affected by economic changes that have occurred since those years. The estimates also depend heavily on several judgments and arbitrary stipulations. It is therefore desirable to see how they are affected if these judgments and stipulations are altered. This question is also considered in this chapter. Other conclusions based on the estimates are developed in the two chapters that follow.

Findings Relating to Employment Effects

In bringing the findings of the whole study together here, we shall summarize separately the findings on the gross and net effects on employment. The minimum, maximum, and quartile values of each effect for the 72 single-industry liberalizations are shown in Table 10.1.

Gross Decreases in Employment

The gross decrease of employment resulting from a million-dollar displacement of domestic output by imports was found to have a median value of 115 employees and a wide dispersion among the cases, ranging from 51 to 224 employees per million-dollar increase of imports valued in 1953 domestic prices. The wide range is partly attributable to the extremely high decrease in a few cases. In three quarters of the 72 cases the gross decrease is less than 135 employees.

The gross decrease in employment that occurs in the liberalized industry is considerably smaller than the gross decrease in all industries. It has a median value of 63 employees and a range of 17 to 194 employees. As is true of the total gross decrease, its range is considerably reduced when the cases with extremely high decreases are eliminated. In only 5 cases of liberalization is the gross employment decrease in the liberalized industry more than 103 employees; the range of 17 to 103 employees for the other 67 cases is less than half the range for all 72 cases.

Generally the cases causing large total decreases are those causing large decreases in the liberalized industry itself. Approximately 25 per cent of the variation in the total gross employment decreases, however, cannot be explained by the variation in the employment decreases in the liberalized industries. Of the 10 cases of liberalization that have the largest total employment decrease, 3 are not among the 10 with highest gross decreases in the liberalized industry.

The facts that the total gross employment decreases often exceed the decreases in the liberalized industry by substantial amounts and that they are imperfectly correlated demonstrate the importance of measuring both effects.[1]

[1] It may be noted that neither the total gross decrease nor the gross decrease in the liberalized industry is measured by the ratio of employment in the liberalized industry to its value added, which is the concept of labor intensiveness frequently used in discussions of the employment effects of liberalization. The total employment effects of a given change in output reflect the labor intensiveness of the liberalized *product,* which can be measured only by a weighted average of the ratios of employment to value added in all the numerous industries participating directly and indirectly in its production. The labor intensiveness of the liberalized *industry* is merely one element, although an important one, in determining this

Not only the absolute amount, but the proportion of the total gross employment decrease that occurs in the liberalized industry varies greatly from case to case, with a high of 86 per cent and a low of 23 per cent, the median proportion being 57 per cent. The variation is not unsystematic, however. It has a positive correlation with the amount of the total gross decrease (r = .45). In 27

Table 10.1

Selected Points in the Array of Employment Effects of 72 Import Liberalizations[a]

(Employment figures represent numbers of employees per million-dollar increase of imports at 1953 domestic port values after payment of duties)[b]

Line Number	Type of Employment Effect	Minimum	1st Quartile	Median	3rd Quartile	Maximum
	Gross decrease:					
1	In all industries................	51	94	115	135	224
2	In liberalized industry..........	17	43	63	84	194
3	*Per cent in liberalized industry..*	*23*	*45*	*57*	*67*	*86*
	Gross increases:					
4	Associated with shipping of imports, all industries.........	0	—[c]	1	2	24[d]
5	Associated with increase of exports, all industries.........	8	19	20	50	70
6	Total, all industries.............	9	21	27	52	78
7	*As per cent of gross decrease..*	*9*	*16*	*26*	*47*	*110*
	Net decrease:					
8	In all industries................	−5[e]	57	86	104	175
9	In liberalized industry..........	17	43	62	84	192

[a] Estimates do not include employment effects of income-induced changes in domestic spending. Line 1 and Lines 4 through 8 of this table come from Table 9.1, Lines 2 and 3 come from Appendix Table F.1, and Line 9 comes from Table 9.2.
[b] Employees include farmers and unpaid farm family workers.
[c] Less than 0.5 employees.
[d] This figure is not regarded as reliable.
[e] Increase.

cases more than half of the total decrease in employment occurs outside the liberalized industry. In one case more than 75 per cent of the employment decline occurs outside it.

The total gross decreases in employment could also be estimated by the crude method of dividing the value of the import increase by the average gross national product per full-time and part-time employee in 1953. This method yields an estimate of 158.5 employees per import increase of $1 million at domestic prices, which

effect. The effect of a given change in output on employment in the liberalized industry reflects the ratio of its employment to the value of its output, not to its value added.

is 38 per cent higher than the median estimate of 114.7 employees obtained by this study. A slightly less crude method, adjusted to conform more closely to the concepts used in this study, comes very little closer, yielding an estimate of 153.0 employees. Using the estimates in this study as a standard, these crude methods overestimate the gross decreases in employment, but they may nevertheless be useful as a method of establishing quickly an upper limit for the gross decreases caused by a diversified reduction of protection.

Gross Increases in Employment

The gross decreases of employment resulting from the displacement of domestic production are partly offset by increases of employment associated with the shipping of the increased imports and with the production and shipment of the additional exports that result from the increase of imports. Of these two types of increases, those resulting from export increases are by far the more important.

The estimates of the increases incidental to the shipment of additional imports are relatively crude, and little reliance should be placed on differences among them in individual cases. As measures of the general tendency, however, they are probably fairly accurate. They indicate that, for the economy as a whole, the increases of employment associated with the process of importation tend to be very small in relation to the gross decreases of employment. In three quarters of the cases they are less than two employees per million dollars of increase in imports and less than 2 per cent of the gross decreases of employment.

These gross increases of employment are highly concentrated in the ocean transportation industry. In that industry, they are large enough in nearly all cases to outweigh the decreases caused by the indirect effects on imports of reductions in domestic output. Thus, even if liberalization gave no stimulus to exports, it would give a net stimulus to employment in the ocean transportation industry.

Under the assumptions made in this study, the employment stimulus from exports is considerably smaller than the displacement of employment resulting from the decrease of domestic production for the home market. It has a median value of 26 employees and ranges from 8 to 70 employees per million-dollar increase of imports.

The large variation among the cases in the employment increases due to exports results mainly from the large variation in export increases per dollar of net increase in the earnings of foreign countries. Little is due either to variation in the net increase in foreign earnings per million-dollar increase of imports or to variation in the employment increase per dollar of export increase.

The large variation in the ratios of the increases in exports to the net increases in foreign dollar earnings implies that, if the assumptions underlying the estimates are valid, a large increase in these earnings is not sufficient to guarantee a correspondingly large increase in United States exports. When foreign countries earn additional dollars, they may merely increase their net international assets, or they may increase their imports from countries other than the United States. If these other countries, or their suppliers in turn, do not increase their imports as much as their earnings increase, and if they obtain small proportions of additional imports from the United States, the expansion of trade reaches its limit before its impact has greatly affected United States exports.

Nevertheless, increases in United States exports that are substantial relative to increases in foreign dollar earnings could occur even if countries receiving them did not spend much of the increase in the United States, for they could develop through multilateral channels. This would happen if the recipients of dollar earnings increased their imports mainly from countries other than the United States and these other countries or their suppliers used a sufficiently large proportion of their additional earnings to expand imports from the United States. In none of the cases examined, however, did a high ratio of United States exports to foreign dollar earnings result from export increases through such multilateral channels. The amount of exports per dollar of net increase in foreign earnings was found to be determined mainly by the percentages of their own additional imports that the major suppliers of liberalized imports obtain from the United States and, to a lesser extent, by their reflection ratios. This export-earnings ratio can be estimated with reasonable accuracy from these two characteristics of the major suppliers, regardless of the identity of the other countries with which they trade.

These findings imply that the variation in the employment stimulus resulting from additions to exports caused by a given increase of imports is not much affected by the independent variations in the ratios of foreign to domestic port value of the liberalized imports, in the output-induced decreases of United States imports, in the identity of countries other than the United States from which the major suppliers obtain their additional imports, or in the reflection ratios and the distribution of imports of countries other than the major suppliers.

The gross increases of employment attributable to exports tend to occur in the same industry groups, no matter what industry's liberalization causes the additional exports. They are concentrated mainly in non-electrical machinery, the wholesale and retail trade group, and iron and steel and their primary products, and to a lesser extent in railroad transportation and coal mining. Liberalized industries share little in the employment increases that result from the exports induced by their own liberalization. In no case do as much as 5 per cent of these increases occur in the liberalized industry.

The process of estimating the amount of exports that would be induced by liberalization forced on our attention the fact that when buying shifts from domestic to foreign products, the net increase in foreign dollar earnings from the sale of all commodity imports is less than the increase in foreign earnings from sale of the liberalized products alone. The difference arises because domestic production contains, directly or indirectly, some foreign ingredients, and imports of these ingredients decline when output of domestic goods is displaced.[2] The estimating process also forced us to note that this deduction from foreign earnings is offset by increases in foreign earnings associated with the shipping of the increased imports.

---

[2] This output-induced offset to the increase in imports of the liberalized products is logically distinct from the further offset resulting from the fact that the displacement of domestic output cuts domestic income and thus expenditure, an income-induced or "multiplier" effect, which was discussed in Chapter 2. It may be noted that the standard concept of the income-expenditure multiplier must be applied to changes in imports or other expenditures *net* of output-induced changes. The multiplier itself includes only *income*-induced changes. See footnote 4, Chap. 2.

Net Effects on Employment

The net effect of liberalization on employment, under the assumptions made about displacement of domestic production and the stimulus to exports, is to decrease employment in all but 2 of the 72 cases; only reductions in the protection of grain mill products and of sugar cause net employment increases. The median net effect is a decrease of 86 employees per million-dollar increase of imports.

The proportion of the gross decrease in employment that is offset by employment increases varies considerably from case to case, having a maximum value of 110 per cent and a minimum of 9 per cent. In more than three quarters of the cases, however, the increase of employment is less than half of the gross decrease and in half of the cases it is approximately one fourth (26 per cent) or less of the gross decrease.

Because the increases in employment caused by liberalization-induced increases in exports and shipping services have a negligible impact on the industries whose protection is reduced, no significant offset to the gross decrease in their employment is caused by their own liberalization. In only two cases do the increases in the liberalized industry exceed 1 per cent of the gross decrease in it, and in no case are they as much as 4 per cent of the gross decrease.

Employment outside the liberalized industry decreases on balance in just over two thirds of the cases and increases on balance in nearly one third. In most industry groups the net change is very small; in 57 of the 72 cases, no more than 4 of the 40 industry groups of the economy experience effects of 3 or more employees per million-dollar increases of imports. Some industry groups are immune to significant effects; 17 of the 40 have net changes of this magnitude either in only one case or in none. On the other hand, non-electrical machinery and iron and steel and their primary products experience changes of this amount in approximately half of the cases. In non-electrical machinery, the large majority of liberalizations cause net increases. In iron and steel and their primary products, net decreases occur in more liberalizations than do net increases.

Effects of Recent Economic Changes on the Estimates

Some of the data underlying the estimates presented in this study are out of date, and the prices used to express them are also out of date. It is necessary to form such judgments as we can about whether the estimates remain valid for shifts of spending from domestic to imported goods that occur at the present time (early 1960). The changes that seem most in need of appraisal are those in the structure of interindustry purchase and sale (input-output) relations and those in the relations between the changes in output and employment in individual industries. Since most of the results have been expressed in relation to import increases of given domestic port value in 1953, it is also desirable to see how they would be affected if they were expressed in prices that have prevailed more recently. This section discusses the effects of these and other changes.

Changes in Interindustry Relations

The estimates of the indirect and total effects of liberalization on domestic output and of their distribution among industries are based on the study by the Bureau of Labor Statistics of the 1947 structure of interindustry relations. As was pointed out in Chapter 4, the B.L.S. adjusted this structure for a few changes in technology and in the composition of production by substituting 1951 or 1953 relationships for those of 1947, and it substituted 1952 for 1947 relationships between domestic and imported sources of the products of each industry. Nevertheless, most of the interindustry relationships are those of 1947. At the beginning of 1955, when this study was begun, data for a more up-to-date structure were not available. Unfortunately, this remains true in 1960; although such data for 1958 are now being prepared in the Department of Commerce, none are yet available for a year later than 1947. As a result, there is no more recent structure with which to compare the one used in this study.

To see more precisely how the lack of this information limits us in appraising the current validity of the estimates of employment effects, we need to recall the role that the pattern of interindustry relations plays in these estimates. We used it to estimate how much the output of every industry would decrease if there were a direct decrease of a million dollars (in 1953 prices) in the output of an import-competing industry as a result of displacement by imports. We also used it to estimate the output changes in every industry that would result from given changes in exports. These output changes were then used, in conjunction with the employment-output coefficients, to determine the gross employment decreases and increases in each industry. Since we do not know if or how the structure of interindustry relations has changed, we cannot know what the distribution of output changes among industries would be and therefore what the distribution of employment effects among industries would be. Moreover, since the relations between changes of output and of employment differ among industries, this means that we also cannot judge how the estimates of total gross employment effects would differ in any specified case of liberalization. So far as changes in the structure of interindustry relations alone are concerned, these employment effects now might be higher or lower than is implied by the interindustry relations of 1947.

Changes in Employment
Per Unit of Output

Changes in employment-output relations affect the current validity of our estimates of employment effects resulting from both direct and indirect changes in output. The changes in employment per unit of output that concern us are those that reflect changes that have occurred since 1953 in methods of producing a given output. Ideally, therefore, we should examine changes in the relationships between employment and real value added in individual industries between periods in which approximately the same percentage of capacity was utilized.[3] The latest year for

[3] Since our estimates of employment effects were made by multiplying the estimated changes in the total value of an industry's output by the ratio of its employment to its total output, it may appear that we should be concerned with changes in this ratio rather than in the ratio of employment to value added. The reason for being concerned with employment-value added relationships is explained in Appendix G.

which data on employment per unit of real value added are available for individual industries is 1956. Even for broad industry divisions, the latest data relate to the recession year 1958, when capacity was less fully used than in 1953. Furthermore, these data represent ratios of employment to total output, not to real value added. For 1959, when the percentage of capacity utilized in most industries more nearly approached that of 1953, the data represent ratios of employment to real value added but are available only for large sectors of the private economy. Since data that are up-to-date, appropriate in concept, and also detailed, are not available, we must examine all the data that bear on the relations between employment and output.

Data for large sectors of the private economy show that approximately 9 per cent fewer employees were required in private non-agricultural industries to produce a unit of output in 1959 than in 1953; and 20 per cent fewer in agricultural industries.[4] These changes indicate that generally the total employment effects resulting from displacement of the same physical quantity of output would probably have been lower in 1959 than our estimates indicate.

This conclusion, however, is based on the average changes in the number of employees required to produce baskets of output that are representative of the total output of agriculture and of nonagricultural industries. The average change for each sector reflects the changes in employment-output relationships in its constituent industries, combined in proportion to their importance in their respective sectors. These proportions are likely to be similar in few, if any, cases to the contributions these industries make to the output of liberalized industries, for this output may differ systematically from that of the economy as a whole. The conclusion therefore may not apply to the total gross employment decreases caused by liberalization, even in most cases, much less to the total gross decreases in any specific case or to the gross decreases in any specific industry in all cases. Before we can make any generalizations about how the changes in employment-output

[4] Computed from employment and output data in Table 2 of U.S. Department of Labor press release USDL-4155, June 28, 1960, headed "Output per Man-Hour in the Private Economy in 1959." For information on sources and methods underlying these data, see U.S. Bureau of Labor Statistics, *Trends in Output per Man-Hour in the Private Economy*, 1909-1958, Bulletin 1249 (December 1959).

relations affect the current validity of the estimates of gross employment decreases, we need to know whether these average changes in major sectors result from changes in the component industries that are in different, or in predominantly the same, direction.

The latest data available for industry divisions cover nearly the whole private economy and give average man-hours per unit of total real output up to 1958. They show that the average of these man-hour requirements fell by more than 10 per cent between 1953 and 1958 in 21 out of 28 industry divisions and rose in only one:

Average Change in Man-Hours per Unit of Total Real Output	Number of Industry Divisions[5]	Number of 200-Order Industries Included
Increase	1[6]	20
Decrease of 0.1–10.0 per cent	6	68
Decrease of 10.1 to 20.0 per cent 13		60
Decrease exceeding 20.0 per cent 8		37
Total 28		185

It is clear that the declines in average employment per unit of total real output since 1953 have been widespread, especially when one considers that in 1958 many industries were operating at smaller percentages of capacity than in 1953. Since it is unlikely that a large proportion of these industry divisions could have experienced declines in the relationship of value added to total output, it is likely that for most industry divisions the ratios of employment to real value added also fell between 1953 and 1958.[7]

There is also evidence that the changes in employment-output relationships for these industry divisions do not reflect shifts in the composition of production among the individual industries within these divisions, at least within the manufacturing divisions. Unpublished information of the Bureau of Labor Statistics for a

---

[5] These divisions represent 20 2-digit manufacturing industries and five 2-digit mining industries in the Standard Industrial Classification, and railroads, agriculture, and services. The data on which the first column of this table is based are shown in Appendix Table G.2.

[6] Increase was 2.0 per cent.

[7] Real value added could decline in relation to total output between 1953 and 1958 for a few individual industries, but a decline of this relationship in a large proportion of these industries could occur only as a result of a wholesale change of industrial structure, a change that could hardly have escaped notice had it occurred.

large number of individual manufacturing industries indicates that even by 1956 the number of man-hours per unit of real value added had fallen since 1953 in 70 per cent of the individual manufacturing industries, had remained approximately unchanged in 6 per cent, and had risen in 24 per cent.[8]

Because employment in relation to real value added decreased between 1953 and 1956 in so large a majority of individual industries, it is safe to conclude that in a period twice as long the decrease in the major sectors of the economy must have reflected widespread decreases in individual industries.

The predominance of decreases in the ratios of employment to real value added for individual industries makes it reasonably certain how these changes alone affect the current validity of the estimates of employment changes: The total gross decreases of employment caused by import increases occurring now (having a domestic port value of a million dollars in 1953) would be less for the vast majority, perhaps for all, of the 72 cases of liberalization than the estimates presented in this study. Similarly, the gross decreases occurring in most individual industries would be less than the estimates indicate for all cases of liberalization in which they are affected, on the assumption that interindustry relations remain approximately the same as in 1947. The changes in employment-output relationships have similar effects on the employment increases caused by increases in exports; if these export increases occurred now, the employment increases associated with them would be smaller than the estimates indicate.

These conclusions concerning the effects of changes in productivity on the employment effects of liberalization apply to most but not necessarily to all of the 72 specific single-industry liberalizations. One reason we cannot be sure they apply to every case is that we do not have information about changes in the relations between employment and real value added in every industry. Even if we knew that this ratio declined in every industry, however, we could not be certain of the direction of the effect in every case unless we also had information about changes in the real value that each industry adds to a unit of output of the industry

---

[8] This information covers almost all manufacturing and refers to 307 individual industries or combinations of industries in the 4-digit Standard Industrial Classification.

liberalized in that case. It is conceivable that the employment required per unit of its own real value added could decrease in every industry in the economy but that the employment effects of a change in the output of an individual liberalized industry still could be higher than before. This result could occur if there were a sufficient increase in the proportion of the total value of the liberalized industry's output that was added in industries whose employment per unit of real value added remained relatively high. There is reason to believe, however, that changes in value-added relationships have not been of this character or have not been sufficiently large to have this effect. Unpublished data indicate that among manufacturing industries those with lower employment per unit of real value added are the ones that have increased in relative importance.[9] We can therefore be reasonably confident that in the vast majority, if not all, of the 72 cases, the gross decreases and gross increases of employment resulting from liberalizations that occured now would be smaller, per million dollar increase of imports valued at 1953 prices, than our estimates indicate.

What does this conclusion imply about the current accuracy of our estimates of net employment effects? Since we cannot say exactly how much lower than our estimates the gross changes would be under present conditions, we can draw no precise conclusions about the effect of the passage of time on the net employment effects. We can, however, state something about the probabilities. The increases in exports that result from a single-industry liberalization come from many industries while the direct displacement of output is assumed to occur in only one industry. Because these exports are more diversified, the increases in output and employment they cause are also much more diversified than the decreases caused by displacement of the output of a single industry. Consequently, in any single case of liberalization chosen at random, it is much more probable that our estimates overstate

[9] It is true that within the nonagricultural sector of the economy there has been some increase in the importance of nonmanufacturing industries relative to manufacturing industries, a shift that tends to increase the relative importance in total output of industries with higher employment per unit of output. This shift, however, must result at least partly and may result mainly from the increase in importance of nonmanufactured products and services in the total production of goods and services rather than from an increase in the contribution of nonmanufacturing industries to the output of specific protected industries.

present gross employment increases than that they overstate present gross decreases. This is particularly true for the liberalizations in which the primary employment effect is concentrated in the liberalized industry because in these cases there is little dispersion of the output decreases. This consequence would make it more likely that our estimates understate rather than overstate the net employment decreases that would result today from any liberalization for which our estimates of the gross decreases and gross increases of employment are of similar magnitudes.

It may be recalled, however, that the gross increases were generally smaller than the gross decreases. In 61 of the 72 cases the estimated gross increase of employment was less than 55 per cent of the estimated gross decrease; in the minimum case it was 9 per cent. In these 61 cases, therefore, the amounts of the net decreases due to liberalizations occurring now could exceed the estimates in this study only if the gross increases occurring now were lower than the estimates of them by a considerably greater percentage than were the gross decreases. It is unlikely that there are many cases in which the overstatement of gross increases exceeds that of gross decreases sufficiently to have this result.[10] It is therefore likely that for most cases of liberalization, our estimates overstate the net decreases as well as the gross changes in employment that would result from liberalization of imports occurring under present conditions.

Changes in Ratios of Imports
to Domestic Output

The effects on total domestic output of the initial decreases in the output of liberalized industries are based in part on 1952 ratios of the imports competing with each industry to its domestic

---

[10] For the actual net decrease to exceed the estimated net decrease in any specific liberalization, the ratio of the overstatement of the gross increase, expressed as a percentage of its estimate, to the overstatement of the gross decrease, expressed as a percentage of its estimate, must exceed the ratio of the estimated gross decrease to the estimated gross increase (the reciprocal of the figure in Column 6 of Table 9.1). Since, in the 61 liberalizations referred to above, the estimated gross increases of employment range from 55 to 9 per cent of the estimated gross decreases, the percentage overstatements of the gross increases would have to be from 1.8 times (1/.55) to 11.1 times (1/.09) the percentage overstatements of the gross decreases for the amounts of the net decreases due to liberalizations occurring now to exceed the estimates of net decreases in this study.

output. These ratios were used to determine how much of the decrease in a liberalized industry's purchases of materials and supplies came from domestic output and how much from imports, how much of its domestic suppliers' purchases, in turn, came from domestic and how much from foreign sources, and so on. Since 1952, the dollar value of total imports has risen in relation to the dollar value of total output.[11] If the quantity of imports has risen in relation to the quantity of corresponding domestic output in all industries, the use of 1952 ratios assigns a larger share of decreased interindustry purchases to domestic sellers than is now appropriate. It thus would tend to make the estimates of gross decreases in employment overstate the gross decreases that would result from liberalization now.

Such increases in import ratios would also cause the estimates to overstate the gross increases in employment associated with export increases and would do so in two ways. In the first place, use of import ratios that are too low would cause an understatement of the decreases of imports and the gross decreases of foreign earnings induced by the decline of domestic production; consequently, it would overstate the net increases of foreign earnings and therefore of United States exports. Furthermore, use of these ratios would overstate the effects of given increases in exports on domestic output and therefore on domestic employment.

These overstatements of gross increases and decreases in domestic employment would occur, however, only if the rises in import ratios since 1952 have been in ratios of physical quantities of imports competing with an industry to physical quantities of its domestic output, if these increases have also occurred over a wide range of industries, and if they have occurred for imports and output that are sold to other industries for use in their current production, not merely for imports and output that are sold to consumers or to buyers of capital equipment. Data on imports are not compiled in a way that permits judging whether recent changes have been of this character. It is clear that at least some of

[11] The ratio of "merchandise imports adjusted" to total output of goods has risen from 5.4 per cent in 1952 and 5.3 per cent in both 1953 and 1954 to 6.2 per cent in 1959. These ratios measure imports and output in current prices. The ratios relevant to the present question, which would measure them in constant prices, are not available for 1959. Import and output data come from U.S. Department of Commerce, *U.S. Income and Output* (1958), Table IV-5 and I-6, and similarly numbered tables in the subsequent July issues of *Survey of Current Business*.

the increases in the share of total domestic supplies that come from abroad have been of consumers' goods, such as automobiles for nonbusiness use, and therefore are not relevant to the current validity of the estimates. It is also true, however, that some of the increases have been of the kind that are relevant, although it is not known how widespread they have been. Without knowing how the quantity of imports has changed in relation to the quantity of output for industry use in a large number of individual industries, it is not possible to make any confident generalization about how these changes affect the applicability of the estimates to present conditions.

Changes in the United States Share
of Earnings from Shipping

In estimating the gross increases of employment associated with the shipping of liberalized imports, it was assumed that the United States ocean shipping and insurance industries obtain 48 per cent of the total revenues associated with ocean transportation of United States imports and that the remaining 52 per cent accrues to foreign countries as increases in their dollar earnings. This distribution was based on data for the three years 1952-1954. There is evidence that since then the United States share of such earnings has declined substantially. By 1956, the most recent year for which a comparable figure is available, the United States share of freight earnings from the carriage of its own imports had declined to 39 per cent.[12] Data based on the proportion of the weight of these imports carried by the United States, which are available for more recent years, suggest that the share of earnings has probably continued to decline. The decrease in the United States share of shipping earnings implies that the estimates of the gross increases of employment from the shipping of liberalized imports overstate the increases that would occur now. Since these increases were in most cases very small in relation to the other employment effects (see Table 9.1), their overstatement has no important effect on the current validity of the estimates of net primary or total net employment effects in all industries.

[12] See U.S. Department of Commerce, *Balance of Payments, 1958, Statistical Supplement to the Survey of Current Business*, p. 107.

The decline in the United States share of shipping earnings implies that the foreign share has risen; the estimated increases of foreign dollar earnings therefore must understate those that would result from liberalization undertaken now, thereby causing an understatement of export increases and of the employment increases associated with them. In all but a few cases, this understatement is also very small relative to the present estimates of employment increases due to exports.

There has also been a decline in the United States share of the revenues earned in the shipment of United States privately controlled exports. This share declined from 42 per cent in 1953 to 28 per cent in 1956 and, judging again from tonnage data, in 1959 it was probably also below that of 1953. The 1953 share, however, was not used to determine the amount of foreign expenditure in the United States but only its distribution between merchandise and shipping. Since the share of shipping was estimated at only 2.7 per cent (see Chap. 8, p. 181), a substantial overstatement of the present United States share affects this distribution very little. Moreover, it merely shifts output effects from industries that participate in the shipping of exports to those that participate in production of exports. It therefore cannot cause the estimates of total gross employment increases associated with exports to be perceptibly in error if applied to present conditions.

Thus, the reductions in the United States share of earnings from the carriage of both imports and exports has effects on the two types of gross employment increases that are both small and offsetting. Their general implications for the current validity of the estimates of total net employment effects in all industries, therefore, may be regarded as insignificant.[13]

Price Changes Since 1953

In considering the effects of decreases in employment per unit of output since 1953 and of other recent economic changes, we were concerned with how accurate the employment estimates

[13] It may be noted, however, that the overstatements of the United States shares of revenue from the carriage of both imports and exports would cause the estimates

would be if they were applied to import increases that occur in 1960. We were envisaging these import increases, however, as quantities worth a million dollars at domestic ports in 1953 prices, not in present prices. It is desirable to know how the estimates would be affected if we changed the unit used to measure import increases so that the estimates referred to import increases worth a million dollars in present prices, assuming that other economic changes had not occurred.

*Effect on Gross Decreases
of Employment*

It will be recalled that the employment estimates are based on the stipulation that import increases of a million dollars at domestic ports in 1953 displace an equal value of domestic output. So long as we maintain this assumption of equal value displacement, the changes in prices that affect the estimates of employment decreases are those affecting the quantity of domestic output of a liberalized industry that is worth a million dollars, *i.e.,* the changes in domestic prices of the liberalized industries.

Using the latest appropriate domestic price data available from the Bureau of Labor Statistics, we can get an average 1958 price index for the domestic output of each liberalized industry that is weighted in the same way as the assumed basket of increases in competing imports. These 72 averages show a median price increase of 11 per cent from 1953 to 1958, with some price increase occurring in 58 of the 72 liberalized industries. Since a million-dollar decrease in the output of these 58 industries represented a smaller quantity in 1958 than did a million dollars' worth in 1953, the gross decreases of employment caused by a million-dollar increase in imports of such products, when measured in 1958 prices, would be lower than the estimates of this study.[14]

---

to overstate both the gross and the net increases of employment in the ocean shipping industry. Although the amounts of these overstatements would be small in relation to the gross changes in all industries, they would be substantial in relation to the estimates of the effects in that industry.

[14] The ratios of 1958 to 1953 average prices of the domestic output of the 72 liberalized industries and the gross decreases of employment, adjusted for the effect of these price changes on the quantity of displaced output valued at a million dollars in 1958, are shown in Appendix Table G.3.

For the other 14 industries, the 1958 average price was lower than that of 1953, although the decline exceeded 5 per cent in only 6 of them. In these 14 cases, a million-dollar increase of imports represented a larger quantity in 1958 than it did in 1953 and therefore would have tended to cause larger employment effects in 1958 than those given in this study for million-dollar increases in 1953 prices. Since the biggest decrease in the average price of liberalized output, that of plastic products, was 15 per cent, this enlargement would in no case exceed 18 per cent $(1.00 \div [1.00 -.15] = 1.18)$.

One of the conclusions drawn from the estimates was that the gross decreases of employment differed greatly in the 72 cases. These decreases ranged from 51 employees to 224 employees per million dollars of import increases, when these increases displaced domestic output worth a million dollars in 1953 prices. Obviously, that this conclusion, like all conclusions that involve comparing the absolute amount of effects in different liberalizations, depends on the relative quantities of the domestic output displaced, and that it may be altered if the million-dollar increases are measured in other prices. How is it affected if we compare the gross employment decreases resulting from shifts of spending worth $1 million in 1958 prices?

If all cases are adjusted for price changes alone, a million-dollar increase of imports of vegetables and fruits continues to cause the maximum gross decrease of employment; this decrease shrinks from 224 to 205 employees. Although prices of most industry outputs rose between 1953 and 1958, there was a decline in the average price of output of the industry whose liberalization caused the minimum gross employment decrease when the measurement was made in 1953 prices, the grain mill products industry. Because of this price decline, the gross decrease of employment caused by liberalization of grain mill products rises from 51 to 54 employees. Liberalization of primary aluminum, the average price of which rose, joins that of grain mill products in causing the minimum gross employment decrease, its effect being diminished from 63 to 54 employees. Thus the range of gross employment decreases narrows because of changes at both extremes. Since the range is determined solely by the extreme items, however, it is not a good measure of the general dispersion. A more reliable one

is the range between the first and third quartiles. When the basis
for valuing the different industry baskets of displaced output is
shifted from a 1953 to a 1958 price basis, this range increases in
amount from 40 to 44 employees and, relative to the median,
rises from 35 per cent to 44 per cent.

Effect on Gross Increases
of Employment

The gross increases of employment associated with import increases valued at a million dollars are influenced by import prices
and domestic prices of exports. Changes in the domestic port
value of liberalized imports affect the quantity of these imports
worth $1 million and therefore the gross increases of domestic
employment associated with shipping them. It is not known how
these domestic port values changed, but the gross employment increases associated with shipping liberalized imports are extremely
small relative to other gross employment effects in all but one
case and must be regarded as unreliable in that one.

Gross employment increases associated with liberalization-induced increases of exports depend on both the dollar amount of
additional foreign spending on our exports and on the quantity
of exports associated with a dollar of such additional spending.
These two elements must be considered separately.

For our present purposes, we may assume that prices affect the
dollar amount of foreign spending on our exports only through
their effect on the net increases of foreign dollar earnings. These
net increases, in turn, consist of gross increases partially offset by
gross decreases. The gross increases are affected not only by the
domestic port values per unit of the liberalized imports but by
the composition of these port values, *i.e.,* by their foreign port
value, the shipping costs, and the average United States tariff
duty. Changes in the domestic port value cause opposite changes
in the quantity of liberalized imports worth a million dollars,
but they do not affect the dollar amount of foreign earnings per
million dollars if they are matched by proportionate changes in
the components that determine the foreign earnings. This condition implies that the average duty rate also changes in proportion
to the domestic port value. The scattered available data indicate

that there has been no clear general movement of import prices of the liberalized imports; since 1953 both increases and decreases have occurred. Most changes in domestic port value of liberalized imports appear to have been 15 per cent or less. There is reason to believe that these changes generally have not reflected disproportionate movements in the duty component of domestic port value. It therefore seems safe to conclude that there is no tendency for the estimated gross increases in foreign dollar earnings in this study systematically to overstate or understate the gross increases of such earnings that would accrue to foreign countries from import increases worth a million dollars at present prices.

The gross decreases of foreign earnings result from the decreases of imports induced by the displacement of domestic output. Since domestic prices of the displaced output have generally risen, the quantity of this output worth a million dollars and therefore the associated quantity of import decreases is less than at the 1953 domestic prices of the displaced output. The effect on foreign dollar earnings of this reduction in the quantity of the import decreases would be offset, however, if the foreign port values and shipping earnings per unit of these imports have risen by as much as the domestic prices of the displaced output. If it is true that there has been no significant *general* movement in the prices of imports used to produce displaced domestic output while there has been a general rise in the domestic prices of this displaced output, our estimates would have a general tendency to overstate the gross decreases in foreign dollar earnings associated with import increases of a million dollars at present prices and correspondingly to understate the net increases in those earnings. This would tend to cause an understatement of export increases and of employment increases associated with them.

It can be seen that a specialized and complex organization of data on import prices would be required to appraise the effects of price changes since 1953 on the dollar amount of net increases in foreign earnings. This influence of price changes, however, has probably been relatively unimportant in most cases. The foreign earnings from the sale and shipment of liberalized imports have probably not changed much since 1953 in relation to the domestic port values of these imports. The losses of foreign dollar earnings from output-induced decreases of imports are affected only by the differences between the price changes of displaced domestic output and of the imports that enter into it. Moreover, in all but one case these decreases in foreign earnings are small compared to gross increases of such earnings from the sale of liberalized products. If price changes have had any general effect on the present applicability of our estimates of the dollar amount of the increase in United States exports, this effect is probably much less than the effect of changes in domestic prices on the quantity of United States exports that foreign countries can buy with a given dollar expenditure.

The prices relevant to these quantities are the domestic prices of the output that is important in liberalization-induced exports. By using domestic price data available from the Bureau of Labor Statistics, we can construct measures of the changes in the average prices of the domestic output of industries important in these exports. The resulting price indexes show that in 24 of the 39 industries most important in exports, the average price of output rose by 5 per cent or more between 1953 and 1958, in 10 others it changed by less than 5 per cent, and in only 5 industries did it fall by more than 5 per cent. Most of the price increases are in the range of 1 to 20 per cent. Since the assumed composition of exports is diversified in nearly all cases, a range of between 5 and 15 per cent is a good approximation of the range of increases in the average cost of the baskets of export increases associated with most of the 72 liberalizations. It is therefore a good indicator of how much the present estimates overstate the physical quantity of exports that would be induced by an increase of imports worth a million dollars at present prices and the gross increases of employment associated with them.

Effect on Net Changes
of Employment

We have found that the percentage price changes relevant to the gross employment increases associated with exports were probably in most cases not much greater or much less than the price changes affecting the gross employment decreases. Since these price changes were generally upward and the estimated gross employment increases were in most cases substantially smaller in absolute amount than the estimated gross employment decreases, adjustments for price changes would, in most cases, diminish the gross increases by less than they would diminish the gross decreases, thereby making the net employment decreases per million dollars of import increases smaller under 1958 than under 1953 prices.

It is possible to test this a priori hypothesis by calculating how great a rise in the average price of the various baskets of exports would be required in each liberalization, given the change in price of the displaced domestic output, to make the net decrease of employment under 1958 price conditions exceed the estimated net decrease under 1953 price conditions. Such a test confirms the hypothesis. It shows that in 44 of the 72 liberalizations, the average price of a basket of exports would have had to rise by more than the rise in price of any of its major components. Since this is an impossible condition, it is clear that in at least these 44 liberalizations, an adjustment of the estimates for the change in prices between 1953 and 1958 would result in smaller estimates of the net employment decreases. In 14 other cases an adjustment for the price changes would almost certainly have made the net decreases larger (and probably converted one of the two net increases into a net decrease), for in these cases only a decrease in the average price of the export basket could avoid this result. In the remaining 14 liberalizations, the direction in which an adjustment for price changes would alter the estimates of net employment effects cannot be judged without a detailed analysis based on the composition of each basket of export increases.

General Conclusions Concerning Applicability
of the Estimates to Current Conditions

We have found that, generally speaking, the effect of changes in output per man-hour since 1953, and probably also that of all recent nonprice changes combined, is to reduce the employment effects of an increase in a given physical quantity of imports below what it would have been in 1953. We have also concluded that, because prices have risen since 1953 in most of the 72 liberalized industries and in most export industries, the employment changes associated with any specified dollar value of import increases would be smaller than our estimates indicate, even if these other changes had not occurred. Taking all changes into account, therefore, it seems quite safe to conclude that in the overwhelming majority, although perhaps not all, of the 72 cases analyzed, liberalization undertaken in 1960 would have smaller gross effects on employment, per increase of imports worth a million dollars in 1960 domestic prices, than is indicated by the estimates presented in this study.

How the combination of these changes would affect the validity of the estimates of net employment effects is less clear. We have already concluded that changes in employment per unit of output would in most cases cause the estimates to overstate the net decreases of employment that would result from liberalization undertaken now. We have also found no evidence that the other nonprice changes have any general tendency to make the estimates either understate or overstate net employment effects. It is probably safe to conclude that all nonprice changes combined would cause the estimates to overstate the net decreases of employment that would result from liberalization occurring now. We have also concluded that in most liberalizations the price changes also cause the estimates to overstate the net decreases. It is possible, of course, that some of the liberalizations for which nonprice changes cause the estimates of the net effects to err in one direction are among those for which the price changes cause them to err in the opposite direction. If there are such cases, the broadly stated conclusions about how the two types of change separately affect the estimates of their net employment changes cannot lead to any conclusion about how their combination affects them. Generally, however, the cases in which nonprice changes cause the estimates of net decreases to be too high are those in which price changes also cause them to be too high, these being generally the liberalizations for which the gross employment increases are substantially smaller than the gross decreases. Consequently, it may be concluded that, in most of the cases analyzed, liberalization undertaken in 1960 would cause smaller net as well as smaller gross effects on employment, per increase of imports worth a million dollars in 1960 domestic prices, than is indicated by the estimates of this study.

Alternative Assumptions About Displacement of Domestic Production and Exports

The findings and conclusions of this study depend on the assumptions underlying its basic estimates. Of these assumptions, the two that are perhaps most likely to be questioned are those relating to the total amount and kind of domestic output directly displaced and to the amount of the increase of exports induced by given increases of imports. One of the virtues of the method of estimating used in this study is that the estimates can be adjusted to different assumptions about displacement and exports by relatively simple procedures.[15] It is of interest to consider how the findings would be affected if different assumptions were made about displacement and exports.

Alternative Assumptions About Displacement of Domestic Production

The assumption of the present estimates regarding displacement of domestic output has two elements that are logically distinct. First, it is assumed that increases of imports resulting from reductions of import barriers displace an amount of domestic output having equal value in 1953 domestic prices. Second, it is assumed that this displacement is entirely in the output of like commodities. For example, imports of synthetic fiber are assumed to displace output of domestic synthetic fibers and are further assumed not to displace output of domestic natural fibers.

Both parts of this general assumption may be, and in fact have been questioned. Professor Don D. Humphrey believes both that "Tariff reductions may create new markets rather than displace old ones" and that "Tariff reductions in one industry may displace production in another."[16] There are grounds for question-

---

[15] How to adjust the estimates to alternative assumptions about these points is explained in Appendix G.

[16] See his "Comment" on the paper "Primary Effects on Employment of Shifts in Demand from Domestic to Foreign Products" by Walter S. Salant with the collaboration of Beatrice N. Vaccara in *Problems of International Economics,* Supplement to *The Review of Economics and Statistics,* Vol. 40, Pt. 2 (February 1958), p. 104.

ing the assumption concerning the total amount of domestic output displaced. It should be recalled that liberalization tends to reduce prices of the liberalized products or to afford domestic buyers a wider choice of available products or both. As was noted in Chapter 2, these effects may result in an increase in total purchasing at given levels of income, so that the total displacement of domestic output may be less than the increase of imports. The estimates of this study do not allow for such an effect, and, to the extent that it occurs, they overstate the gross and net employment decreases. As to the kind of output displaced, it seems less likely that imports would not displace output of the domestic industry producing the corresponding product and yet displace output of other domestic industries. There is little evidence about the industries in which displacement would occur or about how much displacement would occur.

Although the combination of assumptions underlying the estimates is the one that seemed most useful, it is only one of numerous combinations that could have been made. Fortunately, the method of estimating effects for one industry at a time permits the user to obtain approximate estimates of the employment effects on different assumptions as to displacement. Modifications of the two elements in our assumption about output displacement are considered separately.

If we were to assume that there is less than full displacement, while retaining the original assumption that it occurs entirely in the industry whose protection is reduced, the original estimate of the gross decrease of employment would be reduced by the same proportion as the assumed output displacement. At the same time, an upward adjustment—in most cases a minor one—would be required in the estimated employment increase due to exports, because the output-induced decreases of imports would be smaller, thereby making the net increases in foreign dollar earnings and in United States exports larger.

Although the size of both these gross employment changes is affected by how much of the output of the liberalized industry we assume is displaced per million-dollar increase of imports, their distribution among the various industries is not.[17] As the decreases

[17] In theory the distribution of the employment increases due to exports would change since the exports bought by the world trade groups, which would be re-

of employment are distributed among industries differently than the increases, however, changes in the amounts of either have the effect of altering the distribution of the *net* changes in employment.

The estimates may also be adjusted to accord with the assumption that part or all of the output displacement occurs in one or more of the 71 accepted industries whose protection is not reduced, while still assuming that the total displacement is equal to the import increase. (It is not possible to adjust the estimates to the assumption that the displacement occurs in an industry not among the 72 accepted for study.) The change of this assumption simply means that the liberalized and the displaced industries are not the same. The gross employment decreases associated in this study with liberalization of an industry should be replaced by a weighted average of the total gross decreases associated with liberalization of the industries in which displacement is assumed to occur, each of these decreases being weighted by the proportion of the million dollar displacement that occurs in that industry. To get net employment effects, this new estimate of the total gross decrease can be combined with the gross employment increases associated with liberalization of the liberalized industry.[18]

Although a change in the assumption about where displacement occurs would alter the absolute amounts of the gross decreases and the net effects on employment, the direction of the change cannot be known unless the location of the displacement is specified. When it is specified, we can say that the gross and net employment decreases in all industries will be raised if the gross decrease that this study associates with liberalization of the displaced industry is larger than the gross decrease it associates with that of the liberalized industry, and that they will be lowered if it is smaller.

Using the procedures just described and the information on the

vised upward, differ in industry composition and employment effect from those bought by the major suppliers. Under the procedure suggested in Appendix G, however, these differences are ignored, and the employment effects of exports are adjusted by the same proportion in all industries.

[18] This procedure assumes that changing the displacement assumption does not affect the gross increases of employment. It thereby neglects the changes that would occur in the output-induced decreases of imports, and thus in the net increases of foreign earnings, exports, and the associated gross employment increases. The procedure given in Appendix G allows for these changes.

distribution of gross employment decreases shown in Appendix Table F.1, we can adjust the gross decrease occurring in any industry or group of industries for the effect of alternative assumptions about both the total amount of domestic output displaced and its distribution among industries. The significant changes resulting from altering the displacement assumptions will be confined (except in the case of cork and cork products) to the estimates of the gross decreases and the net changes of employment, and to their distributions among industries. The effects of liberalization on foreign earnings, on exports, and on the employment increases associated with exports will be altered only slightly in most cases.

Alternative Assumptions About the Amount of Induced Exports

The second main assumption about which the range of opinions could be wide is the one used to derive the increase in United States exports from the net increase in foreign earnings. This assumption is actually an implication of a whole set of assumptions concerning the merchandise reflection ratios of foreign countries and the distribution of their additional imports among the United States and the four world trade groups. It will be recalled that the reflection ratios, based on judgments concerning the probable reactions of each country, range from .46 to 1.0. As a result of the values assigned to these ratios and to the assumed distributions of additional imports of foreign countries, the increase in United States exports turned out to be less than 30 per cent of the net increase of foreign earnings in half of the 72 cases and less than 53 per cent in three quarters of them. While the merchandise reflection ratio and import distribution attributed to each country were regarded as the most plausible ones, it may readily be conceded that, taken together, they result in a stimulus to exports that some people will regard as implausibly low. An assumption often regarded as more appropriate is that the increase in United States exports would be equal to the net increase in the dollar earnings of foreign countries.[19]

---

[19] This assumption implies that an average of the individual merchandise reflec-

By a simple procedure, the present estimates of employment increases due to exports may be revised to take account of this or any other substitute assumption about the ratio of the increase in United States exports to the net increase in foreign dollar earnings. It is necessary only to multiply the net increase in foreign dollar earnings for that case (shown in Column 2 of Table 5.1) by the ratio of export increase to net increases in foreign earnings that one wishes to assume, and to multiply the product (which is the assumed export increase) by the figure .107, the median employment increase per thousand dollars of export increase.[20] This procedure gives a substitute estimate of the increase in employment due to exports on the assumption that the employment increase per dollar of export increase is the same as the median increase in the 72 cases. Since the average variation in this figure is relatively small, this is probably a good approximation for any distribution of export increases that covers a wide range of industries. The resulting revised estimate of the employment increases associated with exports may then be substituted for the original estimates in order to get a revised estimate of net employment effects in all industries.

How would the conclusions summarized in the first section of this chapter be affected if the estimated employment increases due to exports were adjusted by this simple procedure to accord with the assumption that the increases in United States exports are equal to the net increases in foreign dollar earnings? The effects

tion ratios of foreign countries, when weighted appropriately, is equal to 1.0. Since the weights appropriate to each case differ, this assumption could hardly be valid in every case unless these ratios were 1.0 for every country. To assume that United States exports would increase by more than the net increase in foreign dollar earnings would imply that the relevantly weighted average of foreign merchandise reflection ratios exceeds 1.0. It is widely believed that this is not the case. Prof. Charles P. Kindleberger, however, has expressed doubt about the grounds for this belief. See his communication "The Foreign-Trade Multiplier, the Propensity to Import and Balance-of-Payments Equilibrium," *American Economic Review*, Vol. 39 (March 1949). See also Arthur I. Bloomfield's response, entitled "Induced Investment, Overcomplete International Adjustment, and Chronic Dollar Shortage" and Kindleberger's "Rejoinder," both in *American Economic Review*, Vol. 39 (September 1949).

[20] The adjustment uses the median ratio of employment increase to export increase, shown in Column 4 of Table 5.1, rather than the ratios for each case, because the latter imply that the export increases have a particular composition. Since this composition depends on the set of assumptions that is being replaced, it would be incorrect to assume that these ratios remain appropriate to the adjusted estimate of the employment effect.

Table 10.2

Effect on Employment Estimates of Assuming Export Increases Equal to Net Increases in Foreign Dollar Earnings

Liberalized Industry		Employment Effects (Number of employees, farmers, and unpaid farm family workers)				Total Gross Increase as Percentage of Gross Decrease[a]	
		Gross Increases Due to Exports		Net Effects[a]		Original Estimate	Alternative Estimate
Code Number	Title	Original Estimate	Alternative Estimate	Original Estimate	Alternative Estimate		
		(1)	(2)	(3)	(4)	(5)	(6)
1	Meat animals and products...	68.53	90.53	−23.63	−1.63	75.3	98.3
8	Vegetables and fruits........	64.93	79.69	−148.97	−134.21	33.6	40.2
13	Lead and zinc mining........	66.93	90.99	−94.15	−70.09	42.9	57.5
21	Meat packing and wholesale poultry...................	54.32	88.35	−52.04	−18.01	51.8	83.3
22	Processed dairy products.....	31.28	88.86	−21.38	36.20	60.6	166.7
24	Grain mill products..........	55.80	91.37	5.03	40.60	109.8	179.4
27	Sugar......................	65.30	86.31	2.95	23.96	104.4	135.6
28	Alcoholic beverages..........	47.58	89.57	−35.17	6.82	58.8	108.0
29	Tobacco manufactures.	34.39	78.83	−34.88	9.56	50.2	113.7
30	Spinning, weaving and dyeing.	19.37	81.15	−116.00	−54.22	15.0	60.3
31	Special textile products......	20.11	77.82	−85.43	−27.72	20.0	74.1
34	Apparel...................	19.55	77.30	−174.63	−116.88	10.6	40.2
35	House furnishings and other non-apparel...............	20.86	77.20	−111.34	−55.00	17.5	59.2
38	Plywood...................	39.65	87.75	−99.43	−51.33	28.6	63.1
40	Wood containers and cooperage	70.47	82.46	−88.86	−76.87	46.7	53.9
41	Wood furniture.............	28.17	87.49	−141.73	−82.41	17.0	51.7
45	Paper and board mills........	48.28	90.03	−35.32	6.43	58.1	107.6
46	Converted paper products....	20.53	80.71	−91.66	−31.48	20.2	72.6
49	Industrial organic chemicals..	16.25	72.24	−58.76	−2.77	26.0	96.5
51	Synthetic rubber............	61.44	87.98	−1.12	25.42	98.3	139.0
52	Synthetic fiber.............	18.52	87.63	−71.68	−2.57	21.5	97.2
54	Drugs and medicines........	18.52	89.51	−99.63	−28.64	16.0	75.8
56	Paints and allied products....	36.28	67.17	−30.31	0.58	66.5	100.6
59	Vegetable oils...............	63.82	84.49	−5.55	15.12	92.2	121.3
61	Miscellaneous chemical industries....................	15.36	82.17	−88.61	−21.80	15.9	79.3
65	Tires and inner tubes.......	10.03	84.70	−81.57	−6.90	11.4	92.5
66	Miscellaneous rubber products	25.75	81.19	−91.11	−35.67	22.3	69.6
67	Leather tanning and finishing.	40.66	92.72	−39.00	13.06	51.3	116.3
69	Footwear, except rubber......	24.01	89.81	−154.11	−88.31	13.7	50.5
70	Glass......................	17.48	78.70	−97.57	−36.35	15.7	68.6
73	Pottery and related products..	17.32	73.26	−171.73	−115.79	9.3	38.9
79.1	Carbon steel works and rolling mills...................	18.77	86.99	−66.26	1.96	27.0	102.2
79.2	Alloy steel works and rolling mills, except stainless......	18.21	85.85	−69.53	−1.89	25.6	98.0
79.3	Stainless steel works and rolling mills.....................	18.92	87.39	−71.93	−3.46	25.5	96.4
85	Primary zinc...............	60.48	86.03	−34.12	−8.57	64.2	91.0
88	Primary aluminum, including alumina..................	57.66	89.51	−4.66	27.19	92.6	143.3
89	Aluminum rolling and drawing	37.49	88.47	−42.02	8.96	47.2	111.3

[a] In calculating Columns 3 to 6, increases associated with the process of importation as well as those resulting from exports are taken into account.

Table 10.2 (continued)

Code Number	Title	Employment Effects (Number of employees, farmers, and unpaid farm family workers)				Total Gross Increase as Percentage of Gross Decrease[a]	
		Gross Increases Due to Exports		Net Effects[a]		Original Estimate	Alternative Estimate
		Original Estimate	Alternative Estimate	Original Estimate	Alternative Estimate		
		(1)	(2)	(3)	(4)	(5)	(6)
93	Tin cans and other tinware...	38.71	90.70	−67.17	−15.18	36.7	85.7
94	Cutlery....................	19.07	79.13	−102.81	−43.35	16.2	64.7
95	Tools and general hardware...	19.20	86.77	−110.98	−43.41	14.0	66.7
103	Lighting fixtures............	20.39	78.37	−117.97	−59.99	14.7	56.6
105	Metal barrels, drums, etc,....	16.71	76.02	−87.22	−27.91	16.1	73.1
106	Tubes and foils..............	14.62	82.00	−85.47	−18.09	15.1	82.0
116	Machine tools and metalworking machinery.............	28.53	93.19	−79.83	−15.17	26.8	86.1
118	Special industrial machinery..	26.38	90.04	−110.51	−46.85	19.7	65.0
123	Industrial machinery n.e.c....	39.53	92.01	−83.56	−31.08	32.3	74.8
127	Ball and roller bearings......	35.37	80.72	−90.02	−38.67	28.5	69.3
131	Motors and generators.......	56.70	90.29	−72.28	−38.69	44.1	70.1
132	Transformers................	22.23	90.64	−90.62	−22.21	19.7	80.3
133	Electrical control apparatus..	21.35	88.49	−93.12	−25.98	18.7	77.3
134	Electrical welding apparatus..	42.96	95.11	−58.96	−6.81	42.2	93.3
135	Electrical appliances........	23.34	88.00	−110.53	−45.87	17.7	65.8
136	Insulated wire and cable.....	44.96	77.33	−50.66	−18.29	49.2	81.7
138	Electric lamps..............	19.54	86.54	−89.79	−22.79	18.0	79.2
139	Radio and related products...	51.21	96.33	−103.67	−58.55	33.2	62.3
141	Communication equipment...	58.69	92.13	−73.68	−40.24	44.4	69.6
142	Storage batteries...........	15.15	79.05	−80.68	−16.78	16.0	82.5
143	Primary batteries...........	53.59	84.07	−64.53	−34.05	45.4	71.2
145.1	Passenger cars and light trucks	25.82	92.17	−97.95	−31.60	21.3	74.6
145.2	Heavy trucks and buses......	57.67	91.07	−55.53	−22.13	51.2	80.6
145.3	Motor vehicle parts and accessories....................	51.38	90.92	−51.51	−11.97	50.3	88.4
148	Aircraft and parts...........	52.16	89.57	−66.28	−28.87	44.7	75.9
152	Motorcycles and bicycles.....	24.42	90.78	−103.64	−37.28	19.9	71.2
154	Optical, ophthalmic and photo equipment...............	26.33	88.28	−101.58	−39.63	20.8	69.1
156	Watches and clocks..........	18.93	75.27	−117.56	−61.22	14.5	55.5
157	Jewelry and silverware.......	13.88	71.90	−122.58	−64.56	10.4	52.8
158	Musical instruments and parts	31.11	87.00	−103.90	−48.01	23.3	64.5
159	Toys and sporting goods.....	16.23	76.18	−141.25	−81.30	10.5	48.5
160	Office supplies..............	17.45	74.93	−111.11	−53.63	17.6	60.2
161	Plastic products.............	34.36	82.05	−87.43	−39.74	28.9	67.7
162	Cork products..............	7.99	39.09	−79.10	−48.00	10.3	45.6
164	Miscellaneous manufactured products.................	22.69	78.81	−132.07	−75.95	16.1	51.7
	Minimum.................	7.99	39.09	5.03[b]	40.60[b]	9.3	38.9
	1st quartile................	19.06	79.09	−57.14	−5.14	16.2	63.8
	Median....................	26.36	86.88	−86.34	−28.76	25.6	74.7
	3rd quartile................	49.74	89.92	−103.66	−48.00	47.0	94.8
	Maximum..................	70.47	96.33	−174.63[b]	−134.21[b]	109.8	179.4
	Inter-quartile range.........	30.68	10.83	46.52	42.86	30.8	31.0

[b] For net effects, "minimum" is maximum net increase and "maximum" is maximum net decrease.

of this adjustment appear in Table 10.2, along with the original estimates. On this assumption, the employment increases resulting from exports would be substantially higher in all 72 cases of liberalization. Their median value would become 87 instead of 26 employees per million-dollar increase of imports at 1953 domestic values. While they would be higher in all cases, they would rise by more in the cases where they were low originally than in those where they were high; the minimum increase, which is 8 employees under the original assumptions, would be 39 employees under the substitute estimate, while the maximum would rise from 70 to 96 employees.

Similarly, the median proportion of the gross decreases of employment that are offset by increases due to both exports and the process of shipping additional imports would become 75 per cent instead of only 26 per cent while the range of this proportion would become 39 to 179 per cent, instead of 9 to 110 per cent, as it was under the original assumptions.

Correspondingly, the absolute amount of the net change in employment, which in the median case is a net decrease of 86 employees under the original assumptions, would be a net decrease of only 29 employees. The maximum net decrease would shrink from 175 to 134 employees while the maximum net increase, which is only 5 employees under the original assumptions, would rise to 41 employees. Employment would increase on balance in 13 of the 72 cases instead of in only 2. What seems most significant about this substitute assumption, however, is that net increases of employment would occur in no more than 13 cases; employment would still decrease on balance in nearly five sixths of the cases.

The effect of the substitute assumption on the distribution of the domestic employment increases resulting from exports depends on the distribution of these exports. This distribution cannot be determined by a simple calculation. If exports do not increase by more than foreign dollar earnings, however, there must still be a net decrease of employment in the liberalized industry. We have found that employment in an industry is most affected, per dollar of direct change in output, when that change is in its own output. Therefore, the maximum gross increase in employment in the liberalized industry would occur if the export increase consisted entirely of its products. Of course it is economically unrealistic to assume that an industry that will have to face an increase in competing imports when its protection is reduced could at the same time be the major, let alone the sole, beneficiary of the export increases that would result from the addition to imports. A more reasonable assumption is that exports would be distributed among many domestic industries. With such a distribution of exports, the gross employment increase in the liberalized industry would not exceed 10 per cent of its gross employment decrease in any of the 72 cases of liberalization.

CHAPTER 11

Implications of Different Types
of Liberalization Programs

I N THIS STUDY we have seen that different liberalizations causing import increases of equal domestic values have different
effects on domestic employment, depending on what domestic
goods are displaced and on what countries supply the imports. The
employment effects are related to the classical economic objective
of reducing import barriers, which is to increase real output per
unit of input by obtaining goods from abroad when fewer resources
are required to pay for them than are required to produce them at
home.[1] In the course of estimating these employment effects, we
also had to estimate the effects of the various liberalizations on
other economic variables. Some of these effects, such as the effects
on the dollar earnings of foreign countries and on United States
exports, are often regarded as major purposes of reductions in import barriers. By comparing the effects of the various industry
liberalizations on the economic variables related to different objectives of liberalization, we can learn a good deal about the policy
implications of the findings.

Since the effects of different liberalizations on employment have
already been compared, the major emphasis of this chapter is
placed on comparing their effects on other important variables.
As a means of studying the implications of these effects, we shall
formulate several hypothetical types of liberalization programs,
each designed to maximize a possible objective of policy and see
how compatible are the maximizations of these objectives.

---

[1] The connection between the employment estimates and this classical objective
cannot be pressed far, however. The classical objective was concerned with economical use of all resources, not only labor, and with differences between kinds of
labor that are scarce and kinds that are abundant. The estimates of the present
study do not show the relative effects of different industry liberalizations in releas-
ing nonlabor resources, and they do not distinguish the different categories of
skills or other qualities of the labor released. Nevertheless, in indicating the relative quantities of labor released within short periods, they are relevant to the
classical objective.

A policy of trade liberalization might be designed to attain any of several positive objectives. Five possible objectives have been selected. One is to reduce the highest tariffs. The second is to provide the maximum net increase of foreign dollar earnings for a given domestic value of import increase. The third and fourth, respectively, are to maximize the net increase in world trade and in the trade of underdeveloped countries. The fifth is to maximize the stimulus to United States exports. These objectives have not been selected with any implication that they are wise objectives of economic policy or that the nontariff objectives, even if wisely chosen, can best be achieved through liberalization, but because they are objectives to which the estimates are relevant. Each of these types of liberalization program is represented by the industry liberalizations that carry out its objective best in relation to a given domestic value of import increase.

Compatibility of Objectives

Under the objective of lowering our highest duty rates, tariffs might be reduced for the 15 industries where the duties on 1953 imports had an average ad valorem equivalent of 25 per cent or more.[2] This type of liberalization program, which we shall call Type A, would reduce barriers to imports that compete with the 15 domestic industries identified in the first column of Table 11.1.

A second plausible objective, represented by programs designated as Type B, would be to provide the maximum net increase in foreign dollar earnings for a given increase of imports. The 15 industries whose liberalizations would provide the maximum net increase of foreign dollar earnings are identified in the second column of Table 11.1.[3]

[2] The average ad valorem equivalent of 1953 duties for an industry is the average of the ad valorem equivalent rates on the accepted commodities in the accepted subindustries. Under this definition, duties high enough to keep imports out altogether have no effect on the average. For the meaning of the terms "accepted commodities" and "accepted subindustries," see Chap. 4, pp. 74-77.

[3] Since there were 15 industries with average duties of 25 per cent or more, this

The first conclusion is that these two types of program include none of the same industries. This means that both their objectives cannot be maximized at once, and in that limited sense, the two programs conflict. Increases in imports competing with industries in which tariffs average 25 per cent or more will of course increase the dollar earnings of foreign countries, but by less than would equal increases in imports competing with 15 other industries.

The reason for this conflict becomes clear when we recall that the net increases of foreign dollar earnings consist of the domestic value of the import increases less (a) the average duty, (b) approximately half of the costs associated with shipping the additional imports, and (c) the decreases of dollar earnings from the output-induced decreases of United States imports. Since the second and third deductions are in nearly all cases small and vary little among the cases, net increases of earnings are inversely correlated with average duty levels.

A liberalization program might also be designed to maximize the net increase in world trade. This increase can be regarded as measured by the increase of foreign earnings of all currencies, thereby taking into account not only the effects on the exports of countries supplying the United States but the increases in exports of other countries that result from the expansion of imports by these supplying countries. For programs with this objective, designated as programs of Type C, 14 industries, identified in Column 3 of Table 11.1, have been included. Of these industries, only one, lighting fixtures, has an average tariff duty of 25 per cent or more and was therefore included in a liberalization program of Type A. The average industry tariff rates of the other 13 industries that might be in such programs range between approximately 9 and 18 per cent. Thus maximization of the objectives of Type A and Type C also tend to be mutually exclusive.

Programs of Type B, which maximizes net increases of foreign dollar earnings, and Type C, which maximizes net increases in

---

number of industry liberalizations was sought in making up the other programs. The specific industry liberalizations selected to attain an objective was determined by ranking the 72 industries in the order of the effects that their liberalizations would have on that objective, and then selecting the top 15 cases. For two types of program, however, the difference between the effects of the fifteenth and sixteenth cases was very small and a more natural cut-off point was found after the fourteenth case. Accordingly, these two types of program include only 14 cases.

Table 11.1
Industries Included in Hypothetical Liberalization Programs

Code Number	Liberalized Industry — Title	Type A: Reduce Duties in Industries with Average Duties of 25 Per Cent or More (15 cases)	Type B: Maximize Net Foreign Dollar Earnings (15 cases)	Type C: Maximize Net Foreign Earnings in All Currencies (14 cases)	Type D: Maximize Net Foreign Earnings in All Currencies of Under-developed Countries (15 cases)	Type E: Maximize United States Exports (14 cases)
1	Meat animals and products	x			x	x
8	Vegetables and fruits				x	x
13	Lead and zinc mining		x			x
21	Meat packing and wholesale poultry					x
22	Processed dairy products			x	x	
24	Grain mill products	x			x	
27	Sugar				x	x
29	Tobacco manufactures	x			x	
30	Spinning, weaving and dyeing	x				
31	Special textile products				x	
34	Apparel	x				
35	House furnishings and other non-apparel			x		
40	Wood containers and cooperage				x	x
41	Wood furniture			x	x	
49	Industrial organic chemicals	x			x	
51	Synthetic rubber					x
59	Vegetable oils				x	x
67	Leather tanning and finishing		x	x	x	
69	Footwear, except rubber			x	x	
70	Glass	x				
73	Pottery and related products	x				
85	Primary zinc					x
88	Primary aluminum, including alumina					x
93	Tin cans and other tin ware	x		x		
94	Cutlery	x				
103	Lighting fixtures	x			x	
105	Metal barrels, drums, etc.	x				
116	Machine tools and metal working machinery		x			
118	Special industrial machinery		x	x		
123	Industrial machinery n.e.c.		x	x		
131	Motors and generators					x
132	Transformers		x	x		
134	Electrical welding apparatus		x	x		
135	Electrical appliances			x	x	
139	Radio and related products		x	x		
141	Communication equipment		x			x
145.1	Passenger cars and light trucks		x	x	x	
145.2	Heavy trucks and buses		x			x
145.3	Motor vehicle parts and accessories		x			
152	Motorcycles and bicycles		x	x	x	
156	Watches and clocks	x				
157	Jewelry and silverware	x				
159	Toys and sporting goods	x				
160	Office supplies	x				
162	Cork products	x				
164	Miscellaneous manufactured products	x				

foreign earnings of all currencies, are more similar; they have seven industries in common. What accounts for the fact that they have no more than seven industries in common?

Net increases in foreign total earnings depend partly on the net increases of foreign dollar earnings, but they depend also on how much of the increases in their dollar earnings the supplying countries spend in other foreign countries and on how much of the resulting increases in their earnings *these* countries spend outside the United States. In other words they depend on the reflection ratios and the distribution of imports of the major suppliers and of the world trade groups described in Chapter 7.[4] Some industry liberalizations in programs of Type B would not be in programs of Type C because the net increases of foreign dollar earnings that they generate, although large, go to suppliers that spend relatively small proportions of these increases in foreign countries; they spend either relatively small proportions anywhere or relatively high proportions in the United States. Conversely, some industry liberalizations in Type C programs would not be in Type B programs because the suppliers in these cases get relatively small increases in dollar earnings, even though these increases generate a large expansion in total world trade. A detailed examination of the individual liberalizations shows that a program that sought to achieve the objectives of Types B and C would have to involve compromises; it could not maximize the achievement of both objectives.

A fourth objective of liberalization might be to maximize the net foreign currency earnings of underdeveloped countries.[5] Of the 15 industry liberalizations that fit best into such programs, designated as Type D programs and identified in Column 4 of Table 11.1, only two are among those in Type A programs and only four (all different from those shared with Type A) are appropriate to Type B programs. Thus, the objectives of these three types are to a high degree mutually exclusive. A liberalization program consisting of the imports most appropriate to either Type

---

[4] It should be recalled that, for reasons explained in Chapter 7, expenditures by foreign countries in the United States are assumed not to generate any further increase in world trade.

[5] For purposes of this computation, the major suppliers considered "underdeveloped" are Argentina, Brazil, Cuba, India, Iran, Mexico, The Philippine Republic, and Turkey. World Trade Groups 1 and 2 are also considered "underdeveloped."

A or Type B programs would increase net foreign earnings of underdeveloped countries by little more than half as much as would a program that increased total imports by the same amount but consisted of imports selected to achieve that objective. (See Column 4 of Table 11.2.)

As might be expected, programs of Types C and D do have some liberalizations in common—slightly more than half of those included in each type. A program designed to maximize the net earnings of all foreign countries, therefore, would be suited to the objective of increasing the net earnings of underdeveloped countries. It would not be the best program for the latter purpose alone, however. Among the five industry liberalizations that would cause the largest net increase in earnings of underdeveloped countries, only one is among those selected to increase the net earnings of all foreign countries.

Finally, we may consider as a possible objective the expansion of United States exports that would be associated with increases of imports of given 1953 domestic value (Type E programs). Of the 14 industries whose liberalizations would contribute most to this objective, all have average tariff rates of less than 21 per cent, so none of them satisfies Type A objectives. Reduction of the highest tariff rates is incompatible with maximum stimulation of exports for the same reason that it is incompatible with maximum stimulation of the dollar or total earnings of foreign countries.

Perhaps more surprising is the fact that of the 15 industries whose liberalizations maximize the net increase in dollar earnings of foreign countries (Type B) and the 14 whose liberalizations maximize the increase in United States exports (Type E), only 5 industries are common to both groups, indicating that there is only moderate correlation between increases in dollar earnings and United States exports.

We have noted that Type E programs have 5 industries in common with Type B programs, and we found earlier that Type C programs have 7 industries in common with Type B. Despite these facts, Type C and Type E programs have no industries in common. Evidently, the programs designed to induce maximum increases in United States exports would be incompatible with those designed to induce maximum net increases in foreign countries' earnings of all currencies.

The extent to which these five types of programs overlap is most clearly seen in the diagram below, where the number of industries selected to maximize the objective of each type is indicated in parentheses and the number shared by two types is shown in the line connecting them.

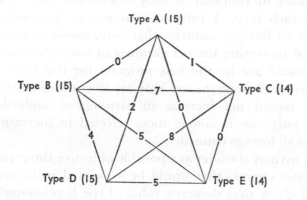

Only 46 of the 72 industry liberalizations analyzed are included in any of the five types of program. Examination of Table 11.1 shows that of these 46 cases, 24 are included in only one type, 17 are included in two types, only 5 are in three types, and no case is in more than three types.

More specific information about each type of program can be obtained by seeing how much it would affect each of the variables discussed. Before these effects can be measured, it must be recognized that the import increases included in each type of program can be combined in many ways and that the effect of a given total of import increases depends on its composition, *i.e.,* on the relative importance of the import increases that it includes. Perhaps the most representative single indicator of how much a type of program affects each variable is the effect of a specific program that causes a total increase of imports in which the imports competing with each of its liberalized industries has equal domestic value, *i.e.,* an unweighted average of the effect of each industry liberalization. These average effects are shown in the first row of each trio of rows in Table 11.2, for programs that increase total imports by a million dollars in 1953 domestic values.

Since different specific programs of a given type may have effects that differ greatly from these average effects, it is important to know the limits of each effect for all possible specific programs of a given type. For that reason, the minimum and maximum amounts of each effect are also shown in Table 11.2 for each type of program. For each type of effect, the programs yielding the maximum (or minimum) amount are programs that increase imports that compete only with the industry whose liberalization has the maximum (or minimum) amount of that effect. It is of course politically unrealistic to assume that a liberalization program may consist entirely of imports competing with one industry. This assumption is made merely to establish the mathematical limits of various effects. The range of effects that it is realistic to consider is narrower than the range thus calculated.

The conflict of the Type A and Type B objectives is brought out clearly by the first two columns of Table 11.2. They show that the maximum net increase of foreign dollar earnings under programs of Type A, $758,000 per increase of imports of a million dollars at domestic prices, is lower than the minimum under programs of Type B, which is $846,000. At the same time, while the lowest average duty of any industry included in Type A programs is, by definition, at least 25 per cent, the highest average duty of any of the industries included in programs of Type B is less than 13 per cent.

Further discussion of what the table shows about the contribution of each type of program to the various objectives is not needed, since the figures in the table relating to these objectives (the first five columns) serve mainly to support and amplify the preceding discussion of their compatibility.[6]

---

[6] Figures for single industry liberalizations corresponding to all the columns of Table 11.2 may be found in the tables from which those columns were derived.

Effects on Foreign Earnings and Employment of

(Per million-dollar increase in

Liberalization Program[b]	Average Duty (Per Cent)	Net Increase of Foreign Earnings (In thousands of 1953 dollars)			Increase in U. S. Exports (In thousands of 1953 dollars)
		Of Dollars, All Countries	Of All Currencies		
			All Countries	Underdeveloped Countries	
	(1)	*(2)*	*(3)*	*(4)*	*(5)*
All liberalized industries					
Average......................	17.9	788.3	1667.7	332.5	312.8
Minimum.....................	5.7	365.3	921.0	65.4	83.9
Maximum.....................	42.3	900.3	2666.2	957.9	627.1
A. Reduce high duties[d]					
Average......................	31.7	692.3	1610.2	324.4	184.0
Minimum.....................	25.5	365.3	921.0	95.5	83.9
Maximum.....................	42.3	758.4	2040.6	768.1	321.4
B. Maximize dollar earnings					
Average......................	11.3	860.2	1754.6	338.6	407.2
Minimum.....................	7.3	846.1	1206.0	124.4	210.1
Maximum.....................	12.8	900.3	2339.9	680.6	611.0
C. Maximize foreign earnings, all currencies					
Average......................	14.7	830.4	2134.8	454.1	275.5
Minimum.....................	8.7	721.5	1921.7	330.2	191.3
Maximum.....................	31.3	888.9	2666.2	680.6	390.5
D. Maximize earnings of underdeveloped countries, all currencies					
Average......................	16.3	802.7	1822.6	603.9	372.8
Minimum.....................	7.7	727.3	1020.6	438.6	191.3
Maximum.....................	31.3	866.5	2666.2	957.9	627.1
E. Maximize U. S. exports					
Average......................	11.6	821.9	1249.9	358.3	553.0
Minimum.....................	5.7	744.8	1020.6	65.4	494.5
Maximum.....................	20.9	861.0	1522.4	957.9	627.1

[a] Sources: Column 1 based on Appendix Table B.2, Column 5; Column 2 based on Table 5.1, Column 2; Column 3 based on Appendix Table F.3, Column 6; Column 4 based on Appendix Table F.4, Column 6; Column 5 based on Appendix Table E.3, Column 2; Column 6 based on Table 9.1, Column 5; Column 7 based on Table 3.2, Column 1; Column 8 based on Appendix Table F.1, Line 2; Column 9 based on Appendix Table F.1, Line 44; Column 10 based on Table 9.1, Column 6; Column 11 based on Table 5.1, Column 2, and Table 3.2, Column 1; Column 12 based on *Employment and Output in Protected Manufacturing Industries,* by Beatrice N. Vaccara, (Brookings Institution, 1960), Table A.7, pp. 89–97, (Col. 10); Column 13 based on Appendix Table B.2, Column 2; Column 14 based on Appendix Table B.2, Column 4.

11.2

Liberalization Programs with Different Objectives[a]

imports at 1953 domestic prices)

	Employment Effects (Number of employees, farmers, and unpaid farm family workers, or percentages)					Average Annual Percentage Change in Employment 1947-54	Value of 1953 Domestic Output (In millions)	1953 Imports as Percentage of 1953 Domestic Output
Net Decrease in All Industries[c]	Gross Decrease		Percentage of Gross Decrease in Liberalized Industry	Total Increase as Percentage of Gross Decrease	Gross Decrease in All Industries per Billion Dollars Net Increase in Foreign Dollar Earnings			
	In All Industries	In Liberalized Industries						
(6)	(7)	(8)	(9)	(10)	(11)	(12)	(13)	(14)
80.85	116.34	66.76	55.5	34.3	149.72	0.7	1892.3	3.8
−5.03	51.15	16.90	22.6	9.3	59.90	−8.9	32.7	e
174.63	224.45	193.63	86.3	109.8	301.36	22.7	17626.3	48.0
111.02	130.92	83.36	62.1	16.9	191.00	−0.3	1589.3	4.0
34.88	69.99	35.19	41.3	9.3	95.00	−3.8	32.7	e
174.63	195.41	163.22	86.2	50.2	276.60	4.4	6695.8	17.8
67.86	113.63	58.19	50.2	43.8	132.03	0.3	2796.0	5.4
−5.03	51.15	16.90	26.2	19.7	59.90	−8.9	135.6	e
103.67	164.85	128.35	78.0	109.8	193.85	9.4	17626.3	48.0
93.46	123.36	61.79	49.4	27.4	149.70	−1.0	2088.5	2.6
21.38	54.27	25.49	26.2	10.7	65.35	−8.9	135.8	e
154.11	178.58	170.50	78.0	60.6	212.77	2.7	17626.3	15.4
78.05	120.83	72.51	58.2	42.6	151.67	−1.6	2651.1	5.2
−2.95	54.27	20.58	26.2	13.7	65.35	−8.9	135.8	e
154.11	224.45	193.63	86.3	104.4	301.36	2.8	17626.3	35.2
46.19	110.60	63.03	51.6	68.0	135.92	0.6	1901.3	1.0
−5.03	51.15	16.90	22.6	33.6	59.90	−3.2	135.6	e
148.97	224.45	193.63	86.3	109.8	301.36	13.4	6083.5	48.0

[b] The industries appropriate to each type of program are indicated in Table 11.1.
[c] Positive figures represent net decreases and negative figures represent net increases.
[d] This type of program reduces protection of industries with duties averaging 25 per cent or more.
[e] Less than .05 per cent.

255

Employment Effects of Different Types
of Liberalization Programs

We may compare the employment effects of different types of programs first from the point of view of net effects, this being the employment effect most closely related to the general level of economic activity. Measured by the "average" effect of the programs within each type, the differences among the various types of program are great. Programs of Type A, designed to reduce tariffs in industries where they average 25 per cent or more, would be likely to cause the largest net decreases of employment. Import increases with a 1953 domestic value of a million dollars and consisting in equal parts of products similar to each of its eligible industries would cause a net employment decrease of 111 employees. (See Column 6 of Table 11.2.) As might be expected, programs designed to increase exports (Type E) are at the other extreme. For them, the net decreases average 46 employees per million-dollar increase of imports. There is not much overlapping, moreover. Only one industry eligible for Type A programs causes a smaller net employment decrease than the average net decrease for Type E programs, and only one industry included in Type E programs causes net decreases exceeding the average for Type A programs. In some programs of Type E (as well as in some of Types B and D), employment would increase on balance.

Most of the differences between the net employment effects of the five types of program result from the differences among them in generating increases of employment. In causing gross decreases of employment, they would not be likely to differ very much.[7] Their average gross decreases range between 131 employees per million-dollar increase in imports for Type A programs and 111 employees for Type E programs. (See Column 7 of Table 11.2.) The range of possible variation in gross decreases among the many possible programs of a given type is very large for all five types; for

---

[7] It was found that the amount of the gross decrease of employment in all industries per million-dollar import increase has a correlation of .39 with the average level of duties protecting the liberalized industry.

each type it covers almost the whole range of effects found among the 72 industries analyzed.

The various types of program are likely to differ more in their effects on gross decreases of employment in the liberalized industries than in their effects on total gross decreases. The average effect on liberalized industries ranges from a high of 83 employees for million-dollar programs of Type A to a low of 58 employees for programs of Type B. (See Column 8 of Table 11.2.) There is an even greater range in their maximum effects. The maximum possible gross decrease in the liberalized industry under Type B programs is only 128 employees and under Type C programs is only 133 employees. This contrasts with possible maxima of 194 employees for both Types D and E.

We may also draw a number of significant conclusions that are independent of the amount of the total import increases. One is the extent to which the gross decreases of employment are concentrated in the liberalized industries, which may be relevant to the geographical location of the effects or to proposals for government or industry action to alleviate hardship. This is shown in Column 9 of Table 11.2.[8] The average of such concentration is highest in programs of Type A, where it is 62 per cent, and lowest in Types B and C, where it is approximately 50 per cent. The minimum concentration in the liberalized industry for Type A programs, moreover, is 41 per cent, which is much higher than the minimum for any other type.

We can also compare the percentages of gross decreases in employment that are offset by increases, which are shown in Column 10 of Table 11.2. Judging by the percentages for programs of "average" composition, this is likely to be much higher in programs of Type E than in those of any other type. This general result is to be expected, since Type E programs were selected to maximize increases in exports. Under no Type E program would less than one third of the gross employment decrease be offset by employment increases. At the other extreme, the likelihood of such offsetting increases is smallest in Type A programs, for which the average offset is only 17 per cent.

[8] The percentage distribution of all employment effects among all industry groups can also be calculated from the estimates presented in Tables 3.3 and 5.2 and Appendix Tables F.1 and F.2.

We may also compare the programs from the point of view of their gross decreases in employment per million dollars of net increase in foreign dollar earnings. (See Column 11 of Table 11.2.) The gross employment decreases associated with increasing foreign dollar earnings is likely to be lowest in programs of Types B and E, those designed to maximize, respectively, foreign dollar earnings and United States exports per million dollars of import increases. The gross employment decreases for such programs average 132 and 136 employees per million dollars net increase in foreign dollar earnings. In contrast, the highest employment decrease associated with given increases of foreign dollar earnings would be likely to occur in programs of Type A, where the average gross decrease is 191 employees per million dollars net increase of foreign dollar earnings.

Perhaps more significant than any of these conclusions, however, is one implied by the wide range of effects on employment of the specific programs within each type. For some types the possible range of some effects is nearly as wide as it is for all of the 72 cases analyzed. This fact implies that even when the choice of industries to be liberalized is restricted to those that best serve a single objective, the employment effects still depend largely on the choice of specific industries to be liberalized.

CHAPTER 12

The Employment Effects in Perspective

THIS BOOK BEGAN with a warning that the effects on aggregate employment are not a good criterion for determining the *level* of import barriers that should be maintained in the long run. The premise underlying this statement is not that the level of employment is unimportant but that in the long run the level of import barriers need not affect it. The economic importance of the continuing level of these barriers lies in its effect on how efficiently resources are allocated among different kinds of output and thus on the amount of real income obtained from a given level of employment.

The process of *changing* import barriers from one level to another, however, generally does have an immediate effect on the level of employment. When the demand for labor is not already excessive, reductions in these barriers cause unemployment. But such unemployment need not persist. Its very existence creates some market pressures that *tend* to restore maximum employment. Moreover, government has the power to encourage these restorative forces, to supplement them, and to discourage forces that cause unemployment to cumulate or persist. If appropriate policies are pursued, therefore, even reductions in import barriers need not involve unemployment in the long run.

Employment effects are nevertheless relevant to decisions regarding changes in import barriers because of their short-run implications. Even apart from the loss of production that occurs when the labor released is not quickly absorbed into new employment, a society that accepts the idea that the welfare of individuals is a legitimate concern of government cannot, consistently with this acceptance, ignore injury that results from governmental action. Such injury is a cost of attaining the benefits expected from these changes. The transitional effects on employment are therefore a factor to be taken into account in deciding whether to make

changes in import barriers, and, when the balance of all considerations indicates that such changes are desirable, they are
relevant to decisions about how the changes should be made. The
findings of this study concerning employment effects are among
the tools needed to evaluate these costs of changing import barriers.

Policy Significance of Different Types of Employment Effects

Before discussing the significance of the employment estimates
presented in this study, we must distinguish the ways in which the
different employment effects are relevant to policy.

First, there are the effects of liberalization on total national
production and employment resulting from its impact on the
aggregate demand for goods and services. These effects, and the
associated effects on profits, are relevant to the question of whether
liberalization would restrain or depress general business activity
and the price level, and, if so, how much. To estimate this influence requires estimating the stimulating as well as the depressing
effects and striking a balance between them. To this concept, the
estimates of total net employment effect are the most relevant of
the estimates presented, for they take account of the stimulating
domestic effects of exports and of the process of shipping additional imports, as well as the depressing effects of intensified
foreign competition on the products whose protection is reduced.
Estimates of net effects, if applied to specified increases of imports,
can be used to judge how much employment needs to be stimulated by other means—whether they are public policy measures
or "natural" market forces—in order to restore the level of employment that would have existed in the absence of liberalization.

Second are the effects of liberalization on the industries whose
protection is reduced and on the communities in which they are
located. Most relevant to these effects are the estimates of net employment changes in the liberalized industry.

Third, if one is concerned with the hardship that may be felt
by individual employees who are displaced when protection is

reduced, the estimates of *gross* employment decreases are the most relevant. We have seen that the employment decreases associated with liberalization, although generally much larger in the liberalized industry than in any other industry, are not confined to it and, in fact, may be large in industries that are direct suppliers of the liberalized industry. To a broad view of the displacement problem, therefore, the estimates of gross decreases of employment in all industries are the most relevant.

The problems of hardship and dislocation are more likely to be serious in the liberalized industry than in other industries, however, because the liberalized industries are less likely than the non-liberalized industries to benefit from the stimulating employment effects of other economic influences such as export increases and general economic growth.[1] Hardship in the liberalized industry is therefore not likely to be averted and may not even be mitigated by expansion of general economic activity. That is why it may be desirable, if import barriers are reduced, to adopt special policy measures, such as adjustment assistance programs, to handle their displacement problem. In forming judgments about the appropriate size of such measures or, more generally, about the portion of displacement that is most likely to present an acute problem, the estimates of gross employment decreases in the liberalized industry are most useful.

To put the estimates of these different employment effects of liberalization in perspective, we may compare them with other corresponding magnitudes in the United States economy. Since these effects have had to be expressed in relation to the volume of import increases that cause them, the comparisons require that we either assume a certain import increase and compare its employment effects with other employment changes or choose specific amounts of employment effects and find what import increases would be required to cause them. Both approaches are useful. In applying them, we shall assume that the estimates of employment

[1] The statement that the liberalized industries are less likely to benefit from export increases is based on the general presumption that firms which have protection against imports do not produce much directly for export. The conclusion about growth is based on the findings of a recent study by Beatrice N. Vaccara, *Employment and Output in Protected Manufacturing Industries* (Brookings Institution, 1960), which indicates that while not all protected manufactured industries have had postwar declines in employment, the industries in which the largest proportions of output are protected and that faced import competition despite their protection were generally laggard in growth between 1947 and 1954.

effects per million dollar increase of imports are valid for import increases of any amount with which we are likely to be concerned. Thus, the employment effects of a billion dollar increase in a specified basket of imports are considered to be one thousand times those of a million-dollar increase in such imports.[2]

Net Employment Effects in Perspective

Since the net short-term effect of import liberalization is generally to decrease employment, it may be compared with the net decreases of employment that have occurred in postwar cyclical recessions. We can also regard this net effect of import liberalization as indicating the amount of expansion in the demand for labor that would be required to offset it. From that point of view, it may be compared with the expansion in the demand for labor that is required in any case to maintain high levels of employment in the face of increases in both output per man and in the labor force.

Comparison with Cyclical Changes in Employment

In comparing the net employment effects of liberalization with the net changes in civilian employment that have occurred in postwar business recessions, we should recall that the estimates of the employment effects of import liberalization measure only its primary effects; they do not include such further effects on employment as may be induced by the changes of income that result from these primary decreases of output and employment. The cyclical decreases of employment, however, represent the net effects on employment of all that happened during the postwar recessions, including, on the one hand, the income-induced effects of the primary decreases that caused the recessions and, on the other hand, the primary and income-induced effects of influences that mitigated them.

[2] It is recognized that this assumption has only limited validity.

We may take the net employment effect of a liberalization program that displaces the output of many different industries to be
represented by the median effect of the 72 single-industry liberalizations. A diversified increase of imports valued at a billion dollars at domestic ports in 1953 would cause a net decrease of 86,000
employees. (An import increase of this size would be approximately one sixth of total dutiable imports in 1953 and probably
about one eleventh of those in 1959.) Such a decrease is one eighth
of one per cent of civilian employment in 1959. The decreases in
employment between the peaks and troughs of employment accompanying the three postwar recessions varied between 3.0 and
3.5 per cent of the respective employment peaks.[3] Evidently the
average net decrease in employment that would result from an
increase in imports valued at a billion dollars in 1953 prices is less
than one twentieth of the smallest cyclical decrease in employment
that has occurred in any of the recessions since World War II.

An alternative way of putting the estimates of employment
effects into perspective is to ask: How large a diversified increase
of imports due to liberalization would have to occur to cause a
net decrease in civilian employment of, say, one per cent of the
1959 level, *i.e.*, a decrease of 656,000 employees? The answer is:
An increase of 7.6 billion dollars, valued in 1953 domestic prices.
This figure exceeds by many times the increase in imports contemplated by any measure that has been officially proposed or that
is possible under the present Trade Agreements Act.[4]

---

[3] Employment levels, seasonally adjusted and expressed in millions, and their
percentage decreases, were as follows:

Peak	Trough	Percentage Decrease
60.0 (July 1948)	58.1 (July 1949)	3.2
62.6 (March 1953)	60.4 (July 1954)	3.5
65.6 (July 1957)	63.6 (July 1958)	3.0

The employment figures are the revised seasonally adjusted estimates of the
Bureau of Labor Statistics, made available in mimeographed tables dated March
1960. They have been adjusted by the B.L.S. for comparability with the definitions of employment and unemployment adopted in January 1957.

[4] The largest possible net decrease of employment per billion-dollar import increase is 175,000 employees and could result only from an increase of imports concentrated entirely on the apparel industry. Because it assumes that the liberalization occurs entirely in the one industry where it would cause the maximum net
decrease of employment, this theoretical maximum far exceeds any practical
maximum. On that unrealistic assumption, the net decrease in employment caused
by a billion-dollar program would be less than one tenth of the smallest postwar
cyclical decrease and an even smaller percentage of its 1959 equivalent. The im-

These conclusions are based on the estimates of net employment effects derived from the judgments described in Chapter 8 about the reactions of individual foreign countries to increased earnings. On the assumption, considered in Chapter 10, that exports would increase in all cases of liberalization by the full amount of the net increase in foreign dollar earnings, the net decrease of employment would be 29,000. This decrease would be less than one twentieth of 1 per cent of 1959 civilian employment, a percentage decline that would be 1½ per cent of the smallest cyclical decrease in employment that has occurred in the postwar period. The increase in imports required to cause a net decrease of employment equal to 1 per cent of the 1959 level would exceed $22 billion, valued in 1953 domestic prices.

Comparison with Employment
Implications of Economic Growth

To offset net decreases of employment, expansion of markets would be required. The need for expansion is, of course, an ever-present one for an economy in which the labor force and output per man are both increasing. The maintenance of full employment in such an economy requires expansion year after year. Whatever expansion of markets is required to offset the employment decreases caused by liberalization, therefore, merely increases the amount of a need that already exists. In contrast to the expansion required by growth, moreover, decreases of employment caused by reductions of import barriers occur only once, when the barriers are reduced.

Considering the once-and-for-all expansion required to offset the net employment effects of a diversified liberalization program that increases imports by a billion dollars in 1953 domestic prices, we may ask the question: How does this expansion compare with the annual expansion required by growth?

Since we have already measured the net employment effects of such a liberalization program, we need only estimate the job increases normally required to employ additions to the labor

---

port increase in that industry required to cause a net decrease in employment of 1 per cent of the 1959 level would have to exceed 3.7 billion dollars in 1953 prices.

force and people released by increases in output per man. For present purposes we may neglect the expansion of employment that would be required to absorb unemployment in excess of some "necessary" or irreducible minimum. We also neglect the expansion required to absorb workers employed in producing goods, such as surplus farm products, and services for which there is no demand at prices that cover costs of production, although a rational economic policy calls for expansion to absorb these workers, too. We may therefore work from a base representing what civilian employment would have been in 1959 if unemployment had been no higher than, say, 4 per cent of the civilian labor force, this being the highest of the figures widely regarded as an acceptable minimum. This definition of "full employment" implied civilian employment of 66.6 million in 1959.

Increases in output per man in civilian employment between the 1955-1957 average and 1965 have been projected by the National Planning Association at an average rate of 2.3 per cent a year.[5] Assuming that this change will occur in each year and applying it to the "full" civilian employment figure of 66.6 million for 1959, we find that employment of 65.1 million will suffice in 1960 to produce the same quantity of output that could have been produced by 66.6 million people in 1959. Thus, 1.5 million more jobs will have to be created merely to offset the net effects of one normal year's change in average output per man with no change in the labor force. The labor force, however, is likely to expand by approximately 1.0 million from 1959 to 1960. Adding these two changes, we find that the total expansion of job opportunities required to maintain maximum employment in the face of these two changes alone will be approximately 2.5 million.[6] To allow for the effects on employment of income-induced changes of expenditure, we may assume that a specified expansion in total em-

[5] This is the net result of a projected average increase of 2.9 per cent a year in total output per civilian man-hour and a projected average decrease of 0.6 per cent a year in hours worked per man. The sources of the projections used in this section, an intermediate one of several alternative projections by The National Planning Association, are given in Appendix Table G.4.

[6] The amount of the annual increases required by these two elements of growth will increase over time even if the percentage changes in output per man are constant, both because growth in the labor force will cause constant percentage changes in output per man to release a growing number of men and because the annual growth of the labor force itself probably will far exceed 1.0 million from

ployment can be obtained by a primary expansion of approximately 40 per cent of the specified total expansion. On that assumption an expansion of 2.5 million in total employment can be obtained by a primary expansion of 1.0 million.

This is the figure with which the net employment effects of a billion dollar liberalization program may be compared. We found the median net effect of such a program would be to release 86,000 employees. Thus, such a program would have the effect of raising the needed annual primary expansion of employment by 8.6 per cent or from 1.0 million to less than 1.1 million, and doing so for only one year.[7]

It thus seems clear that, from the point of view of its effect on the economy as a whole, the problem created by increases of imports resulting from a reduction of import barriers would add relatively little to the problem—if it is a problem—created by normal growth of the labor force and rising output per man. If we solve the "growth problem," the effects of import liberalization on the level of employment cannot be significant for the economy as a whole.

Gross Employment Decreases in Perspective

The conclusion that decreases of employment caused by liberalization cannot be significant for the economy as a whole of course does not imply that they do not involve a substantial problem of finding jobs for the individuals who are displaced. If markets do

---

1962 until at least 1975. (See Gertrude Bancroft, *The American Labor Force: Its Growth and Changing Composition*, the Census monograph series (John Wiley and Sons, Inc., 1958), p. 145, and U. S. Department of Labor, *Population and Labor Force Projections for the United States, 1960 to 1975*, Bulletin No. 1242, 1959, especially Table 10.) Thus, the absolute amount of expansion required by growth will increase persistently, although perhaps not steadily.

[7] It should be noted that these estimates of the net decreases of employment assume export increases that are much less than the net increases of foreign dollar earnings. On the alternative assumption that exports increase by as much as the net increase in foreign dollar earnings, diversified liberalization would, for one year, add approximately 2.9 per cent to the job expansion required to maintain maximum employment.

expand sufficiently to keep up with the increasing output per man of an increasing labor force, the expansion does not necessarily solve the problems of the industries and localities in which the displacement occurs, particularly those that are directly affected. They may not participate in the general expansion.

Comparison with Technological Improvement

In this respect the dislocations resulting from import liberalization do not differ from those resulting from improvements in productive techniques. The average decreases in labor requirements per unit of output for the economy as a whole that result from such improvements are not distributed uniformly over industry but reflect substantial reductions in some industries and very small reductions or none at all in others. General expansion of markets benefits the labor and capital that is displaced by such increases in productivity because it increases the alternative employment opportunities available to them, but it does not prevent their displacement if the industries that employ them do not participate in the general expansion. Similarly, a reduction of import barriers may reduce employment in producing an import-competing commodity below what it was before if there is little or no growth in the demand for it. Both types of change create the opportunity, when the resources displaced can be absorbed elsewhere, to attain a higher output or more leisure; neither contains any guaranty that the opportunity will be used instead of being dissipated in involuntary unemployment.[8] If the industry affected is an expanding one, both technological

[8] The effects of improvements in productive techniques and of reductions in trade barriers are similar in that they may be regarded as two different ways of increasing national income per person employed. The late Professor A. C. Pigou pointed out the similarity long ago in his classic work *The Economics of Welfare*. In discussing the effects of inventions or improvements in processes or methods on the size and distribution of the national income he said: "It is interesting to observe that exactly the same analysis is appropriate when the initiating cause is, not an invention in the ordinary sense, but a development which enables a country to obtain some commodity more cheaply than before by making something else with which to purchase it from elsewhere, instead of making the commodity itself. Here too more of what people want is made available; and here too the proportionate parts played by labour and capital in production may be changed." (1st ed. Macmillan and Co. Ltd., London, 1920, pp. 716-17.)

change and import liberalization may not cause any actual displacement but only a relative one; they may merely cause employment to be lower than it would otherwise have been at the expanded level of output without causing it to be lower than it was before they occurred.

In the probability that their displacement effects will be offset by growth, the two types of change do differ. Technological improvement itself often gives some impetus to growth of an industry's output because it lowers costs and thereby permits price reductions or because it improves the product. Import liberalization, although it may stimulate price reductions and improvement of products, does not ordinarily induce growth of the liberalized industry's domestic output. Moreover, technological improvements appear to occur most frequently in industries that are expanding independently of the improvements. A recent study shows that, at least in 1947 to 1954, protected industries that also had sizable import competition generally had declining employment.[9] Consequently, it cannot be assumed that growth will prevent employees in these industries from being displaced by liberalization, although growth in the economy as a whole will certainly alleviate the adjustment problems of many of them.

Comparison with Normal Turnover

As we have already noted, the problem of displacement is best measured by gross decreases of employment. The most appropriate magnitude with which to compare these decreases in order to put them in perspective is the number of different people who have been unemployed at some time during a year of high employment. Estimates of their number show that even in 1955 and 1956, years that were free of recession and important strikes, 9.8 and 8.8 million different persons who had worked during the year were

[9] See *Employment and Output in Protected Manufacturing Industries* by Beatrice N. Vaccara (Brookings Institution, 1960). That study examines the relation between the extent and degree of protection of manufacturing industries in 1954 and their average annual changes in employment and production between 1947 and 1954. It should be noted that the finding cited above does not apply to protected manufacturing industries that did not have sizable import competition. In Mrs. Vaccara's study, protected manufacturing industries are those with at least 75 per cent of output protected by tariff duties having ad valorem equivalents of 10 per cent or more in 1954. Industries considered import-competing are those for which imports of corresponding commodities equaled or exceeded 5 per cent of domestic output in 1954.

unemployed or "on layoff" at some time during the year.[10] Since 1955 and 1956 were both good years, these figures are apparently not abnormally high. They indicate that it is usual for a large number of people—approximately one for every eight—who work at some time during a year to be out of a job and looking for one some time during that year. Projecting the number of such people on the basis of their relationship to the civilian labor force, we get 10 million as an estimate of the minimum number of different persons who will work but will be unemployed or laid off at some time during a normal future year.

The other side of this picture is that vacancies are constantly being created by discharges, retirements, deaths, and voluntary withdrawals from the labor force as well as by the creation of new jobs. In relation to the 10 million or more vacancies that will be normally required to absorb these people, the additional vacancies that would be required to absorb the median of 115,000 employees who could be displaced by a diversified billion-dollar increase of imports is little more than 1 per cent.

Finally, to get perspective on the magnitude of displacement in the liberalized industries, we may compare the displacement in them caused by liberalization with the number who leave them in a normal year for reasons other than discharge or layoff. This comparison is of interest because the number leaving for other reasons gives some indication of how fast an industry could shrink in response to increased import competition without laying employees off by merely failing to replace those who leave otherwise.

For 68 of the 72 industries analyzed, we can estimate, although only crudely, the annual number of such separations associated with their 1959 levels of employment on the assumption that those who leave are not replaced. We can, therefore, compute the maximum increase of imports that could occur without causing gross decreases of employment in the liberalized industry to exceed such separations from it.[11]

---

[10] These figures include a relatively small proportion of people who were laid off with instructions to return to work within 30 days and were presumably not looking for work. Their number is not available separately. The figures exclude 880,000 people in 1955 and 1 million in 1956 who did not work during the year but were looking for work. The figures, based on annual surveys begun in 1955, are taken from the report on "Work Experience of the Population in 1957," Current Population Reports, Labor Force, Series P-50, No. 86, by the U. S. Bureau of the Census (September 1958), Table J.

[11] See Appendix Table G.5 for the sources and methods of these estimates.

Such a computation shows that for 14 of the 72 industries this maximum level of import increases is less than $50 million per year at 1953 domestic prices. Among these industries are some of those that have been most vigorous either in opposing tariff reductions or requesting increased protection from imports—lead and zinc, pottery and related products, cutlery, motorcycles and bicycles, watches and clocks, musical instruments and parts, and toys and sporting goods.

For another 31 industries, this maximum level is between $50 and $200 million a year. There are 3 industries—apparel, passenger cars and light trucks, and aircraft and parts—for which imports of the corresponding products could increase by $1¼ billion or more without causing gross displacement in them that exceeds the number of these employee separations in a normal year.

These comparisons are intended to put the estimates of the employment effects of import liberalization in perspective. They suggest that the domestic employment decreases that would result from a program of import liberalization—even one drastic enough to cause an increase of competitive imports of several billion dollars—would not be large enough to have a serious dislocating effect on the economy of the nation as a whole. They would be far smaller than the employment decreases that result from many other economic changes that we have come to take for granted. Some of these other changes, such as the alternations between prosperity and minor recessions, are recognized as evils that we have apparently not yet learned to avoid. Others, such as technological improvements, are recognized as economically beneficial to the nation as a whole; the employment decreases incidental to them are regarded not as "displacement"—a word with unfavorable connotations—but as a "release" of labor that is no longer needed to produce the output previously produced by less economical methods and is thereby made available for other production, a release that adds to national income if the released labor is re-employed. Of these two types of change, decreases of import barriers are in the latter category. Like improvements in productivity, they provide the nation with the opportunity to have more goods and services for the same amount of work or the same goods and services and more leisure, in short the opportunity to attain a higher average standard of living, although they do not guarantee that we shall use the opportunity.

For the individuals and the industries affected, however, and where these industries are geographically concentrated, for individual localities, reductions of import barriers may cause decreases in the employment of labor and capital that are serious. This possibility is one that a nation concerned with individual hardship cannot dismiss lightly.

Even these difficulties, however, may be made less serious by proper management of liberalization itself and by measures to deal with the dislocations. If import barriers are reduced gradually, the gradual but persistent expansion of demand for the products of other industries that accompanies good economic management of a potentially growing economy provides alternative opportunities for the employment of labor and capital. In a growing economy, moreover, a gradual reduction of import barriers may involve only a relative and not an absolute contraction of some industries. Even where absolute contraction is required, it can often be accomplished gradually and without widespread injury to individual employees by failure to attract new entrants to replace workers who retire, die, or leave in the normal course of events. Beyond the exercise of skill in managing liberalization with the already available tools is the possibility of new measures to assist labor and capital in transferring to other industries or localities when such transfer is believed to be necessary.

It is outside the scope of this study to analyze the potential long-run effects of liberalization on the size of real national income, its distribution and other effects, to analyze the possible measures for reducing its undesirable transitional effects, or to balance the costs and benefits of these effects and measures against each other. To answer these questions of public policy would require research on matters not considered in this study, such as the geographical concentration of dislocations, to name only one, and the balancing of conflicting interests. Any answer to these larger questions, however, must include answers to the questions analyzed in this study.

Appendices

Code Numbers of Industries and Their Classification in 40-Order Industry Groups[a]

Industry
Code
Number   *Industry Group and Industry*

1–10   Agriculture, forestry and fishing
1............   Meat animals and products
2............   Poultry and eggs
3............   Farm dairy products
4............   Food grains and feed crops
5............   Cotton
6............   Tobacco
7............   Oil-bearing crops
8............   Vegetables and fruits
9............   All other agricultural (tree nuts, legumes and grass seeds,
                   sugar and syrup crops, miscellaneous crops, forest products,
                   greenhouse and nursery products, and agricultural services)
10..........   Fisheries, hunting and trapping

11–15   Metal mining
11............   Iron ore mining
12............   Copper mining
13..........   Lead and zinc mining
14..........   Bauxite mining
15..........   Other metal mining (gold and silver and ferro-alloy ores)

16   Coal mining

17   Crude petroleum and natural gas

18–20   Other nonmetallic minerals
18..........   Stone, sand, clay and abrasives
19..........   Sulfur
20..........   Other nonmetallic minerals (chemical and fertilizing mineral
                   mining, fluorspar, phosphate rock, rock salt, and miscellaneous
                   nonmetallic minerals)

21–28   Processed foods and alcoholic beverages
21..........   Meat packing and wholesale poultry
22..........   Processed dairy products
23..........   Canning, preserving and freezing
24..........   Grain mill products
25..........   Bakery products

[a] Industry titles are from "Industry Classification List—Mobilization Model," Bureau of Labor Statistics, Division of Interindustry Economics, May 13, 1953. (Mimeo.)

Appendix A (*continued*)

Industry Code Number	Industry Group and Industry
26..........	Miscellaneous food products (confectionery products, chocolate-cocoa products, chewing gum, bottled soft drinks, liquid, frozen and dried eggs, leavening compounds, shortening and cooking oils, oleomargarine, corn products, flavorings, vinegar and cider, manufactured ice, macaroni and spaghetti, food preparations, miscellaneous)
27..........	Sugar
28..........	Alcoholic beverages
29	Tobacco manufactures
30	Spinning, weaving and dyeing
34	Apparel
31–33, 35	All other textile products
31..........	Special textile products (carpets and rugs, miscellaneous felt goods, lace goods, paddings and upholstery filling, processed textile waste, miscellaneous textile goods)
32..........	Jute, linen, cordage and twine
33..........	Canvas products
35..........	House furnishings and other non-apparel (hard-surface floor covering, coated fabrics, curtains and draperies, miscellaneous housefurnishings, textile bags, fabricated textile products, n.e.c.)
36–43	Lumber, wood products and furniture
36..........	Logging
37..........	Sawmills, planing and veneer mills
38..........	Plywood
39..........	Fabricated wood products (millwork, prefabricated wood products, lasts and related products, mirror and picture frames, wood products, miscellaneous)
40..........	Wood containers and cooperage
41..........	Wood furniture
42..........	Metal furniture
43..........	Partitions, screens, shades, etc.
44–46	Pulp, paper, and paper products
44..........	Pulp mills
45..........	Paper and board mills
46..........	Converted paper products
47	Printing and publishing
48–50, 53	Industrial chemicals (except synthetic rubber and fiber)
48.1	Sulfuric acid
48.2	Other inorganic chemicals, excluding alumina
49..........	Industrial organic chemicals
50..........	Plastics materials
53..........	Explosives and fireworks

Appendix A (*continued*)

Industry Code Number	*Industry Group and Industry*
51–52	Synthetic rubber and synthetic fiber
51	Synthetic rubber
52	Synthetic fiber
54–61	All other chemicals and allied products
54	Drugs and medicines
55	Soap and related products
56	Paints and allied products
57	Gum and wood chemicals
58	Fertilizers
59	Vegetable oils
60	Animal oils
61	Miscellaneous chemical industries (printing ink, essential oils, toilet preparations, glue and gelatin, carbon black, compressed and liquefied gas, insecticides, salt, chemical products, n.e.c.)
62–64	Products of petroleum and coal
62	Petroleum products
63	Coke and products
64	Paving and roofing materials
65–66	Tires, inner tubes, and miscellaneous rubber products
65	Tires and inner tubes
66	Miscellaneous rubber products (rubber footwear, reclaimed rubber, rubber industries, n.e.c.)
67–69	Leather and products and footwear (excluding rubber)
67	Leather tanning and finishing
68	Other leather products (industrial leather belting, leather gloves, luggage, handbags and purses, small leather goods, saddlery, harness and whips, miscellaneous leather goods)
69	Footwear (excluding rubber)
70	Glass
73	Pottery and related products
71, 72, 74–77	Stone and clay products
71	Cement
72	Structural clay products
74	Concrete and plaster products
75	Abrasive products
76	Asbestos products
77	Other miscellaneous nonmetallic minerals (graphite and statuary goods, minerals, ground or treated, and non-clay refractories)
78–81, 92	Iron and steel and their primary products
78	Blast furnaces
79.1	Carbon steel works and rolling mills
79.2	Alloy steel works and rolling mills, except stainless

Appendix A (*continued*)

Industry Code Number	Industry Group and Industry
79.3	Stainless steel works and rolling mills
79.4	Nonferrous forgings and metal powders
80..........	Iron foundries
81..........	Steel foundries
92..........	Iron and steel forgings
82–91.4	Nonferrous metals and their primary products
82..........	Primary copper
83..........	Copper rolling and drawing
84..........	Primary lead
85..........	Primary zinc
86..........	Primary metals, n.e.c.
87..........	Nonferrous metal rolling, n.e.c.
88..........	Primary aluminum, including alumina
89..........	Aluminum rolling and drawing
90..........	Secondary nonferrous metals
91.1	Copper foundries
91.2	Aluminum foundries
91.3	Magnesium foundries
91.4	Other nonferrous foundries
93–109	Fabricated metal products
93..........	Tin cans and other tinware
94..........	Cutlery
95..........	Tools and general hardware
96..........	Hardware, n.e.c.
97..........	Metal plumbing and vitreous fixtures
98..........	Heating equipment
99..........	Structural metal products
100.1	Boiler shop products
100.2	Fabricated pipe
101..........	Metal stampings
102..........	Metal coating and engraving
103..........	Lighting fixtures
104..........	Fabricated wire products
105..........	Metal barrels, drums, etc.
106..........	Tubes and foils
107..........	Miscellaneous fabricated metal products
108..........	Steel springs
109..........	Nuts, bolts, and screw machine products
110–128	Machinery, except electrical
110..........	Steam engines and turbines
111..........	Internal combustion engines
112..........	Farm and industrial tractors
113..........	Farm equipment
114..........	Construction and mining machinery
115..........	Oil-field machinery and tools
116..........	Machine tools and metalworking machinery
117..........	Cutting tools, jigs and fixtures
118..........	Special industrial machinery (food products machinery, textile

Appendix A (*continued*)

Appendix A (*continued*)

Industry Code Number	Industry Group and Industry
150.........	Locomotives
151.........	Railroad equipment
152.........	Motorcycles and bicycles
153–156	Instruments, optical and photographic equipment, watches and clocks
153.........	Instruments, etc. (laboratory, scientific, and engineering instruments, mechanical measuring and controlling instruments)
154.........	Optical, ophthalmic, and photographic equipment
155.........	Medical and dental instruments and supplies
156.........	Watches and clocks
157–164	Miscellaneous manufactures
157.........	Jewelry and silverware
158.........	Musical instruments and parts
159.........	Toys and sporting goods
160.........	Office supplies
161.........	Plastic products
162.........	Cork products
163.........	Motion picture production
164.........	Miscellaneous manufactured products (phonograph records, artificial flowers, buttons, needles, pins and fasteners, brooms and brushes, matches, candles, jewelry and instrument cases, lamp shades, morticians' goods, signs and advertising displays, hair work, umbrellas, parasols, and canes, tobacco pipes, models and patterns, miscellaneous products, n.e.c.)
167–168	Electric light and power, and gas
167.........	Electric light and power
168.........	Natural, manufactured and mixed gas
169	Railroad transportation
169.1	Railroad freight activity
169.2	Railroad passenger activity
172	Ocean transportation
170, 171, 173– 175, 178	Transportation (except railroad and ocean transportation) and allied services
170.........	Trucking
171.........	Warehousing and storage
173.........	Other water transportation
174.........	Air transportation
175.........	Pipeline transportation
178.........	Local and highway transportation
176–177	Wholesale and retail trade
176.........	Wholesale trade
177.........	Retail trade

Appendix A (*continued*)

Industry
Code
Number   *Industry Group and Industry*

179, 181, 186 and
187   Communications, finance, and business services
   179.......... Telephone and telegraph
   181.......... Banking, finance, and insurance
   186.......... Advertising, including radio and television
   187.......... Business services (credit and collection agencies, building main-
               tenance services, miscellaneous business services, wholesale
               sales offices and agents)

188–189   Auto and other repair services
   188.......... Auto repair services and garages
   189.......... Other repair services (electrical repair shops, watch, clock and
               jewelry repair, armature rewinding shops, miscellaneous re-
               pair services)

182–185, 190–192   Other services
   182.......... Hotels
   183.......... Real estate and rentals
   184.......... Laundries and dry cleaning
   185.......... Other personal services (photographic studios, barber and
               beauty shops, shoe repair and hat cleaning, funeral services,
               pressing, alteration and garment repair, miscellaneous per-
               sonal services)
   190.......... Motion pictures and other amusements
   191.......... Medical, dental and other professional services (medical and
               health services, miscellaneous professional services, hospitals)
   192.......... Nonprofit institutions

Appendix Table B.1

Output, Imports, and Duties of Liberalized Industries and Accepted Subindustries

Code Number	Liberalized Industry Accepted Sub-Industry	Shipments of Accepted Commodities as Percentage of Total Shipments[a]	Estimated Value of 1953 Domestic Output of Accepted Commodities[b] (In millions of dollars)	Foreign Port Value of Imports of Accepted Commodities, 1953		Duties as Percentage of Foreign Port Value of Imports, 1953
				Millions of Dollars	Percentage of Estimated Domestic Output	
		(1)	(2)	(3)	(4)	(5)
1	Meat animals and products......	56.9	5757.9	201.4	3.5	12.3
	Meat animals................	56.2	5548.0	18.4	.3	12.1
	Other livestock and products...	99.0	209.9	183.0	83.3	18.9
8	Vegetables and fruits...........	69.0	2493.6	34.9	1.4	20.9
	Vegetables...................	97.1	2493.6	34.9	1.4	20.9
13	Lead and zinc mining...........	100.0	135.6	65.1	48.0	9.7
	Lead and zinc ores[c]...........	100.0	135.6	65.1	48.0	9.7
21	Meat packing and wholesale poultry........................	44.2	w.	9.9	.2	13.3
	Meat packing, wholesale......	65.3	w.	9.9	.2	13.3
22	Processed dairy products........	59.0	2081.9	26.8	1.3	13.6
	Creamery butter.............	100.0	1033.5	.1	*	10.0
	Natural cheese..............	86.7	442.7	25.3	5.7	18.0
	Concentrated milk...........	73.7	605.7	1.4	.2	15.4
24	Grain mill products.............	33.6	w.	.3	*	11.8
	Flour and meal..............	71.2	w.	.3	*	10.4
	Rice cleaning and polishing....	94.0	w.	*	*	18.6
27	Sugar.........................	94.5	1222.6	430.8	35.2	7.7
	Raw cane sugar..............	72.3	w.	5.7	5.8	6.3
	Cane sugar refining...........	97.9	w.	425.1	49.5	8.0
	Beet sugar..................	89.0	w.	—	—	—
28	Alcoholic beverages.............	82.6	2807.7	125.1	4.5	13.6
	Malt liquors.................	99.3	1938.7	7.2	.4	8.7
	Distilled liquors, except brandy	97.6	869.0	117.9	13.6	24.5
29	Tobacco manufactures..........	93.5	3186.9	84.9	2.7	28.0
	Cigarettes...................	100.0	w.	*	*	34.8
	Cigars......................	100.0	w.	2.8	.7	22.2
	Tobacco stemming and redrying	100.0	w.	82.1	7.1	19.9
30	Spinning, weaving, and dyeing...	73.3	6695.8	104.6	1.6	25.5
	Yarn mills, wool, except carpet.	75.0	254.0	6.9	2.7	24.6
	Woolen and worsted fabrics....	100.0	1386.0	46.8	3.4	35.0
	Thread mills.................	93.6	163.2	1.0	.6	10.8
	Yarn mills, cotton system.....	100.0	837.6	3.8	.4	18.6
	Cotton broad-woven fabrics....	88.0	2868.6	29.5	1 0	23.0
	Rayon and related broad-woven fabrics....................	79.0	1186.4	16.6	1.4	28.0
31	Special textile products.........	58.7	643.4	45.3	7.0	24.2
	Wool carpets and rugs........	84.0	w.	21.6	5.0	23.5
	Carpets and rugs, n.e.c.......	90.0	w.	12.0	8.8	17.1
	Lace goods..................	100.0	w.	11.7	16.5	43.4
34	Apparel.......................	48.9	5087.5	49.4	1.0	31.2
	Seamless hosiery mills.........	90.0	367.5	4.2	1.1	28.1
	Knit underwear mills.........	100.0	381.4	.1	*	30.1
	Knit fabric mills.............	100.0	369.5	.6	.2	26.6
	Fur-felt hats and hat bodies...	71.2	65.9	1.1	1.7	23.4
	Straw hats..................	100.0	w.	8.7	39.0	16.7

* Less than 0.05.

w. = Withheld to prevent inference of data not available for publication.

[a] The figures for accepted subindustries in this column represent the value of shipments in 1947, wherever produced, of accepted commodities primary to an accepted subindustry, expressed as a percentage of total shipments in 1947, wherever produced, of all commodities primary to that subindustry. The figures for liberalized industries represent the value of shipments of accepted commodities as a percentage of shipments of all commodities primary to all subindustries in an industry, whether accepted or rejected. Data for shipments on a commodity basis for any year after 1947 were not available when these percentages had to be calculated. Shipments data were used because sufficiently detailed data for output were not available, even for 1947.

[b] Estimated by multiplying total 1953 domestic output for a given subindustry, shown in Column 2 of Table D.1, by the percentage shown in Column 1 of this table. These estimates thus assume that the ratio of accepted to total output in 1953 was the same as the ratio of accepted to total shipments in 1947.

[c] This is the subindustry title used in Census of Manufactures. It covers the same output as the industry, the title of which comes from the BLS Interindustry Classification.

Code Number	Liberalized Industry Accepted Sub-Industry	Shipments of Accepted Commodities as Percentage of Total Shipments[a]	Estimated Value of 1953 Domestic Output of Accepted Commodities[b] (In millions of dollars)	Foreign Port Value of Imports of Accepted Commodities, 1953		Duties as Percentage of Foreign Port Value of Imports, 1953
				Millions of Dollars	Percentage of Estimated Domestic Output	
		(1)	(2)	(3)	(4)	(5)
	Men's dress shirts and nightwear	84.9	697.0	.1	*	24.5
	Women's and misses' outerwear	75.0	2419.4	15.2	.6	33.1
	Corsets and allied garments....	100.0	445.2	.2	*	29.4
	Millinery....................	90.0	151.1	1.8	1.2	57.5
	Suspenders and garters........	90.0	w.	*	*	17.5
	Leather and sheep-lined clothing	80.7	w.	.1	.2	17.3
	Handkerchiefs..............	100.0	44.8	15.8	35.3	29.1
	Schiffli-machine embroideries...	50.0	21.8	1.3	6.0	53.7
	Embroideries, except Schiffli-machine....................	50.0	34.0	.2	.6	42.0
35	Housefurnishings and other non-apparel.....................	46.2	914.7	9.2	1.0	17.3
	Hard-surface floor coverings....	100.0	184.3	.5	.3	13.0
	Coated fabrics, except rubberized	66.5	205.2	4.2	2.0	12.3
	Housefurnishings, n.e.c........	78.5	525.2	4.5	.9	20.7
38	Plywood......................	100.0	466.9	20.0	4.3	17.3
	Plywood plants[c]	100.0	466.9	20.0	4.3	17.3
40	Wood containers and cooperage..	73.1	w.	*	*	16.7
	Wooden boxes, (except cigar boxes).....................	100.0	w.	*	*	16.7
41	Wood furniture................	64.5	1301.9	6.5	.5	16.6
	Wood furniture, except uphol-stered....................	100.0	1301.9	6.5	.5	16.6
45	Paper and board mills..........	65.6	2672.7	25.7	1.0	9.5
	Paper and board mills.........	65.6	2672.7	25.7	1.0	9.5
46	Converted paper products.......	51.5	2701.0	4.2	.2	15.4
	Paper coating and glazing.....	70.7	505.7	1.8	.4	10.9
	Envelopes....................	100.0	194.6	.1	.1	18.8
	Paperboard boxes............	88.2	1925.8	.2	*	15.7
	Wallpaper...................	100.0	w.	1.5	3.8	12.4
	Pulp goods, pressed and molded	100.0	w.	.6	1.7	13.8
49	Industrial organic chemicals.....	88.3	2661.7	22.2	.8	32.0
	Organic chemicals, n.e.c.[c]......	88.3	2661.7	22.2	.8	32.0
51	Synthetic rubber..............	100.0	462.0	7.5	1.6	10.0
	Synthetic rubber.............	100.0	462.0	7.5	1.6	10.0
52	Synthetic fiber................	100.0	1270.5	23.2	1.8	15.2
	Synthetic fiber...............	100.0	1270.5	23.2	1.8	15.2
54	Drugs and medicines...........	59.6	1183.2	7.5	.6	13.7
	Medicinal chemicals..........	82.4	295.1	6.1	2.1	17.9
	Pharmaceutical chemicals.....	59.1	888.1	1.4	.2	12.7
56	Paints and allied products.......	74.8	1472.0	.2	*	11.4
	Paints and varnishes..........	94.0	1472.0	.2	*	11.4
59	Vegetable oils.................	83.1	1339.8	47.6	3.6	8.4
	Cottonseed oil mills...........	86.0	w.	4.6	.8	10.7
	Soybean oil mills.............	97.0	w.	1.7	.3	7.2
	Vegetable oil mills, n.e.c.	90.2	w.	41.3	24.0	4.4
61	Miscellaneous chemical industries.	39.7	731.6	6.7	.9	19.2
	Toilet preparations...........	100.0	w.	2.5	.4	20.2
	Glue and gelatin.............	100.0	w.	3.7	4.8	19.2
	Salt.........................	100.0	w.	.5	.7	11.8
65	Tires and inner tubes..........	98.1	2049.0	3.2	.2	10.0
	Tires and inner tubes.........	98.1	2049.0	3.2	.2	10.0
66	Miscellaneous rubber products...	64.4	1334.9	5.1	.4	21.1
	Rubber footwear.............	100.0	225.5	.7	.3	18.3
	Rubber industries, n.e.c........	61.0	1109.4	4.4	.4	21.4
67	Leather tanning and finishing.....	60.7	471.5	16.2	3.4	11.5
	Leather tanning and finishing..	60.7	471.5	16.2	3.4	11.5
69	Footwear, except rubber.........	62.3	1494.1	9.3	.6	14.6
	Footwear, except rubber.......	76.2	1494.1	9.3	.6	14.6
70	Glass........................	100.0	1737.3	29.6	1.7	31.8
	Flat glass....................	100.0	340.3	18.9	5.6	16.5
	Glass containers..............	100.0	613.1	.3	.1	41.8
	Pressed and blown glassware, n.e.c.....................	100.0	357.7	9.4	2.6	36.1
	Products of purchased glass....	100.0	426.2	1.0	.2	26.7

Code Number	Liberalized Industry Accepted Sub-Industry	Shipments of Accepted Commodities as Percentage of Total Shipments[a]	Estimated Value of 1953 Domestic Output of Accepted Commodities[b] (In millions of dollars)	Foreign Port Value of Imports of Accepted Commodities, 1953		Duties as Percentage of Foreign Port Value of Imports, 1953
				Millions of Dollars	Percentage of Estimated Domestic Output	
		(1)	(2)	(3)	(4)	(5)
73	Pottery and related products.....	70.8	258.9	30.2	11.7	42.3
	Vitreous-china food utensils....	100.0	w.	5.8	12.5	49.3
	Earthenware food utensils.....	88.9	w.	11.6	19.2	54.6
	Porcelain electrical supplies....	93.0	86.9	.1	.1	35.0
	Pottery products, n.e.c........	100.0	w.	12.7	19.5	34.8
79.1	Carbon steel works and rolling mills					
	Carbon steel works and rolling mills......................		10181.8			
79.2	Alloy steel works and rolling mills excluding stainless............	82.8		159.0	1.3	11.5
	Alloy steel works and rolling mills, excluding stainless.....		1333.3			
79.3	Stainless steel works and rolling mills......................					
	Stainless steel works and rolling mills......................		606.1			
85	Primary zinc..................	84.3	237.6	50.8	21.4	5.7
	Primary zinc..................	84.3	237.6	50.8	21.4	5.7
88	Primary aluminum, including alumina.........................	100.0	488.1	115.8	23.7	6.3
	Primary aluminum[c]...........	100.0	488.1	115.8	23.7	6.3
89	Aluminum rolling and drawing....	100.0	968.0	18.6	1.9	10.1
	Aluminum rolling and drawing..	100.0	968.0	18.6	1.9	10.1
93	Tin cans and other tinware	97.3	1292.4	.4	*	12.1
	Tin cans and other tinware	97.3	1292.4	.4	*	12.1
94	Cutlery......................	100.0	200.7	6.3	3.1	31.7
	Cutlery......................	100.0	200.7	6.3	3.1	31.7
95	Tools and general hardware......	52.7	248.1	3.2	1.3	20.5
	Hand tools, n.e.c..............	61.9	w.	2.1	1.2	24.8
	Files.......................	100.0	w.	.3	1.4	12.4
	Hand saws and saw blades.....	50.0	w.	.8	1.7	8.7
103	Lighting fixtures..............	100.0	764.2	1.0	.1	31.3
	Lighting fixtures.............	100.0	764.2	1.0	.1	31.3
105	Metal barrels, drums, etc.......	100.0	204.0	*	*	35.0
	Metal barrels, drums, etc......	100.0	204.0	*	*	35.0
106	Tubes and foils................	63.5	120.6	1.9	1.6	20.1
	Metal foil....................	89.9	120.6	1.9	1.6	20.1
116	Machine tools and metalworking machinery...................	100.0	2376.4	37.2	1.6	12.1
	Machine tools................	100.0	1542.2	30.0	2.0	11.0
	Metalworking machinery......	100.0	834.2	7.2	.9	14.1
118	Special industrial machinery.....	61.1	1121.6	17.7	1.6	15.3
	Food products machinery.....	100.0	359.9	1.2	.3	14.6
	Textile machinery............	100.0	341.0	5.8	1.7	18.5
	Woodworking machinery......	100.0	196.4	1.8	.9	13.5
	Printing-trades machinery.....	100.0	224.3	8.9	4.0	13.1
123	Industrial machinery, n.e.c.......	54.5	360.9	28.3	7.8	12.8
	General industrial machinery, n.e.c......................	74.7	360.9	28.3	7.8	12.8
127	Ball and roller bearings.........	100.0	634.3	2.5	.4	20.1
	Ball and roller bearings.......	100.0	634.3	2.5	.4	20.1
131	Motors and generators.........	100.0	1697.4	10.3	.6	14.5
	Motors and generators........	100.0	1697.4	10.3	.6	14.5
132	Transformers.................	100.0	716.8	1.1	.2	12.5
	Transformers.................	100.0	716.8	1.1	.2	12.5
133	Electrical control apparatus......	61.1	752.0	1.0	.1	17.6
	Electrical control apparatus....	61.1	752.0	1.0	.1	17.6
134	Electrical welding apparatus.....	48.9	191.7	1.4	.7	8.7
	Electrical welding apparatus...	100.0	191.7	1.4	.7	8.7
135	Electrical appliances...........	41.9	765.2	25.3	3.3	16.9
	Domestic laundry equipment...	75.9	449.2	.6	.1	17.5
	Sewing machines.............	100.0	137.0	24.6	18.0	10.0
	Vacuum cleaners.............	95.7	179.0	.1	*	20.0

Code Number	Liberalized Industry Accepted Sub-Industry	Shipments of Accepted Commodities as Percentage of Total Shipments[a]	Estimated Value of 1953 Domestic Output of Accepted Commodities[b] (In millions of dollars)	Foreign Port Value of Imports of Accepted Commodities, 1953		Duties as Percentage of Foreign Port Value of Imports, 1953
				Millions of Dollars	Percentage of Estimated Domestic Output	
		(1)	(2)	(3)	(4)	(5)
136	Insulated wire and cable.........	100.0	1422.9	1.9	.1	17.0
	Insulated wire and cable......	100.0	1422.9	1.9	.1	17.0
138	Electric lamps..............	69.3	315.8	.9	.3	20.0
	Electric lamps..............	100.0	315.8	.9	.3	20.0
139	Radio and related products.....	73.3	w.	3.7	.1	7.3
	Radios and related products[c]..	73.3	w.	3.7	.1	7.3
141	Communication equipment......	89.9	827.5	3.0	.4	12.8
	Telephone and telegraph equipment......................	100.0	827.5	3.0	.4	12.8
142	Storage batteries..............	100.0	372.0	.2	.1	19.4
	Storage batteries.............	100.0	372.0	.2	.1	19.4
143	Primary batteries..............	100.0	151.3	*	*	17.5
	Primary batteries.............	100.0	151.3	*	*	17.5
145.1	Passenger cars and light trucks...	91.8	w.	42.1	.2	10.0
	Passenger cars and light trucks..	98.7	w.	42.1	.2	10.0
145.2	Heavy trucks and buses.........	91.8	w.	.6	*	12.0
	Heavy trucks and buses.......	98.7	w.	.6	*	12.0
145.3	Motor vehicle parts and accessories	91.8	w.	9.1	.3	12.4
	Motor vehicle parts and accessories....................	98.7	w.	9.1	.3	12.4
148	Aircraft and parts..............	100.0	11745.2	28.2	.2	15.0
	Aircraft....................			10.3	.2	15.0
	Aircraft propellers, and equipment, n.e.c..................	100.0	11745.2	16.9	.2	15.0
	Aircraft engines.............			1.0	.2	15.0
152	Motorcycles and bicycles.......	75.3	135.8	20.9	15.4	12.1
	Motorcycles and bicycles.......	100.0	135.8	20.9	15.4	12.1
154	Optical, ophthalmic, and photo equipment...................	100.0	1208.3	28.7	2.4	16.9
	Optical instruments and lenses.	100.0	145.2	9.3	6.4	29.8
	Ophthalmic goods...........	100.0	173.6	.7	.4	21.1
	Photographic equipment......	100.0	889.5	18.7	2.1	14.0
156	Watches and clocks.............	89.2	418.4	74.6	17.8	34.1
	Watches and clocks..........	100.0	418.4	74.6	17.8	34.1
157	Jewelry and silverware.........	95.8	896.8	19.7	2.2	32.4
	Jewelry, precious metals.......	100.0	279.5	1.5	.5	26.4
	Jewelers' findings............	100.0	w.	.3	.3	16.4
	Silverware and plated ware....	100.0	w.	6.3	2.9	22.2
	Costume jewelry.............	100.0	w.	11.6	4.0	51.2
158	Musical instruments and parts....	59.7	w.	.4	.3	20.0
	Pianos......................	100.0	w.	.3	.3	19.8
	Piano and organ parts........	89.3	w.	.1	.3	20.3
159	Toys and sporting goods........	91.4	811.7	17.8	2.2	33.4
	Games and toys..............	100.0	360.9	10.1	2.8	36.6
	Dolls......................	100.0	w.	1.6	.9	42.8
	Children's vehicles...........	62.4	w.	.2	.4	21.7
	Sporting and athletic goods....	93.0	w.	5.9	2.5	25.8
160	Office supplies................	67.2	w.	.5	.2	31.3
	Pens and mechanical pencils...	100.0	w.	.1	.1	33.9
	Lead pencils and crayons......	100.0	w.	.4	.8	22.4
161	Plastic products...............	75.0	779.6	2.0	.3	24.5
	Plastic products..............	75.0	779.6	2.0	.3	24.5
162	Cork products.................	85.0	w.	4.2	12.8	29.1
	Cork products................	85.0	w.	4.2	12.8	29.1
164	Miscellaneous manufactured products.........................	43.2	673.0	12.2	1.8	26.2
	Phonograph records...........	93.3	85.8	2.0	2.3	14.7
	Artificial flowers.............	100.0	w.	5.5	11.7	53.9
	Needles, pins, and fasteners....	99.0	224.5	1.6	.7	26.0
	Brooms and brushes..........	100.0	189.2	.8	.4	24.6
	Matches....................	100.0	53.8	1.3	2.4	26.8
	Candles.....................	100.0	w.	.2	.6	28.0
	Umbrellas, parasols and canes..	100.0	w.	.8	2.2	24.8

Estimation of Total Domestic Output Effects of Stipulated Output Changes

Choice of Input-Output Matrix[1]

It was noted in footnote 9 of Chapter 4 that the effect of a direct change in the domestic output of one industry on the outputs of all other industries was estimated from an arrangement of data on inter-industry relations (*i.e.*, an input-output matrix) that shows the relation between the direct total output (or "final demand") of each industry and the direct and indirect total output of every industry. "Total" in this context means that output is defined to include both an industry's domestic output and the imports of similar products. Such matrices are called matrices with a total output base. As the footnote explained, when an inverse matrix of this type is used to estimate the effects of initial changes in output, the question it answers is, How much does a stipulated direct or initial change in the total supply of products of any one industry affect the total supply of every industry? The same data are available in forms that relate the direct *domestic* output of each industry to the direct and indirect *domestic* output of every industry on the assumption that input requirements are met entirely from domestic sources. These are called matrices with a domestic output base. An inverse matrix with a domestic output base can be used to answer the question, How much does a stipulated initial change in the domestic output of any one industry affect the domestic output of every industry? Since the concern of this study is with effects on domestic employment and not on domestic plus foreign employment and since the assumed cause of these effects is an initial curtailment of an industry's domestic output, it may appear that a matrix with a domestic output base would have been the more appropriate one to use.

Use of such a matrix would have involved difficulties of its own, however. First, the estimates of total effects on every industry obtained from such a matrix imply that these effects fall entirely on domestic output and that there are no indirect effects on imports. Because this assumption is unrealistic for most industries, the estimates obtained

[1] The problems involved in the choice of a matrix and the treatment of imports were greatly clarified by discussions with Messrs. Sidney Jaffe and W. Duane Evans of the Bureau of Labor Statistics.

from such a matrix would overstate domestic output decreases and thereby lead to an overstatement of domestic employment decreases. They would also fail to show any output-induced decreases of imports and would thereby lead to overestimates of the net increases of foreign earnings and thus of the employment stimulus from exports. To avoid these errors, the primary domestic output effects would have to be adjusted downward and corresponding values would have to be assigned to decreases of imports competing with each industry.

At first it may appear that the correct domestic output could be obtained merely by reducing the matrix estimates of the effects on the output of every industry (other than the liberalized one) by the 1953 ratio of its competing imports to the sum of these imports and the industry's domestic output and that the resulting figure could be used to obtain a valid estimate of effects on domestic employment. Such an adjustment would not be sufficient, however. It would correct the error of the matrix in distributing the estimated requirements for an industry's products between its domestic output and imports, but it would not take into account the fact that these estimated requirements would themselves be overstated. In other words, it would not take into account the cumulative character of the error, which arises from the fact that the matrix reflects chains of relationships, every link of which implies that imports are constant. A theoretically correct adjustment would have to take account of the matrix overstatement of requirements for domestic output at all points in the network of input-output relationships.

This course was neither feasible nor necessary. Since there was available an inverse matrix on a total output base in which total supplies of each industry's products were assumed to be distributed between domestic output and imports in accordance with 1952 import ratios, its use would avoid the overstatements of domestic output implicit in the matrix with a domestic output base. It is true that most of the data used in the study relate to 1953, so that implicitly or explicitly the study seeks to estimate the effects of liberalization in 1953 rather than 1952. The estimated requirements for each industry would therefore be in error to the extent that the ratios of imports to domestic output in 1953 differed from those in 1952. These differences appeared likely to be much smaller in most industries, however, than those between the 1953 import proportions and the proportion implicit in the matrix with a domestic output base, which is zero. More important was the fact that the errors in assuming zero import proportions would all be in the same direction and would certainly bias the results, while the errors in using 1952 import proportions would not be in the same direction in all industries and would therefore tend to cancel each other at least partially. This is why a matrix with a total output base was used.

Use of Matrix with Total Output Base

Since the matrix used relates an initial level of *total* supplies of one industry to requirements for the *total* supply of every industry, the procedures used to get the effects of an initial *domestic* output in one industry on *domestic* output in all industries had to be adapted to this characteristic. This required three adjustments of the procedure normally used in applying input-output methods.

The first adjustment is in the initial change to be stipulated. We wished to know the effects of an initial displacement of domestic output worth a million dollars in 1953 prices. If we had stipulated a decrease in final demand equivalent to that amount (converted into 1947 prices because the matrix expresses relationships in those prices) and if the total supply of the stipulated products came from domestic output to the extent of a fraction k and from imports to the extent of 1-k, the output results given by the matrix would have implied a stipulated change in the domestic output of that industry of only k times one million dollars. It was therefore necessary to inflate the stipulated final demand for output sufficiently to make the portion of it consisting of domestic output equal to a million dollars. This was done by dividing a million dollars by the fraction k before converting it from 1953 into 1947 prices. For example, where imports similar to products of the liberalized industry were 20 per cent of total supply, the final demand change stipulated the 1947 equivalent of a million dollars divided by 80 per cent, *i.e.,* the 1947 equivalent of $1,250,000. The direct impact on the domestic output of the liberalized industry thus was the amount we wanted.

Since we were examining the effects of reducing barriers for only one industry at a time, the import proportions that are built into the matrix for other industries may be taken as correct. It follows, therefore, that the outputs of other industries generated by an assumed decrease in final demand for the liberalized industry equivalent to $\frac{\$1 \text{ million}}{k}$ in 1953 prices are the same as those that would be generated by a decrease of demand of a million dollars in its domestic output alone. There is, however, one exception to this statement that was of some quantitative significance. The matrix with a total output base implies that part of the stipulated decrease in output of the liberalized industry takes the form of a decrease in imports of its products. Consequently, the output results from such a matrix include output decreases in the ocean transportation industry and in other industries affected by ocean transportation that are generated by this implied decrease of imports of the liberalized products. Since, in the present problem, these imports are assumed to increase rather than to decrease, the decreases of output in ocean transportation and other industries shown by the matrix contain an element that is fictitious. Elimination of this fictitious import-generated output was the second adjustment made necessary by the fact that the matrix had a total output base.

More important quantitatively than either of these two points is the fact that the output levels obtained from the matrix were the total effects on domestic output and imports combined. To eliminate the imported element in these output results and get the domestic output effects alone required a third adjustment, a reduction of these levels by the fraction 1-k, as described in pages 84 to 86 of Chapter 4.

This adjustment was not applied to the indirect output of the liberalized industry, however. It was assumed instead that the indirect effect on its total output fell entirely on the domestic portion, imply-ing that there are no output-induced effects on its imports and that the gross and net decreases of imports are equal. The matrix, however, implies that indirect effects on the liberalized industry are distributed between domestic output and imports in 1952 proportions. For this reason, the output changes in every industry that are generated by these indirect effects are smaller than those implied by our assumption and the employment effects associated with them are correspondingly smaller than it implies. The amount of this understatement depends on the size of the indirect output effect in the liberalized industry and the difference between 100 per cent, the domestic proportion of total output we assumed, and the 1952 proportion implied by the matrix. In only 26 of the 72 cases was the indirect output effect in the liberal-ized industry as much as 10 per cent of the stipulated change in its output. In 23 of these cases the domestic portion of total output im-plied by the matrix was over 90 per cent. Thus in almost all cases the inconsistency between our assumption and the assumption built into the matrix involves little difference in the output and therefore in the employment results. Unfortunately in one case, that of sugar liberaliza-tion, the feedback to the liberalized industry is large and the propor-tion of total output coming from domestic production is only 58 per cent. In this case, the assumption that output-induced decreases in the liberalized industry affect only domestic production implies consider-ably larger indirect domestic output effects of sugar liberalization on all industries than are yielded by the matrix and total indirect em-ployment effects correspondingly larger than the present estimates.

It should be noted that discrepancies between the estimates and the effects implied by our assumption about the distribution of the liberalized industry's indirect output may not be errors in the sense of discrepancies between the estimates and the actual effects of liberali-zation, for our assumption may be in error. If indirect output effects in the liberalized industry are distributed between domestic output and imports in 1952 proportions, as the matrix implies, the estimates of indirect effects in the non-liberalized industries are correct but the estimates of such effects in the liberalized industries are too high.

Elimination of Effects of Fictitious
Changes in Agricultural Output

Under this heading in Chapter 4, it was noted that the output changes obtained from the matrix of interindustry relations included changes in the output of six agricultural industries that are assumed to be unresponsive to changes of demand in the short period—farm dairy products, food grains and feed crops, cotton, tobacco, oil-bearing crops, and "all other agricultural products." All of the output changes in these industries, as obtained from the matrix, and whatever component of the changes in output of all other industries was generated by them, were therefore fictitious from the point of view of the present study. All these fictitious changes could have been eliminated by adjusting the output results obtained from the matrix, but in some cases of liberalization, they were so small that they were not worth eliminating.

In the case of primary output effects, *i.e.*, those resulting from displacement of domestic output, the criterion used to determine whether these fictitious output effects were large enough to warrant an adjustment in any specific case of liberalization was that the combined change in the *domestic* output of the 6 unresponsive agricultural industries, as obtained from the matrix and modified by the deduction of imports, amounted to $100,000 or more in 1947 prices, the prices in which matrix output results were expressed. This criterion was met in liberalizations of the following 12 industries:

Meat animals and products (#1)
Meat packing and wholesale poultry (#21)
Processed dairy products (#22)
Grain mill products (#24)
Sugar (#27)
Alcoholic beverages (#28)
Tobacco manufactures (#29)
Spinning, weaving, and dyeing (#30)
Apparel (#34)
House furnishings and other non-apparel (#35)
Paints and allied products (#56)
Vegetable oils (#59)

Although primary output effects yielded by the matrix were adjusted in all these cases, the adjustment was confined to eliminating the domestic output of those of the 6 industries whose domestic output decreased by more than $10,000 and that portion of the total output decrease in other industries that was generated by the direct input requirements of those industries. The output decreases generated by their indirect input requirements, *i.e.*, through the input requirements of their direct suppliers, were too small to be worth eliminating.

It should be noted that it is only the domestic outputs of these 6 agricultural industries and not the competing imports that are regarded as unresponsive in the short period to changes in demand. The output results obtained from the matrix included these effects on competing imports and the effects they generate on the domestic output of the ocean transportation industry and on foreign earnings. Since these effects were not regarded as fictitious, they did not have to be eliminated.

The problem of fictitious output generated by unresponsive agricultural industries also arose in estimating the output effects of increases in exports, described in Chapter 8. Failure to eliminate these effects would have tended to cause overstatement of the employment stimulus of exports. To avoid this overstatement an adjustment was made in those cases of liberalization in which the matrix showed a combined change in total output (*i.e.,* domestic output plus competing imports) for the 6 unresponsive agricultural industries of $50,000 or more in 1947 prices. This criterion was met only in the case of sugar liberalization. The adjustment was confined to the output generated by those of the 6 agricultural industries whose output changes, according to the matrix, exceed $5,000. As in the case of the primary effects, only the fictitious outputs of these industries and of their direct suppliers were eliminated.

Relation between Changes in Output and Changes in Imports

It was noted in Chapter 4 (page 85) that, for commodities obtained from both domestic and foreign sources, changes in United States requirements for the products of an industry may have a greater percentage impact on its domestic output than on competing imports, despite the often expressed view that the reverse is generally true. The assumption that imports provide the "marginal" supply of most commodities, insofar as it is not based on the fallacy that countries import only what they "cannot" produce themselves, may reflect conclusions drawn from statistical analyses that relate changes of specific imports to changes in some variant of total national output. This relationship is not relevant to the present question because it is composed of two other relationships, one between the specific imports and the total (*i.e.,* domestic plus imported) supply of them and another between this supply and total national output. In this study we are concerned only with the first of these component relationships. The results obtained in most published studies, besides being concerned with the composite relationship, are generally dominated by its second component.

Theoretical considerations suggest no important reasons for imports to vary in greater proportion than total requirements. When demand for a product sold under competitive conditions falls, the decline will affect the purchases from different sources of supply in accordance with the rate of fall in their marginal total costs (including costs of delivery to the buyer). Sales of supplies whose marginal costs fall least with decreases in output will suffer most. Insofar as quantities of their inputs are concerned, there appears to be no more reason for the marginal costs of imports to decline more or less than those of domestic supplies when United States demand declines. It is true that their marginal costs may fall less if changes in United States demand have a smaller effect on the *prices* of the foreign inputs than they do on those used by United States producers, but it is not clear that they generally do. With regard to costs of delivery to the buyer, it may be argued that international transportation costs are likely to be constant in the face of changes in United States demand for particular products, but this is probably equally true of domestic transportation costs. The only element of cost to United States buyers for which the case for a greater decline of imports appears clear a priori is protective tariff duties levied on a specific basis.

Empirical evidence also indicates that imports do not bear a disproportionate share of changes in domestic demand. An unpublished statistical study by Mrs. M. Holzman for the International Monetary Fund dated February 11, 1949, "The U. S. Demand for Imports of Certain Individual Commodities in the Interwar Period" found elasticities of imports to changes in total consumption or output of the corresponding commodities amounting to less than 1.0 for several commodities: copper (0.57), woodpulp (0.83), unmanufactured tobacco (0.49) and furs (0.39).

The Department of Commerce, in its review of 1957, points out that prior to the middle of 1957, imports of many industrial materials (other than petroleum) failed to rise in proportion to the output of the industries using them, because the proportion of supplies obtained from domestic sources rose.

> The rising share of domestically produced goods in the total consumption of such materials may indicate that the dependence by (sic) the United States on imported materials has declined. It may also signify, however, that for some commodities domestically produced goods are used to supply the peak demand and that as demand declines imports would again supply a rising share of the market. The latter would be the case where domestic sources of supply are being gradually depleted, and costs of production are rising more than abroad, or where foreign prices are more flexible than those of domestically produced goods. In these instances imports would be expected to be more stable than the activity of those industries which use the imported materials.[2]

Similarly, during the first two months of 1958, when business ac-

[2] See *Survey of Current Business* (February 1958), p. 28.

tivity was declining, the department, in discussing changes in imports of copper, lead, zinc, and iron ore, observed that "The decline in consumption of these metals was absorbed partly by a decline in domestic mine production and partly by rising inventories. . . . For these products the decline in domestic output indicates that through the first 2 months of this year at least domestic rather than foreign producers were the marginal suppliers." Further developments led the department to observe later that "Despite the weakening in imports [of some metals, particularly aluminum, copper, lead, zinc, and manganese] most of the impact of the decline in domestic demand was still absorbed by domestic producers and through increases in inventories" and that a rise in domestic demand for many metals may not raise imports proportionally, not only because some of the additional demand may be met by reducing inventories but because "a rising share of the market is likely to be supplied by domestic producers who will re-enter the market as prices firm up."[3]

The relative behavior of selected United States imports and corresponding United States production was studied by R. A. Degen to determine whether imports of these commodities from all countries have been affected more favorably or less favorably than their home-produced counterparts during the recessions of the last three decades. All the commodities were among the leading imports for 1957, and all were produced domestically to an important extent. The commodities examined were newsprint, wood pulp, lumber, petroleum, iron ore, aluminum, copper, whisky, and zinc. Agricultural imports were not considered. Comparing changes of imports and domestic output in terms of volume, Degen finds that

> in the five recessions that occurred in the entire thirty-year period, it is apparent that imports of the commodities examined have not generally suffered losses relatively larger than those experienced by domestic production. In forty-three comparisons involving the nine commodities, imports unambiguously suffered a relative reduction in their share of the market twelve times, or in 28 per cent of the total. Thus in the vast majority of the cases imports either held the share of the market that they had had before the recession or else increased it. In seventeen instances, or 40 per per cent of the total, imports gained a larger share.

Summarizing his results, he says:

> It must be concluded that United States recessions do not operate so as to injure foreign exporters more than domestic suppliers of the commodities examined. Post-war experience indicates the opposite to be more often true. Indeed, exports to the United States have increased or held their own in absolute volume in a majority of the post-war cases covered.[4]

[3] For the first quotation in this paragraph, see *Survey of Current Business* (June 1958), p. 11. The second comes from the issue of September 1958, p. 10.
[4] R. A. Degen, "United States Recessions and Selected Imports", *Canadian Journal of Economics and Political Science,* Vol. 25, No. 2, (May, 1959).

Estimation of Employment Changes from Output Changes

Relation of Employment to
Output Changes

Burgess Cameron studied the relationship between the ratio of output to employment (in man-years) and levels of output in Australian manufacturing industries with approximately homogeneous outputs. In a survey of his results, he reported that for the 45 industries with sufficient data, the time series for 5 industries showed no correlation between the output-employment ratio and the level of output, in 33 there was a marked correlation, and in the other 7 a clear but less marked correlation. Perhaps because his concern was to test merely whether the ratio remained constant, he does not say in how many cases the ratio was positively and in how many it was negatively correlated with output. He concludes that "The hypothesis of a constant employment coefficient is certainly incorrect for the majority of the industries examined."[1] Although Cameron does not say so, the charts shown for 9 industries and his interpretive comments indicate that the correlations were positive in most if not all cases, indicating that changes in man-years of employment generally were less than proportional to changes in the volume of output. The amount of this deviation from proportionality, which is in the direction referred to in Chapter 4 (p. 87), cannot be judged since Cameron does not give the regression coefficients.

George W. Wilson studied the relationships between percentage changes of employment and of output in Canada at various levels of industry aggregation and using monthly, quarterly, and annual data.[2] He questions that there is any stable relationship of percentage changes, especially over very short periods of time. He finds that the relationship becomes more stable as one moves from monthly to quarterly and annual data. He concedes that most of the erratic behavior of the monthly data and some of that of the quarterly and annual data reflect inadequacy of the statistics, but believes they also reflect instability of the actual relationships. Although the more ag-

[1] "The Production Function in Leontief Models", *The Review of Economic Studies*, Vol. 20 (1) (1952-53), page 66.
[2] "The Relationship Between Output and Employment", *Review of Economics and Statistics*, Vol. 42 (February 1960) and other studies cited therein.

gregated data are affected by changes in the composition of output among industries with differing employment-output relationships, Wilson tested the relationship for five individual industries and found them to be less stable than for more aggregated data. He attributes the actual instability to labor requirements that do not vary with production, business men's expectations that the declines will not persist and consequent unwillingness to release workers, and other familiar considerations. Such factors are not likely to be as important a factor in output changes due to liberalization as in output changes in general because the latter include, if they are not dominated by, cyclical movements, the duration of which is hard to forecast and which can be expected to reverse themselves. In general, Wilson's conclusions appear to be more skeptical than would be justified in connection with changes due to liberalization. The monthly data are poor. All the data include the effects of changes in technique.

The Bureau of Labor Statistics, in its latest publication on output per man-hour in individual industries, also presents data on output per employee man-year.[3] Inspection of these data suggests that if rough allowance is made for improvements in the technique of production, total employment might be found to vary by a smaller proportion than output in only about half of the non-agricultural industries for which man-year employment data are available and in about equal proportion in the remaining ones.

We are not aware of any attempts to measure the multiple regression of employment (either in man-years or man-hours) on output and any other variable, such as time, which might be regarded as a surrogate, however poor, for changes of technique. It is our impression, however, that if one could eliminate the effects of technical change from the time series in order to isolate the effects on employment of changes in output due to demand changes alone, the assumption that employment changes are proportional to output changes would be a good approximation for many commodity-producing industries. Insofar as this assumption causes error in the estimates of this study, the error is in the direction of overstating the employment effects associated with given changes of output.

Adjustment for Matrix Duplication of Domestic Output

In footnote 19 of Chapter 4, it was noted that the estimates of industry outputs obtained from the input-output matrix include the value of the industry's output plus output of products that are primary

---

[3] See U. S. Department of Labor, *Indexes of Output per Man-Hour for Selected Industries, 1939 and 1947-59* (July 1960). This study is one of an annual series.

to it but produced in other industries.[4] The employment-output coefficients to be applied to them were based on output data that did not
contain such duplication. To apply them to the matrix output results
without adjustment would therefore have caused overstatement of
employment effects. To avoid such overstatement, it was necessary to
reduce the estimates of output obtained from the matrix for every
industry in all the 72 cases of liberalization by the ratio of the duplication to the output including the duplication. Since the percentage of
duplication in the output of every industry is the same in every case,
the effect of adjusting an industry's output 72 times was obtained with
less computation by making a corresponding adjustment in the employment-output coefficients applied to each industry's output. (The
employment-output coefficients shown in Appendix Tables D.1, D.2,
and D.3 are the unadjusted coefficients based on unduplicated output.)

The duplication occurs in the estimates of the total output of every
non-liberalized industry and in both the direct and the indirect components of the output of the liberalized industry. It may appear surprising that any adjustment is needed to offset duplication in the direct
output of the liberalized industry. Since the direct decrease in the
domestic output of the liberalized products was stipulated as being the
equivalent of one million dollars in 1953 dollars, why could that
amount of the liberalized industry's output, as obtained from the
matrix, not have been regarded as an accurate estimate containing no
duplication? The reason is that part of the production of liberalized
products occurs outside the liberalized industry, which is defined as
the industry producing them as primary products. Despite the fact that
we stipulated the direct decrease of output as occurring entirely in the
liberalized industry, its impact on the industries that produce it as a
secondary product is taken into account because the matrix treats the
output of liberalized products produced as a secondary product by a
non-liberalized industry as an input purchased by the liberalized industry. Therefore if we had treated the matrix-estimated output of the
liberalized industry as including all the direct output we would have
overstated the amount of it that is really produced in that industry.
Suppose, for example, that 10 per cent of the output of liberalized
products is produced outside the liberalized industry and 90 per cent
is produced in it. To assume that the matrix estimate of the liberalized
industry's output includes a million dollars of direct output would
imply a direct output of one million dollars in the liberalized industry
and $100,000 in other industries or a total of $1.1 million and would

[4] See "The Interindustry Relations Study for 1947" by W. Duane Evans and
Marvin Hoffenberg, *Review of Economics and Statistics*, Vol. 34, (May 1952) p. 137.
As this article points out, the output estimates also include imports of competitive
products and inventory depletions of products primary to but held outside the in-
dustry. The adjustment made in this study to eliminate imports was described in
Chapter 4. No adjustment was made to eliminate inventory depletion.

overstate the portion really produced in the liberalized industry by $\dfrac{1.00}{.90}$. To avoid this error, the direct employment effect in the liberalized industry would have to be estimated as one million dollars times the direct employment-output coefficient reduced by 10 per cent. An adjustment to take account of this duplication was made in converting the estimated output changes in every industry into the associated employment.

An equal percentage adjustment was made in computing the employment effect of the liberalized industry's indirect output. Although the percentage duplication in the total output of the liberalized industry may differ from that in the portion of its output that we assumed to be affected by the liberalization, the overstatement of the industry's total output, as yielded by the matrix, depends on the former percentage.

(See Tables D.1-D.3 on following pages)

Derivation of Direct Employment-Output Ratios and 1953
Price Indices for Liberalized Industries

	Liberalized Industry Accepted Subindustry	Average Number of Employees 1953 (In thousands)	Value of 1953 Domestic Output (In millions of dollars)	1953 Employment-Output Ratio[a]	Index of 1953 Prices of Output (1947=100)
		(1)	(2)	(3)	(4)
1	Meat animals and products.................	676.3[b]	10084.0	.0669	91.2
	Meat animals..........................	599.2[b]	9872.0	.0607	90.6
	Other livestock and products.............	77.1[b]	212.0	.3636	109.0
8	Vegetables and fruits.......................	480.7	2568.1	.1872	89.3
	Vegetables..............................	480.7	2568.1	.1872	89.3
13	Lead and zinc mining.....................	17.4	135.6	.1283	87.6
	Lead and zinc ores[c]......................	17.4	135.6	.1283	87.6
21	Meat packing and wholesale poultry.........	w.	n.a.p.	.0232	94.7
	Meat packing, wholesale.................	w.	n.a.p.	.0232	94.7
22	Processed dairy products....................	52.9	2365.9	.0224	103.1
	Creamery butter.......................	25.0	1033.5	.0241	94.1
	Natural cheese.........................	11.4	510.6	.0223	99.5
	Concentrated milk......................	16.5	821.8	.0201	120.4
24	Grain mill products.......................	w.	w.	.0156	95.9
	Flour and meal.........................	w.	w.	.0159	94.8
	Rice cleaning and polishing...............	n.a.p.	n.a.p.	.0140	101.6
27	Sugar....................................	32.2	1311.5	.0246	105.0
	Raw cane sugar........................	n.a.p.	n.a.p.	.0403	102.0
	Cane sugar refining....................	w.	w.	.0176	105.4
	Beet sugar.............................	w.	w.	.0377	105.4
28	Alcoholic beverages........................	106.2	2842.8	.0374	114.2
	Malt liquors...........................	84.8	1952.4	.0434	124.6
	Distilled liquors, except brandy............	21.4	890.4	.0241	96.4
29	Tobacco manufactures.....................	88.1	3186.9	.0276	120.2
	Cigarettes.............................	w.	w.	.0184	128.8
	Cigars.................................	w.	w.	.1049	103.8
	Tobacco stemming and redrying...........	n.a.p.	n.a.p.	.0148	115.2
30	Spinning, weaving, and dyeing..............	642.6	7498.3	.0857	89.9
	Yarn mills, wool, except carpet..........	24.2	338.7	.0715	125.8
	Woolen and worsted fabrics..............	95.8	1386.0	.0691	120.4
	Thread mills...........................	14.8	174.4	.0848	106.8
	Yarn mills, cotton system...............	84.0	837.6	.1003	89.4
	Cotton broad-woven fabrics..............	318.2	3259.8	.0976	88.6
	Rayon and related broad-woven fabrics....	105.6	1501.8	.0703	70.1
31	Special textile products....................	51.2	741.6	.0690	128.1
	Wool carpets and rugs..................	w.	n.a.p.	.0628	139.1
	Carpets and rugs, n.e.c.................	w.	w.	.0685	118.9
	Lace goods.............................	n.a.p.	n.a.p.	.1158	90.8
34	Apparel..................................	701.4	6171.7	.1137	97.1
	Seamless hosiery mills..................	63.5	408.3	.1555	107.7
	Knit underwear mills....................	40.7	381.4	.1067	109.8
	Knit fabric mills.......................	15.2	369.5	.0412	92.8
	Fur-felt hats and hat bodies.............	10.2	92.5	.1102	86.3
	Straw hats.............................	n.a.p.	n.a.p.	.1074	86.6
	Men's dress shirts and nightwear..........	108.7	821.0	.1324	91.4
	Women's and misses' outerwear...........	371.6	3225.9	.1152	94.6
	Corsets and allied garments..............	41.6	445.2	.0934	110.0
	Millinery...............................	19.0	167.9	.1131	115.7
	Suspenders and garters..................	n.a.p.	n.a.p.	.0998	113.2
	Leather and sheep-lined clothing..........	n.a.p.	n.a.p.	.0877	109.9
	Handkerchiefs..........................	n.a.p.	44.8	.0871	91.4
	Schiffli-machine embroideries.............	n.a.p.	43.5	.1034	96.1
	Embroideries, except Schiffli-machine......	n.a.p.	67.9	.1869	96.1
35	House furnishings and other non-apparel.....	64.4	1161.9	.0554	96.0
	Hard-surface floor coverings.............	10.4	184.3	.0565	114.8

n.a.p.=Data not available for publication.

w.=Withheld to prevent inference of data not available for publication.

[a] This ratio represents number of employees per $1,000 of output. It is obtained by dividing Column 1 by Column 2, but figures may not equal the quotient exactly because of rounding.

[b] Includes farmers and unpaid farm family workers.

[c] This is the sub-industry title used by Census of Manufactures. It covers the same output as the industry, the title of which comes from BLS Interindustry classification.

Liberalized Industry Accepted Subindustry	Average Number of Employees 1953 (In thousands)	Value of 1953 Domestic Output (In millions of dollars)	1953 Employment Output Ratio[a]	Index of 1953 Prices of Output (1947 = 100)
	(1)	(2)	(3)	(4)
Coated fabrics, except rubberized..........	11.8	308.5	.0382	90.8
House furnishings, n.e.c...................	42.2	669.1	.0630	94.2
38 Plywood...............................	39.1	466.9	.0837	116.7
Plywood plants[c].......................	39.1	466.9	.0837	116.7
40 Wood containers and cooperage............	w.	w.	.1017	126.2
Wooden boxes (except cigar boxes)........	n.a.p.	n.a.p.	.1017	126.2
41 Wood furniture...........................	142.6	1301.9	.1095	117.5
Wood furniture, except upholstered........	142.6	1301.9	.1095	117.5
45 Paper and board mills.....................	162.0	4074.3	.0398	132.2
Paper and board mills....................	162.0	4074.3	.0398	132.2
46 Converted paper products.................	186.3	3168.3	.0588	108.1
Paper coating and glazing................	31.2	715.4	.0435	111.4
Envelopes..............................	w.	w.	.0832	111.6
Paperboard boxes.......................	132.2	2183.4	.0605	106.7
Wallpaper..............................	n.a.p.	n.a.p.	.0962	111.6
Pulp goods, pressed and molded...........	n.a.p.	n.a.p.	.0820	111.6
49 Industrial organic chemicals...............	99.6	3014.4	.0331	111.2
Organic chemicals, n.e.c.[c],.............	99.6	3014.4	.0331	111.2
51 Synthetic rubber........................	10.0	462.0	.0216	124.3
Synthetic rubber.......................	10.0	462.0	.0216	124.3
52 Synthetic fiber..........................	71.9	1270.5	.0566	109.8
Synthetic fiber.........................	71.9	1270.5	.0566	109.8
54 Drugs and medicines.....................	89.7	1860.8	.0482	83.1
Medicinal chemicals.....................	15.9	358.1	.0444	48.7
Pharmaceutical preparations.............	73.8	1502.7	.0491	100.0
56 Paints and allied products.................	60.8	1566.0	.0388	112.3
Paints and varnishes....................	60.8	1566.0	.0388	112.3
59 Vegetable oils...........................	23.1	1468.4	.0158	72.2
Cottonseed oil mills.....................	w.	w.	.0221	74.2
Soybean oil mills.......................	w.	w	.0092	69.6
Vegetable oil mills, n.e.c................	n.a.p.	n.a.p.	.0151	74.2
61 Miscellaneous chemical industries...........	31.4	731.6	.0429	111.2
Toilet preparations.....................	w.	w.	.0400	108.5
Glue and gelatin.......................	w.	w.	.0488	117.9
Salt..................................	n.a.p.	n.a.p.	.0590	128.7
65 Tires and inner tubes.....................	97.0	2088.7	.0464	127.9
Tires and inner tubes...................	97.0	2088.7	.0464	127.9
66 Miscellaneous rubber products..............	170.4	2044.2	.0834	126.3
Rubber footwear.......................	25.4	225.5	.1126	122.3
Rubber industries, n.e.c.................	145.0	1818.7	.0797	126.8
67 Leather tanning and finishing..............	46.4	776.7	.0598	88.2
Leather tanning and finishing............	46.4	776.7	.0598	88.2
69 Footwear, except rubber..................	232.5	1960.7	.1186	116.6
Footwear, except rubber.................	232.5	1960.7	.1186	116.6
70 Glass..................................	144.7	1737.3	.0833	136.6
Flat glass..............................	25.8	340.3	.0758	129.2
Glass containers........................	50.6	613.1	.0826	154.5
Pressed and blown glassware, n.e.c........	39.7	357.7	.1110	135.2
Products of purchased glass...............	28.6	426.2	.0671	122.8
73 Pottery and related products...............	45.4	272.9	.1664	121.9
Vitreous-china food utensils..............	n.a.p.	n.a.p.	.1808	116.7
Earthenware food utensils................	w.	w.	.2152	129.0
Porcelain electrical supplies..............	11.4	93.4	.1221	119.6
Pottery products, n.e.c..................	w.	w.	.1687	122.1
79.1 Carbon steel works and rolling mills........			.0403	155.0
Carbon steel works and rolling mills.......			.0403	155.0
79.2 Alloy steel works and rolling mills, excluding stainless...............................	589.2[d]	14639.2	.0403	155.0
Alloy steel works and rolling mills, excluding stainless...............................			.0403	155.0
79.3 Stainless steel works and rolling mills........			.0403	155.0
Stainless steel works and rolling mills.......			.0403	155.0

[d] Although the *Annual Survey of Manufactures, 1953*, presents separate statistics for the value of shipments of carbon steel, alloy steel, and stainless steel, it does not give the corresponding employment data separately. The separate employment figures and the corresponding employment-output relationships were derived by apportioning the relevant total employment figure in proportion to the relative importance of shipments of carbon, alloy and stainless steel. This procedure implicitly assumes that employment-output ratios are the same for these three types of steel.

	Liberalized Industry Accepted Subindustry	Average Number of Employees 1953 (In thousands)	Value of 1953 Domestic Output (In millions of dollars)	1953 Employment Output Ratio[a]	Index of 1953 Prices of Output (1947=100)
		(1)	(2)	(3)	(4)
85	Primary zinc	11.4	281.8	.0405	105.0
	Primary zinc	11.4	281.8	.0405	105.0
88	Primary aluminum, including alumina	19.6	488.1	.0401	143.3
	Primary aluminum[c]	19.6	488.1	.0401	143.3
89	Aluminum rolling and drawing	39.1	968.0	.0404	141.3
	Aluminum rolling and drawing	39.1	968.0	.0404	141.3
93	Tin cans and other tinware	55.7	1328.3	.0419	140.8
	Tin cans and other tinware	55.7	1328.3	.0419	140.8
94	Cutlery	17.3	200.7	.0862	124.5
	Cutlery	17.3	200.7	.0862	124.5
95	Tools and general hardware	39.1	405.7	.0964	147.0
	Hand tools, n.e.c.	w.	w.	.0980	150.0
	Files	n.a.p.	n.a.p.	.1305	154.4
	Hand saws and saw blades	w.	w.	.0836	137.0
103	Lighting fixtures	54.5	764.2	.0713	118.2
	Lighting fixtures	54.5	764.2	.0713	118.2
105	Metal barrels, drums, etc.	10.0	204.0	.0490	140.3
	Metal barrels, drums, etc.	10.0	204.0	.0490	140.3
106	Tubes and foils	5.5	134.2	.0410	130.3
	Metal foil	5.5	134.2	.0410	130.3
116	Machine tools and metalworking machinery	157.6	2376.4	.0663	153.0
	Machine tools	99.5	1542.2	.0645	160.2
	Metalworking machinery	58.1	834.2	.0697	141.4
118	Special industrial machinery	104.0	1121.6	.0927	132.9
	Food products machinery	30.8	359.9	.0856	132.9
	Textile machinery	38.3	341.0	.1123	132.9
	Woodworking machinery	15.3	196.4	.0779	133.0
	Printing-trades machinery	19.6	224.3	.0874	132.9
123	Industrial machinery, n.e.c.	33.6	483.1	.0695	132.9
	General industrial machinery, n.e.c.	33.6	483.1	.0695	132.9
127	Ball and roller bearings	58.5	634.3	.0922	124.2
	Ball and roller bearings	58.5	634.3	.0922	124.2
131	Motors and generators	129.3	1697.4	.0762	123.7
	Motors and generators	129.3	1697.4	.0762	123.7
132	Transformers	45.4	716.8	.0634	129.1
	Transformers	45.4	716.8	.0634	129.1
133	Electrical control apparatus	88.4	1230.7	.0718	136.8
	Electrical control apparatus	88.4	1230.7	.0718	136.8
134	Electrical welding apparatus	8.0	191.7	.0417	128.7
	Electrical welding apparatus	8.0	191.7	.0417	128.7
135	Electrical appliances	53.9	915.8	.0588	110.5
	Domestic laundry equipment	27.4	591.8	.0463	107.8
	Sewing machines	16.0	137.0	.1168	122.0
	Vacuum cleaners	10.5	187.0	.0562	111.4
136	Insulated wire and cable	62.2	1422.9	.0437	130.1
	Insulated wire and cable	62.2	1422.9	.0437	130.1
138	Electric lamps	21.2	315.8	.0671	137.8
	Electric lamps	21.2	315.8	.0671	137.8
139	Radio and related products	w.	n.a.p.	.0711	95.5
	Radios and related products[c]	w.	n.a.p.	.0711	95.5
141	Communication equipment	66.1	827.5	.0799	132.9
	Telephone and telegraph equipment	66.1	827.5	.0799	132.9
142	Storage batteries	17.3	372.1	.0465	123.4
	Storage batteries	17.3	372.1	.0465	123.4
143	Primary batteries	12.3	151.3	.0813	118.3
	Primary batteries	12.3	151.3	.0813	118.3
145.1	Passenger cars and light trucks			.0333	130.2
	Passenger cars and light trucks			.0333	130.2
145.2	Heavy trucks and buses			.0333	130.2
	Heavy trucks and buses	n.a.p.	n.a.p.	.0333	130.2
145.3	Motor vehicle parts and accessories			.0338	130.2
	Motor vehicle parts and accessories			.0338	130.2
148	Aircraft and parts	817.4	11745.2	.0696	132.9
	Aircraft	439.4			
	Aircraft engines	187.4	n.a.p.	n.a.p.	n.a.p.
	Aircraft propellers	18.0			
	Aircraft equipment, n.e.c.	172.6			

Liberalized Industry Accepted Subindustry	Average Number of Employees 1953 (In thousands)	Value of 1953 Domestic Output (In millions of dollars)	1953 Employment Output Ratio[a]	Index of 1953 Prices of Output (1947 = 100)
	(1)	(2)	(3)	(4)
152 Motorcycles and bicycles..................	9.3	135.8	.0685	132.9
Motorcycles and bicycles................	9.3	135.8	.0685	132.9
154 Optical, ophthalmic, and photographic equipment................................	97.0	1208.3	.0803	115.8
Optical instruments and lenses...........	16.4	145.2	.1129	108.0
Ophthalmic goods.......................	20.4	173.6	.1175	108.0
Photographic equipment.................	60.2	889.5	.0677	119.0
156 Watches and clocks.......................	29.3	418.4	.0700	109.0
Watches and clocks.....................	29.3	418.4	.0700	109.0
157 Jewelry and silverware....................	78.3	896.8	.0873	101.1
Jewelry, precious metals..................	21.8	279.8	.0779	96.4
Jewelers' findings.......................	n.a.p.	n.a.p.	.0711	96.4
Silverware and plated ware..............	w.	w.	.0829	119.2
Costume jewelry.......................	n.a.p.	n.a.p.	.1054	96.4
158 Musical instruments and parts.............	w.	w.	.0865	116.2
Pianos...............................	n.a.p.	n.a.p.	.0873	116.2
Piano and organ parts..................	n.a.p.	n.a.p.	.0843	116.2
159 Toys and sporting goods..................	92.5	857.4	.1079	115.7
Games and toys.......................	41.6	360.9	.1153	112.1
Dolls................................	w.	w.	.0994	126.3
Children's vehicles.....................	n.a.p.	n.a.p.	.0961	110.6
Sporting and athletic goods..............	w.	w.	.1066	116.0
160 Office supplies..........................	w.	w.	.0889	98.4
Pens and mechanical pencils.............	n.a.p.	n.a.p.	.0862	94.4
Lead pencils and crayons................	n.a.p.	n.a.p.	.0978	114.7
161 Plastic products........................	85.1	1039.4	.0819	126.1
Plastic products.......................	85.1	1039.4	.0819	126.1
162 Cork products..........................	w.	w.	.0623	119.6
Cork products........................	n.a.p.	n.a.p.	.0623	119.6
164 Miscellaneous manufactured products........	69.2	681.5	.1016	111.3
Phonograph records....................	6.6	92.0	.0717	126.3
Artificial flowers......................	n.a.p.	n.a.p.	.1428	119.6
Needles, pins, and fasteners..............	26.5	226.8	.1168	89.2
Brooms and brushes....................	16.3	189.2	.0862	126.6
Matches.............................	5.8	53.8	.1077	146.7
Candles..............................	n.a.p.	n.a.p.	.1083	127.5
Umbrellas, parasols, and canes...........	n.a.p.	n.a.p.	.0955	115.6

Derivation of Total Employment-Output Ratios and 1953 Indices of Total Output for All Commodity-Producing Industries

Industry		Average Number of Employees, 1953 (In thousands)	Value of 1953 Domestic Output (In millions of dollars)	1953 Employment-Output Ratio[a]	Index of 1953 Prices of Output (1947=100)
Code Number	Title				
		(1)	(2)	(3)	(4)
1	Meat animals and products....................	676.3[b]	10,084.0	.0669	91.2
2	Poultry and eggs............................	471.4[b]	5,104.9	.0923	102.0
3	Farm dairy products.........................	1,104.7[b]	5,377.3	c	101.5
4	Food grains and feed crops....................	845.8[b]	10,032 0	c	83.3
5	Cotton......................................	710.3[b]	2,814.6	c	91.2
6	Tobacco.....................................	308.3[b]	993.6	c	114.9
7	Oil-bearing crops...........................	66.9[b]	1,012.8	c	84.8
8	Vegetables and fruits........................	742.0[b]	3,971.0	.1869	97.9
9	All other agricultural products................	n.a.	n.a.	c	n.a.
10	Fisheries, hunting and trapping...............	41.6	d	d	n.a.
11	Iron ore mining.............................	39.8	712.7	.0559	173.5
12	Copper mining..............................	28.6	434.5	.0658	136.3
13	Lead and zinc mining........................	17.4	135.6	.1283	87.6
14	Bauxite mining	} 19.9	16.7	.1130[e]	149.6
15	Other metal mining..........................		d	d	n.a.
16	Coal mining.................................	338.4	2,211.3	.1530	128.9
17	Crude petroleum and natural gas..............	294.5	7,651.9	.0385	140.5
18	Stone, sand, clay and abrasives..............		d	d	n.a.
19	Sulfur......................................	}123.9	122.5	.0647[f]	149.9
20	Other nonmetallic minerals...................		d	d	n.a.
21	Meat packing and wholesale poultry...........	298.6	11,767.1	.0254	94.0
22	Processed dairy products.....................	98.4	3,453.5	.0285	113.5
23	Canning, preserving and freezing..............	206.3	3,777.8	.0546	98.7
24	Grain mill products..........................	107.9	5,307.9	.0204	92.8
25	Bakery products.............................	286.1	3,710.9	.0771	117.4
26	Miscellaneous food products...................	310.6	7,567.8	.0410	117.8
27	Sugar.......................................	w.	w.	.0246	105.0
28	Alcoholic beverages..........................	115.0	3,244.5	.0355	111.0
29	Tobacco manufactures........................	w.	w.	.0287	120.5
30	Spinning, weaving, and dyeing.................	781.4	9,198.5	.0850	93.8
31	Special textile products......................	79.5	1,194.7	.0666	120.3
32	Jute, linen, cordage and twine................	19.6	245.3	.0799	101.8
33	Canvas products.............................	14.4	157.8	.0913	96.0
34	Apparel and furs............................	1,380.4	12,657.8	.1091	98.1
35	House furnishings and other nonapparel.........	115.5	1,959.7	.0590	92.6
36	Logging.....................................	80.9	764.9	.1058	121.2
37	Sawmills, planing and veneer mills..............	411.1	4,072.5	.1009	125.2
38	Plywood.....................................	39.1	466.9	.0837	116.7
39	Fabricated wood products.....................	124.9	1,442.4	.0866	143.0
40	Wood containers and cooperage.................	63.9	609.5	.1048	124.6
41	Wood furniture..............................	207.0	2,004.8	.1032	117.9
42	Metal furniture.............................	98.3	1,270.2	.0774	122.1
43	Partitions, screens, and shades.................	55.5	663.8	.0837	120.2

n.a. =not available.

n.a.p. =not available for publication.

w =withheld to prevent inference of figures not available for publication.

[a] This ratio represents the number of employees per $1,000 of output. It is obtained by dividing Column 1 by Column 2, but figures may not equal the quotient exactly because of rounding.

[b] Includes farmers and unpaid farm family workers.

[c] No employment-output ratio was used for these industries because it was assumed, for the purposes of this study, that in the short period their output and therefore their employment remain unchanged.

[d] The value of 1953 output of this industry was derived from the value of 1947 output and is available only in 1947 prices. Since it was not possible to derive the value of output in 1953 prices, the employment-output coefficient could not be expressed in 1953 prices. For use in connection with the interindustry relations matrix, however, its expression in 1947 prices was sufficient.

[e] To get the 1953 employment-output ratio with output expressed in 1953 prices for industry no. 14, the combined ratio for industries nos. 14 and 15, with output expressed in 1947 prices, was divided by the 1953 price index for industry no. 14.

[f] To get the 1953 employment-output ratio with output expressed in 1953 prices for industry no. 19, the combined ratio for industries nos. 18, 19, and 20, with output expressed in 1947 prices, was divided by the 1953 price index for industry no. 19.

Table D.2 (*continued*)

Code Number	Title	Average Number of Employees, 1953 (In thousands)	Value of 1953 Domestic Output (In millions of dollars)	1953 Employment-Output Ratio[a]	Index of 1953 Prices of Output (1947 = 100)
		(1)	(2)	(3)	(4)
44	Pulp mills	55.1	1,469.6	.0375	114.1
45	Paper and board mills	162.0	4,074.0	.0398	132.2
46	Converted paper products	316.3	5,399.3	.0586	111.3
47	Printing and publishing	760.3	9,018.7	.0843	128.7
48.1	Sulfuric acid	n.a.p.	n.a.p.	.0426	129.7
48.2	Other inorganic chemicals, excluding alumina	n.a.p.	n.a.p.	.0438	133.0
49	Industrial organic chemicals	99.6	3,013.6	.0331	111.2
50	Plastic materials	43.0	1,261.1	.0341	126.1
51	Synthetic rubber	10.0	462.0	.0216	124.3
52	Synthetic fiber	71.9	1,270.5	.0566	109.8
53	Explosives and fireworks	n.a.p.	n.a.p.	.0936	124.6
54	Drugs and medicines	94.0	1,923.8	.0489	83.2
55	Soap and related products	47.4	1,480.6	.0320	87.4
56	Paints and allied products	74.6	1,938.4	.0385	113.5
57	Gum and wood chemicals	8.6	180.3	.0477	102.6
58	Fertilizers	34.8	908.9	.0383	118.3
59	Vegetable oils	25.0	1,586.5	.0157	70.5
60	Animal oils	13.8	275.5	.0501	53.3
61	Miscellaneous chemical industries	86.4	2,012.5	.0429	115.5
62	Petroleum products	168.7	11,890.2	.0142	125.3
63	Coke and products	42.7	1,747.6	.0244	145.4
64	Paving and roofing materials	19.9	476.6	.0417	115.8
65	Tires and inner tubes	97.0	2,088.2	.0464	127.9
66	Miscellaneous rubber products	172.8	2,075.0	.0833	126.3
67	Leather tanning and finishing	46.4	777.0	.0598	88.2
68	Other leather products	64.5	602.1	.1071	104.5
69	Footwear (excluding rubber)	264.5	2,318.3	.1141	111.2
70	Glass	144.8	1,737.3	.0833	136.6
71	Cement	37.8	752.1	.0503	133.0
72	Structural clay products	72.2	567.2	.1273	135.3
73	Pottery and related products	54.6	378.4	.1443	127.5
74	Concrete and plaster products	87.5	1,231.4	.0710	121.5
75	Abrasive products	24.8	403.6	.0614	125.0
76	Asbestos products	38.0	544.6	.0698	119.5
77	Other miscellaneous nonmetallic minerals	28.1	408.3	.0688	132.2
78	Blast furnaces	59.5	4,130.3	.0144	164.5
79.1	Carbon steel works and rolling mills			.0403	155.0
79.2	Alloy steel works and rolling mills, excluding stainless	589.2[g]	14639.2[g]	.0403	155.0
79.3	Stainless steel works and rolling mills			.0403	155.0
79.4	Nonferrous forgings and metal powders	30.1	754.0	.0399	137.6
80	Iron foundries	173.0	1,871.1	.0925	137.1
81	Steel foundries	76.9	841.6	.0914	144.8
82	Primary copper	13.4	807.4	.0166	136.2
83	Copper rolling and drawing	54.3	1,833.3	.0387	143.0
84	Primary lead	4.7	306.3	.0153	92.0
85	Primary zinc	11.4	281.8	.0405	105.0
86	Miscellaneous primary metals	8.7	206.7	.0421	121.1
87	Miscellaneous nonferrous metal rolling	12.3	368.5	.0334	143.1
88	Primary aluminum, including alumina	19.6	488.1	.0401	143.3
89	Aluminum rolling and drawing	39.1	968.0	.0404	141.3
90	Secondary nonferrous metals	12.8	713.8	.0179	118.4
91.1	Copper foundries	83.7	1,055.5	.0793	134.7
91.2	Aluminum foundries	83.7	1,055.5	.0793	134.7
91.3	Magnesium foundries	83.7	1,055.5	.0793	134.7
91.4	Other nonferrous foundries	83.7	1,055.5	.0793	134.7
92	Iron and steel forgings	55.9	907.0	.0616	146.9
93	Tin cans and other tinware	55.7	1,328.7	.0419	140.8
94	Cutlery	17.3	200.7	.0862	124.5
95	Tools and general hardware	47.3	479.6	.0986	145.6
96	Miscellaneous hardware	93.4	1,129.3	.0827	140.2
97	Metal plumbing and vitreous fixtures	41.8	531.8	.0786	120.8
98	Heating (including cooking) equipment	89.0	1,283.2	.0693	121.3
99	Structural metal products	199.7	3,056.3	.0653	120.8
100.1	Boiler shop products	72.7	1,119.3	.0650	118.7
100.2	Fabricated pipe	12.9	211.4	.0610	148.9

[g] See footnote [d] to Appendix Table D.1.

	Industry	Average Number of Employees, 1953 (In thousands)	Value of 1953 Domestic Output (In millions of dollars)	1953 Employment-Output Ratio[a]	Index of 1953 Prices of Output (1947 =100)
Code Number	Title				
		(1)	(2)	(3)	(4)
101	Metal stampings	170.3	2,462.8	.0692	141.4
102	Metal coating and engraving	49.2	444.7	.1107	126.0
103	Lighting fixtures	54.5	764.2	.0713	118.2
104	Fabricated wire products	70.2	903.2	.0777	146.7
105	Metal barrels, drums, etc	10.0	204.0	.0490	140.3
106	Tubes and foils	9.6	169.0	.0568	124.9
107	Miscellaneous fabricated metal products	21.1	283.2	.0745	152.3
108	Steel springs	8.1	138.8	.0583	138.0
109	Nuts, bolts, and screw machine products	103.8	1,392.7	.0745	158.6
110	Steam engines and turbines	30.0	426.9	.0702	131.4
111	Internal combustion engines	68.0	1,178.8	.0577	143.2
112	Farm and industrial tractors	101.1	1,960.0	.0516	135.7
113	Farm equipment	83.0	1,273.9	.0651	137.1
114	Construction and mining machinery	99.1	1,555.2	.0638	143.2
115	Oil-field machinery and tools	34.7	504.8	.0688	133.2
116	Machine tools and metalworking machinery	157.6	2,376.4	.0663	153.0
117	Cutting tools, jigs and fixtures	137.4	1,711.1	.0803	126.6
118	Special industrial machinery	176.7	2,060.1	.0858	132.9
119	Pumps and compressors	60.7	913.2	.0665	140.1
120	Elevators and conveyors	42.3	648.7	.0652	139.1
121	Blowers and fans	16.4	231.8	.0708	156.0
122	Power transmission equipment	56.2	715.9	.0785	132.8
123	Industrial machinery, n.e.c.	43.3	665.5	.0651	134.4
124	Commercial machines and equipment, n.e.c.	117.8	1,272.4	.0926	116.0
125	Refrigeration equipment	134.2	2,385.3	.0562	120.6
126	Valves and fittings	79.0	1,009.8	.0782	137.4
127	Ball and roller bearings	58.5	634.3	.0922	124.2
128	Machine shops	118.5	1,259.6	.0940	132.7
129	Wiring devices and graphite products	58.4	793.0	.0737	132.9
130	Electrical measuring instruments	38.1	395.5	.0963	130.2
131	Motors and generators	129.3	1,697.4	.0762	123.7
132	Transformers	45.4	716.8	.0634	129.1
133	Electrical control apparatus	88.4	1,230.2	.0719	136.8
134	Electrical welding apparatus	19.8	327.4	.0605	130.4
135	Electrical appliances	111.6	1,814.5	.0615	113.2
136	Insulated wire and cable	62.2	1,423.0	.0437	130.1
137	Engine electrical equipment	53.0	631.9	.0839	132.9
138	Electric lamps	29.1	423.0	.0688	135.5
139	Radio and related products	n.a.p.	n.a.p.	.0711	95.5
140	Electronic tubes	83.2	783.2	.1062	132.9
141	Communication equipment	78.5	965.4	.0813	132.9
142	Storage batteries	17.3	372.1	.0465	123.4
143	Primary battteries	12.3	151.3	.0813	118.3
144	X-ray and therapeutic apparatus	5.5	73.8	.0745	133.0
145.1	Passenger cars and light trucks	n.a.p.	n.a.p.	.0333	130.2
145.2	Heavy trucks and buses	n.a.p.	n.a.p.	.0333	130.2
145.3	Motor vehicle parts and accessories	n.a.p.	n.a.p.	.0338	130.2
146	Truck trailers	19.4	390.6	.0497	132.9
147	Automobile trailers	12.5	240.7	.0519	132.9
148	Aircraft and parts	817.4	11,745.2	.0696	132.9
149	Ship and boat building and repairing	148.9	1,438.9	.1035	132.9
150	Locomotives	28.6	602.2	.0475	133.0
151	Railroad equipment	45.6	837.9	.0544	132.9
152	Motorcycles and bicycles, and miscellaneous transportation equipment	11.3	164.8	.0686	130.7
153	Instruments, etc.	110.3	1,303.0	.0847	132.3
154	Optical, ophthalmic, and photo equipment	97.0	1,208.3	.0803	115.8
155	Medical and dental instruments and supplies	44.5	607.4	.0733	126.4
156	Watches and clocks	33.7	468.4	.0719	107.5
157	Jewelry and silverware	80.3	972.7	.0826	101.1
158	Musical instruments and parts	n.a.p.	n.a.p.	.0870	115.6
159	Toys and sporting goods	92.5	857.5	.1079	115.7
160	Office supplies	33.3	386.9	.0860	106.8
161	Plastic products	85.1	1,039.7	.0818	126.1
162	Cork products	n.a.p.	n.a.p.	.0623	119.6
163	Motion picture production	52.0	864.2	.0602	n.a.
164	Miscellaneous manufactured products	181.7	1,800.9	.1009	115.3

Appendix Table D.3

Employment-Output Relationships for 1953 and 1947–1954 for Non-Commodity Producing Industries[a]

Industry		1953 Employment (In millions)	Value of 1953 Output (In billions of 1947 dollars)	1953 Ratio[b]	Regression of Employment on Output, 1947–1954			
					Coefficients		Coefficient of Determination (r²)	Standard Error of Slope[c]
Code Number	Title				Constant	Slope[c]		
		(1)	(2)	(3)	(4)	(5)	(6)	(7)
167	Electric light and power.......	.360	6.408	.0562	.3103	.0080*	.97	.0007
168	Natural, manufactured and mixed gas......................	.192	3.165	.0607	.1339	.0171*	.94	.0017
169.1	Railroad freight activity	1.206	7.696	.1567	.3487[e]	.0890*	.85	
169.2	Railroad passenger activity					.2614		
170	Trucking...................	.640	7.966	.0803	.2814	.0439*	.94	.0048
171	Warehousing and storage......	.143	.703	.2034		d*		
172	Overseas transportation.......	.130	.956	.1360	.0669	.0644*	.89	.0101
173	Other water transportation....	.136	1.296	.1050	.0291	.0784*	.92	.0108
174	Air transportation............	.109	1.285	.0851	.0610	.0352*	.90	.0049
175	Pipeline transportation........	.027	.521	.0517		d*		
176	Wholesale trade..............	2.784	19.145	.1454	.4636	.1231*	.83	.0228
177	Retail trade..................	7.744	30.507	.2538	1.8747	.1920*	.98	.0109
178	Local and highway transportation......................	.282	1.291	.2184	.1556	.0996*	.99	.0050
179	Telephone and telegraph......	.677	3.825	.1770	.4072	.0674*	.85	.0143
181	Banking, finance and insurance.	1.413	16.236	.0870	.3434	.0057*	.99	.0030
182	Hotels......................	.439	.864	.5082	.2830	.1744*	.89	.0253
183	Real estate and rentals........	.459	37.236	.0123		d*		
184	Laundries and dry cleaning....	.505	1.959	.2578*				
185	Other personal services........	.361	2.274	.1588*	−.0095	.1666	.44	.0761
186	Advertising, including radio and TV.....................	.169	1.909	.0885*				
187	Business services.............	.297	1.236	.2403	.0107	.2297*	.99	.0091
188	Auto repair services..........	.234	1.404	.1667	.0967	.0987*	.78	.0068
189	Other repair services..........	.146	1.751	.0834	.0485	.0560*	.89	.0079
190	Motion pictures and other amusements....................	.467	2.113	.2210	.1057	.1698*	.82	.0404
191	Medical, dental and other professional services..........	1.111	5.566	.1996*	−.2614	.6708		
192	Non-profit institutions........	3.093	8.545	.3620*	−.5177	.4251		

* Indicates the figure that was used in this study to represent ratio of employment change to output change, measured in 1947 prices.
[a] Source: Derivation is explained in immediately following pages.
[b] Employees per $1,000 of output in 1947 prices.
[c] Slope and standard error converted to per $1,000 basis in 1947 prices.
[d] No effect on employment of changes in output.
[e] Multiple regression.

Derivation of Employment-Output Relations for
Non-Commodity Producing Industries

As was explained in Chapter 4, changes of output in commodity-producing industries were converted into the associated employment changes on the assumption that the ratios of employment changes to output changes in those industries were the same as the ratios of their total employment to their total output. This assumption was not regarded as a safe one to apply to non-commodity producing industries. The relationships used for these industries were determined after examining the postwar relationships of employment to output in constant prices from 1947 to 1954 and deriving from them linear approximations of the regression of employment on output.[5]

In selecting the data from which to estimate these relationships, primary emphasis was placed on obtaining data for employment and output that were comparable in coverage. Wherever possible, both sets of data were obtained from the same source even if they did not cover the entire industry, provided, of course, that the segment covered was sufficiently large to justify the assumption that it was representative of the whole.[6] In most cases, however, no single source was available for both employment and output; estimates of output had to be reconciled with available employment data. This reconciliation generally involved one of two types of adjustments. In the first type, the employment data covered the whole industry but output indexes could be derived for only part of the industry. Usually the output data covered a substantial part of the industry, and the output level was brought up to the industry level by applying the available output indexes to the absolute level of output of the entire industry in 1947. (Total 1947 output was available for all industries from BLS industry reports.)

In other cases the reverse was true—output information was available for a larger segment than for employment. Here the output level was adjusted to make it comparable by removing the output of that part that was not covered by the employment data. This procedure

[5] The statistical and analytical work here described was done by Mrs. Eva Jacobs.

[6] Since the coefficients were to be applied to output changes derived from a Bureau of Labor Statistics input-output matrix, output had to be defined and industries had to be classified as they were in the B.L.S. study. (See Appendix C of *The Mobilization Model Matrix*, mimeographed memorandum dated March 15, 1954, by Division of Interindustry Economics, Bureau of Labor Statistics, U. S. Department of Labor.) Since that study expressed output in 1947 prices, output data were converted into 1947 prices in determining these coefficients and are so expressed in the regression equations given in Appendix Table D.3.

involves the possibility of error because the slope of the regression for a segment of an industry will differ from that of the whole industry if the segment's share of the industry's employment differs from its share of the industry's output. Any such errors were probably not large, however, because the segments were generally large parts of their industries, so that their shares of its employment and of its output probably did not differ much.

The decision that the 1953 employment-output ratios for non-commodity producing industries could not be assumed to represent the ratios of their employment-output changes did not imply an *a priori* decision that regression coefficients would necessarily represent these incremental relationships better. Regression coefficients based on time series also have deficiencies in representing the true relation between employment and output because they reflect the effects of changes in technique as well as in output. In many industries increases in total output and employment-saving changes of technique were both correlated with time during the postwar period; there was no way of separating their effects on the regression. Where improvement of techniques reduced employment and output was rising, the regression coefficient gives an apparent change of employment per unit change of output that is lower than the true relation of the change in employment to the change of output with given productive technique. Whether to use the coefficient of the regression equation or the 1953 employment-output ratio for each industry was decided after studying the equations and considering other factors, such as adequacy of the data, the trend of the employment-output ratios over time, and comparison of these ratios with the regression coefficients.

For 20 of the 27 industries the coefficient chosen for use was the one obtained from the regression. For these industries, the coefficients derived from the slopes of the regressions are lower than the 1953 ratio. The differences are substantial for those industries with high fixed labor expenses, such as public utilities. Differences that appear to be small, such as in wholesale trade, may make significant differences in the resulting employment effects if the industry has relatively large output changes. For two of these 20 industries (pipelines and real estate) the data showed that moderate short-run changes in output had no effect on employment, *i.e.,* the slope of the regression was approximately zero. The data for the period analyzed showed little or no change in employment while output was rising steadily and substantially.

For six of the industries, the 1953 ratio of total employment and output was used. For three of these industries, the regressions were rejected because they had negative constants, implying negative employment at a level of no output, with slopes therefore considerably higher than the 1953 ratios. Such a result was ruled out on theoretical grounds as not indicating the true relation between employment and output, the statistical result presumably reflecting the effect on employment of factors other than output. The regressions for three other industries were rejected because the slopes were not statistically significant or because there was not sufficient change in output and employment during the period of observation to reveal the relationship.

For one industry (warehousing and storage), the data pointed to no clear output-employment relationship; neither the equation nor the 1953 ratio appeared reasonable. The data were questionable, and it is a relatively small industry. It was therefore assumed that changes in output have no effect on employment.

Appendix Table D.3 summarizes the results of the analysis. Columns 1, 2, and 3 show, respectively, the actual number of employees in 1953, the 1953 output in 1947 prices, and the corresponding employment-output ratios. Columns 4 and 5 show, respectively, the constant and the slope of the regression equations. Column 6 shows the coefficient of determination, the proportion of total variance that has been explained by the equation. Column 7 shows the standard error of the slope, an indication of its statistical significance.

Output Data

In general, the output data were obtained by developing production indexes, applying them to the 1947 value of subindustry output to obtain subindustry output in 1947 dollars for the years 1947-1954, and adding the output of the subindustries in an industry to obtain the industry output.

The Bureau of Labor Statistics, in appraising the 1947 pattern of interindustry relations, had developed a series of production indexes for these subindustries for the years 1947-1952. Where these indexes were appropriate for our purposes, they were used and extrapolated to 1953 or 1954. Where, as in some of the service industries, the BLS indexes for output of an industry (or a substantial part thereof) were based on the movement of its employment, they were not used; independent indexes were calculated instead.

Wherever possible, as for the utility and transportation industries, production indexes were derived from physical measures. For the service industries, it was necessary to deflate values in current prices to obtain production indexes. The particular data used to determine value of output varied with the industry, depending on what available series would best indicate the movement of output. In general, the data used were national income originating in the industry or personal consumption expenditures on its products. Among the factors considered in choosing the most appropriate measure were whether the service was primarily consumed by households or business, whether an appropriate deflator was available, and which measure most closely matched the definition of the industry.

The Consumer Price Index for individual items provided most of the deflators. In a few instances it was necessary to use the National Income Division's implicit price deflator for services, one of the "Implicit Price Deflators for Gross National Product". It was felt that, despite the aggregative character of this deflator, it adequately indicated the *movement* of prices in a narrower sector.

Employment Data

The definition of industries used in the Bureau of Labor Statistics interindustry relations study and in this book differs from that used in the employment series published by the Bureau of Labor Statistics or the National Income Division of the Department of Commerce.[7] In general it is less aggregative; an industry, as defined here, might consist of a part of one industry or of several industries as defined by the National Income Division. To obtain data on employment in industries as they are defined here, the components of the published industry employment figures had to be analyzed and, in some cases, re-combined.

In most cases it was possible to break down the employment data of the National Income Division on the basis of the detailed industry statistics contained in the Bureau of Employment Security (BES) publication *Average Employment and Total Wages of Workers Covered by State Unemployment Insurance Laws*. Inherent in this technique for estimating employment in individual industries is a crucial and questionable assumption. The BES figures are understated by the number of workers not covered by state unemployment insurance laws. In using BES data to determine the industry composition of the more aggregative grouping used by the National Income Division, we assume that the undercoverage for each industry within an industry group was the same. While BES has estimated undercoverage for some industries for selected periods, such estimates were not available for the service industries. The assumption was therefore unavoidable. Any resulting error in the estimates is probably minimized by the fact that most of the disaggregation was within groups the components of which are fairly homogeneous.

[7] See *Handbook of Labor Statistics,* 1950 edition for BLS data for 1947 and *Employment and Earnings,* May 1954 and May 1955 for BLS data for 1948-54. For National Income Division data for 1947-51 see U. S. Department of Commerce *National Income,* 1954 edition and for 1952-1954 data see *Survey of Current Business,* July 1955.

Relationship Between Ideal and Applied Concepts of Reflection Ratios

Estimates of reflection ratios were needed to estimate how much more every country would spend, per dollar of increase in its earnings, both in the United States for goods and services that create employment and in third countries in ways that generate income in these countries. Ideally, therefore, the numerator of the ratio should include all changes in a foreign country's current account spending in the United States except for payments of income on United States investments and all changes of current account spending in other countries, including income on the investments of these countries. It was explained in Chapter 7 that the statistical data required to use this concept of the reflection ratio at the next stage of the estimating process were not available and that for this reason no effort was made to estimate it. Instead, we sought to measure how much more every country would spend, per dollar of increase in its earnings, on merchandise alone. It was also explained in Chapter 7 that even the merchandise reflection ratios were not measured in the theoretically correct way because that way requires distinguishing changes in foreign payments that are induced directly by a country's export changes from those that are induced by its domestic income changes, a distinction that could not be made statistically. It is of interest to find the conditions under which the merchandise reflection ratios, as they were actually derived, would be equal to the ideal ratio, which includes services and investment income paid to countries other than the United States. These conditions can be most clearly seen if the various ratios are expressed algebraically.

We use the following notation:

$Y \equiv$ change in national income
$E \equiv$ change in export earnings
$M \equiv$ change in imports of (*i.e.*, current payments for) all goods and services, including income on foreign capital invested in the country. Its components are designated as M with subscripts containing numbers and letters (*e.g.*, M_{1e}) as follows:

1 $\equiv$ goods and services other than income paid on foreign capital.

2 $\equiv$ income on foreign capital paid to the United States.

3 $\equiv$ income on foreign capital paid to third countries;

e ≡ payments generated directly by export changes;

y ≡ payments generated by domestic income changes.

$$m_{1e} \equiv \frac{M_{1e}}{E}$$

$$m_{2e} \equiv \frac{M_{2e}}{E}$$

$$m_{3e} \equiv \frac{M_{3e}}{E}$$

$$m_{1y} \equiv \frac{M_{1y}}{Y}$$

$$m_{2y} \equiv \frac{M_{2y}}{Y}$$

$$m_{3y} \equiv \frac{M_{3y}}{Y}.$$

d ≡ the country's export multiplier, generated by the part of E that gets into the income stream, operating through internal mechanisms, whether through direct effects of income changes on internal spending or otherwise, *e.g.*, through income-induced changes of credit policy. Thus

$$d \equiv \frac{Y}{E(1 - m_{1e} - m_{2e} - m_{3e})}$$

To avoid going through the familiar exercise of deriving the foreign trade multiplier, various versions of which are derived in the works cited in footnote 1 of Chapter 7, it may simply be asserted that

$$d = \frac{1}{1 - b + m_{1y} + m_{2y} + m_{3y}} \quad \text{where}$$

b is the ratio of changes in domestic spending on goods and services to changes in income. (The figures in the columns of Appendix Tables E.1 and E.3 designated as the "Marginal Non-spending: Income Ratio" thus represent 1-b.)

The total reflection ratio, R, which includes investment income paid to the United States as well as other countries, is

$$\frac{M_{1e} + M_{1y} + M_{2e} + M_{2y} + M_{3e} + M_{3y}}{E}.$$

It follows from the definitions of the m's and d that $M_{1y} = m_{2y}Y$, $M_{2y} = m_{2y}Y$, $M_{3y} = m_{3y}Y$, and $Y = dE(1 - m_{1e} - m_{2e} - m_{3e})$. Therefore

$$\frac{M_{1y} + M_{2y} + M_{3y}}{E} = (m_{1y} + m_{2y} + m_{3y})d(1 - m_{1e} - m_{2e} - m_{3e}).$$

Also,

$$\frac{M_{1e} + M_{2e} + M_{3e}}{E} = m_{1e} + m_{2e} + m_{3e}.$$

Therefore the total reflection ratio

$$R\left(\equiv\frac{M_{1e} + M_{1y} + M_{2e} + M_{2y} + M_{3e} + M_{3y}}{E}\right)$$

$$= m_{1e} + m_{2e} + m_{3e} + (1 - m_{1e} - m_{2e} - m_{3e})d(m_{1y} + m_{2y} + m_{3y}).$$

$$= m_{1e} + m_{2e} + m_{3e} + (1 - m_{1e} - m_{2e} - m_{3e})\frac{m_{1y} + m_{2y} + m_{3y}}{1 - b + m_{1y} + m_{2y} + m_{3y}}.$$

To estimate expenditures of other countries in the United States that generate employment directly, we need a reflection ratio that excludes investment income paid to the United States, *i.e.*, that excludes

$$\frac{M_{2e} + M_{2y}}{E}.$$

This modified total reflection ratio, which we have referred to as the theoretically correct ratio for our problem and which we may call R′, is therefore

$$R'\left(\equiv\frac{M_{1e} + M_{1y} + M_{3e} + M_{3y}}{E}\right)$$

$$= m_{1e} + m_{3e} + (1 - m_{1e} - m_{2e} - m_{3e})d(m_{1y} + m_{3y})$$

$$= m_{1e} + m_{3e} + (1 - m_{1e} - m_{2e} - m_{3e})\frac{m_{1y} + m_{3y}}{1 - b + m_{1y} + m_{2y} + m_{3y}}.$$

In the first form of the right hand side of this equation, the sum of the first two terms is the component of R′ designated on page 155 in Chapter 7 as (1), the first factor in its last term is the component designated as (2a), the factor d is the one designated as (2b), and the last factor is the one designated as (2c). This is the ratio with which we now want to compare the ratios actually obtained.

It will be noted that this formula requires distinguishing the sum $m_{2e}+m_{3e}$ from the sum $m_{2y}+m_{3y}$. To distinguish these two sums statistically, it would be necessary to distinguish $M_{2e}+M_{3e}$ from $M_{2y}+M_{3y}$. There was no statistical basis for making the latter distinction and therefore no basis for determining some of the values called for by this formula.

In computing the merchandise reflection ratios for all countries, therefore, we actually estimated

$$\frac{M_{2e} + M_{2y} + M_{3e} + M_{3y}}{E},$$

designated in Appendix Tables E.1 and E.3 as the "Marginal Dividends: Export Ratio."

For some countries, the merchandise reflection ratios were derived by assuming that their total reflection ratios, R, $= 1$. (This assumption can be regarded as an inference from the assumption that $1 - b = 0$, although it would also be true if $M_{1e} + M_{2e} + M_{3e} = 1$.) The merchandise reflection ratios that were used for these countries, designated as R'_M, were computed as

$$R'_M \equiv 1 - \frac{M_{2e} + M_{2y} + M_{3e} + M_{3y}}{E}$$

In terms of the parameters, this formula becomes

$$R'_M = 1 - \left[m_{2e} + m_{3e} + \frac{(1 - m_{1e} - m_{2e} - m_{3e})(m_{2y} + m_{3y})}{1 - b + m_{1y} + m_{2y} + m_{3y}} \right].$$

This ratio is equal to the modified total reflection ratio R' when, in addition to the condition $1 - b = 0$, it is also true that $M_{2y} = M_{3e} = M_{3y} = 0$, for then

$$R'_M = 1 - m_{2e} = R'.$$

Expressed verbally, these conditions are that increases of income generate equal increases of spending on goods and services, investment income paid to the United States is not affected by the country's domestic income changes, and investment income paid to other countries is not affected by export changes, either directly or through export-induced changes in national income. This implies that changes in income paid on foreign investments are confined to United States investments in export industries.

For other countries, a value less than 1 was assigned to b and the merchandise reflection ratio (designated in these cases as R''_M) was computed by the formula

$$R''_M \equiv \left(1 - \frac{M_{2e} + M_{2y} + M_{3e} + M_{3y}}{E} \right) \left(\frac{1}{1 - b + \dfrac{M'_{1e} + M'_{1y}}{Y}} \right)$$

$$\cdot \left(\frac{M'_{1e} + M'_{1y}}{Y} \right)$$

where M'_{1e} and M'_{1y} represent the merchandise and shipping cost components of M_{1e} and M_{1y}, respectively. When expressed in terms of the parameters, this general formula becomes too complicated to reproduce.

However, when not only $M_{2y}=M_{3e}=M_{3y}=0$ but in addition, $M'_{1e}=M_{1e}$ and $M'_{1y}=M_{1y}$, it is equal to the modified total reflection ratio because then

$$R''_M = \frac{m_{1e}(1-b) + m_{1y}(1-m_{2e})}{1-b+m_{1y}} = R'.$$

These conditions include those implied by the formula for the first group of countries except for the assumption that characterized those countries, viz., that changes of domestic income generate equal changes of spending on goods and services. In place of this condition, the additional condition for the ratio used to be equal to the ideal one is simply that all changes in imports of goods and services consist of merchandise and shipping services.

The conditions under which the actually computed merchandise reflection ratios are equal to the theoretically correct way of estimating the merchandise reflection ratio can be derived in a similar way. The exclusion of other produced services and investment income makes the correct formula for the merchandise reflection, R_M, the following:

$$R_M = m'_{1e} + (1 - m_{1e} - m_{2e} - m_{3e}) \frac{m'_{1y}}{1-b+m_{1y}+m_{2y}+m_{3y}}.$$

R'_M, the ratio used for the countries whose total reflection ratios were assumed to equal 1, is equal to this theoretically correct merchandise reflection ratio when, in addition to the condition $1-b=0$, the conditions $M'_{1e}=M_{1e}$ and $M'_{1y}=M_{1y}$ are also fulfilled, because then

$$R'_M = \frac{m_{1e}(m_{2y}+m_{3y}) + m_{1y}(1-m_{2e}-m_{3e})}{m_{1y}+m_{2y}+m_{3y}} = R_M.$$

In other words, if all increases in domestic income are spent on goods and services, the only additional condition is that there are no changes in imports of services other than shipping. No limitations need be placed on the values of any of the types of investment income.

Similarly, R''_M, the ratio used for other countries, is equal to the theoretically correct merchandise reflection ratio when $M'_{1e}=M_{1e}$ and $M'_{1y}=M_{1y}$ even if $1-b>0$ because then

$$R''_M = \frac{m_{1e}(1-b+m_{2y}+m_{3y}) + m_{1y}(1-m_{2e}-m_{3e})}{1-b+m_{1y}+m_{2y}+m_{3y}} = R_M.$$

This indicates that all the assumptions described in Chapter 7 as having been made when the ratios for these countries were estimated were not necessary to make the formula equivalent to a theoretically correct merchandise reflection ratio.

Whether we consider the set of conditions under which the formulae used are equivalent to the formula for R' or the set of those under which they are equivalent to R_M—and some of the conditions are the same—

two things about them are worth noting. Although these conditions presumably are fully met in few if any countries, the net effect of deviations from them is probably sufficiently small in most countries to make the formulae used fairly close approximations to them. This conclusion is supported partly by the fact that one of the deviations offsets another. Consider the conditions $M_{2y} = M_{3y} = 0$, two of the conditions required for the formulae used to be equivalent to R'. If changes in the host country's domestic income do generate changes in investment income paid to foreign countries so that $M_{2y} + M_{3y} > 0$, the formulae we have used understate the leakages from domestic incomes and thereby overstate the export multipliers. We have treated such changes of investment income as though they arose directly from exports, thereby overstating $M_{2e} + M_{3e}$ by as much as we have understated $M_{2y} + M_{3y}$. Since the overstated changes were deducted from the export earnings to which the export multipliers were applied, the overstatement of $M_{2e} + M_{3e}$ introduces an understatement into the computed reflection ratio that offsets (although not necessarily exactly) the corresponding understatement of $M_{2y} + M_{3y}$.

Moreover, deviations of the conditions $M'_{1e} = M_{1e}$ and $M'_{1y} = M_{1y}$ from reality appear unlikely to be large. In both 1953 and 1954, foreign countries' imports from the United States of merchandise and services other than payments of investment income, as measured by United States exports of such goods and services, consisted of merchandise and shipping services to the extent of 92 per cent.[1] Thus, insofar as one can judge by expenditures that other countries make in the United States, the services excluded by the formulae used were only about 8 per cent of the total in 1953. They do not seem to be significantly different now.

[1] See *Balance of Payments Yearbook*, Vol. 8, published by the International Monetary Fund, p. 211. Insurance is assumed to be entirely on merchandise. Transportation is divided between merchandise and persons on the basis of Table C, page 213, total port expenditures being distributed in accordance with the distribution of freight receipts and passenger fares.

Appendix Table E.1
Reflection Ratios of Major Suppliers of Liberalized Imports[a]

Country	Number of Cases in Which Country Is Major Supplier	World Trade Group	Determinants of Merchandise Reflection Ratio					
			Total Reflection Ratio	Marginal Dividends Export Ratio	Marginal Non-Spending: Income Ratio	Marginal Import: Income Ratio[b]	Export Multiplier[b]	Merchandise Reflection Ratio
	(1)	(2)	(3)	(4)	(5)	(6)	(7)	(8)
Argentina	1	2	1.00	0	0			1.00
Australia	2	2	1.00	0	0			1.00
Austria	1	4	—	0	.15	.21	2.78	.58
Bahamas	1	4	—	n.a.	.10[c]	n.a.	n.a.	.67[c]
Belgium-Luxembourg	9	4	—	0	.15	.36	1.96	.71
Brazil	2	2	1.00	.05	0			.95
Canada	36	3	—	.05	.05	.23	3.57	.78
Cuba	2	1	1.00	.15	0			.85
Finland	2	2	1.00	0	0			1.00
France	16	4	—	0	.15	.13	3.57	.46
Germany (Federal Republic)	26	4	—	0	.15	.15	3.33	.50
Hong Kong	2	4	—	.15	.15	.80	1.05	.72
India	1	2	1.00	0	0			1.00
Iran	1	4	1.00	.20	0			.80
Italy	6	2	1.00	0	0			1.00
Japan	21	4	—	0	.15	.14	3.45	.48
Mexico	6	1	1.00	.10	0			.90
Netherlands	7	4	—	0	.15	.47	1.61	.76
New Zealand	1	2	1.00	0	0			1.00
Norway	1	2	1.00	0	0			1.00
Philippine Republic	1	1	1.00	.15	0			.85
Portugal	1	4	—	0	.15	.22	2.70	.59
Spain	2	2	1.00	0	0			1.00
Sweden	4	4	—	0	.15	.22	2.70	.59
Switzerland	12	4	—	0	.15	.24	2.56	.61
Turkey	1	2	1.00	0	0			1.00
United Kingdom	43	4	—	0	.10	.23	3.03	.70

n.a. = not available.

[a] Sources: Column 1 from Appendix Table E.4. Column 2 based on Column 8 of this table and Column 1 of Appendix Table E.2, in accordance with criteria described in Chapter 7. Columns 3 and 5 based on criteria described in Chapter 7. Columns 4 and 6 represent judgments based on data from *Balance of Payments Yearbooks* of the International Monetary Fund and *Statistics of National Income and Expenditure*, published by the United Nations. Column 7 is equal to 1.00 divided by the sum of Columns 5 and 6. Column 8: Where Column 3 figure is 1.00, Column 8 is 1.00 less Column 4. For other countries it is equal to 1.00 less Column 4, multiplied by Columns 6 and 7.

[b] For countries whose marginal non-spending: income ratio, as shown in Column 5, is zero, no figure is shown in Columns 6 and 7 because none is required to obtain Column 8. See Chapter 7.

[c] Since a marginal import : income ratio was not available for this country, its merchandise reflection ratio could not be computed. Its marginal non-spending ratio was used merely to help determine whether it belonged in a world trade group containing countries with merchandise reflection ratios exceeding .85 or not. The merchandise reflection ratio assigned to it was the unweighted average ratio of the countries in World Trade Groups 3 and 4.

Appendix Table E.2

Percentage Distribution of Imports and Total Exports of Major Suppliers of Liberalized Imports[a]

Country	Percentage of 1953 Imports Coming From: United States	World Trade Group 1	World Trade Group 2	World Trade Group 3	World Trade Group 4	Total 1953 Exports (In millions of dollars)	Weight in Exports of Its World Trade Group
	(1)	(2)	(3)	(4)	(5)	(6)	(7)
Argentina	14.4	7.9	23.4	7.5	46.8	1109	.0722
Australia	12.6	0.1	14.9	4.8	67.6	2014	.1309
Austria	12.7	2.3	31.4	1.0	52.6	538	.0164
Bahamas	47.7[b]	0[b]	4.5[b]	11.4[b]	36.4[b]	c	c
Belgium-Luxembourg	10.3	3.0	16.3	2.9	67.5	2259	.0689
Brazil	27.8	1.0	20.3	10.2	40.7	1539	.1001
Canada	73.8	2.1	4.1	4.0	16.0	4184	.6642
Cuba	76.1	2.2	6.5	2.4	12.8	640	.1742
Finland	5.4	0.8	49.5	0.2	44.1	572	.0372
France	9.8	1.4	22.6	3.4	62.8	3784	.1154
Germany (Federal Republic)	10.4	4.5	29.2	4.6	51.3	4422	.1848
Hong Kong	5.9	2.5	43.4	1.5	46.7	483	.0147
India	15.8	0.1	23.5	5.6	55.0	1116	.0726
Iran	17.2	6.3	11.7	0.6	64.2	115	.0035
Italy	13.4	1.7	26.1	5.4	53.4	1507	.0981
Japan	31.5	12.2	32.5	9.4	14.4	1275	.0389
Mexico	83.3	0.3	2.8	1.7	11.9	496	.1351
Netherlands	10.1	2.4	20.5	2.3	64.7	2150	.0655
New Zealand	7.6	0	21.0	1.4	70.0	660	.0429
Norway	8.5	0.6	13.1	5.3	72.5	509	.0331
Philippine Republic	78.8	0	3.5	3.6	14.1	391	.1065
Portugal	9.9	0.9	8.8	5.8	74.6	219	.0067
Spain	12.0	4.3	15.6	13.9	54.2	486	.0316
Sweden	8.1	1.9	21.6	2.1	66.3	1470	.0451
Switzerland	12.3	3.1	22.4	4.5	57.7	1202	.0366
Turkey	11.4	0	26.2	3.4	59.0	396	.0258
United Kingdom	7.7	2.4	38.3	9.5	42.1	7525	.2292

[a] Sources: Columns 1–6 based on *Direction of International Trade, 1938, 1948, and 1951–1954*, published jointly by the United Nations, the International Monetary Fund, and the International Bank for Reconstruction and Development (Statistical Papers, Series T, Vol. VI, No. 10). Column 7 is the ratio of Column 6 to total 1953 exports of all countries in the same world trade group.

[b] The distribution of imports by the Bahamas was based on data provided by the International Monetary Fund covering 1950 and 1951 imports from major sources of supply. Complete or later information was not available when the estimates were made.

[c] Since no independently determined merchandise reflection ratio was available for this country, it was not included in determining the weighted average merchandise reflection ratio of World Trade Group 4.

Reflection Ratios, Percentages of Imports Purchased from the United States and Other Data for Countries Not Major Suppliers of Liberalized Imports[a]

Country (1953 Name)	World Trade Group	Total Reflection Ratio	Determinants of Merchandise Reflection Ratio					Percentage of 1953 Merchandise Imports From U.S.	Total 1953 Exports (In millions of dollars)	Weight in Exports of its World Trade Group
			Marginal Dividends: Export Ratio	Marginal Non-Spending: Income Ratio	Marginal Import: Income Ratio[b]	Export Multiplier[b]	Merchandise Reflection Ratio			
(1)	(1)	(2)	(3)	(4)	(5)	(6)	(7)	(8)	(9)	(10)
Aden and British Protected States in Persian Gulf	4	1.00	.35	0			.65	10.8	1115	.0340
Albania	2	1.00	0	0			1.00	n.a.	n.a.	n.a.
Algeria	4	1.00	.20	0			.80	2.8	397	.0121
Anglo-Egyptian Sudan	2	1.00	0	0			1.00	2.6	128	.0083
Angola	4	—	0	.15[c]	n.a.	n.a.	.62[c]	15.0	123	d
Belgian Congo	4	—	0	.15	.42	1.75	.74	23.0	412	.0126
Bolivia	1[c]	1.00	0	0			1.00	31.8	125	.0341
British Guiana	4	—	.10	.15	.30	2.22	.60	11.3	49	.0015
Bulgaria	2	1.00	0	0			1.00	n.a.	29	.0019
Burma	2	1.00	0	0			1.00	4.0	238	.0155
Ceylon	2	1.00	0	0			1.00	3.2	329	.0214
Chile	1	1.00	.10	0			.90	52.7	415	.1130
China (Mainland)	2	1.00	0	0			1.00	n.a.	332	.0216
China (Formosa)	1	1.00	.05	0			.95	39.3	128	.0349
Colombia	1	1.00	.10	0			.90	61.8	596	.1624
Costa Rica	1	1.00	0	0			1.00	60.1	80	.0218
Cyprus	2	1.00	0	0			1.00	5.4	43	.0028
Czechoslovakia	2	1.00	0	.15	.31	2.17	.67	n.a.	200	.0130
Denmark	4	—	0	0			.90	4.5	894	.0273
Dominican Republic	1	1.00	.10	0			.90	67.9	104	.0283
Ecuador	1	1.00	.10	0			.90	59.8	76	.0207
Egypt	2	1.00	.10	0			.90	15.8	394	.0256
El Salvador	1	1.00	0	0			1.00	61.1	90	.0245
Ethiopia	2	1.00	0	0			1.00	13.5	71	.0046

French Cameroons	4	—	0	.15a	n.a.	n.a.	.62b	5.0	75	a
French Equatorial Africa	4	—	.20	.15a	n.a.	n.a.	.62c	8.6	57	d
French Morocco	4	1.00	.20	0			.80	8.2	269	.0082
French West Africa	4	1.00	0	0			.80	3.9	267	.0081
Germany, East	2	1.00	.15	.15	.40	1.82	1.00	1.0	98	.0064
Gold Coast	4	—	0	0			.62	5.5	251	.0077
Greece	2	1.00	0	0			1.00	16.7	132	.0086
Guatemala	1	1.00	.05	0			1.00	64.5	89	.0242
Haiti	1	1.00	.15	0			.95	67.0	38	.0104
Honduras	1	1.00	0	0			.85	71.6	67	.0183
Hungary	2	1.00	0	.15	.43		1.00	n.a.	58	.0038
Iceland	4	1.00	0	0			.74	26.5	43	.0013
Indo-China	2	1.00	.25	0			1.00	4.5	96	.0062
Indonesia	2	1.00	0	0			1.00	18.2	840	.0547
Iraq	4	1.00	.05	0		1.72	.75	15.2	406	.0124
Ireland, Republic of	2	1.00	0	0			1.00	9.0	319	.0208
Israel	2	1.00	.10	.10e			.95	31.7	58	.0038
Jamaica	4	—	0	.15	n.a.	n.a.	.62c	16.5	72	d
Kenya	4	1.00	0	0	.41	1.79	.66	5.2	64	.0020
Korea, South	1	1.00	0	0			1.00	35.9	41	.0112
Lebanon	2	1.00	.15	.15e			1.00	14.3	25	.0016
Madagascar	4	—	0	.15e	n.a.	n.a.	.62c	3.4	85	d
Malaya and Singapore	4	—	0	.15	.50	.50	.65	4.3	987	.0301
Mauritius	4	—	0	.15e	n.a.	n.a.	.62c	1.5	58	d
Mozambique	4	—	0	.15e	n.a.	n.a.	.62c	18.6	56	d
Netherlands Antilles	4	—	0	.15e	n.a.	n.a.	.62c	10.3	715	d
Nicaragua	1	1.00	0	0			1.00	65.1	55	.0150

n.a. = not available.

a Sources: Column 1 based on Columns 7 and 8, in accordance with criteria described in Chapter 7. Countries for which Column 8 data were not available are all in the Soviet bloc and are known to obtain less than one-third of their imports from the United States. Columns 2 and 4 based on criteria described in Chapter 7. Columns 3 and 5 represent judgments based on data from *Balance of Payments Yearbooks* of the International Monetary Fund and *Statistics of National Income and Expenditure*, published by the United Nations. Column 6 is equal to 1.00 divided by the sum of Columns 4 and 5. Column 7: Where Column 2 figure is 1.00, Column 7 is 1.00 less Column 3. For other countries it is equal to 1.00 less Column 3, multiplied by Columns 5 and 6. Columns 3 and 9 based on *Direction of International Trade, 1938, 1948 and 1951–1954,* published jointly by the United Nations, the International Monetary Fund, and the International Bank for Reconstruction and Development. (Statistical Papers, Series T, Vol. VI, No. 10). Column 10 is the ratio of Column 9 to total 1953 exports of all countries in the same world trade group.

b For countries whose marginal non-spending:income ratio, as shown in Column 4

is zero, no figure is shown in Columns 5 and 6 because none is required to obtain Column 7. See Chapter 7.

c Since a marginal import:income ratio was not available for this country, its merchandise reflection ratio could not be computed. Its marginal non-spending:income ratio was used merely to help determine whether it belonged in a world trade group containing countries with merchandise reflection ratios exceeding .85 or not. The merchandise reflection ratio assigned to it was the unweighted average ratio of the countries in World Trade Group 4.

d Since no independently determined merchandise reflection ratio was available for this country, it was not included in determining the weighted average merchandise reflection ratio of World Trade Group 4.

e Although Bolivia obtained slightly less than one-third of its imports from the United States in 1953, it was assigned to World Trade Group 1 instead of World Trade Group 2 because the 1953 percentage appeared subnormal. See Appendix Table E.3a for 1952 and 1954 percentages.

Table E.3 (continued)

		Determinants of Merchandise Reflection Ratio							
Country (1953 Name)	World Trade Group	Total Reflection Ratio	Marginal Dividends: Export Ratio	Marginal Non-Spending: Income Ratio	Marginal Import: Income Ratio[b]	Export Multiplier[b]	Merchandise Reflection Ratio	Percentage of 1953 Merchandise Imports From U.S.	Total 1953 Exports (In millions of dollars)	Weight in Exports of its World Trade Group
	(1)	(2)	(3)	(4)	(5)	(6)	(7)	(8)	(9)	(10)
Nigeria	4	—	0	.15	.16	3.23	.52	3.9	348	.0106
Pakistan	2	1.00	0	0			1.00	4.9	439	.0286
Panama, Republic of	1	1.00	0	0			1.00	64.0	18	.0049
Paraguay	2	1.00	.10	0			1.00	19.8	34	.0022
Peru	1	1.00	0	0			.90	54.5	222	.0605
Poland	2	1.00	0	0			1.00	0.3	264	.0172
Rhodesia and Nyasaland, Federation of	4	—	.15	.15	.50	1.54	.65	5.0[f]	451[g]	.0137
Romania	2	1.00	0	0			1.00	n.a.	61	.0040
Sarawak	4	1.00	.20	0			.80	0.3	139	.0042
Saudi Arabia	3	1.00	.35	0			.65	47.5	597	.0948
Sierra Leone	4	—	.10	.15[c]	n.a.	n.a.	.62[c]	2.9	34	d
South West Africa	4	—	.15	.15[c]	n.a.	n.a.	.62[c]	3.0	97	d
Syria	2	1.00	.20	0			1.00	12.2	104	.0068
Tanganyika	4	1.00	.20	0			.80	7.0	101	.0031
Thailand	2	1.00	0	0			1.00	18.9	349	.0227
Trinidad and Tobago	4	1.00	.20	0			.80	8.1	150	.0046
Tunisia	4	1.00	.20	0			.80	4.7	111	.0034
Uganda	4	—	.15	.15	.25	2.50	.53	2.8	94	.0029
U.S.S.R.	2	1.00	0	0			1.00	n.a.	364	.0237
Union of South Africa	4	—	.15	.15	.25	2.50	.53	18.4	805	.0245
Uruguay	2	1.00	0	0			1.00	17.8	270	.0176
Venezuela	3	1.00	.25	0			.75	66.2	1518	.2410
Yugoslavia	2[h]	1.00	0	0			1.00	34.4	186	.0121

f The Federation of Rhodesia and Nyasaland was not formed until September 1953. The percentage given in the table is the percentage of the total imports of Northern and Southern Rhodesia that came from the United States. Separate figures permitting computation of the corresponding percentage for Nyasaland are not available but its imports are known to have been a very small proportion of the total for the three areas.

g From United Nations Monthly Bulletin of Statistics.
h Although Yugoslavia obtained slightly more than one-third of its imports from the United States in 1953, it was assigned to World Trade Group 2 instead of World Trade Group 1 because the 1953 figure was abnormally high. See Appendix Table E.3a for 1952 and 1954 percentages.

Appendix Table E.3a

Percentages of Foreign Countries' Imports Obtained from the United States, 1952–1954[a]

Country	1952	1953	1954
	(1)	(2)	(3)
Aden and British Protected States in Persian Gulf..............................	12.6	10.8	11.4
Albania...............................	n.a.	n.a.	n.a.
Algeria...............................	4.5	2.8	3.2
Anglo-Egyptian Sudan..................	2.8	2.6	1.8
Angola................................	13.5	15.0	16.2
Argentina.............................	17.5	14.3	14.5
Australia.............................	14.4	12.5	11.5
Austria...............................	18.3	12.7	8.8
Bahamas..............................	n.a.	n.a.	n.a.
Belgian Congo.........................	24.6	23.0	18.9
Belgium-Luxembourg...................	14.7	10.3	10.3
Bolivia...............................	40.9	31.8	42.9
Brazil................................	41.8	27.8	32.9
British Guiana........................	16.0	11.3	13.5
Bulgaria..............................	n.a.	n.a.	n.a.
Burma................................	5.3	4.0	4.1
Canada...............................	74.0	73.7	72.7
Ceylon...............................	8.8	3.2	2.6
Chile.................................	51.6	52.7	40.7
China (Mainland)......................	n.a.	n.a.	n.a.
China (Formosa).......................	13.4	39.3	46.7
Colombia.............................	67.1	61.8	62.8
Costa Rica............................	63.3	60.1	58.2
Cuba.................................	74.8	75.7	76.7
Cyprus...............................	4.9	5.4	4.2
Czechoslovakia........................	n.a.	n.a.	0.6
Denmark..............................	8.3	4.5	4.9
Dominican Republic....................	70.1	67.9	65.8
Ecuador..............................	61.9	59.8	53.3
Egypt................................	16.4	15.8	11.1
El Salvador...........................	62.6	61.1	59.1
Ethiopia..............................	18.6	13.5	14.4
Finland...............................	7.7	5.4	4.9
France...............................	10.0	9.8	9.0
French Cameroons.....................	9.6	5.0	5.5
French Equatorial Africa...............	9.3	8.6	6.6
French Morocco.......................	8.8	8.2	9.7
French West Africa....................	4.7	3.9	3.5
Germany, East........................	0.8	1.0	0.4
Germany (Federal Republic)............	15.5	10.4	11.6

n.a. = not available.

[a] Source: *Direction of International Trade, 1938, 1948, 1951–1954* published jointly by the United Nations, the International Monetary Fund, and the International Bank for Reconstruction and Development (Statistical Papers, Series T, Vol. VI, No. 10).

Table E.3a (*continued*)

Country	1952	1953	1954
	(1)	(2)	(3)
Gold Coast..........................	7.2	5.5	3.8
Greece.............................	21.9	16.7	13.9
Guatemala.........................	62.9	64.5	64.4
Haiti..............................	70.1	67.0	64.4
Honduras..........................	73.8	71.6	68.5
Hong Kong.........................	5.8	5.8	8.2
Hungary...........................	n.a.	n.a.	2.2
Iceland............................	20.3	26.5	20.2
India..............................	34.3	15.7	12.5
Indochina..........................	5.1	4.5	7.2
Indonesia..........................	17.1	18.2	14.4
Iran...............................	22.3	17.1	23.8
Iraq...............................	18.3	15.2	13.9
Ireland, Republic of................	10.8	9.0	6.7
Israel..............................	36.5	31.7	27.4
Italy...............................	21.1	13.4	12.1
Jamaica............................	21.5	16.5	16.7
Japan..............................	37.9	31.4	35.4
Kenya.............................	6.3	5.2	2.8
Korea, South.......................	56.5	35.9	39.5
Lebanon...........................	15.9	14.3	14.8
Madagascar........................	4.5	3.4	3.1
Malaya and Singapore...............	4.7	4.3	4.7
Mauritius..........................	2.1	1.5	1.3
Mexico............................	82.8	83.1	80.9
Mozambique........................	11.5	13.6	17.4
Netherlands........................	12.6	9.8	11.8
Netherlands Antilles................	10.8	10.3	9.6
New Zealand.......................	9.3	7.4	8.2
Nicaragua..........................	71.3	65.1	64.9
Nigeria............................	4.6	3.9	4.7
Norway............................	11.2	8.5	8.4
Pakistan...........................	6.0	4.9	6.4
Panama, Republic of................	65.6	64.0	62.6
Paraguay...........................	29.9	27.6	19.8
Peru...............................	56.1	54.5	51.9
Philippine Republic.................	73.5	78.6	68.0
Poland.............................	0.1	0.3	0.7
Portugal...........................	13.7	9.8	8.3
Rhodesia and Nyasaland, Federation of....	n.a.	n.a.	4.5
Romania...........................	n.a.	n.a.	0.2
Sarawak...........................	0.1	0.3	1.2
Saudi Arabia.......................	48.4	47.5	34.0
Sierra Leone.......................	2.8	2.9	1.9
South West Africa..................	5.5	3.0	3.1
Spain..............................	16.7	12.0	18.3
Sweden............................	9.6	8.1	7.9

Table E.3a (*continued*)

Country	1952	1953	1954
	(1)	(2)	(3)
Switzerland..............................	16.2	12.3	12.8
Syria...................................	14.5	12.2	12.0
Tanganyika..............................	4.4	7.0	3.2
Thailand................................	18.7	18.9	15.9
Trinidad and Tobago.....................	9.1	8.1	8.6
Tunisia.................................	5.8	4.7	3.8
Turkey..................................	8.4	11.3	15.0
Uganda.................................	2.2	2.8	3.3
U.S.S.R.................................	n.a.	n.a.	n.a.
Union of South Africa....................	20.9	18.4	19.8
United Kingdom.........................	9.2	7.6	8.4
Uruguay................................	23.6	17.8	16.5
Venezuela...............................	68.5	66.2	61.6
Yugoslavia..............................	10.3	34.4	28.8

Distribution Among Foreign Countries of Increases in Foreign Dollar Earnings and in United States Exports[a]

		Gross Increase in Dollar Earnings		Increase in U. S. Exports	
Code Number	Title	Total (In Thousands of 1953 Dollars)	Percentage Distribution	Total (In Thousands of 1953 Dollars)	Percentage Distribution
		(1)	(2)	(3)	(4)
1	Meat animals and products.........	862.9		611.0	
	Mexico.........................		49.5		52.5
	Canada........................		47.5		38.6
	Australia......................		3.0		0.5
	World as a whole..............		—		8.4
8	Vegetables and fruits..............	762.8		577.5	
	Mexico........................		79.0		78.2
	Canada........................		21.0		16.0
	World as a whole..............		—		5.8
13	Lead and zinc mining..............	883.8		596.0	
	Canada........................		72.4		61.8
	Mexico........................		27.6		30.7
	World as a whole..............		—		7.5
21	Meat packing and wholesale poultry.	865.1		494.5	
	Canada........................		77.5		78.0
	Australia......................		22.5		5.0
	World as a whole..............		—		17.0
22	Processed dairy products...........	862.7		301.3	
	New Zealand...................		51.5		11.2
	Italy..........................		15.1		5.8
	Argentina......................		14.9		6.1
	Netherlands....................		11.6		2.6
	Switzerland....................		6.9		1.5
	World as a whole..............		—		72.8
24	Grain mill products................	890.1		510.0	
	Canada........................		83.0		83.4
	Japan.........................		17.0		4.5
	World as a whole..............		—		12.1
27	Sugar..........................	886.7		604.2	
	Cuba..........................		78.0		74.1
	Philippine Republic.............		22.0		21.6
	World as a whole..............		—		4.3
28	Alcoholic beverages................	859.1		427.6	
	Canada........................		64.7		74.9
	West Germany.................		18.5		1.9
	United Kingdom...............		16.8		1.8
	World as a whole..............		—		21.4
29	Tobacco manufactures..............	775.8		321.4	
	United Kingdom...............		47.7		6.2
	Cuba..........................		27.6		43.2
	Turkey........................		24.7		6.8
	World as a whole..............		—		43.8

[a] Money figures represent increases per $1 million increase of imports.

Liberalized Industry		Gross Increase in Dollar Earnings		Increase in U. S. Exports	
Code Number	Title	Total (In Thousands of 1953 Dollars)	Percentage Distribution	Total (In Thousands of 1953 Dollars)	Percentage Distribution
		(1)	(2)	(3)	(4)
30	Spinning, weaving, and dyeing	788.3		205.8	
	Japan		38.1		22.1
	United Kingdom		38.0		7.8
	Switzerland		12.4		3.5
	France		11.5		2.0
	World as a whole		—		64.6
31	Special textile products	793.4		194.8	
	Belgium		52.3		15.6
	Iran		25.5		14.3
	Japan		12.2		7.5
	France		10.0		1.8
	World as a whole		—		60.8
34	Apparel	753.2		210.2	
	Japan		34.8		20.8
	United Kingdom		35.2		6.8
	Italy		11.0		5.3
	France		9.7		1.6
	Switzerland		5.7		1.5
	World as a whole		—		64.0
35	Housefurnishings and other nonapparel	834.2		216.4	
	United Kingdom		41.1		8.5
	Japan		25.3		14.8
	Italy		21.9		11.3
	Netherlands		11.7		3.5
	World as a whole		—		61.9
38	Plywood	851.0		384.7	
	Canada		44.2		56.3
	Japan		40.1		13.4
	Finland		15.7		1.9
	World as a whole		—		28.4
40	Wood containers and cooperage	805.7		627.1	
	Mexico		100.0		96.4
	World as a whole		—		3.6
41	Wood furniture	849.5		270.7	
	Hong Kong		44.5		5.9
	Italy		37.3		15.7
	United Kingdom		18.2		3.1
	World as a whole		—		75.3
45	Paper and board mills	905.0		437.8	
	Canada		58.4		69.5
	Finland		28.6		3.2
	Sweden		13.0		1.3
	World as a whole		—		26.0
46	Converted paper products	847.0		201.6	
	West Germany		39.5		8.6
	United Kingdom		34.3		7.8

Liberalized Industry		Gross Increase in Dollar Earnings		Increase in U. S. Export	
Code Number	Title	Total (In Thousands of 1953 Dollars)	Percentage Distribution	Total (In Thousands of 1953 Dollars)	Percentage Distribution
		(1)	(2)	(3)	(4)
	Japan		18.1		11.5
	Canada		8.1		19.6
	World as a whole		—		52.5
49	Industrial organic chemicals	736.1		148.5	
	West Germany		46.0		11.9
	Switzerland		32.2		11.9
	United Kingdom		21.8		5.9
	World as a whole		—		70.3
51	Synthetic rubber	887.4		546.8	
	Canada		100.0		93.4
	World as a whole		—		6.6
52	Synthetic fiber	856.2		173.8	
	West Germany		43.2		11.0
	Belgium		34.3		12.4
	France		22.5		5.0
	World as a whole		—		71.6
54	Drugs and medicines	875.0		185.1	
	France		40.9		8.7
	Switzerland		36.0		12.7
	Japan		12.2		8.8
	United Kingdom		10.9		2.8
	World as a whole		—		67.0
56	Paints and allied products	711.1		326.3	
	Canada		62.0		77.8
	United Kingdom		38.0		4.5
	World as a whole		—		17.7
59	Vegetable oils	902.5		570.4	
	Mexico		44.0		52.2
	Canada		43.0		39.1
	Brazil		7.0		2.9
	India		6.0		1.5
	World as a whole		—		4.3
61	Miscellaneous chemical industries	825.5		148.9	
	France		76.1		19.0
	Bahamas		10.0		17.7
	United Kingdom		7.4		2.2
	West Germany		6.5		1.9
	World as a whole		—		59.2
65	Tires and inner tubes	903.3		105.2	
	France		100.0		38.7
	World as a whole		—		61.3
66	Miscellaneous rubber products	821.9		264.7	
	Japan		46.7		21.9
	United Kingdom		31.3		5.3
	Canada		16.9		30.3
	Netherlands		5.1		1.2
	World as a whole		—		41.3

	Liberalized Industry	Gross Increase in Dollar Earnings		Increase in U. S. Exports	
Code Number	Title	Total (In Thousands of 1953 Dollars)	Percentage Distribution	Total (In Thousands of 1953 Dollars)	Percentage Distribution
		(1)	(2)	(3)	(4)
67	Leather tanning and finishing.......	892.3		377.0	
	United Kingdom................		48.4		6.2
	Brazil.........................		30.7		19.2
	Canada........................		20.9		28.4
	World as a whole...............		—		46.2
69	Footwear (except rubber)...........	867.7		237.9	
	United Kingdom...............		66.3		13.0
	Japan.........................		17.4		9.6
	Switzerland....................		16.3		4.5
	World as a whole...............		—		72.9
70	Glass.........................	753.5		173.7	
	West Germany.................		30.3		6.9
	Belgium......................		21.0		6.7
	France.......................		20.0		3.9
	United Kingdom...............		17.0		4.0
	Japan.........................		11.7		7.6
	World as a whole...............		—		70.9
73	Pottery and related products........	700.7		183.9	
	Japan.........................		42.4		24.4
	West Germany.................		29.4		5.8
	United Kingdom...............		28.2		5.8
	World as a whole...............		—		64.0
79.1	Carbon steel works and rolling mills..	852.6		132.9	
	Belgium......................		44.6		20.9
	France.......................		28.7		8.3
	West Germany.................		26.7		8.9
	World as a whole...............		—		61.9
79.2	Alloy steel works and rolling mills, excluding stainless.................	852.6		132.9	
	Belgium......................		44.6		20.9
	France.......................		28.7		8.3
	West Germany.................		26.7		8.9
	World as a whole...............		—		61.9
79.3	Stainless steel works and rolling mills.	852.6		132.9	
	Belgium......................		44.6		20.9
	France.......................		28.7		8.3
	West Germany.................		26.7		8.9
	World as a whole...............		—		61.9
85	Primary zinc....................	935.9		542.3	
	Canada.......................		69.4		68.9
	Mexico.......................		17.6		22.8
	Italy.........................		13.0		3.0
	World as a whole...............		—		5.3
88	Primary aluminum including alumina	935.5		513.1	
	Canada.......................		88.3		92.7
	West Germany.................		11.7		1.1
	World as a whole...............		—		6.2

Liberalized Industry		Gross Increase in Dollar Earnings		Increase in U. S. Export	
Code Number	Title	Total (In Thousands of 1953 Dollars)	Percentage Distribution	Total (In Thousands of 1953 Dollars)	Percentage Distribution
		(1)	(2)	(3)	(4)
89	Aluminum rolling and drawing......	908.6		344.1	
	United Kingdom................		64.2		9.1
	Canada........................		35.8		54.5
	World as a whole...............		—		36.4
93	Tin cans and other tinware.........	889.6		352.2	
	Canada........................		34.8		50.6
	United Kingdom................		34.8		4.7
	Netherlands....................		30.4		5.9
	World as a whole...............		—		38.8
94	Cutlery.........................	757.8		185.7	
	West Germany..................		61.6		13.2
	United Kingdom................		27.6		6.0
	Italy..........................		10.8		5.9
	World as a whole...............		—		74.9
95	Tools and general hardware.........	827.9		188.0	
	West Germany..................		58.8		13.5
	Sweden........................		13.4		2.8
	Japan.........................		12.2		8.1
	United Kingdom................		6.8		1.6
	Norway........................		4.8		1.8
	Switzerland....................		4.0		1.3
	World as a whole...............		—		70.9
103	Lighting fixtures..................	761.5		191.3	
	Hong Kong.....................		86.8		14.7
	West Germany..................		13.2		2.7
	World as a whole...............		—		82.6
105	Metal barrels, drums, etc...........	740.7		161.6	
	France........................		87.2		18.0
	Canada........................		12.8		33.7
	World as a whole...............		—		48.3
106	Tubes and foils...................	827.4		137.9	
	France........................		44.7		12.1
	West Germany..................		37.6		11.7
	Switzerland....................		17.7		8.0
	World as a whole...............		—		68.2
116	Machine tools and metalworking machinery.........................	884.0		259.0	
	West Germany..................		45.0		8.0
	Switzerland....................		29.4		7.5
	Canada........................		15.6		30.6
	United Kingdom................		10.0		1.9
	World as a whole...............		—		52.0
118	Special industrial machinery........	860.3		244.4	
	United Kingdom................		49.9		9.5
	West Germany..................		40.5		7.4

Liberalized Industry		Gross Increase in Dollar Earnings		Increase in U. S. Exports	
Code Number	Title	Total (In Thousands of 1953 Dollars)	Percentage Distribution	Total (In Thousands of 1953 Dollars)	Percentage Distribution
		(1)	(2)	(3)	(4)
	Canada		9.6		19.4
	World as a whole		—		63.7
123	Industrial machinery, n.e.c.	883.0		357.8	
	Netherlands		42.5		8.0
	Canada		34.6		49.3
	United Kingdom		22.9		3.0
	World as a whole		—		39.7
127	Ball and roller bearings	828.0		320.5	
	Canada		41.7		62.0
	Sweden		36.3		4.5
	West Germany		22.0		3.0
	World as a whole		—		30.5
131	Motors and generators	870.8		508.0	
	Canada		85.0		83.8
	United Kingdom		15.0		1.4
	World as a whole		—		14.8
132	Transformers	888.8		210.1	
	Switzerland		59.4		18.9
	United Kingdom		21.3		4.8
	Austria		19.3		6.0
	World as a whole		—		70.3
133	Electrical control apparatus	850.7		197.6	
	Switzerland		72.5		23.5
	France		16.2		3.1
	United Kingdom		11.3		2.6
	World as a whole		—		70.8
134	Electrical welding apparatus	919.0		390.5	
	Canada		40.9		55.5
	United Kingdom		34.1		4.3
	Netherlands		25.0		4.5
	World as a whole		—		35.7
135	Electrical appliances	851.1		228.9	
	United Kingdom		77.8		15.6
	West Germany		12.5		2.4
	Japan		9.7		5.5
	World as a whole		—		76.5
136	Insulated wire and cable	826.6		413.3	
	Canada		66.9		77.0
	Spain		18.9		4.5
	United Kingdom		14.2		1.5
	World as a whole		—		17.0
138	Electric lamps	831.6		241.5	
	Japan		100.0		52.0
	World as a whole		—		48.0
139	Radio and related products	928.3		461.7	
	Canada		60.8		70.4

Liberalized Industry		Gross Increase in Dollar Earnings		Increase in U. S. Export	
Code Number	Title	Total (In Thousands of 1953 Dollars)	Percentage Distribution	Total (In Thousands of 1953 Dollars)	Percentage Distribution
		(1)	(2)	(3)	(4)
	Netherlands		19.7		3.1
	United Kingdom		19.5		2.1
	World as a whole		—		24.4
141	Communication equipment	885.1		524.7	
	Canada		87.8		85.3
	Belgium		12.2		1.5
	World as a whole		—		13.2
142	Storage batteries	835.0		145.9	
	Sweden		82.2		22.5
	United Kingdom		17.8		5.5
	World as a whole		—		72.0
143	Primary batteries	851.1		479.5	
	Canada		85.7		87.5
	United Kingdom		14.3		1.4
	World as a whole		—		11.1
145.1	Passenger cars and light trucks	900.6		246.7	
	United Kingdom		100.0		19.7
	World as a whole		—		80.3
145.2	Heavy trucks and buses	884.6		515.9	
	Canada		85.9		84.8
	United Kingdom		14.1		1.3
	World as a whole		—		13.9
145.3	Motor vehicle parts and accessories	881.5		463.5	
	Canada		69.5		76.1
	United Kingdom		30.5		3.1
	World as a whole		—		20.8
148	Aircraft and parts	845.8		470.2	
	Canada		74.2		77.6
	United Kingdom		25.8		2.6
	World as a whole		—		19.8
152	Motorcycles and bicycles	876.2		231.7	
	United Kingdom		82.2		16.7
	West Germany		17.8		3.5
	World as a whole		—		79.8
154	Optical, ophthalmic, and photographic equipment	851.7		244.4	
	West Germany		58.5		10.6
	Canada		16.9		33.8
	Belgium		16.7		4.3
	Japan		7.9		4.2
	World as a whole		—		47.1
156	Watches and clocks	738.4		170.1	
	Switzerland		100.0		32.6
	World as a whole		—		67.4

Liberalized Industry		Gross Increase in Dollar Earnings		Increase in U. S. Exports	
Code Number	Title	Total (In Thousands of 1953 Dollars)	Percentage Distribution	Total (In Thousands of 1953 Dollars)	Percentage Distribution
		(1)	(2)	(3)	(4)
157	Jewelry and silverware.............	753.2		147.9	
	United Kingdom................		29.9		8.2
	France........................		25.8		5.9
	Japan.........................		24.0		18.5
	West Germany.................		20.3		5.3
	World as a whole..............		—		62.1
158	Musical instruments and parts......	830.0		288.4	
	United Kingdom................		62.1		9.6
	Canada.......................		21.3		35.3
	West Germany.................		16.6		2.5
	World as a whole..............		—		52.6
159	Toys and sporting goods...........	747.2		181.5	
	Japan.........................		49.7		31.1
	United Kingdom................		17.7		3.9
	France........................		17.4		3.2
	West Germany.................		15.2		3.2
	World as a whole..............		—		58.6
160	Office supplies....................	731.1		176.4	
	West Germany.................		40.9		8.8
	United Kingdom...............		36.1		8.0
	Japan.........................		23.0		14.4
	World as a whole..............		—		68.8
161	Plastic products..................	792.3		327.1	
	United Kingdom................		40.8		5.3
	Canada.......................		36.8		51.4
	Japan.........................		22.4		8.1
	World as a whole..............		—		35.2
162	Cork products....................	766.1		83.9	
	Portugal......................		78.8		26.1
	Spain.........................		21.2		15.3
	World as a whole..............		—		58.6
164	Miscellaneous manufactured products	777.7		217.8	
	United Kingdom................		46.6		9.0
	West Germany.................		26.0		4.8
	Japan.........................		9.9		5.4
	Canada.......................		9.5		19.5
	Belgium.......................		8.0		2.1
	World as a whole..............		—		59.2

Effect of One Dollar Initial Increase in Exports on Total Exports
of World Trade Groups and United States[a]

(In dollars)

Sector Affected	Effect on Exports of $1 Initial Net Increase in Export Earnings of:				
	Group 1	Group 2	Group 3	Group 4	United States
Group 1................	1.0405	.0500	.0228	.0421	0
Group 2................	.1733	1.6113	.1123	.3996	0
Group 3................	.0586	.1359	1.0491	.0994	0
Group 4................	.4764	1.3962	.3066	1.8661	0
United States..........	.7095	.4162	.6285	.2592	1.0000
Total.................	2.4583	3.6096	2.1193	2.6664	1.0000
Total, Groups 1 through 4	1.7488	3.1934	1.4908	2.4072	0
Total, Groups 1 and 2....	1.2138	1.6613	.1351	.4417	0

[a] This table is the inverse matrix derived from the direct trade relationships shown in Table 7.1.

Percentage Distribution Among Industry Groups of United States Exports to Major Supplying Countries and World as a Whole, Actual for 1953 and Assumed Increases

Line Num-ber	Industry Group	Argentina		Australia		Austria	
		Percentage Distribution of U.S. Exports		Percentage Distribution of U.S. Exports		Percentage Distribution of U.S. Exports	
		Actual, 1953	Assumed Increases	Actual, 1953	Assumed Increases	Actual, 1953	Assumed Increases
		(1)	(2)	(3)	(4)	(5)	(6)
1	Agriculture, forestry and fishing (1–10)	.54	.33	18.17	18.17	68.43	43.73
2	Metal mining (11–15)	*	*	*	*	.16	.30
3	Coal mining (16)	5.19	5.20	—	—	.99	1.88
4	Crude petroleum and natural gas (17)	3.11	3.12	—	—	—	—
5	Other nonmetallic minerals (18–20)	.53	.53	2.98	3.00	.99	1.88
6	Processed foods and alcoholic beverages (21–28)	.22	.20	.42	.07	5.01	8.36
7	Tobacco manufactures (29)	.01	.01	.62	.62	.44	—
8	Spinning, weaving, and dyeing (30)	.48	.48	.95	.95	.56	1.06
9	Apparel (34)	.02	.02	.01	.01	.44	.84
10	All other textile products (31–33, 35)	.09	.09	.07	.07	.06	.12
11	Lumber, wood products, and furniture (36–43)	*	*	3.14	3.15	.19	.36
12	Pulp, paper, and paper products (44–46)	.27	.27	.50	.50	.04	.08
13	Printing and publishing (47)	.02	.02	.54	.54	.06	.12
14	Industrial chemicals (except synthetic rubber and fiber) (48–50, 53)	6.14	6.15	1.71	1.72	.88	1.66
15	Synthetic rubber and synthetic fiber (51, 52)	.75	.75	.26	.26	.14	.26
16	All other chemicals and allied products (54–61)	14.77	14.80	4.18	4.20	3.02	4.12
17	Products of petroleum and coal (62–64)	5.73	5.74	6.16	6.19	1.13	2.14
18	Tires, inner tubes, and miscellaneous rubber products (65, 66)	.27	.27	.28	.28	.21	.39
19	Leather and products and footwear (excluding rubber) (67–69)	.01	.01	.01	.01	.06	.11
20	Glass (70)	.08	.08	.09	.09	.02	.04
21	Pottery and related products (73)	.01	.01	*	*	*	*
22	Stone and clay products (71, 72, 74–77)	.18	.18	.66	.66	.18	.34
23	Iron and steel and their primary products (78–81, 92)	10.24	10.26	5.05	5.07	2.19	4.15
24	Nonferrous metals and their primary products (82–91)	2.71	2.72	.82	.82	.45	.85
25	Fabricated metal products (93–109)	.98	.98	1.71	1.72	.09	.18
26	Machinery, except electrical (110–128)	24.62	24.69	38.17	38.35	12.40	23.49
27	Electrical machinery and products (129–138, 142–144)	2.66	2.68	2.38	2.39	.72	1.36
28	Communication equipment and products (139–141)	5.13	5.14	.55	.55	.05	.10
29	Motor vehicles, parts, and accessories (145–147)	5.66	5.67	5.91	5.93	.25	.47
30	Other transportation equipment (148–152)	7.93	7.95	2.73	2.74	*	.01
31	Instruments, optical and photographic equipment, watches and clocks (153–156)	1.46	1.46	1.29	1.30	.76	1.44
32	Miscellaneous manufactures (157–164)	.19	.19	.64	.64	.08	.16
33	Total purchases: Per cent	100.00	100.00	100.00	100.00	100.00	100.00

* Less than .005 per cent.

Table E.6 (continued)

Line Number	Bahamas Percentage Distribution of U.S. Exports		Belgium Percentage Distribution of U.S. Exports		Brazil Percentage Distribution of U.S. Exports		Canada Percentage Distribution of U.S. Exports		Cuba Percentage Distribution of U.S. Exports	
	Actual, 1953	Assumed Increases	Actual, 1953	Assumed Increases	Actual, 1953	Assumed Increases	Actual, 1953	Assumed Increases	Actual, 1953	Assumed Increases
	(7)	(8)	(9)	(10)	(11)	(12)	(13)	(14)	(15)	(16)
1	2.76	2.62	26.05	2.74	4.67	4.00	5.38	5.32	5.75	5.76
2	—	—	.01	.01	.05	.05	1.08	1.08	*	*
3	—	—	2.52	3.72	2.85	2.89	7.28	7.30	.21	.21
4	—	—	—	—	—	—	1.60	1.60	1.94	1.95
5	.10	.10	.79	1.16	.86	.87	.87	.87	.17	.17
6	12.94	12.42	5.71	2.92	1.27	.78	3.12	3.09	27.76	27.87
7	1.51	1.52	1.60	—	.01	—	.08	.08	.30	—
8	1.86	1.88	1.68	2.48	1.14	1.15	2.76	2.76	7.07	7.09
9	3.76	3.79	1.47	2.17	.10	.10	.74	.74	1.20	1.20
10	1.19	1.20	.22	.32	.05	.05	.97	.97	1.20	1.20
11	6.54	6.59	.54	.80	.13	.13	1.46	1.46	1.44	1.44
12	1.64	1.65	.61	.90	.79	.80	1.30	1.30	3.78	3.79
13	.64	.65	.18	.27	.47	.48	1.74	1.74	.44	.44
14	.15	.15	2.51	3.70	3.49	3.53	3.22	3.23	1.72	1.73
15	—	—	.16	.24	.17	.17	.20	.20	.05	.05
16	2.56	2.55	8.83	9.05	6.55	6.61	3.76	3.70	6.74	6.76
17	1.87	1.89	4.09	6.04	4.90	4.96	4.52	4.53	3.41	3.42
18	.54	.54	.60	.89	.15	.15	.85	.85	1.09	1.09
19	1.36	1.37	.19	.28	.01	.01	.42	.42	1.20	1.20
20	.59	.59	.15	.22	.16	.16	1.04	1.04	1.53	1.53
21	.22	.22	.01	.01	.04	.04	.20	.20	.39	.39
22	.93	.94	.54	.79	.58	.59	1.39	1.39	.87	.87
23	.85	.86	2.85	4.20	6.08	6.16	5.87	5.88	2.71	2.72
24	.15	.15	.36	.53	3.19	3.23	.76	.76	.33	.33
25	4.89	4.93	1.38	2.04	3.20	3.24	4.85	4.86	3.62	3.63
26	10.26	10.34	11.97	17.66	27.34	27.69	22.95	23.01	8.79	8.82
27	20.57	20.75	2.72	4.02	7.26	7.35	3.91	3.92	3.61	3.62
28	15.69	15.82	1.51	2.23	1.65	1.67	2.19	2.19	1.99	2.00
29	3.19	3.22	14.56	21.48	12.15	12.31	10.66	10.68	6.66	6.68
30	.50	.50	3.64	5.37	7.41	7.50	1.16	1.16	.91	.91
31	1.02	1.03	2.00	2.95	2.07	2.10	1.97	1.97	1.20	1.20
32	1.72	1.73	.55	.81	1.21	1.23	1.70	1.70	1.92	1.93
33	100.00	100.00	100.00	100.00	100.00	100.00	100.00	100.00	100.00	100.00

Table E.6 (*continued*)

Line Number	Finland Percentage Distribution of U.S. Exports		France Percentage Distribution of U.S. Exports		Hong Kong Percentage Distribution of U.S. Exports		India Percentage Distribution of U.S. Exports		Iran Percentage Distribution of U.S. Exports	
	Actual, 1953	Assumed Increases	Actual, 1953	Assumed Increases	Actual, 1953	Assumed Increases	Actual, 1953	Assumed Increases	Actual, 1953	Assumed Increases
	(17)	(18)	(19)	(20)	(21)	(22)	(23)	(24)	(25)	(26)
1	9.84	9.75	31.54	30.25	17.95	18.20	33.34	.08	.41	.43
2	*	*	.41	.43	*	*	—	—	—	—
3	—	—	1.04	1.09	—	—	—	—	—	—
4	—	—	.43	.45	—	—	—	—	—	—
5	.17	.17	.80	.84	.01	.01	.96	1.45	.03	.03
6	1.18	—	1.54	—	10.24	8.58	.92	1.37	6.41	1.08
7	.38	.39	.76	.80	9.11	9.30	.76	1.14	.03	.03
8	1.03	1.05	1.84	1.93	14.71	15.02	.03	.04	7.28	7.70
9	1.08	1.10	.62	.65	6.93	7.08	.01	.02	.84	.89
10	.12	.12	.04	.04	.88	.90	.02	.03	.79	.83
11	.17	.17	.62	.05	.62	.63	.27	.41	.40	.42
12	.04	.04	.70	.73	2.01	2.05	.07	.11	.26	.27
13	.10	.10	.20	.21	.67	.68	.43	.64	.22	.23
14	2.54	2.59	2.11	2.21	1.08	1.10	2.06	3.09	3.42	3.62
15	.21	.21	.66	.69	.01	.01	.03	.04	—	—
16	3.97	3.44	5.64	5.45	6.97	7.02	8.60	12.67	12.51	13.22
17	2.09	2.13	1.87	1.96	1.47	1.50	11.78	17.71	1.77	1.87
18	.30	.31	.37	.39	.48	.49	.66	.99	12.88	13.61
19	—	—	.16	.17	1.14	1.16	.11	.16	.03	.03
20	.09	.00	.14	.15	.68	.69	.05	.08	1.00	1.06
21	.21	.21	.01	.01	.08	.08	.14	.21	.03	.03
22	.80	.82	.52	.55	.32	.33	.73	1.10	.64	.68
23	8.00	8.10	1.71	1.79	5.37	5.48	3.39	5.09	5.35	5.66
24	6.25	6.38	3.59	3.77	.05	.05	1.05	1.58	.05	.05
25	9.88	10.09	.97	1.02	1.75	1.79	1.50	2.25	2.79	2.95
26	35.59	36.37	26.04	27.33	4.49	4.59	19.69	29.59	16.03	16.95
27	3.85	3.93	3.87	4.06	2.35	2.40	4.00	6.02	4.81	5.08
28	.34	.35	2.16	2.27	.35	.36	.33	.50	2.90	3.07
29	7.13	7.28	1.89	1.98	.94	.96	7.17	10.77	15.32	16.19
30	7.88	8.05	6.01	6.31	.03	.03	.25	.38	1.67	1.77
31	1.46	1.49	1.12	1.17	3.86	3.94	1.42	2.14	1.46	1.54
32	.21	.21	.62	.65	5.45	5.57	.23	.34	.67	.71
33	100.00	100.00	100.00	100.00	100.00	100.00	100.00	100.00	100.00	100.00

Table E.6 (*continued*)

Line Number	Italy Percentage Distribution of U.S. Exports		Japan Percentage Distribution of U.S. Exports		Mexico Percentage Distribution of U.S. Exports		Netherlands Percentage Distribution of U.S. Exports		New Zealand Percentage Distribution of U.S. Exports	
	Actual, 1953	Assumed Increases	Actual, 1953	Assumed Increases	Actual, 1953	Assumed Increases	Actual, 1953	Assumed Increases	Actual, 1953	Assumed Increases
	(27)	(28)	(29)	(30)	(31)	(32)	(33)	(34)	(35)	(36)
1	31.05	21.35	42.37	43.73	12.74	4.28	34.86	3.69	15.33	15.52
2	.03	.04	.75	.77	.04	.04	*	*	—	—
3	6.30	7.31	5.35	5.53	.05	.05	4.16	6.51	—	—
4	.38	.44	.35	.36	.39	.43	—	—	—	—
5	.66	.76	.60	.62	.25	.28	1.20	1.88	9.03	9.16
6	2.44	1.51	13.29	10.57	3.87	3.22	10.99	12.22	1.44	.10
7	.54	.63	.10	—	.39	.43	.42	—	*	*
8	.80	.93	2.49	2.57	1.41	1.56	1.27	1.99	.33	.33
9	.53	.62	.23	.24	.94	1.04	1.01	1.59	.09	.09
10	.23	.27	.05	.05	.56	.62	.08	.13	.02	.02
11	.64	.74	1.17	1.21	1.60	1.78	.52	.81	.86	.87
12	.33	.38	.62	.64	1.71	1.90	.24	.37	1.38	1.40
13	.18	.21	.18	.19	.57	.63	.17	.27	1.09	1.11
14	3.04	3.53	2.29	2.37	4.87	5.40	1.59	2.49	.44	.45
15	.71	.82	.23	.24	.23	.26	.20	.32	.03	.03
16	8.18	9.49	6.70	6.92	7.18	7.97	10.94	17.11	2.62	2.65
17	2.26	2.62	4.77	4.93	5.93	6.58	1.82	2.85	15.35	15.56
18	.09	.11	.08	.08	.72	.80	.11	.17	.39	.40
19	.25	.29	.06	.06	.28	.31	.14	.22	.01	.01
20	.16	.18	.05	.05	.48	.53	.29	.45	.06	.06
21	.01	.01	.01	.01	.10	.11	.01	.01	.01	.01
22	.33	.38	.66	.68	1.41	1.56	.17	.27	.40	.41
23	4.78	5.54	.98	1.01	5.77	6.40	5.47	8.56	5.60	5.68
24	3.13	3.63	.33	.34	.49	.54	2.81	4.40	.03	.03
25	1.63	1.89	.73	.75	3.67	4.07	.68	1.06	1.90	1.93
26	21.05	24.41	9.14	9.44	19.83	22.00	7.62	11.92	37.59	38.09
27	3.28	3.80	.74	.76	4.02	4.46	1.25	1.95	1.44	1.46
28	2.37	2.75	.86	.89	2.05	2.27	.78	1.22	.20	.20
29	.57	.66	3.21	3.32	13.38	14.85	3.20	5.01	1.98	2.01
30	2.01	2.33	.32	.33	2.02	2.24	7.05	11.03	.48	.49
31	1.61	1.87	.79	.82	1.78	1.98	.73	1.15	1.19	1.21
32	.43	.50	.50	.52	1.27	1.41	.22	.35	.71	.72
33	100.00	100.00	100.00	100.00	100.00	100.00	100.00	100.00	100.00	100.00

Line Num-ber	Norway		Philippine Republic		Portugal		Spain		Sweden	
	Percentage Distribution of U.S. Exports		Percentage Distribution of U.S. Exports		Percentage Distribution of U.S. Exports		Percentage Distribution of U.S. Exports		Percentage Distribution of U.S. Exports	
	Actual, 1953	Assumed Increases	Actual, 1953	Assumed Increases	Actual, 1953	Assumed Increases	Actual, 1953	Assumed Increases	Actual, 1953	Assumed Increases
	(37)	(38)	(39)	(40)	(41)	(42)	(43)	(44)	(45)	(46)
1	29.00	31.74	4.21	1.33	26.08	10.25	50.36	38.17	12.17	12.17
2	—	—	*	*	—	—	—	—	.37	.37
3	1.36	1.49	—	—	.35	.43	.55	.69	.51	.51
4	—	—	—	—	—	—	—	—	—	—
5	.07	.08	.21	.23	.02	.02	.02	.02	.57	.57
6	7.61	—	15.62	13.75	1.09	1.24	1.84	1.76	4.94	4.91
7	1.15	1.26	1.47	—	2.98	3.62	3.47	4.36	4.61	4.61
8	1.67	1.83	21.29	23.04	.83	1.01	3.12	3.92	3.49	3.49
9	.13	.14	.88	.95	.59	.72	.35	.44	.27	.27
10	.11	.12	2.06	2.23	.12	.14	.03	.04	.11	.11
11	.72	.79	.31	.34	.54	.66	.10	.13	.24	.24
12	.12	.13	3.93	4.25	.22	.27	.25	.31	.27	.27
13	.29	.32	.97	1.05	.21	.25	.07	.09	.31	.31
14	1.62	1.78	1.52	1.64	1.86	2.26	1.21	1.52	2.33	2.33
15	.14	.15	.01	.01	.15	.18	.14	.17	.93	.93
16	3.55	2.66	7.50	7.87	7.86	9.55	2.14	2.69	3.24	3.24
17	8.07	8.84	1.64	1.78	4.89	5.94	4.39	5.52	8.36	8.36
18	.30	.43	1.93	2.09	.45	.55	.14	.18	.43	.43
19	.28	.31	1.51	1.63	.03	.04	.01	.01	.01	.01
20	.07	.08	.85	.92	.11	.13	.03	.04	.29	.29
21	.23	.25	.17	.18	.01	.01	.01	.01	.04	.04
22	.81	.89	.43	.46	.36	.44	.12	.15	1.36	1.36
23	8.33	9.13	3.60	3.90	10.08	12.25	3.83	4.81	5.92	5.92
24	3.67	4.02	.51	.55	.05	.06	.74	.93	.24	.24
25	1.43	1.57	4.33	4.69	1.20	1.46	1.34	1.68	1.80	1.80
26	17.71	19.41	11.25	12.18	19.65	23.88	14.44	18.15	17.26	17.28
27	3.57	3.91	3.63	3.93	4.58	5.56	7.51	9.44	2.71	2.71
28	2.01	2.20	.91	.98	5.74	6.98	.53	.67	.62	.62
29	3.81	4.18	5.20	5.63	4.97	6.04	1.59	2.00	15.55	15.56
30	.49	.54	.89	.96	1.76	2.14	.77	.97	8.81	8.81
31	1.42	1.56	1.72	1.86	2.50	3.04	.57	.72	2.01	2.01
32	.17	.19	1.45	1.57	.72	.88	.33	.41	.23	.23
33	100.00	100.00	100.00	100.00	100.00	100.00	100.00	100.00	100.00	100.00

Line Num-ber	Switzerland Percentage Distribution of U.S. Exports		Turkey Percentage Distribution of U.S. Exports		United Kingdom Percentage Distribution of U.S. Exports		Germany (Federal Republic) Percentage Distribution of U.S. Exports		World as a Whole Percentage Distribution of U.S. Exports	
	Actual, 1953	Assumed Increases	Actual, 1953	Assumed Increases	Actual, 1953	Assumed Increases	Actual, 1953	Assumed Increases	Actual, 1953	Assumed Increases
	(47)	(48)	(49)	(50)	(51)	(52)	(53)	(54)	(55)	(56)
1	12.57	1.07	1.78	*	47.66	1.75	53.98	2.30	17.63	9.30
2	.01	.01	—	—	.61	1.26	.42	.93	.39	.44
3	1.38	1.85	—	—	—	—	8.60	19.07	3.00	3.38
4	—	—	—	—	.23	.47	—	—	.59	.67
5	.63	.85	*	*	1.05	2.16	.69	1.53	.62	.70
6	8.45	—	.30	—	3.07	—	8.11	14.85	6.66	6.00
7	1.59	—	—	—	.26	—	.55	—	.68	.44
8	2.73	3.67	.87	.89	.09	.19	.06	.14	3.53	3.98
9	10.57	14.21	.36	.37	.12	.25	.24	.54	1.09	1.23
10	.48	.65	.11	.11	.01	.02	.06	.13	.60	.68
11	.27	.36	.34	.35	1.24	2.55	.82	1.82	1.13	1.27
12	.59	.79	.24	.25	1.81	3.70	.54	1.20	1.34	1.51
13	.25	.33	.19	.19	.78	1.60	.19	.43	.75	.84
14	2.97	3.99	.41	.42	3.25	6.66	2.11	4.69	2.62	2.95
15	.43	.58	—	—	.58	1.19	1.09	2.42	.23	.26
16	9.17	7.19	4.09	4.18	3.65	5.27	7.80	17.29	5.73	6.17
17	1.19	1.60	5.18	5.29	7.35	15.06	1.83	4.05	4.12	4.64
18	1.01	1.36	2.56	2.61	.05	.11	.07	.15	.73	.82
19	2.25	3.03	.01	.01	.10	.21	.02	.05	.42	.47
20	.35	.47	.11	.11	.02	.04	.18	.39	.59	.66
21	.01	.01	.20	.20	.11	.23	.01	.03	.13	.15
22	.74	1.00	.27	.28	.37	.75	.22	.48	.81	.91
23	5.32	7.15	10.71	10.94	1.76	3.60	.60	1.32	4.39	4.95
24	3.09	4.16	2.26	2.31	3.90	7.99	3.28	7.27	1.16	1.31
25	1.33	1.79	5.06	5.17	.83	1.71	.19	.43	3.34	3.76
26	12.58	16.93	40.65	41.48	17.57	36.00	5.66	12.55	19.14	21.57
27	1.95	2.62	7.28	7.44	1.17	2.40	.53	1.18	3.60	4.06
28	.69	.93	3.62	3.70	.26	.53	.25	.56	1.50	1.69
29	6.68	8.98	11.10	11.34	.52	1.07	.22	.48	8.57	9.66
30	2.95	3.97	.30	.31	.41	.83	.64	1.43	2.15	2.42
31	2.52	3.39	1.42	1.45	.71	1.45	.72	1.59	1.53	1.72
32	5.25	7.06	.58	.60	.46	.95	.32	.70	1.23	1.39
33	100.00	100.00	100.00	100.00	100.00	100.00	100.00	100.00	100.00	100.00

Appendix Table E.6a

Code Numbers of Industries Whose Products are Excluded from Assumed Increases in United States Exports to Major Suppliers

Country	Code Numbers of Excluded Industries[a]			
	Agriculture, Forestry and Fishing	Processed Foods and Alcoholic Beverages	Tobacco Manufactures	All Other Chemicals and Allied products
Argentina................	1–7, 9	21–25, 27, 28		60
Australia.................	1–4	21–25, 27		60
Austria..................	1–4, 7, 9	22, 24, 25, 27, 28	29	60
Bahamas.................	1, 4, 5, 7	22, 27		59, 60
Belgium..................	1–7, 9	21, 22, 24–28	29	60
Brazil...................	1–3, 5, 7–9	21, 25–27	29	59, 60
Canada..................	3, 6	22, 27		60
Cuba....................	6, 7	27	29	
Finland..................	1–4, 7–9	21–28		59, 60
France...................	1–4	21–28		60
Hong Kong...............	1–4	21, 22, 25, 27		59, 60
India....................	1–8	21, 25, 27, 28		59, 60
Iran.....................		27		
Italy....................	2–4, 7–9	23–28		
Japan...................	1–3	21, 23, 25, 27	29	
Mexico..................	1, 3–7	24–27		59
Netherlands..............	1–7, 9	22, 24–28	29	
New Zealand.............	1–5, 7	21–23, 27		59, 60
Norway..................	2, 3, 9	21–28		59, 60
Philippine Republic........	3, 4, 6, 7	23, 25, 27	29	59
Portugal.................	1–5, 7–9	23, 25, 27, 28		59
Spain....................	1–4, 7–9	23–25, 27, 28		
Sweden..................	2, 3, 7	22, 24, 25, 27, 28		60
Switzerland..............	1–9	21–28	29	59, 60
Turkey..................	1–9	21–28	29	59, 60
United Kingdom..........	1–9	21–28	29	59, 60
Germany (Federal Republic).	2–7	22, 24, 25, 27, 28	29	

[a] Titles of industries corresponding to code numbers are shown in Appendix A.

339

Distribution of Gross Primary Employment Decreases Resulting from Liberalization, by Industry Groups[a]

(Number of employees, farmers, and unpaid farm family workers)

Line Num-ber	Industry Group Affected and Code Numbers of Industries in Group	Liberalized Industry	
		Meat Animals and Products	Vegetables and Fruits
		(1)	(8)
1	Total, all industries...	95.84	224.45
2	Liberalized industry...	74.38	193.63
3	Other industries—total...	21.46	30.82
4	Agriculture, forestry, and fishing (1–10)..........................	1.84*	.08*
5	Metal mining (11–15)..	.04	.06
6	Coal mining (16)..	.32	.54
7	Crude petroleum and natural gas (17).............................	.62	.60
8	Other nonmetallic minerals (18–20)...............................	.13	.44
9	Processed foods, and alcoholic beverages (21–28)...................	.95	.26
10	Tobacco manufactures (29).......................................	—	—
11	Spinning, weaving, and dyeing (30)...............................	.25	.60
12	Apparel (34)..	—	—
13	All other textile products (31–33, 35).............................	.13	.54
14	Lumber, wood products, and furniture (36–43)......................	.26	7.63
15	Pulp, paper, and paper products (44–46)..........................	.35	.38
16	Printing and publishing (47).....................................	.49	.46
17	Industrial chemicals (except synthetic rubber and fiber) (48–50, 53)....	.31	.91
18	Synthetic rubber and synthetic fiber (51, 52)......................	.04	.07
19	All other chemicals and allied products (54–61)....................	.37	1.81
20	Products of petroleum and coal (62–64)...........................	.23	.52
21	Tires, inner tubes, and miscellaneous rubber products (65, 66)........	.22	.38
22	Leather and products and footwear (excluding rubber) (67–69).......	.01	.02
23	Glass (70)..	.04	.06
24	Pottery and related products (73)................................	—	.01
25	Stone and clay products (71, 72, 74–77)..........................	.05	.11
26	Iron and steel and their primary products (78–81, 92)..............	.55	.57
27	Nonferrous metals and their primary products (82–91)..............	.11	.12
28	Fabricated metal products (93–109)..............................	.26	.52
29	Machinery, except electrical (110–128)...........................	.45	.48
30	Electrical machinery and products (129–138, 142–144)..............	.12	.11
31	Communication equipment and products (139–141)..................	.02	.02
32	Motor vehicles, parts, and accessories (145–147)..................	.25	.38
33	Other transportation equipment (148–152)........................	.08	.10
34	Instruments, optical and photographic equipment, watches and clocks (153–156)..	.04	.03
35	Miscellaneous manufactures (157–164)............................	.17	.13
36	Electric light and power, and gas (167, 168)......................	.04	.05
37	Railroad transportation (169)....................................	2.00	1.94
38	Ocean transportation (172)......................................	.08	.28
39	Transportation (except railroad and ocean transportation) and allied services (170, 171, 173–175, 178).............................	1.32	.76
40	Wholesale and retail trade (176, 177)............................	5.74	6.36
41	Communication, finance, business services (179, 181, 186, 187)........	1.56	1.83
42	Auto and other repair services (188, 189).........................	.61	1.27
43	Other services (182–185, 190–192)...............................	1.41	.39
44	Percent of total decrease occurring in liberalized industry (Line 2 ÷ Line 1)	77.6	86.3

* Excludes employment effects in the liberalized industry, which is part of this industry group. The employment effect in the liberalized industry is shown in Line 2.

[a] Figures are gross decreases of employment per million-dollar increase of imports. Dashes represent decreases that are less than .005 employees, including some that are zero.

Table F.1 (*continued*)

Line Number	Liberalized Industry						
	Lead and Zinc Mining (13)	Meat Packing and Wholesale Poultry (21)	Processed Dairy Products (22)	Grain Mill Products (24)	Sugar (27)	Alcoholic Beverages (28)	Tobacco Manufactures (29)
1.....	164.85	107.99	54.27	51.15	67.38	85.39	69.99
2.....	128.35	24.41	25.49	16.90	46.17	43.21	42.54
3.....	36.50	83.58	28.78	34.25	21.21	42.18	27.45
4.....	.06	58.42	2.21	1.03	.09	4.24	.11
5.....	.18*	.06	.10	.08	.04	.11	.05
6.....	1.91	.54	1.00	.68	1.87	1.18	.58
7.....	.85	.56	.52	.66	.46	.34	.18
8.....	.09	.12	.12	.18	.21	.14	.14
9.....	.06	1.44*	2.58*	2.44*	.12*	1.43*	.41
10....	—	—	—	—	—	—	—*
11....	.10	.26	.30	1.93	.70	.17	.15
12....	—	.08	—	.02	.01	—	—
13....	.04	.13	.18	1.92	.69	.09	.08
14....	6.53	.90	.81	.46	.26	2.75	2.06
15....	.23	.50	2.83	1.99	1.42	2.58	4.09
16....	.35	.80	1.10	2.36	1.24	4.21	3.95
17....	4.37	.32	.35	.51	.33	.57	.72
18....	.02	.15	.04	.17	.06	.06	.04
19....	.58	.56	.59	.86	.24	.35	.42
20....	.67	.24	.25	.25	.24	.24	.13
21....	.50	.30	.26	.34	.08	.33	.18
22....	.03	.02	.02	.12	.01	.02	.01
23....	.04	.18	.23	.17	.03	4.30	.08
24....	.01	—	—	—	—	.01	—
25....	.31	.07	.10	.09	.12	.24	.05
26....	3.81	.88	1.40	.96	.42	1.52	.43
27....	.49	.14	.15	.20	.10	.19	.22
28....	1.41	.81	1.50	.68	.21	2.55	.72
29....	4.29	.75	.58	1.06	.42	.49	.35
30....	.36	.18	.12	.22	.09	.10	.06
31....	.02	.03	.03	.03	.02	.03	.02
32....	.11	.24	.19	.19	.08	.11	.06
33....	.56	.08	.09	.11	.41	.06	.05
34....	.04	.04	.05	.05	.04	.05	.04
35....	.12	.21	.20	.29	.17	.50	.34
36....	.62	.08	.12	.11	.19	.11	.04
37....	1.66	2.39	1.99	4.74	2.59	2.60	1.69
38....	.12	.10	.10	.06	.24	.10	.04
39....	.48	1.42	.74	1.33	.53	.88	.58
40....	2.88	6.52	3.77	3.31	2.31	2.37	3.34
41....	1.83	2.08	2.45	3.44	4.31	5.75	5.12
42....	.49	.72	.82	.51	.30	.50	.22
43....	.28	1.26	.77	.70	.56	.91	.70
44....	77.9	22.6	47.0	33.0	68.5	50.6	60.8

Line Num-ber	Liberalized Industry						
	Spinning, Weaving, and Dyeing (30)	Special Textile Products (31)	Apparel (34)	House Furnishings and Other Non-apparel (35)	Plywood (38)	Wood Containers and Cooperage (40)	Wood Furniture (41)
1.....	136.41	106.85	195.41	134.91	139.24	166.64	170.72
2.....	97.57	73.57	133.87	47.74	80.93	93.87	102.76
3.....	38.84	33.28	61.54	87.17	58.31	72.77	67.96
4.....	4.30	4.53	3.35	2.33	.10	.03	.33
5.....	.08	.02	.05	.12	.09	.14	.23
6.....	1.74	.90	.84	1.32	.70	.92	1.07
7.....	.49	.19	.23	.38	.40	.35	.26
8.....	.18	.06	.08	.15	.10	.07	.10
9.....	.58	.60	.25	.78	.18	.04	.11
10....	—	—	—	—	—	—	—
11....	—*	9.96	29.34	46.97	.16	.15	4.64
12....	—	—*	.33	—	—	.37
13....	.61	1.36*	1.06	1.25*	.06	.06	2.08
14....	1.40	.35	.77	2.20	36.06*	48.85*	29.83*
15....	1.32	1.34	1.58	1.99	.38	.45	.75
16....	1.08	1.09	1.87	1.40	.76	.84	1.29
17....	2.19	.61	.92	2.00	1.86	.17	.48
18....	7.67	1.65	3.46	3.63	.04	.02	.40
19....	.76	.24	.36	1.85	1.25	.25	1.33
20....	.31	.14	.16	.26	.36	.44	.32
21....	.20	.22	.48	1.15	.50	.43	.64
22....	.04	.01	.39	.03	.13	.14	.17
23....	.61	.20	.20	.36	.08	.08	1.09
24....	—	—	—	.01	.01	.01	.02
25....	.10	.04	.06	.12	.38	.52	.53
26....	.67	.23	.38	.63	.88	2.23	2.33
27....	.16	.05	.12	.18	.19	.21	.47
28....	.29	.18	.33	.43	1.19	1.65	4.94
29....	1.13	.26	.55	.88	1.29	1.11	1.04
30....	.11	.05	.24	.11	.20	.23	.20
31....	.02	.02	.02	.02	.02	.02	.02
32....	.10	.06	.06	.09	.21	.21	.13
33....	.07	.05	.10	.08	.09	.10	.07
34....	.04	.02	.04	.04	.05	.06	.06
35....	.37	.14	2.06	1.12	.20	.14	.48
36....	.20	.09	.10	.15	.10	.10	.12
37....	2.25	1.29	1.49	2.18	3.00	3.91	2.71
38....	.06	.20	.06	.20	.07	.11	.06
39....	.72	.44	.42	.57	1.76	2.00	1.08
40....	4.78	3.72	6.10	7.68	1.72	2.78	3.80
41....	2.90	1.98	2.82	2.87	2.41	2.36	3.06
42....	.39	.34	.28	.42	.67	.92	.57
43....	.92	.65	.92	.89	.66	.67	.78
44....	71.5	68.9	68.5	35.4	58.1	56.3	60.2

Line Num-ber	Paper and Board Mills (45)	Converted Paper Products (46)	Industrial Organic Chemicals (49)	Synthetic Rubber (51)	Synthetic Fiber (52)	Drugs and Medicines (54)	Paints and Allied Products (56)
Liberalized Industry							
1.....	84.29	114.88	79.41	65.20	91.32	118.58	90.55
2.....	39.98	59.62	35.19	19.25	55.10	52.29	42.09
3.....	44.31	55.26	44.22	45.95	36.22	66.29	48.46
4.....	.13	.13	.88	.69	.30	1.41	.46
5.....	.07	.09	.71	.20	.21	.18	2.80
6.....	3.14	1.99	5.04	1.65	3.60	1.61	1.97
7.....	.54	.61	1.31	5.95	.56	.52	1.06
8.....	.50	.31	.78	.34	.47	.30	.96
9.....	.40	.33	1.90	.75	.79	1.39	1.31
10.....	—	—	—	—	—	—	—
11.....	.64	.67	.23	.12	.12	.24	.26
12.....	—	—	—	—	—	.01	—
13.....	.51	.53	.10	.06	.04	.12	.13
14.....	8.46	4.04	2.82	.77	3.21	.99	.93
15.....	10.00*	24.11*	1.35	1.48	3.53	5.87	2.04
16.....	.62	1.39	.96	1.26	.86	11.41	1.44
17.....	.90	1.20	4.78*	7.93	8.11	4.89	7.63
18.....	.09	.08	.20	.06*	.01*	.20	.14
19.....	.53	.79	3.26	3.81	1.55	2.45*	3.08*
20.....	.38	.45	1.85	4.20	.54	.51	1.01
21.....	.17	.49	.52	.35	.25	.58	.50
22.....	.06	.04	.03	.03	.02	.04	.03
23.....	.05	.07	.68	.23	.17	4.57	.25
24.....	.01	—	.01	.01	—	.02	.01
25.....	.25	.18	.26	.17	.18	.29	1.08
26.....	.75	.96	1.94	1.02	1.06	.97	2.73
27.....	.18	.25	.03	.36	.31	.44	1.34
28.....	.59	.60	1.24	.71	.43	1.06	2.67
29.....	1.31	1.07	1.08	1.55	.92	.88	2.13
30.....	.14	.12	.14	.11	.10	.11	.29
31.....	.02	.02	.02	.02	.02	.05	.03
32.....	.13	.09	.08	.05	.11	.12	.09
33.....	.15	.11	.21	.35	.13	.12	.14
34.....	.03	.19	.06	.10	.04	.13	.26
35.....	.14	.64	.19	.18	.50	1.01	.58
36.....	.20	.15	.37	.23	.13	.16	.18
37.....	3.66	4.26	4.08	2.96	3.17	2.70	3.35
38.....	.16	.10	.20	.29	.10	.09	.18
39.....	1.32	1.13	1.00	1.14	.86	.92	.72
40.....	5.46	4.10	1.82	3.06	.96	5.02	3.09
41.....	1.60	1.92	2.20	2.73	1.83	12.87	2.55
42.....	.47	.44	.40	.35	.32	.44	.35
43.....	.55	.71	.67	.68	.71	1.60	.69
44.....	47.4	51.9	44.3	29.5	60.3	44.1	46.5

Line Number	Vegetable Oils (59)	Miscellaneous Chemical Industries (61)	Tires and Inner Tubes (65)	Miscellaneous Rubber Products (66)	Leather Tanning and Finishing (67)	Footwear (Except Rubber) (69)	Glass (70)
			Liberalized Industry				
1.....	71.12	105.32	92.07	117.26	80.10	178.58	115.75
2.....	20.58	35.77	44.68	76.62	62.50	132.58	86.73
3.....	50.54	69.55	47.39	40.64	17.60	46.00	29.02
4....	1.37	2.20	.86	.48	.45	.31	.04
5....	.11	.32	.10	.14	.06	.04	.12
6....	1.05	2.05	1.41	1.22	1.24	.72	1.26
7....	.87	1.26	.97	.65	.20	.16	.52
8....	.21	1.64	.26	.23	.08	.07	1.27
9....	11.01	1.96	.30	.23	.38	.21	.06
10....	—	.02	—	—	—	—	—
11....	.82	.48	14.91	6.92	.14	2.18	.26
12....	.01	.01	—	—	—	.06	—
13....	.68	.31	.12	.17	.06	.47	.05
14....	.49	1.15	.52	1.47	.55	2.11	1.80
15....	1.22	5.02	1.08	2.14	.25	2.76	4.99
16....	1.49	8.28	1.42	1.15	.47	1.42	1.03
17....	.80	6.49	2.10	1.84	1.29	.80	1.85
18....	.15	.31	3.38	1.67	.03	.22	.03
19....	.79*	5.37*	1.88	1.86	2.48	1.26	.29
20....	.28	.75	.71	.50	.16	.13	.31
21....	.46	.65	4.25*	5.18*	.28	2.60	.32
22....	.10	.37	.02	.02	.32*	17.21*	.05
23....	.52	1.77	.18	.34	.06	.08	—*
24....	—	.02	—	.01	.01	—	.16
25....	.13	.76	.15	.40	.16	.20	2.91
26....	1.40	1.78	.78	1.42	.29	.37	1.04
27....	.28	.74	.18	.32	.08	.11	.22
28....	1.13	1.81	.36	1.58	.22	.46	.61
29....	1.17	1.57	1.00	1.68	.20	.38	.90
30....	.18	.16	.08	.18	.05	.06	.10
31....	.05	.05	.02	.03	.01	.02	.02
32....	.24	.09	.08	.26	.05	.05	.06
33....	.16	.12	.09	.08	.04	.04	.07
34....	.06	.77	.05	.06	.02	.04	.10
35....	.33	.91	.18	.16	.10	.62	.17
36....	.18	.20	.16	.16	.07	.08	.55
37....	3.55	3.01	1.96	1.93	2.12	1.72	2.26
38....	.33	.16	.19	.11	.08	.05	.05
39....	1.04	.80	.44	.40	.78	.45	.78
40....	11.51	3.90	3.86	2.92	2.39	3.33	2.34
41....	4.54	10.59	2.37	1.81	1.67	4.31	1.46
42....	.75	.50	.33	.29	.24	.22	.38
43....	1.08	1.20	.64	.63	.52	.68	.59
44.....	28.9	34.0	48.5	65.3	78.0	74.2	74.9

Line Number	Pottery and Related Products (73)	Carbon Steel Works and Rolling Mills (79.1)	Alloy Steel Works and Rolling Mills Except Stainless (79.2)	Stainless Steel Works and Rolling Mills (79.3)	Primary Zinc (85)	Primary Aluminum Including Alumina (88)	Aluminum Rolling and Drawing (89)
				Liberalized Industry			
1.....	189.43	90.79	93.50	96.61	95.40	62.72	79.51
2.....	163.22	51.36	53.75	72.82	36.29	29.95	43.85
3.....	26.21	39.43	39.75	23.79	59.11	32.77	35.66
4.....	.05	.02	.02	.02	.03	.02	.02
5.....	.21	3.28	3.45	1.43	27.52	3.04	1.66
6.....	1.03	6.07	6.02	2.70	3.07	1.90	1.59
7.....	.41	.71	.72	.35	.81	.78	.52
8.....	2.67	.52	.50	.19	.22	.34	.16
9.....	.08	.04	.04	.03	.03	.03	.02
10.....	—	—	—	—	—	—	—
11.....	.12	.04	.04	.03	.05	.04	.03
12.....	—	—	—	—	—	—	—
13.....	.04	.02	.02	.02	.02	.02	.01
14.....	.81	.79	.56	.44	1.51	.23	.67
15.....	2.08	.18	.20	.14	.18	.17	.13
16.....	.71	.52	.46	.41	.49	.37	.42
17.....	.80	.41	.42	.27	1.11	1.42	.66
18.....	.02	.01	.01	.01	.01	.01	.01
19.....	1.94	.27	.29	.20	.27	.18	.17
20.....	.27	2.54	2.49	.92	.65	.69	.49
21.....	.22	.09	.08	.05	.26	.16	.16
22.....	.01	.02	.02	.01	.01	.01	.01
23.....	.17	.03	.03	.02	.03	.03	.02
24.....	—*	.02	.02	.01	.02	—	—
25.....	3.47	1.87	2.12	.80	1.84	.30	.17
26.....	.90	7.73*	5.90*	2.59*	1.40	1.60	1.12
27.....	.29	.82	.96	.74	4.40*	8.48*	18.15*
28.....	.39	.48	.39	.65	.52	.31	.27
29.....	.44	1.09	.68	.55	1.55	.94	.71
30.....	1.64	.34	.40	.48	.17	.12	.13
31.....	.05	.02	.02	.02	.02	.02	.02
32.....	.05	.06	.07	.05	.08	.08	.12
33.....	.06	.33	.33	.18	.21	.17	.12
34.....	.04	.03	.05	.03	.03	.02	.02
35.....	.16	.12	.13	.11	.09	.08	.06
36.....	.33	.26	.30	.26	.68	.72	.44
37.....	2.08	4.65	5.70	4.38	5.21	3.32	2.30
38.....	.07	.28	.34	.10	.32	.63	.29
39.....	.59	1.14	1.28	.70	.52	.39	.29
40.....	1.38	2.59	3.68	3.01	3.58	4.42	2.97
41.....	1.64	1.29	1.28	1.17	1.37	1.08	1.07
42.....	.34	.30	.31	.26	.37	.29	.23
43.....	.65	.45	.42	.46	.46	.36	.43
44.....	86.2	56.6	57.5	75.4	38.0	47.8	55.2

Liberalized Industry

Line Number	Tin Cans and Other Tinware (93)	Cutlery (94)	Tools and General Hardware (95)	Lighting Fixtures (103)	Metal Barrels, Drums, etc. (105)	Tubes and Foils (106)	Machine Tools and Metal-working Machinery (116)
1.....	106.10	122.70	130.39	138.36	103.93	100.62	109.05
2.....	42.11	82.61	89.16	66.70	42.89	43.95	62.90
3.....	63.99	40.09	41.23	71.66	61.04	56.67	46.15
4.....	.06	.09	.03	.07	.04	.04	.03
5.....	1.96	.52	.63	1.00	1.52	1.37	.49
6.....	3.48	.97	1.26	1.31	2.80	1.28	1.13
7.....	.50	.20	.25	.30	.39	.36	.21
8.....	.33	.10	.14	.19	.25	.12	.15
9.....	.09	.08	.03	.08	.06	.06	.03
10.....	—	—	—	—	—	—	—
11.....	.07	.26	.20	.32	.07	.08	.19
12.....	—	—	—	—	—	—	—
13.....	.04	.06	.03	.12	.03	.04	.05
14.....	1.66	1.54	2.72	2.09	.58	.78	.60
15.....	2.22	3.58	.62	2.83	.40	1.63	.31
16.....	.73	2.09	.44	1.03	.61	.71	.56
17.....	.55	.56	.20	.77	.36	.67	.17
18.....	.02	.03	.02	.06	.02	.02	.03
19.....	1.63	.38	.29	.64	1.00	.72	.21
20.....	1.41	.32	.45	.45	1.13	.37	.42
21.....	.14	.36	.34	.47	.24	.32	1.03
22.....	.02	.44	.02	.10	.02	.02	.11
23.....	.05	.06	.07	4.27	.04	.06	.05
24.....	.01	.01	.03	.23	.01	.01	.04
25.....	1.04	.65	1.38	.68	.91	.26	.77
26.....	30.71	7.32	9.59	7.30	25.15	2.64	13.12
27.....	.86	1.39	1.25	4.74	1.15	26.08	1.92
28.....	1.73*	6.62*	8.65*	11.98*	10.70*	6.82*	2.75
29.....	1.20	1.36	4.26	1.85	1.68	1.24	11.10*
30.....	.26	.31	.68	14.43	.37	.34	3.01
31.....	.04	.04	.05	.80	.09	.04	.10
32.....	.07	.06	.09	.11	.39	.11	.06
33.....	.20	.07	.10	.11	.17	.11	.13
34.....	.05	.07	.07	.32	.04	.07	.12
35.....	.16	2.14	.36	.90	.17	.13	.24
36.....	.23	.13	.16	.19	.20	.30	.12
37.....	4.46	1.48	1.67	2.31	3.62	2.87	1.50
38.....	.16	.05	.05	.07	.13	.14	.05
39.....	.86	.34	.42	.56	.67	.44	.33
40.....	4.39	2.28	2.46	5.84	3.68	3.97	2.48
41.....	1.59	3.12	1.40	2.03	1.48	1.52	1.74
42.....	.43	.25	.26	.34	.33	.28	.22
43.....	.58	.76	.56	.77	.54	.65	.58
44.....	39.7	67.3	68.4	48.2	41.3	43.7	57.7

Table F.1 (*continued*)

Line Number	Liberalized Industry						
	Special Industrial Machinery (118)	Industrial Machinery, n.e.c. (123)	Ball and Roller Bearings (127)	Motors and Generators (131)	Transformers (132)	Electrical Control Apparatus (133)	Electrical Welding Apparatus (134)
1.....	137.54	123.42	125.86	129.23	112.85	114.47	102.03
2.....	84.98	55.66	94.46	73.76	60.50	67.39	31.10
3.....	52.56	67.76	31.40	55.47	52.35	47.08	70.93
4.....	.06	.05	.03	.05	.10	.05	.09
5.....	.64	.91	.62	1.11	1.63	.89	1.08
6.....	1.26	1.40	1.43	1.58	1.34	.80	1.21
7.....	.19	.23	.30	.24	.43	.20	.28
8.....	.14	.18	.17	.29	.15	.18	.19
9.....	.04	.05	.02	.05	.07	.06	.10
10.....	—	—	—	—	—	—	—
11.....	.62	.31	.16	.40	1.30	.25	.28
12.....	—	—	—	—	.01	.01	.01
13.....	.05	.07	.03	.07	1.12	.07	.10
14.....	1.52	1.05	.62	1.13	1.22	.79	1.56
15.....	.70	.45	.26	.66	1.27	.93	1.62
16.....	.50	.82	.48	.60	.58	.58	.96
17.....	.28	.42	.15	.61	.42	1.21	.64
18.....	.08	.06	.03	.05	.12	.04	.05
19.....	.26	.53	.18	.41	.67	.51	1.55
20.....	.44	.49	.55	.50	.54	.29	.44
21.....	1.20	1.58	.35	.55	.53	.41	.74
22.....	.10	.12	.20	.06	.02	.02	.04
23.....	.10	.08	.03	.09	.07	.11	.21
24.....	.02	.06	.02	.14	1.92	2.51	.55
25.....	.50	1.90	1.26	1.88	.47	.33	.65
26.....	13.42	13.78	11.40	12.03	7.68	5.03	8.72
27.....	2.52	3.76	.84	4.34	5.76	4.09	3.85
28.....	3.57	5.99	.80	3.92	4.09	4.24	4.04
29.....	12.21*	20.49*	4.13*	5.08	1.51	1.98	3.54
30.....	3.27	2.83	.34	5.82*	6.44*	9.24*	20.08*
31.....	.11	.14	.03	2.03	2.18	2.13	6.62
32.....	.06	.06	.04	.07	.06	.06	.08
33.....	.12	.16	.09	.30	.11	.26	.14
34.....	.26	1.03	.04	.22	.10	.19	.12
35.....	.60	.28	.14	1.90	.54	1.50	.80
36.....	.12	.14	.20	.14	.13	.10	.14
37.....	1.82	2.10	1.89	2.20	2.22	1.47	2.12
38.....	.06	.07	.06	.07	.08	.05	.07
39.....	.40	.43	.39	.48	.51	.34	.45
40.....	2.92	3.46	2.19	3.50	4.41	3.29	4.63
41.....	1.51	2.02	1.09	1.97	1.65	1.74	2.20
42.....	.27	.30	.21	.25	.26	.21	.28
43.....	.62	.66	.63	.68	.64	.63	.70
44.....	61.8	45.1	75.1	57.1	53.6	58.9	30.5

347

Line Number	Liberalized Industzy						
	Electrical Appliances (135)	Insulated Wire and Cable (136)	Electric Lamps (138)	Radio and Related Products (139)	Communication Equipment (141)	Storage Batteries (142)	Primary Batteries (143)
1.....	134.30	99.71	109.48	155.15	132.53	96.09	118.12
2.....	52.61	43.90	72.74	80.46	91.95	46.52	80.39
3.....	81.69	55.81	36.74	74.69	40.58	49.57	37.73
4.....	.08	.09	.05	.10	.05	.12	.05
5.....	.88	4.91	.74	.62	.80	3.59	2.60
6.....	1.39	1.00	.54	.90	.77	.96	1.07
7.....	.28	.37	.20	.26	.16	.37	.22
8.....	.19	.10	.19	.19	.07	.26	.17
9.....	.08	.07	.05	.08	.06	.21	.11
10.....	—	—	—	—	—	—	—
11.....	.50	1.08	.39	1.13	.45	.79	.15
12.....	.01	—	—	.04	.01	—	—
13.....	.09	.32	.04	.54	.09	.05	.04
14.....	3.09	3.64	.65	13.27	1.72	3.61	.61
15.....	1.36	.66	1.40	1.88	.69	.66	1.27
16.....	2.04	.48	1.57	2.56	.86	.78	.53
17.....	.80	1.19	.63	.88	.84	1.62	2.16
18.....	.11	.33	.13	.16	.09	.18	.10
19.....	.68	.61	.39	.48	.56	5.74	.46
20.....	.47	.34	.16	.29	.21	.36	.25
21.....	1.73	.57	.71	.97	.44	7.09	.81
22.....	.12	.07	.02	.10	.03	.01	.01
23.....	.19	.07	9.70	.74	.20	.10	.07
24.....	.15	.08	.04	.30	.06	.01	.10
25.....	1.21	.55	.54	.42	.22	.40	.31
26.....	9.91	2.47	1.20	3.21	3.24	1.00	1.55
27.....	6.07	19.02	1.96	2.84	3.34	7.00	8.51
28.....	12.10	2.87	2.56	7.83	3.24	.72	1.21
29.....	10.81	1.69	.85	2.14	1.18	1.05	.69
30.....	9.28*	3.47*	2.56*	7.54	5.50	.11*	6.91*
31.....	1.32	.20	1.20	8.02*	6.72*	.02	.40
32.....	.11	.14	.27	.16	.05	.11	.04
33.....	.55	.11	.05	.08	.38	.08	.08
34.....	1.11	.04	.05	.30	.05	.05	.03
35.....	2.67	.19	1.20	2.92	.80	2.39	.34
36.....	.16	.16	.19	.13	.08	.18	.14
37.....	2.43	2.41	1.29	2.19	1.37	2.70	2.14
38.....	.08	.15	.05	.05	.04	.12	.16
39.....	.55	.54	.32	.64	.34	.48	.31
40.....	4.77	3.76	1.78	5.24	3.02	3.93	2.09
41.....	3.15	1.27	2.22	4.06	1.93	1.77	1.22
42.....	.34	.29	.23	.44	.26	.37	.24
43.....	.83	.50	.62	.99	.66	.58	.58
44.....	39.2	44.0	66.4	51.9	69.4	48.4	68.1

Table F.1 (*continued*)

Line Number	Passenger Cars and Light Trucks (145.1)	Heavy Trucks and Buses (145.2)	Motor Vehicle Parts and Accessories (145.3)	Aircraft and Parts (148)	Motorcycles and Bicycles (152)	Optical, Ophthalmic, and Photo Equipment (154)	Watches and Clocks (156)
			Liberalized Industry				
1.....	124.48	113.90	103.59	119.80	129.43	128.26	137.54
2.....	32.67	32.90	32.81	76.31	67.66	83.92	94.82
3.....	91.81	81.00	70.78	43.49	61.77	44.34	42.72
4.....	.23	.13	.06	.06	.07	.12	.07
5.....	.94	.82	1.18	.49	.80	.34	.65
6.....	1.82	1.61	1.95	.83	1.72	1.08	.58
7.....	.45	.39	.32	.28	.30	.24	.15
8.....	.26	.22	.23	.08	.17	.24	.23
9.....	.10	.09	.06	.05	.05	.14	.06
10....	—	—	—	—	—	—	—
11....	3.04	1.66	.70	.30	.83	.69	.34
12....	.57	.01	.01	.04			
13....	1.09	.29	.53	.11	.06	.23	.16
14....	1.07	2.96	.98	1.46	1.19	1.50	1.04
15....	.92	.77	.82	1.10	1.30	2.94	1.61
16....	1.32	1.35	1.14	1.36	.71	1.79	3.31
17....	.67	.60	.45	.28	.33	3.28	.54
18....	.43	.37	.16	.05	.18	.08	.04
19....	1.10	1.11	.64	.48	.53	.99	.35
20....	.67	.59	.72	.33	.65	.26	.15
21....	4.30	5.37	1.58	.71	2.85	.51	.24
22....	.14	.14	.26	.03	.17	.18	.51
23....	1.96	1.04	.15	.09	.09	2.48	1.42
24....	.00	.03	.03	.02	.03	.03	.01
25....	1.58	1.25	1.18	.47	.65	.57	.50
26....	13.23	12.16	20.38	7.71	15.95	1.81	1.42
27....	2.88	2.58	4.11	3.66	1.52	1.36	3.67
28....	12.66	8.28	6.57	4.78	4.29	4.75	3.54
29....	6.98	6.15	10.27	4.54	9.57	1.59	1.48
30....	5.15	5.28	4.86	2.20	2.21	2.60	.62
31....	.44	.12	.13	.64	.06	.39	.08
32....	14.05*	14.15*	.02*	.79	3.52	.05	.05
33....	.98	.37	.32	.46*	2.62*	.07	.07
34....	.98	.57	.54	2.30	.12	1.21*	1.87*
35....	.80	.53	.31	.30	.16	2.49	5.07
36....	.19	.13	.16	.14	.14	.14	.09
37....	3.72	3.25	3.46	1.51	2.53	1.78	1.43
38....	.09	.08	.09	.04	.19	.06	.24
39....	.76	.67	.71	.34	.54	.44	.34
40....	3.11	2.67	2.64	2.34	3.15	3.57	5.52
41....	2.03	2.12	2.01	2.54	1.61	3.27	4.11
42....	.35	.35	.35	.22	.29	.26	.26
43....	.67	.69	.68	.36	.62	.81	.90
44....	26.2	28.9	31.7	63.7	52.3	65.4	68.9

349

	Liberalized Industry						
Line Number	Jewelry and Silverware (157)	Musical Instruments and Parts (158)	Toys and Sporting Goods (159)	Office Supplies (160)	Plastic Products (161)	Cork Products (162)	Miscellaneous Manufactured Products (164)
1.....	136.76	135.38	157.86	134.79	123.05	88.16	157.31
2.....	90.95	97.42	100.12	87.41	77.79	48.61	77.21
3.....	45.81	37.96	57.74	47.38	45.26	39.55	80.10
4.....	.18	.11	.16	.25	.41	.12	.91
5.....	1.58	.23	.54	.20	.12	.24	.39
6.....	.59	1.01	.92	.74	1.16	.84	1.03
7.....	.26	.14	.25	.26	.28	.36	.32
8.....	3.71	.08	.13	.17	.17	.08	.16
9.....	.04	.06	.12	.23	.32	.62	.46
10.....	—	—	—	—	—	—	—
11.....	.19	1.38	1.73	1.42	5.68	.18	1.80
12.....	—	—	—	—	—	—	.01
13.....	.05	.06	1.15	.10	.18	.07	.51
14.....	1.82	7.06	6.38	9.52	2.25	.82	6.63
15.....	1.34	.87	4.01	3.10	2.93	.64	7.48
16.....	3.44	3.55	2.47	2.73	1.40	1.30	21.71
17.....	.42	.48	1.49	1.28	7.57	.25	1.44
18.....	.03	.12	.24	.17	.49	.03	.38
19.....	.22	.47	1.09	1.69	1.11	.22	1.16
20.....	.21	.19	.26	.23	.27	.32	.30
21.....	.41	.42	4.02	2.49	1.12	.18	.42
22.....	.08	.05	1.11	.05	.04	.03	.22
23.....	.18	.05	.35	.16	.13	.07	.42
24.....	.01	.01	.02	.01	.01	.01	.03
25.....	.40	.25	.48	.51	4.08	.29	.34
26.....	.83	2.24	2.44	.92	.74	2.75	2.15
27.....	9.44	.54	1.98	.82	.27	.82	1.46
28.....	2.84	1.52	3.33	1.88	.44	12.90	3.54
29.....	.92	.74	1.95	.92	.79	.97	2.21
30.....	.12	.14	.70	.20	.12	.27	1.23
31.....	.03	.02	.05	.03	.02	.13	.07
32.....	.07	.05	.32	.37	.12	.09	.11
33.....	.09	.05	.53	.08	.07	.37	.09
34.....	.04	.05	.21	.06	.04	.04	.17
35.....	3.42*	6.53*	9.78*	7.11*	4.90*	5.87*	7.13*
36.....	.14	.10	.14	.11	.14	.13	.13
37.....	2.01	1.41	1.71	1.59	1.66	.93	2.31
38.....	.18	.06	.07	.24	.05	2.69	.11
39.....	.33	.44	.49	.59	.45	.24	.65
40.....	4.48	2.11	2.93	3.05	2.91	1.34	8.55
41.....	4.57	4.31	3.13	2.98	1.89	2.66	2.64
42.....	.27	.25	.30	.31	.27	.17	.48
43.....	.87	.81	.76	.81	.66	.51	.95
44.....	66.5	72.0	63.4	64.8	63.2	55.1	49.1

Appendix Table F.2

Distribution of Net Employment Effects of Liberalization
by Industry Groups[a]

(Number of employees, farmers, and unpaid farm family workers.)

		Liberalized Industry	
Line Number	Industry Group Affected and Code Numbers of Industries in Group	Meat Animals and Products (1)	Vegetables and Fruits (8)
1	Total, all industries...	−23.63	−148.97
2	Liberalized industry..	−73.78	−191.99
3	Other industries—total...	50.15	43.02
4	Agriculture, forestry, and fishing (1–10)............................	.65*	1.38*
5	Metal mining (11–15)..	.52	.45
6	Coal mining (16)..	2.45	1.22
7	Crude petroleum and natural gas (17)..............................	.51	.58
8	Other nonmetallic minerals (18–20)................................	.27	−.08
9	Processed food and alcoholic beverages (21–28)......................	−.02	.63
10	Tobacco manufactures (29).......................................	.06	.08
11	Spinning, weaving, and dyeing (30)................................	1.59	1.02
12	Apparel (34)..	.65	.67
13	All other textile products (31–33, 35).............................	.23	−.18
14	Lumber, wood products, and furniture (36–43)......................	1.64	−5.72
15	Pulp, paper, and paper products (44–46)...........................	.87	.85
16	Printing and publishing (47).....................................	1.00	1.00
17	Industrial chemicals (except synthetic rubber and fiber) (48–50, 53)....	1.00	.45
18	Synthetic rubber and synthetic fiber (51, 52)......................	.18	.14
19	All other chemicals and allied products (54–61)....................	1.48	.24
20	Products of petroleum and coal (62–64)............................	.65	.41
21	Tires, inner tubes, and miscellaneous rubber products (65, 66)........	.66	.51
22	Leather and products and footwear (excluding rubber) (67–69)........	.30	.24
23	Glass (70)..	.54	.48
24	Pottery and related products (73).................................	.14	.09
25	Stone and clay products (71, 72, 74–77)...........................	.97	.90
26	Iron and steel and their primary products (78–81, 92)...............	5.76	5.47
27	Nonferrous metals and their primary products (82–91)..............	1.04	.99
28	Fabricated metal products (93–109)...............................	3.27	2.87
29	Machinery, except electrical (110–128)............................	10.24	9.52
30	Electrical machinery and products (129–138, 142–144)..............	2.51	2.50
31	Communication equipment and products (139–141)..................	1.22	1.18
32	Motor vehicles, parts, and accessories (145–147)...................	2.73	2.76
33	Other transportation equipment (148–152).........................	1.08	1.46
34	Instruments, optical and photographic equipment, watches and clocks (153–156)...	.96	.93
35	Miscellaneous manufactures (157–164)............................	.87	.92
36	Electric light and power, and gas (167, 168).......................	.05	.05
37	Railroad transportation (169).....................................	1.42	1.41
38	Ocean transportation (172).......................................	3.35	7.27
39	Transportation (except railroad and ocean transportation) and allied services (170, 171, 173–175, 178)...............................	−.52	.04
40	Wholesale and retail trade (176, 177).............................	.31	−.57
41	Communication, finance, and business services (179, 181, 186, 187)....	.70	1.58
42	Auto and other repair services (188, 189).........................	−.29	−.95
43	Other services (182–185, 190–192)................................	−.89	.23

* Excludes employment effects in the liberalized industry, which is a part of this industry group.

[a] Figures are net changes of employment per million-dollar increase of imports, after subtraction of increases associated with the process of importation and with exports. They are obtained by subtracting primary decreases shown in Table 3.3 from increases associated with exports shown in Table 5.3. Dashes represent effects of less than .005 employees, including some that are zero.

351

Line Number	Lead and Zinc Mining (13)	Meat Packing and Wholesale Poultry (21)	Processed Dairy Products (22)	Grain Mill Products (24)	Sugar (27)	Alcoholic Beverages (28)	Tobacco Manufactures (29)
			Liberalized Industry				
1.....	−94.15	−52.04	−21.38	5.03	2.95	−35.17	−34.88
2.....	−128.27	−24.30	−25.44	−16.80	−46.13	−43.18	−42.52
3.....	34.12	−27.74	4.06	21.83	49.08	8.01	7.64
4.....	2.81	−56.55	−1.15	1.26	5.10	−2.24	1.95
5.....	.47*	.52	.22	.53	.24	.43	.26
6.....	1.63	2.98	.29	3.18	−.82	1.99	.34
7.....	.26	.27	.01	.20	.55	.41	.39
8.....	.34	.32	.23	.26	.03	.22	.03
9.....	.86	−.81*	−2.05*	−1.71*	3.93*	−.73*	.97
10.....	.04	.03	.04	.02	.01	.03	—*
11.....	1.84	1.48	.89	−.14	5.73	1.42	1.59
12.....	.60	.35	.53	.43	.78	.39	.40
13.....	.34	.16	−.05	−1.62	.03	.18	.17
14.....	−4.72	.52	−.12	.95	1.43	−1.54	−1.15
15.....	.93	.36	−2.32	−1.08	.64	−1.78	−3.29
16.....	1.19	.46	−.50	−1.04	.22	−3.02	−3.29
17.....	−3.19	.51	.15	.36	.63	.19	−.20
18.....	.21	.04	.09	.03	.49	.11	.14
19.....	.96	.45	.43	.21	1.82	.61	.56
20.....	.17	.37	.16	.38	.34	.31	.25
21.....	.33	.33	.08	.30	.75	.21	.25
22.....	.28	.22	.10	.12	.77	.19	.26
23.....	.55	.30	−.01	.35	.87	−3.88	.28
24.....	.14	.14	.05	.14	.24	.11	.08
25.....	.69	.68	.21	.71	.45	.40	.30
26.....	2.27	4.10	1.33	3.98	3.00	2.66	2.03
27.....	.65	.80	.39	.74	.65	.65	.34
28.....	2.05	1.95	−.18	2.18	2.56	−.19	.79
29.....	6.07	8.12	4.72	7.55	4.73	7.01	4.28
30.....	2.13	1.76	.95	1.74	1.87	1.56	1.14
31.....	1.20	.91	.47	.95	.93	.76	.55
32.....	2.44	1.54	.73	1.59	1.56	1.41	.97
33.....	.54	.58	.56	.51	.47	.62	.40
34.....	.92	.72	.35	.74	.63	.61	.33
35.....	.90	.59	.13	.54	1.01	.22	.16
36.....	−.53	−.01	−.08	−.04	−.11	−.05	—
37.....	1.70	.31	−.45	−1.97	.93	−.21	.06
38.....	3.70	2.22	1.85	1.23	4.07	1.81	1.19
39.....	.31	−.80	−.37	−.69	.35	−.32	−.14
40.....	3.08	−1.64	−.93	1.68	3.88	1.95	−.13
41.....	−.08	−.65	−1.47	−2.16	−1.75	−3.69	−4.15
42.....	−.17	−.46	−.66	−.24	.05	−.26	−.02
43.....	.21	−.91	−.56	−.34	.02	−.54	−.45

Table F.2 (*continued*)

Line Number	Spinning, Weaving, and Dyeing (30)	Special Textile Products (31)	Apparel (34)	House Furnishings and Other Non-apparel (35)	Plywood (38)	Wood Containers and Cooperage (40)	Wood Furniture (41)
1.....	−116.00	−85.43	−174.63	−111.34	−99.43	−88.86	−141.73
2.....	−96.66	−73.55	−133.48	−47.68	−80.91	−93.62	−102.72
3.....	−19.34	−11.88	−41.15	−63.66	−18.52	4.76	−39.01
4.....	−3.66	−3.89	−2.72	−1.53	1.43	3.44	.78
5....	.16	.17	.20	.15	.33	.34	.09
6....	−.84	−.10	.10	−.25	1.84	.30	.20
7....	−.16	.08	.09	—	.21	.92	.13
8....	−.05	.05	.04	−.01	.17	.26	.07
9....	−.13	−.21	.21	−.27	.54	.91	.47
10....	.02	.02	.02	.03	.02	.09	.09
11....	—*	−8.98	−28.48	−46.16	1.26	1.51	−3.33
12....	.39	.27	—*	−.11	.36	.74	.06
13....	−.52	−1.27*	−.97	−1.20*	.16	.30	−1.95
14....	−.89	.08	−.31	−1.66	−35.10*	−47.00*	−29.22*
15....	−.98	−1.00	−1.25	−1.64	.27	.01	−.26
16....	−.70	−.70	−1.48	−.98	.13	.61	−.74
17....	−1.83	−.26	−.56	−1.62	−1.22	1.38	−.01
18....	−7.57	−1.54	−3.36	−3.53	.12	.20	−.26
19....	−.15	.49	.25	−1.14	−.36	2.17	−.48
20....	−.06	.08	.09	.02	.09	.58	−.01
21....	.01	.16	−.27	−.93	−.05	.55	−.34
22....	.05	.07	−.31	.05	.06	.13	−.03
23....	−.48	−.02	−.07	−.23	.26	.49	−.88
24....	.02	.02	.02	.01	.07	.10	.03
25....	.09	.16	.13	.08	.12	.60	−.23
26....	.82	1.38	1.14	1.03	2.54	4.86	−.07
27....	.18	.28	.23	.21	.48	.97	.03
28....	.47	.67	.46	.42	.75	2.01	−3.77
29....	1.99	2.65	2.66	2.60	4.89	9.68	3.41
30....	.49	.68	.37	.58	1.16	2.62	.82
31....	.24	.33	.26	.29	.65	1.25	.41
32....	.49	.88	.52	.48	1.09	3.49	.65
33....	.28	.39	.26	.49	.46	1.44	.45
34....	.20	.25	.21	.23	.51	.99	.36
35....	−.11	.10	−1.82	−.86	.35	.93	−.06
36....	−.17	−.06	−.07	−.12	−.05	.01	−.08
37....	−1.30	−.29	−.52	−1.09	−1.03	−.35	−1.29
38....	1.21	1.33	1.39	1.94	.78	5.74	1.16
39....	−.48	−.20	−.18	−.30	−1.30	−1.14	−.74
40....	−3.03	−1.89	−4.31	−5.73	1.85	3.41	−1.18
41....	−2.26	−1.32	−2.16	−1.89	−1.48	.46	−2.27
42....	−.29	−.24	−.18	−.31	−.48	−.57	−.43
43....	−.79	−.51	−.78	−.71	−.40	−.07	−.59

Liberalized Industry

Line Number	Paper and Board Mills (45)	Converted Paper Products (46)	Industrial Organic Chemicals (49)	Synthetic Rubber (51)	Synthetic Fiber (52)	Drugs and Medicines (54)	Paints and Allied Products (56)
1.....	−35.32	−91.66	−58.76	−1.12	−71.68	−99.63	−30.31
2.....	−39.68	−59.48	−35.06	−19.22	−55.03	−52.11	−41.82
3.....	4.36	−32.18	−23.70	18.10	−16.65	−47.52	11.51
4.....	1.77	.79	−.17	1.87	.57	−.85	1.03
5.....	.46	.20	−.47	.49	.01	.05	−2.34
6.....	−.13	−.75	−4.19	2.66	−2.60	−.85	.43
7.....	.18	−.24	−1.24	−4.98	−.31	−.27	−.18
8.....	−.17	−.16	−.67	.12	−.36	−.17	−.66
9.....	.31	.19	−1.50	.08	−.32	−1.05	−.76
10.....	.04	.02	.02	.02	.02	.03	.02
11.....	1.02	.06	.42	1.90	.64	.68	.93
12.....	.42	.19	.53	.47	.23	.67	.29
13.....	−.26	−.43	−.01	.30	.05	−.03	.16
14.....	−7.30	−4.41	−2.42	.78	−2.81	−.58	.16
15.....	−9.54*	−23.90*	−1.06	−.48	−3.23	−5.55	−1.36
16.....	.48	−.93	−.59	.25	−.53	−11.06	−.22
17.....	−.16	−.83	−4.61*	−6.99	−7.79	−4.57	−7.01
18.....	.09	.01	−.12	.13*	.01*	−.10	−.01
19.....	.42	−.14	−2.72	−2.74	−.93	−2.09*	−2.58*
20.....	.15	−.18	−1.63	−3.50	−.33	−.31	−.39
21.....	.39	−.27	−.34	.37	−.02	−.35	−.07
22.....	.17	.05	.07	.27	.06	.07	.13
23.....	.38	.07	−.57	.34	−.04	−4.43	.08
24.....	.11	.02	.01	.13	.02	—	.07
25.....	.40	.03	−.10	.71	—	−.11	−.55
26.....	3.57	.67	−.71	4.52	.35	.48	.62
27.....	.70	.13	−.32	.69	.03	−.10	−.65
28.....	1.89	.28	−.56	2.47	.31	−.33	−.63
29.....	6.35	2.15	1.34	8.02	1.76	2.02	3.86
30.....	1.57	.54	.36	2.03	.51	.51	1.03
31.....	.78	.25	.17	1.07	.25	.21	.60
32.....	1.49	.53	.38	1.95	.60	.46	1.07
33.....	.60	.35	.35	.46	.28	.30	1.69
34.....	.65	.06	.18	.77	.22	.13	.28
35.....	.54	−.36	.13	.78	−.26	−.68	.12
36.....	−.14	−.12	−.35	−.15	−.11	−.14	−.12
37.....	−1.28	−3.18	−3.20	.12	−2.24	−1.90	−1.10
38.....	1.35	1.99	2.87	2.47	1.20	.61	15.67
39.....	−.77	−.87	−.78	−.43	−.63	−.71	−.21
40.....	−1.16	−2.17	−.27	2.45	.77	−3.35	.43
41.....	−.53	−.96	−1.13	−1.01	−1.23	−12.34	1.92
42.....	−.24	−.33	−.31	−.06	−.22	−.35	−.15
43.....	−.24	−.53	−.49	−.25	−.58	−1.47	−.09

Line Number	Vegetable Oils (59)	Liberalized Industry					
		Miscellaneous Chemical Industries (61)	Tires and Inner Tubes (65)	Miscellaneous Rubber Products (66)	Leather Tanning and Finishing (67)	Footwear (Except Rubber) (69)	Glass (70)
1.....	−5.55	−88.61	−81.57	−91.11	−39.00	−154.11	−97.57
2.....	−20.52	−35.69	−44.65	−76.42	−62.44	−132.54	−86.61
3.....	14.97	−52.92	−36.92	−14.60	23.44	−21.57	−10.96
4.....	1.42	−1.60	−.58	.50	.78	.46	.69
5.....	.42	−.14	.04	.17	.49	.29	.11
6.....	1.50	−1.53	−1.05	.30	.74	.25	−.35
7.....	.19	−1.07	−.84	−.22	.43	.25	−.26
8.....	.17	−1.55	−.18	−.06	.22	.11	−1.16
9.....	−10.18	−1.65	−.15	.35	.17	.25	.37
10.....	.06	.02	.02	.02	.03	.03	.02
11.....	.88	.08	−14.53	−6.00	1.11	−1.23	.49
12.....	.58	.25	.11	.23	.36	.48	.20
13.....	−.35	−.24	−.09	−.04	.12	.36	.03
14.....	1.19	−.67	−.29	−.82	.36	−1.49	−1.41
15.....	−.11	−4.76	−.92	−1.70	.42	−2.33	−4.70
16.....	−.14	−8.02	−1.23	−.59	.37	−.94	−.71
17.....	.41	−6.27	−1.93	−1.39	−.61	−.35	−1.55
18.....	.06	−.25	−3.34	−1.56	.12	−.11	.06
19.....	.90*	−5.05*	−1.59	−1.16	−1.47	−.55	.29
20.....	.53	−.60	−.61	−.17	.33	.18	−.10
21.....	.34	−.49	−4.17*	−5.09*	.18	−2.33	−.13
22.....	.16	−.27	.02	.10	−.21*	−17.13*	.02
23.....	.02	−1.66	−.11	−.15	.25	.08	−*
24.....	.13	—	.02	.03	.06	.04	−.14
25.....	.79	−.61	−.05	−.08	.34	.06	−2.75
26.....	4.49	−.63	.03	.67	3.40	1.56	.32
27.....	.79	−.38	.03	.12	.78	.37	.10
28.....	2.12	−1.13	.07	−.45	1.75	.56	.10
29.....	8.84	.82	.86	2.42	6.80	3.64	1.81
30.....	2.28	.60	.31	.63	1.63	.74	.47
31.....	1.09	.59	.16	.38	.62	.31	.22
32.....	2.57	.30	.20	.58	1.35	.68	.57
33.....	.75	.21	.23	.29	.77	.40	.99
34.....	.88	−.59	.08	.29	.55	.26	.11
35.....	.59	−.73	−.06	.19	.46	−.27	.02
36.....	−.10	−.18	−.15	−.13	−.01	−.05	−.53
37.....	−.43	−2.28	−1.47	−.64	−.14	−.56	−1.38
38.....	2.16	1.30	.40	.74	.99	.79	.89
39.....	−.30	−.62	−.32	−.09	−.31	−.17	−.57
40.....	−5.92	−2.54	−2.95	−.60	1.17	−1.21	−.70
41.....	−2.71	−10.06	−2.06	−1.14	−.06	−3.66	−.94
42.....	−.45	−.42	−.28	−.16	−.05	−.10	−.29
43.....	−.65	−1.10	−.57	−.46	−.25	−.52	−.47

Liberalized Industry

Line Num- ber	Pottery and Related Products (73)	Carbon Steel Works and Rolling Mills (79.1)	Alloy Steel Works and Rolling Mills, Except Stainless (79.2)	Stainless Steel Works and Rolling Mills (79.3)	Primary Zinc (85)	Primary Aluminum, Including Alumina (88)	Aluminum Rolling and Drawing (89)
1.....	−171.73	−66.26	−69.53	−71.93	−34.12	−4.66	−42.02
2.....	−163.20	−50.70	−53.67	−72.77	−36.25	−29.91	−43.81
3.....	−8.53	−15.56	−15.86	.84	2.13	25.25	1.79
4.....	.62	.82	.80	.83	2.61	2.45	1.38
5.....	.04	−3.08	−3.26	−1.23	−26.90	−2.38	−1.19
6.....	−.04	−5.08	−5.06	−1.70	.43	2.22	.54
7.....	−.11	−.37	−.39	−.01	.14	.10	.11
8.....	−2.56	−.38	−.36	−.04	.19	.08	.12
9.....	.42	.40	.38	.41	.78	.79	.54
10.....	.02	.03	.03	.03	.04	.02	.03
11.....	.55	.64	.62	.65	1.68	1.80	1.30
12.....	.19	.27	.26	.27	.42	.43	.34
13.....	.05	.08	.08	.08	.29	.31	.19
14.....	−.36	−.32	−.10	.03	.06	1.18	.31
15.....	−1.77	.14	.11	.18	.82	.74	.52
16.....	−.37	−.10	−.05	.01	.88	1.01	.44
17.....	−.47	−.08	−.10	.06	−.08	−.53	−.02
18.....	.06	.07	.07	.07	.20	.20	.14
19.....	−1.35	.38	.34	.45	1.06	.85	.63
20.....	−.05	−2.28	−2.24	−.66	.06	−.05	−.03
21.....	−.04	.13	.14	.18	.46	.50	.28
22.....	.06	.04	.04	.05	.26	.25	.16
23.....	−.05	.09	.09	.10	.51	.50	.29
24.....	—*	.01	.01	.02	.12	.13	.07
25.....	−3.30	−1.67	−1.93	−.60	−.96	.50	.31
26.....	.39	−6.91*	−4.54*	−1.15*	4.06	3.55	2.15
27.....	.02	−.46	−.61	−.38	−3.42*	−7.53*	−17.49*
28.....	.27	.37	.43	.20	2.53	2.62	1.46
29.....	2.24	1.76	2.08	2.32	7.91	8.03	5.54
30.....	−1.10	.33	.25	.20	2.05	1.88	1.17
31.....	.18	.23	.23	.24	1.09	1.00	.57
32.....	.45	.71	.68	.73	2.14	1.78	1.05
33.....	.23	.50	.49	.66	.53	.46	.38
34.....	.17	.24	.22	.25	.83	.78	.48
35.....	.04	.12	.10	.13	.82	.78	.46
36.....	−.31	−.24	−.28	−.24	−.60	−.64	−.39
37.....	−1.20	−3.59	−4.67	−3.32	−2.23	−.46	−.46
38.....	.62	3.86	3.79	4.05	1.39	.70	.35
39.....	−.37	−.89	−1.04	−.45	.18	.26	.15
40.....	.24	−.79	−1.93	−1.20	1.82	.74	.36
41.....	−1.16	−.11	−.11	.02	.10	.21	−.22
42.....	−.25	−.19	−.21	−.15	−.08	−.02	−.05
43.....	−.53	−.24	−.22	−.25	−.06	.01	−.18

			Liberalized Industry				
Line Number	Tin Cans and Other Tinware (93)	Cutlery (94)	Tools and General Hardware (95)	Lighting Fixtures (103)	Metal Barrels, Drums, etc. (105)	Tubes and Foils (106)	Machine Tools and Metalworking Machinery (116)
1.....	−67.17	−102.81	−110.98	−117.97	−87.22	−85.47	−79.83
2.....	−42.05	−82.60	−89.08	−66.67	−42.87	−43.95	−62.39
3.....	−25.12	−20.21	−21.90	−51.30	−44.35	−41.52	−17.44
4.....	1.70	.84	.89	.90	.55	.57	1.20
5.....	−1.51	−.24	−.38	−.81	−1.32	−1.18	−.15
6.....	−1.16	.17	−.11	−.48	−1.97	−.50	.57
7.....	.12	.09	.03	−.04	−.15	−.18	.19
8.....	−.05	.02	−.03	−.09	−.13	.04	.04
9.....	.62	.44	.53	.42	.20	.28	.55
10.....	.03	.02	.03	.12	.02	.02	.02
11.....	1.24	.38	.61	.93	.58	.54	.95
12.....	.38	.22	.30	.44	.18	.43	.65
13.....	.16	.03	.06	−.02	.05	.02	.10
14.....	−.68	−1.02	−2.26	−1.63	−.18	−.46	.07
15.....	−1.60	−3.26	−.31	−2.45	−.13	−1.40	.16
16.....	.11	−1.72	−.09	−.62	−.27	−.45	.03
17.....	.08	−.19	.14	−.43	−.10	−.43	.32
18.....	.13	.06	.08	.06	.04	.05	.11
19.....	−.70	.28	.36	−.02	−.60	−.24	.57
20.....	−.95	−.09	−.23	−.24	−.95	−.22	−.11
21.....	.29	−.15	−.14	−.24	−.05	−.17	−.70
22.....	.15	−.86	.06	.02	.04	.05	.04
23.....	.21	.00	.07	−4.11	.08	.04	.17
24.....	.06	.01	−.01	−.21	.03	.01	—
25.....	−.56	−.44	−1.19	−.48	−.71	−.13	−.46
26.....	−27.39	−5.82	−8.15	−5.75	−23.71	−1.54	−10.85
27.....	−.17	−1.01	−.91	−4.42	−.84	−25.80	−1.41
28.....	−*	−5.84*	−8.00*	−11.16*	−9.96*	−6.28*	−1.51
29.....	4.86	1.69	−1.46	.91	1.11	.92	−7.38*
30.....	1.05	.30	−.10	−13.76	.20	.13	−2.12
31.....	.57	.22	.19	−.54	.22	.17	.30
32.....	1.14	.48	.47	.50	.14	.31	.83
33.....	.53	.29	.29	.23	.20	.22	.32
34.....	.47	.17	.14	−.02	.20	.13	.27
35.....	.38	−1.88	−.14	−.53	.05	.08	.23
36.....	−.18	−.10	−.14	−.16	−.18	−.28	−.08
37.....	−2.56	−.48	−.69	−1.28	−2.79	−2.14	−.08
38.....	.72	.50	.49	.28	.17	.55	1.05
39.....	−.42	−.10	−.18	−.32	−.48	−.27	.01
40.....	−.92	−.42	−.63	−3.92	−2.18	−2.60	.14
41.....	−.71	−2.62	−.90	−1.51	−1.09	−1.06	−1.01
42.....	−.24	−.15	−.16	−.24	−.25	−.20	−.08
43.....	−.32	−.62	−.43	−.63	−.43	−.55	−.39

Table F.2 (*continued*)

Line Number	Liberalized Industry						
	Special Industrial Machinery (118)	Industrial Machinery, n.e.c. (123)	Ball and Roller Bearings (127)	Motors and Generators (131)	Transformers (132)	Electrical Control Apparatus (133)	Electrical Welding Apparatus (134)
1.....	−110.51	−83.56	−90.02	−72.28	−90.62	−93.12	−58.96
2.....	−84.39	−55.49	−94.26	−73.21	−60.47	−67.32	−31.04
3.....	−26.12	−28.07	4.24	.93	−30.15	−25.80	−27.92
4.....	1.06	1.83	1.48	2.26	.61	.59	1.80
5.....	−.27	−.45	−.26	−.47	−1.36	−.63	−.58
6.....	.19	.89	.81	2.23	−.50	−.11	1.32
7.....	.24	.36	.24	.64	−.13	.07	.38
8.....	.02	.10	.08	.15	—	−.04	.12
9.....	.52	.72	.60	.73	.29	.26	.66
10.....	.03	.03	.05	.02	.03	.02	.03
11.....	.32	.99	1.11	1.44	−.31	.74	1.12
12.....	.27	.38	.31	.46	.91	.98	.38
13.....	.07	.13	.16	.23	−1.04	.04	.13
14.....	−.85	−.08	.24	.31	−.76	−.34	−.48
15.....	−.24	.19	.32	.27	−.89	−.55	−.91
16.....	.05	.04	.31	.74	−.16	−.17	−.01
17.....	.19	.21	.40	.27	−.04	−.85	.06
18.....	.03	.09	.11	.15	—	.08	.11
19.....	.49	.44	.58	.62	−.05	.10	−.55
20.....	−.12	−.05	−.16	.14	−.30	−.07	.05
21.....	−.91	−1.14	.06	.11	−.26	−.16	−.25
22.....	—	.06	−.06	.19	.12	.15	.15
23.....	.09	.25	.28	.43	.09	.05	.16
24.....	.02	.01	.05	—	−1.89	−2.49	−.46
25.....	−.20	−.71	−.82	−1.08	−.24	−.29	−.10
26.....	−11.28	−10.40	−8.32	−6.96	−5.89	−3.35	−4.98
27.....	−2.02	−3.06	−.23	−3.35	−5.34	−3.69	−3.09
28.....	−2.43	−4.17	.91	−1.02	−3.17	−3.35	−1.99
29.....	−8.51*	−14.58*	1.08*	3.86	2.00	1.20	3.23
30.....	−2.38	−1.49	.91	−4.36*	−5.75*	−8.62*	−18.67*
31.....	.27	.49	.54	−1.04	−1.93	−1.84	−5.93
32.....	.71	1.15	1.16	1.73	.64	.65	1.28
33.....	.30	.66	.47	.35	.34	.21	.56
34.....	.08	−.45	.46	.59	.26	.13	.46
35.....	−.26	.28	.34	−1.06	−.05	−1.00	−.19
36.....	−.08	−.09	−.15	−.07	−.10	−.07	−.08
37.....	−.51	−.15	−.13	.60	−1.14	−.45	.01
38.....	.98	.89	1.00	1.09	.31	.32	.77
39.....	−.08	.03	.03	.17	−.26	−.10	.05
40.....	−.51	.10	1.01	1.55	−2.43	−1.40	−.77
41.....	−.82	−1.07	−.29	−.69	−1.11	−1.22	−1.22
42.....	−.14	−.10	−.04	.02	−.16	−.11	−.07
43.....	−.44	−.40	−.40	−.32	−.49	−.49	−.42

Table F.2 (*continued*)

Line Number	Electrical Appliances (135)	Insulated Wire and Cable (136)	Electric Lamps (138)	Radio and Related Products (139)	Communication Equipment (141)	Storage Batteries (142)	Primary Batteries (143)
				Liberalized Industry			
1	−110.53	−50.66	−89.79	−103.67	−73.68	−80.68	−64.53
2	−52.52	−43.83	−72.72	−80.03	−91.70	−46.49	−80.38
3	−58.01	−6.83	−17.07	−23.64	18.02	−34.19	15.85
4	.75	1.71	.59	2.14	2.36	.43	2.16
5	−.55	−4.42	−.52	−.04	−.15	−3.39	−1.98
6	−.37	1.96	.68	2.33	3.19	−.41	2.58
7	.14	.38	.15	.52	.74	−.11	.62
8	—	.24	−.07	.19	.36	−.17	.23
9	.40	.56	.62	.75	.75	.09	.61
10	.03	.05	.02	.03	.02	.07	.02
11	.31	.36	.45	.57	1.48	−.17	1.52
12	.24	.38	.20	.40	.50	.15	.42
13	.01	−.07	.06	−.27	.23	.02	.25
14	−2.49	−2.52	−.16	−11.99	−.30	−3.28	.75
15	−.94	.09	−1.07	−1.06	.25	−.40	−.41
16	−1.58	.63	−1.19	−1.40	.52	−.49	.74
17	−.37	−.48	−.27	−.08	.06	−1.36	−1.33
18	−.01	−.17	−.03	.03	.12	−.10	.09
19	.03	.30	.33	.59	.52	−5.35	.49
20	−.15	.22	.10	.28	.44	−.16	.36
21	−1.47	−.05	−.50	−.38	.25	−6.91	−.18
22	−.02	.13	.06	.14	.23	.06	.23
23	−.03	.33	−9.56	−.28	.34	.01	.43
24	−.09	.02	−.02	−.19	.07	.01	.02
25	−.96	.08	−.31	.26	.60	−.24	.45
26	−8.02	1.59	.18	1.29	2.04	.31	3.27
27	−5.60	−18.22	−1.66	−1.94	−2.33	−6.73	−7.56
28	−11.09	−.56	−1.81	−5.31	−.22	−.04	1.53
29	−6.82	5.51	2.01	5.88	7.92	1.37	7.78
30	−8.57*	−1.86*	−2.00*	−5.74	−3.45	.40*	−5.02*
31	−1.00	.59	−.91	−7.59*	−5.94*	.18	.54
32	.58	1.31	.34	1.46	1.97	.47	1.67
33	−.13	.66	.26	.65	.30	.38	.50
34	−.82	.60	.18	.42	.81	.17	.71
35	−2.37	.40	−.95	−2.17	.07	−2.22	.40
36	−.13	−.10	−.16	−.06	—	.16	−.07
37	−1.28	−.13	−.30	.33	1.53	−1.96	.51
38	.69	3.29	.54	1.04	1.10	.41	.74
39	−.27	−.01	−.07	−.05	.32	−.30	.30
40	−2.67	.24	.02	−.66	2.22	−2.59	2.70
41	−2.50	.26	−1.70	−2.88	−.64	−1.40	−.05
42	−.22	−.07	−.12	−.19	.02	−.30	.01
43	−.67	−.15	−.48	−.66	−.28	−.48	−.24

Table F.2 (*continued*)

Line Number	Liberalized Industry						
	Passenger Cars and Light Trucks (145.1)	Heavy Trucks and Buses (145.2)	Motor Vehicle Parts and Accessories (145.3)	Aircraft and Parts (148)	Motorcycles and Bicycles (152)	Optical, Ophthalmic, and Photo Equipment (154)	Watches and Clocks (156)
1.....	−97.95	−55.53	−51.51	−66.28	−103.64	−101.58	−117.56
2.....	−32.50	−32.75	−31.63	−76.17	−67.65	−83.80	−94.80
3.....	−65.45	−22.78	−19.88	9.89	−35.99	−17.78	−22.76
4.....	.62	2.23	2.00	2.03	.85	1.16	.48
5....	−.55	−.15	−.61	.10	−.44	−.04	−.41
6.....	−.85	2.25	1.35	2.57	−.69	1.66	.11
7.....	.02	.50	.49	.54	.13	.14	.06
8.....	−.06	.22	.16	.30	.02	−.08	−.12
9.....	.34	.70	.66	.68	.43	.49	.21
10.....	.03	.02	.03	.03	.03	.02	.02
11.....	−2.10	.19	.99	1.42	.01	.17	.64
12.....	−.29	.46	.41	.39	.27	.26	1.06
13.....	−.98	.02	−.25	.18	.05	−.11	−.06
14.....	−.35	−1.50	.32	−.16	−.54	−.84	−.67
15.....	−.43	.17	.03	−.24	−.85	−2.52	−1.29
16.....	−.78	.01	.07	−.14	−.23	−1.25	−2.96
17.....	−.19	.29	.37	.55	.12	−2.84	−.22
18.....	−.32	−.17	.03	.14	−.08	.03	.07
19.....	−.39	−.07	.34	.50	.19	−.22	.18
20.....	−.31	.06	−.13	.26	−.32	.03	.03
21.....	−4.02	−4.69	−.98	−.11	−2.58	−.21	—
22.....	−.03	.12	−.03	.20	−.07	−.06	−.32
23.....	−1.78	−.51	.32	.38	.09	−2.26	−1.27
24.....	−.02	.05	.06	.09	.03	.01	.01
25.....	−1.28	−.44	−.47	.23	−.40	−.26	−.30
26.....	−11.08	−6.97	−15.80	−3.04	−13.97	.29	.06
27.....	−2.34	−1.57	−3.21	−2.75	−1.03	−.90	−3.30
28.....	−11.54	−5.35	−3.98	−2.17	−3.25	−3.60	−2.77
29.....	−2.39	2.94	−2.02	3.79	−5.34	2.25	1.21
30.....	−4.24	−3.26	−3.06	−.37	−1.36	−1.76	−.04
31.....	−.09	.89	.73	.24	.28	.01	.14
32.....	−13.46*	−12.42*	.45*	.95	−2.81	.87	.59
33.....	−.53	.27	.29	.01*	−2.21*	.35	.34
34.....	−.66	.25	.18	−1.57	.19	−.99*	−1.59*
35.....	−.44	.33	.45	.46	.15	−2.14	−4.57
36.....	−.15	−.05	−.09	−.07	−.11	−.11	−.07
37.....	−2.46	−.40	−.93	1.07	−1.32	−.45	−.54
38.....	1.01	1.51	1.39	2.03	1.47	.71	.99
39.....	−.46	−.01	−.12	.26	−.25	−.12	−.13
40.....	−.84	2.48	1.94	2.33	−.95	−1.12	−3.87
41.....	−1.33	−.78	−.80	−1.23	−.88	−2.60	−3.52
42.....	−.23	−.08	−.11	.03	−.17	−.12	−.17
43.....	−.50	−.32	−.35	−.02	−.45	−.63	−.77

Line Number	Jewelry and Silverware (157)	Musical Instruments (158)	Toys and Sporting Goods (159)	Office Supplies (160)	Plastic Products (161)	Cork Products (162)	Miscellaneous Manufactured Products (164)
			Liberalized Industry				
1.....	−122.58	−103.90	−141.25	−111.11	−87.43	−79.10	−132.07
2.....	−90.93	−97.40	−100.09	−87.38	−77.67	−48.61	−77.12
3.....	−31.65	−6.50	−41.16	−23.73	−9.76	−30.49	−54.95
4.....	.36	1.11	.43	.50	.89	−.04	—
5.....	−1.40	.17	−.33	.05	.28	−.18	−.10
6.....	.14	.66	−.01	.27	.89	−.61	.18
7.....	−.03	.38	.02	.11	.29	−.24	.11
8.....	−3.62	.13	−.03	−.05	.07	−.06	−.01
9.....	.32	.49	.35	.27	.26	−.55	.02
10.....	.02	.03	.02	.02	.03	.11	.02
11.....	.40	−.32	−1.05	−.75	−4.51	.05	−.95
12.....	.15	.30	.15	.19	.30	.07	.22
13.....	.01	.09	−1.08	—		−.05	−.39
14.....	−1.48	−6.26	−5.98	−9.03	−1.34	.66	−6.06
15.....	−1.10	−.33	−3.73	−2.78	−2.35	−.53	−7.07
16.....	−3.19	−2.88	−2.16	−2.30	−.63	−1.15	−21.21
17.....	−.16	.06	−1.20	−.95	−7.00	−.13	−1.03
18.....	.03	.01	−.16	−.09	−.36	—	−.28
19.....	.25	.32	−.52	−1.08	−.33	.08	−.50
20.....	−.03	.19	−.05	.04	.15	−.20	.01
21.....	−.27	−.06	−3.84	−2.31	−.73	−.09	−.16
22.....	−.03	.10	−1.04	.02	.13	−.02	−.12
23.....	−.08	.19	−.24	−.04	.16	−.02	−.25
24.....	.01	.04		.01	.06	—	—
25.....	−.26	.14	−.31	−.32	−3.63	−.22	−.10
26.....	.24	.40	−1.24	.44	2.21	−1.85	−.26
27.....	−9.18	.05	−1.69	−.49	.34	−.68	−1.04
28.....	−2.32	−.09	−2.69	−1.16	1.19	−12.58	−2.54
29.....	1.40	4.43	.58	1.00	4.80	.46	1.45
30.....	.30	.93	−.20	.35	1.07	.23	−.49
31.....	.14	.44	.19	.17	.51	.22	.23
32.....	.33	.89	.17	.13	.96	.11	.68
33.....	.18	.41	−.23	.58	.39	−.25	.43
34.....	.11	.36	−.01	.17	.45	.11	.11
35.....	−3.28*	−6.11*	−9.63*	−6.89*	−4.52*	−5.77*	−6.94*
36.....	−.12	−.00	−.12	−.00	−.10	−.12	.10
37.....	−1.32	.13	−.89	−.59	.03	−.57	−1.12
38.....	.35	.80	.60	4.00	1.69	−1.59	1.95
39.....	−.16	−.08	−.29	−.36	−.05	−.15	−.37
40.....	−3.21	.68	−1.43	−1.34	.15	−.72	−6.45
41.....	−4.18	−3.54	−2.66	−1.51	−.98	−2.31	−1.70
42.....	−.20	−.10	−.21	−.21	−.10	−.14	−.36
43.....	−.77	−.60	−.65	−.59	−.43	−.45	−.76

Derivation of Net Increase in Earnings of All Currencies by All Foreign Countries

(In thousands of 1953 dollars per $1 million increase of United States imports)

Liberalized Industry		Gross Increase in Dollar Earnings of Major Suppliers[a]	Change in Earnings of World Trade Groups				Total Net Increase in Earnings by All Countries[e]
			Increase Due to Spending by Major Suppliers[b]	Output-Induced Decrease	Net Increase[c]	Multiplied Net Increase[d]	
Code Number	Title						
		(1)	(2)	(3)	(4)	(5)	(6)
1	Meat animals and products...	862.9	170.6	16.8	153.8	371.8	1234.7
8	Vegetables and fruits........	762.8	123.4	18.0	105.4	257.8	1020.6
13	Lead and zinc mining........	883.8	167.5	33.4	134.1	322.1	1205.7
21	Meat packing and wholesale poultry...................	865.1	307.1	39.4	267.7	657.6	1522.7
22	Processed dairy products.....	862.7	733.5	32.2	701.3	1803.5	2666.2
24	Grain mill products..........	890.1	200.6	36.2	164.4	400.0	1290.1
27	Sugar......................	886.7	175.6	80.1	95.5	255.3	1142.0
28	Alcoholic beverages..........	859.1	277.9	22.0	255.9	645.7	1504.8
29	Tobacco manufactures........	775.8	452.4	39.1	413.3	1091.1	1866.9
30	Spinning, weaving, and dyeing	788.3	382.3	29.9	352.4	922.0	1710.3
31	Special textile products.......	793.4	463.0	66.1	396.9	1010.4	1803.8
34	Apparel....................	753.2	391.5	30.8	360.7	943.9	1697.1
35	House furnishings and other non-apparel...............	834.2	515.8	112.7	403.1	1087.5	1921.7
38	Plywood...................	851.0	315.3	30.9	284.4	751.7	1602.7
40	Wood containers and cooperage	805.7	121.1	35.0	86.1	218.3	1024.0
41	Wood furniture.............	849.5	630.2	31.8	598.4	1598.4	2447.9
45	Paper and board mills........	905.0	416.8	63.6	353.2	965.4	1870.4
46	Converted paper products....	847.0	401.9	92.7	309.2	837.3	1684.3
49	Industrial organic chemicals...	736.1	382.2	61.0	321.2	852.1	1588.2
51	Synthetic rubber............	887.4	181.3	65.2	116.1	281.4	1168.8
52	Synthetic fiber..............	856.2	432.8	37.2	395.6	1018.9	1875.1
54	Drugs and medicines.........	875.0	414.0	38.5	375.5	974.8	1849.8
56	Paints and allied products	711.1	264.6	83.3	181.3	486.2	1197.3
59	Vegetable oils...............	902.5	227.9	112.9	115.0	308.7	1211.2
61	Miscellaneous chemical industries.....................	825.5	353.0	57.6	295.4	772.4	1597.9
65	Tires and inner tubes........	903.0	374.7	111.7	263.0	715.1	1618.1
66	Miscellaneous rubber products	821.9	349.4	63.1	286.3	757.4	1579.3
67	Leather tanning and finishing.	892.3	505.0	25.8	479.2	1232.0	2124.3
69	Footwear, except rubber......	867.7	497.1	28.4	468.7	1230.6	2098.3
70	Glass......................	753.5	377.2	18.0	359.2	926.9	1680.4
73	Pottery and related products..	700.7	317.7	16.0	301.7	786.1	1486.8
79.1	Carbon steel works and rolling mills....................	852.6	445.8	39.6	406.2	1042.0	1894.6
79.2	Alloy steel works and rolling mills, except stainless......	852.6	445.8	50.3	395.5	1018.6	1871.2
79.3	Stainless steel works and rolling mills....................	852.6	445.8	35.9	409.9	1050.1	1902.7
85	Primary zinc................	935.9	263.0	131.9	131.1	354.1	1290.0
88	Primary aluminum, including alumina..................	935.5	217.9	99.0	118.9	305.2	1240.7
89	Aluminum rolling and drawing	908.6	443.2	81.8	361.4	964.5	1873.1
93	Tin cans and other tinware...	889.6	448.3	41.9	406.4	1051.6	1941.2
94	Cutlery....................	757.8	415.0	18.3	396.7	1036.7	1794.5
95	Tools and general hardware...	827.9	401.8	17.0	384.8	994.0	1821.9

[a] From Column 7 of Table 6.1.

[b] Based on distribution among major suppliers of gross increase in dollar earnings, their merchandise reflection ratios, and distribution of their imports among world trade groups.

[c] Column 2 less Column 3.

[d] Based on distribution among world trade groups of gross increases and decreases shown in Columns 2 and 3 and inverse coefficients of world trade matrix shown in Appendix Table E.5.

[e] Column 1 plus Column 5.

	Liberalized Industry	Gross Increase in Dollar Earnings of Major Suppliers[a]	Change in Earnings of World Trade Groups				Total Net Increase in Earnings by All Countries[e]
Code Number	Title		Increase Due to Spending by Major Suppliers[b]	Output-Induced Decrease	Net Increase[c]	Multiplied Net Increase[d]	
		(1)	(2)	(3)	(4)	(5)	(6)
103	Lighting fixtures............	761.5	492.9	29.1	463.8	1279.0	2040.5
105	Metal barrels, drums, etc.....	740.7	287.4	30.2	257.2	665.2	1405.9
106	Tubes and foils..............	827.4	371.1	61.0	310.1	818.0	1645.4
116	Machine tools and metalworking machinery.............	884.0	402.4	13.1	389.3	999.8	1883.8
118	Special industrial machinery..	860.3	450.4	18.8	431.6	1129.0	1989.3
123	Industrial machinery, n.e.c....	883.0	449.4	23.1	426.3	1090.7	1973.7
127	Ball and roller bearings......	828.0	315.2	17.5	297.7	754.4	1582.4
131	Motors and generators......	870.8	235.6	27.0	208.6	515.8	1386.6
132	Transformers..............	888.8	490.0	41.7	448.3	1173.4	2062.2
133	Electrical control apparatus...	850.7	449.0	23.7	425.3	1094.1	1944.8
134	Electrical welding apparatus..	919.0	436.4	30.1	406.3	1044.5	1963.5
135	Electrical appliances........	851.1	502.7	28.7	474.0	1251.3	2102.6
136	Insulated wire and cable.....	826.6	326.4	103.9	222.5	561.9	1388.5
138	Electric lamps..............	831.6	273.5	22.8	250.7	644.0	1475.6
139	Radio and related products...	928.3	357.4	28.0	329.4	833.8	1762.1
141	Communication equipment...	885.1	227.6	24.1	203.5	490.5	1375.6
142	Storage batteries...........	835.0	468.3	96.2	372.1	993.7	1828.7
143	Primary batteries...........	851.1	227.6	65.4	162.2	411.5	1262.6
145.1	Passenger cars and light trucks	900.6	581.7	39.2	542.5	1439.6	2340.2
145.2	Heavy trucks and buses......	884.6	235.8	33.5	202.3	501.0	1385.6
145.3	Motor vehicle parts and accessories....................	881.5	298.8	31.8	267.0	678.4	1559.9
148	Aircraft and parts..........	854.8	272.1	17.7	254.4	637.9	1492.7
152	Motorcycles and bicycles.....	876.2	535.2	27.8	507.4	1339.9	2216.1
154	Optical, ophthalmic, and photo equipment................	851.7	365.4	26.7	338.7	869.8	1721.5
156	Watches and clocks..........	738.4	394.9	34.9	360.0	925.8	1664.2
157	Jewelry and silverware.......	753.2	354.1	81.2	272.9	738.2	1491.4
158	Musical instruments and parts	830.0	431.0	16.9	414.1	1080.4	1910.4
159	Toys and sporting goods.....	747.2	312.4	35.2	277.2	726.5	1473.7
160	Office supplies..............	731.1	359.8	30.8	329.0	866.3	1597.4
161	Plastic products.............	792.3	326.9	25.5	301.4	779.4	1571.7
162	Cork products..............	481.9[f]	293.4	116.6	176.8	439.1	921.0
164	Miscellaneous manufactured products.................	777.7	404.8	41.2	363.6	950.5	1734.2

[f] Represents *net* earnings of major suppliers.

Derivation of Net Increase in Earnings of All Currencies by Underdeveloped Countries

(In thousands of 1953 dollars per $1 million increase of United States imports)

	Liberalized Industry	Gross Increase in Dollar Earnings of Under-developed Major Suppliers[b]	Change in Earnings of World Trade Groups 1 and 2[a]				Total Net Increase in Earnings of Under-developed Countries[g]
			Increase Due to Spending by All Major Suppliers[c]	Output-Induced Decrease[d]	Net Increase[e]	Multi-plied Net Increase[f]	
Code Number	Title						
		(1)	(2)	(3)	(4)	(5)	(6)
1	Meat animals and products......	427.2	35.7	7.5	28.2	95.6	522.8
8	Vegetables and fruits...........	602.6	24.7	7.9	16.8	64.0	666.6
13	Lead and zinc mining...........	244.0	37.8	14.8	23.0	81.1	325.1
21	Meat packing and wholesale poultry.......................	—	61.7	17.4	44.3	165.1	165.1
22	Processed dairy products........	128.5	196.5	14.2	182.3	523.0	651.5
24	Grain mill products.............	—	68.2	16.0	52.2	124.4	124.4
27	Sugar........................	886.7	56.8	35.4	21.4	71.0	957.7
28	Alcoholic beverages.............	—	94.8	9.7	85.1	204.7	204.7
29	Tobacco manufactures..........	405.9	171.4	17.3	154.1	362.2	768.1
30	Spinning, weaving, and dyeing...	—	175.0	13.2	161.8	335.8	335.8
31	Special textile products..........	202.3	115.5	29.1	86.4	276.8	479.1
34	Apparel......................	—	175.4	13.6	161.8	340.0	340.0
35	House furnishings and other non-apparel......................	—	210.8	49.8	161.0	371.2	371.2
38	Plywood......................	—	158.6	13.7	144.9	287.4	287.4
40	Wood containers and cooperage..	805.7	22.5	15.4	7.1	48.3	854.0
41	Wood furniture................	—	257.0	14.0	243.0	550.2	550.2
45	Paper and board mills...........	—	172.2	28.0	144.2	332.4	332.4
46	Converted paper products.......	—	175.4	40.9	134.5	296.4	296.4
49	Industrial organic chemicals.....	—	139.6	27.0	112.6	276.1	276.1
51	Synthetic rubber...............	—	42.9	28.8	14.1	65.4	65.4
52	Synthetic fiber.................	—	124.0	16.4	107.6	300.2	300.2
54	Drugs and medicines............	—	138.8	17.0	121.8	306.4	306.4
56	Paints and allied products.......	—	98.2	36.8	61.4	155.2	155.2
59	Vegetable oils.................	514.3	55.5	49.8	5.7	66.3	580.6
61	Miscellaneous chemical industries.	—	98.3	25.4	72.9	220.5	220.5
65	Tires and inner tubes...........	—	99.7	49.4	50.3	191.0	191.0
66	Miscellaneous rubber products...	—	169.7	27.9	141.8	285.5	285.5
67	Leather tanning and finishing.....	273.9	187.6	11.4	176.2	406.7	680.6
69	Footwear, except rubber.........	—	218.3	12.6	205.7	438.6	438.6
70	Glass........................	—	132.3	7.9	124.4	298.9	298.9
73	Pottery and related products.....	—	154.8	7.1	147.7	295.3	295.3
79.1	Carbon steel works and rolling mills	—	117.6	17.5	100.1	296.9	296.9
79.2	Alloy steel works and rolling mills, except stainless..............	—	117.6	22.2	95.4	288.4	288.4
79.3	Stainless steel works and rolling mills.......................	—	117.6	15.9	101.7	299.8	299.8
85	Primary zinc..................	164.8	69.9	58.3	11.6	81.3	246.1
88	Primary aluminum, including alumina....................	—	58.4	43.8	14.6	72.6	72.6

[a] The trade groups consist entirely of underdeveloped countries.
[b] Based on Columns 1 and 2 of Table E.4.
[c] Based on distribution among all major suppliers of gross increases in dollar earnings, their merchandise reflection ratios, and the distribution of their imports among World Trade Groups 1 and 2.
[d] Equal to 44.2 percent of output-induced decreases shown in Column 3 of Appendix Table F.3, which represents share of World Trade Groups 1 and 2 in these decreases.
[e] Column 2 less Column 3.
[f] Based on distribution among world trade groups of gross increases and decreases shown in Columns 2 and 3 and the inverse coefficients of world trade matrix which give ratios of total earnings of World Trade Groups 1 and 2 to net increase in earnings of each world trade group. See Rows 1 and 2 of Appendix Table E.5.
[g] Column 1 plus Column 5.

Liberalized Industry		Gross Increase in Dollar Earnings of Under-developed Major Suppliers[b]	Change in Earnings of World Trade Groups 1 and 2[a]				Total Net Increase in Earnings of Under-developed Countries[g]
Code Number	Title		Increase Due to Spending by All Major Suppliers[c]	Output-Induced Decrease[d]	Net Increase[e]	Multiplied Net Increase[f]	
		(1)	(2)	(3)	(4)	(5)	(6)
89	Aluminum rolling and drawing...	—	181.8	36.1	145.7	330.5	330.5
93	Tin cans and other tinware......	—	150.2	18.5	131.7	330.2	330.2
94	Cutlery.......................	—	161.0	8.0	153.0	349.3	349.3
95	Tools and general hardware......	—	145.4	7.5	137.9	325.1	325.1
103	Lighting fixtures..............	—	235.4	12.9	222.5	472.3	472.3
105	Metal barrels, drums, etc........	—	75.9	13.3	62.6	188.9	188.9
106	Tubes and foils................	—	116.0	27.0	89.0	246.0	246.0
116	Machine tools and metalworking machinery....................	—	139.3	5.8	133.5	321.2	321.2
118	Special industrial machinery.....	—	185.0	8.3	176.7	390.2	390.2
123	Industrial machinery, n.e.c......	—	137.7	10.2	127.5	332.2	332.2
127	Ball and roller bearings........	—	89.1	7.8	81.3	222.2	222.2
131	Motors and generators..........	—	73.0	11.9	61.1	155.4	155.4
132	Transformers..................	—	169.1	18.4	150.7	373.9	373.9
133	Electrical control apparatus......	—	138.4	10.5	127.9	334.0	334.0
134	Electrical welding apparatus.....	—	147.5	13.3	134.2	330.4	330.4
135	Electrical appliances...........	—	224.3	12.7	211.6	449.1	449.1
136	Insulated wire and cable........	—	91.3	45.9	45.4	150.3	150.3
138	Electric lamps.................	—	178.4	10.1	168.3	286.8	286.8
139	Radio and related products......	—	110.7	12.4	98.3	253.5	253.5
141	Communication equipment......	—	52.4	10.6	41.8	130.4	130.4
142	Storage batteries..............	—	137.6	42.4	95.2	287.8	287.8
143	Primary batteries..............	—	69.8	28.8	41.0	117.9	117.9
145.1	Passenger cars and light trucks...	—	256.5	17.3	239.2	513.4	513.4
145.2	Heavy trucks and buses.........	—	72.2	14.8	57.4	149.2	149.2
145.3	Motor vehicle parts and accessories	—	106.2	14.0	92.2	218.3	218.3
148	Aircraft and parts.............	—	93.5	7.8	85.7	203.2	203.2
152	Motorcycles and bicycles........	—	231.5	12.3	219.2	473.8	473.8
154	Optical, ophthalmic, and photo equipment...................	—	124.8	11.8	113.0	276.4	276.4
156	Watches and clocks............	—	114.8	15.4	99.4	274.1	274.1
157	Jewelry and silverware.........	—	150.3	35.9	114.4	257.2	257.2
158	Musical instruments and parts...	—	178.7	7.4	171.3	375.1	375.1
159	Toys and sporting goods	—	150.8	15.6	135.2	272.3	272.3
160	Office supplies.................	—	161.5	13.6	147.9	312.2	312.2
161	Plastic products...............	—	144.3	11.3	133.0	278.0	278.9
162	Cork products.................	—	42.0	22.0	13.8	95.5	95.5
164	Miscellaneous manufactured products......................	—	165.9	18.2	147.7	329.4	329.4

Uses and Current Validity of the Estimates

This appendix deals with a number of technical questions that relate to the use of the estimates and to the appraisal of their current validity. It gives specific instructions to readers who wish to adjust the estimates to different assumptions about the size or industry locus of the domestic output displacement and discusses some limitations on the uses of the estimates.

Alternative Assumptions About
Displacement of Domestic Production

As Chapter 10 explained, although the present estimates assume that an increase of a million dollars in imports, valued at 1953 domestic port values, displaces an equal value of domestic output of the liberalized industry and none of the domestic output of other industries, they may be used to obtain estimates based on other assumptions as to both the total value of domestic output displaced and its identity, so long as the displaced output is in one of the 72 accepted industries.

The procedure for doing so is indicated and illustrated below. This procedure takes into account the effects on output-induced decreases of foreign dollar earnings, which are generally small and were neglected in the procedure described verbally in Chapter 10 (page 239).

Both the wording of the instructions for applying this procedure and the example assume that the displacement occurs entirely in one industry. Where it is assumed that displacement occurs in several industries, it is necessary only to enter as Lines 1 and 3f the sums of the separate products for each displaced industry that the instructions for these lines indicate.

It may also be noted that, although the example assumes that the displacement occurs in one of the non-liberalized industries, the procedure applies equally when the displacement occurs in the liberalized industry. On that assumption and on the further assumption of this study that $p_i = 1.0$, application of the procedure should give the estimates it has presented.

Gross employment decreases experienced by specific industry groups may be estimated by multiplying by p_i the figure in Appendix Table F.1 located in the line for the industry group in which the employment effect is desired and the column for the industry whose domestic

Method of Estimating Gross and Net Employment Effects for Any Assumed Amount of Domestic Output Displacement in Any of 72 Accepted Industries

Variable to be Estimated[a]	Source of Estimate (Effect in All Industries)	Example: Liberalized Industry: #34; Displaced Industry (i): #31; p_i[b]$=.8$
1. Gross employment decrease	$p_i \times$Column 1, Table 9.1 (line for displaced industry)[c]	85.48
2. Gross primary employment increase	Column 2, Table 9.1 (line for liberalized industry)	1.23
3. Gross employment increase from exports:		
a. Bilateral increase in exports	Column 2 of Table 7.3 (line for liberalized industry)	75.6
b. Net multilateral increase in exports	Column 3 of Table 7.3 (line for liberalized industry)	134.6
c. Original output-induced decrease in foreign dollar earnings[d]	Column 3, Appendix Table F.3 (line for liberalized industry)	66.1
d. Original output-induced decrease in U.S. exports[d]	$.4948 \times$Line 3c[e]	32.7
e. Gross multilateral increase in exports	Lines 3b+3d	167.3
f. Alternative output-induced effects on foreign dollar earnings	$p_i \times$Column 3, Appendix Table F.3 (line for displaced industry)	23.9
g. Alternative output-induced effects on U.S. exports	$.4948 \times$Line 3f[e]	11.8
h. Total effect on U.S. exports	Lines 3a+3e −3g	231.1
i. Employment increase per $1000 of exports	Column 4 of Table 5.1 (line for liberalized industry)	.0930
j. Gross employment increase from exports	Lines 3h×3i	21.49
4. Net employment effect (− represents net decrease)	Lines 2+3j−1	−62.76

[a] The variables in the table are expressed in the same units that are used in the source tables.

[b] p is the value in 1953 prices of domestic output displaced per one million dollars of liberalized imports valued at domestic ports in 1953, and expressed as a ratio to one million dollars. The subscript i identifies the industry in which displacement is assumed to occur. Thus $p_{31}=.8$ means that $800,000 of the domestic output of Industry #31 is displaced per one million dollar increase of imports of the liberalized industry, both valuations being in 1953 prices.

[c] The gross employment decrease in any one industry group can be determined by multiplying the appropriate figure in Appendix Table F.1 by p_i.

[d] These lines are needed only to derive the gross multilateral increase in U.S. exports, which is implied but not shown explicitly in the book.

[e] The figure .4948 is the average of the figures in the first column of Table 7.2, weighted by each group's share of the total output-induced decrease of dollar earnings. These shares were assumed to be the same in all cases except when domestic output of the cork and cork products industry is displaced.

output is displaced. (If this industry group happens to contain the liberalized industry, as indicated by an asterisk, the effect on the liberalized industry, which may be approximated as p_i times the figure in Line 2 of Appendix Table F.1, should be added.) When liberalization displaces the output of several industries, the gross employment decrease occurring in any industry or group of industries is the sum of the gross decreases obtained by multiplying the figures in the relevant columns of Appendix Table F.1 by the different values for p_i appropriate to them. These values represent the fraction of one million dollars displaced in the industry designated in the column heading.

Altering Composition of Individual
Industry Import Increases

It will be recalled that the estimates of this study assume that the import increase caused by liberalization of an industry consists of a basket of output of its "accepted subindustries," combined in proportion to their relative importance in domestic output. If the reader wants a corresponding estimate of the *direct* employment decreases caused by displacement of domestic output corresponding to any subindustry component of this basket, he may get it by multiplying the displacement he wishes to assume (expressed in 1953 prices) by the 1953 direct employment-output coefficient for that subindustry given in Column 3 of Appendix Table D.1. These estimates may be combined to get the direct employment effect of a basket having any desired composition of accepted subindustries.

It should be noted that the present estimates cannot be used to obtain reliable estimates of the *indirect* employment effects of liberalizations that combine the imports of subindustries in an industry in proportions different from those assumed in this study. The estimates of indirect effects are based on a procedure that implicitly assumes that the output of the entire industry changes. The tests we applied in accepting an industry for analysis enabled us to assume that this procedure gives accurate estimates of indirect effects when an industry basket of imports has the composition we specified, but that assumption cannot safely be made when the industry basket has a substantially different composition.

Simultaneous Liberalizations in
Two or More Industries

The effects of liberalizing imports competing with several of the 72 accepted industries can be estimated by combining the estimated separate effects of liberalizing the individual industries. The hypothetical liberalization programs presented in Chapter 11 were obtained in this way. In principle, however, to add the estimates of the effects of single-industry liberalizations is inconsistent with the assumptions of the study because the study estimates indirect domestic output effects on the assumption that liberalization does not occur in other industries. More strictly, it assumes that changes in imports obtained from industries other than the one liberalized come from domestic output and imports in 1952 proportions, which were generally the pre-liberalization proportions when the study was begun. For cases in which they are still the pre-liberalization proportions, liberalization of supplying industries, by reducing the import proportion, would make this assumption less valid and cause the estimates to overstate the actual domestic effect and understate the effect on imports. If the liberalized industries are few in number, however, or if they are unimportant as suppliers of each other or if the liberalization is moderate enough to have little effect on the relative importance of imports, the error from this source will be small. In general, it will be less, the closer the post-liberalization ratios of changes in imports to changes in total requirements for an industry's products are to the 1952 ratios of total imports to total requirements.

It should also be noted that imports of raw and other materials and of more finished goods that use them as inputs compete with each other. Liberalization of materials may expand the domestic output of finished goods that use them and thus reduce imports of such goods. This effect is not taken into account. The converse effect that liberalizing finished goods has on imports of their material components is taken into account in the estimates as an output-induced effect on imports but on the assumption that barriers against these material imports remain unchanged. If imports of both materials and the finished goods are liberalized simultaneously, any interaction of these liberalizations should be taken into account in determining the size of the import increase to which the estimates are applied.

Use of Employment-Value Added Relationships
in Appraising Current Validity of Estimates

It was noted in Chapter 10 that the effect on the current validity of the employment estimates of changes in employment per unit of output since 1953 may best be judged by examining the changes that have occurred since 1953 in the relationships between employment and real value added. Even though the estimates were made by multiplying the estimated value of the output change in an industry by the ratio of employment to the total value of its output, it would not be correct to judge the current validity of the estimates from changes in the latter ratio. That ratio is the product of two ratios, Employment : Value added and Value added : Total value of output, and would change if only the second component had changed since 1953. A change occurring for that reason would not necessarily affect the current validity of our employment estimates. For example, an industry might cease to produce components for its own products, reduce its employment correspondingly, and purchase the components from another industry. This change would decrease its ratio of employment to total value of output but it would not necessarily cause the total employment effects to be less because the effects in the industry that now produces the component would be greater. If both industries use the same number of employees to produce the components, the two changes would exactly offset each other. Whether changes in employment-total output relations are of this kind or are of greater significance for total employment effects can be known only if changes in employment-output relations and in interindustry relations are both known. In the absence of data for changes in interindustry relations, changes in ratios of employment to total output cannot be used even to draw inferences about the probable *direction* of the effect on employment because, as this illustration makes clear, some changes in interindustry relations may offset them. The ratio of employment to value added would not be affected by a change such as that mentioned; the decline of employment in the industry that stopped producing its own components would be offset by a decline in its value added.

It is true that every dollar of the total value of one industry's output represents value added in some industry. Thus the direct and indirect employment involved in one industry's output depends on an average of the employment-value added relationships in all the industries directly and indirectly involved in its production, weighted by the ratio of the value they have contributed to the total value of that output. To know how the total employment involved in one industry's output has been affected by changes in employment per unit of output over time, therefore, one would have to know how the ratios of employment to value added have changed in all the industries that contribute to its output and also how the weights that should be given to these ratios have changed. If changes in these ratios sometimes did and sometimes did not reflect factors that cause offsetting changes in these weights, as is the case with changes in ratios of employment to total value of output, we could draw no conclusions from observing them alone. Fortunately, however, this is generally not the case. Changes in the ratio of employment to value added in an industry over periods of several years result mainly from factors relevant to efficiency and generally affect the total employment involved in the outputs to which it adds value in the same direction. Therefore, a substantial decline in the ratios of employment to value added in all or most industries can be counted on to imply that the total employment involved in a given output change has declined. This would fail to be true only if large increases occur in the weights appropriate to industries whose employment-value added ratios remain high. In that case the weighted average of all the relevant ratios may not decline or may actually rise, even though all its components fall. Such changes are not likely to occur, however. Therefore general conclusions can be drawn from changes in the ratios of employment to value added. That is why it is preferable to examine those changes rather than changes in the ratios of employment to total value of output.

Short-Cut Estimates of Average Gross Primary Decreases of Employment Per Million-Dollar Decrease in Domestic Output, 1953 and 1959[a]

	Gross Product Originating (In billions of dollars)	Number of Full and Part-Time Employees (In millions)	Employees per $1 Million Gross Product Originating (Number)	Gross Product Originating, per Employee (In dollars)
	(1)	(2)	(3)	(4)
A. 1953				
1. Total economy...................	365.4	57.93	158.5	6,308
2. Less: General government........	31.8	9.64	303.5	3,295
3. Private non-business[b].......	12.2	2.77	227.1	4,404
4. Plus: Non-employees engaged in farming......................	—	3.66	—	—
5. Equals: Private business..........	321.4	49.18	153.0[c]	6,536[c]
6. Less: Farms....................	20.9	5.60[c]	267.8[c]	3,735[c]
7. Equals: Private non-farm business..	300.5	43.58	145.0	6,895
Addendum: Estimates for 1953 by inter-industry relations method:				
8. Median of all 72 liberalizations....			114.7[d]	8,718
9. Median of the 60 liberalizations not adjusted for fictitious effects of changes in agricultural output...			124.0[d]	8,065
B. 1959 in 1953 prices				
10. Total economy...................	423.7	60.24	142.2	7,033
11. Less: General government........	32.7	9.90	302.6	3,305
12. Private non-business[b].......	16.8	3.44	204.7	4,885
13. Plus: Non-employees engaged in farming......................	—	3.06	—	—
14. Equals: Private business..........	374.2	49.96	133.5[c]	7,489[c]
15. Less: Farms....................	22.9	4.98[c]	217.6[c]	4,597[c]
16. Equals: Private non-farm business..	351.3	44.98	128.0	7,810
C. 1959 in 1959 prices				
17. Total economy...................	482.1	60.24	125.0	8,002
18. Less: General government........	44.0	9.90	224.8	4,449
19. Private non-business........	19.7	3.44	174.7	5,725
20. Plus: Non-employees engaged in farming......................	—	3.06	—	—
21. Equals: Private business..........	418.4	49.96	119.4[c]	8,373[c]
22. Less: Farms....................	20.4	4.98[c]	244.3[c]	4,094[c]
23. Equals: Private non-farm business..	398.0	44.98	113.0	8,847

[a] Sources: Column 1 figures come from Tables I-12 and I-15 of *U. S. Income and Output* (1958) and *Survey of Current Business* (July 1960), Office of Business Economics, U. S. Department of Commerce, except for 1959 in 1953 prices, which are derived as indicated in Appendix Table G.1a. Column 2 figures for 1953 come from Table VI-14 of *U. S. Income and Output* and those for 1959 from Table 53, page 29, of *Survey of Current Business* for July 1960. Column 3 equals Column 2 divided by Column 1, and Column 4 equals Column 1 divided by Column 2 (equivalent to $1,000,000 divided by Column 3, except for discrepancies due to rounding).

[b] Consists of households, non-profit institutions n.e.c., and rest of world.

[c] Includes non-employees engaged in farming.

[d] From Table 3.2 of this study.

Derivation of 1959 Gross National Product in 1953 Prices, by Economic Sectors[a]

	1959 in 1954 Prices	Ratio of Implicit Price Deflators, 1953:1954	1959 in 1953 Prices[b]
	(1)	(2)	(3)
1. Total economy.....................	428.0	99.0	423.7
2. Less: General government..........	33.8	96.7	32.7
3. Private non-business[c].........	17.4	n.a.	16.8[d]
4. Equals: Private business...........	376.8	99.3	374.2
5. Less: Farms......................	21.3	107.4	22.9
6. Equals: Private non-farm business....	355.6	n.a.	351.3[d]

n.a. = not available.

[a] Source: Column 1 figures come from Tables 10 and 11 of *Survey of Current Business*, July 1960 (National Income Supplement). Column 2 figures come from Tables VII-8 and VII-11 of *U. S. Income and Output*.

[b] Column 3 equals Column 1 times Column 2, except where otherwise noted.

[c] Consists of households, non-profit instituitons n.e.c., and rest of world.

[d] Determined residually from other figures in Column 3.

Change in Man-Hours per Unit of Output, 1953 to 1958, for Major Sectors and Industry Divisions[a]

S.I.C. Code Number	Title	Number of 200-Order Industries Included[b]	Index of Output per Man-hour (1947–49=100)			Per Cent Change in Man-hours per Unit of Output from 1953 to:	
			1953	1957	1958	1957	1958
		(1)	(2)	(3)	(4)	(5)	(6)
	Manufacturing[c]		116.1	131.1	133.1	−11.4	−12.8
	Manufacturing[d]		118.3	127.7	e	− 7.4	e
20	Food and kindred products....	8	109.6	126.1	130.7	−13.1	−16.2
21	Tobacco manufactures........	1	120.4	137.1	152.5	−12.2	−21.0
22	Textile mill products..........	3+	117.4	137.9	144.0	−14.9	−18.5
23	Apparel and other finished fabric products..................	3−	104.8	114.4	118.3	− 8.4	−11.4
24	Lumber and wood products, except furniture..............	5	120.3	137.6	145.9	−12.6	−17.6
25	Furniture and fixtures........	3	107.0	127.3	128.2	−16.0	−16.5
26	Paper and allied products.....	3	113.0	128.1	135.4	−12.8	−16.6
27	Printing, publishing, and allied products..................	1	105.8	114.6	114.0	− 7.7	− 7.2
28	Chemicals and allied products..	14+	129.9	160.9	166.4	−19.3	−21.9
29	Petroleum refining and related industries.................	3−	119.7	134.5	133.8	−11.0	−10.5
30	Rubber and miscellaneous plastic products...............	2	111.6	122.1	126.0	− 8.6	−11.4
31	Leather and leather products...	3	107.5	122.8	124.4	−12.5	−13.6
32	Stone, clay, and glass products..	8	115.6	130.1	133.2	−11.2	−13.2
33	Primary metals...............	21	112.4	117.8	112.8	− 4.6	− .4
34	Fabricated metals............	18−	105.9	109.4	112.0	− 3.2	− 5.4
35	Nonelectrical machinery.......	20−	115.2	112.7	112.9	+ 2.2	+ 2.0
36	Electrical machinery..........	15+	119.7	136.3	131.9	−11.2	− 9.2
37	Transportation equipment.....	10	113.9	137.9	139.5	−17.4	−18.4
38	Instruments.................	4	119.2	137.7	139.7	−13.4	−14.7
39	Miscellaneous manufactures....	6	112.5	136.1	140.9	−17.3	−20.4
	Mining.......................		129.8	150.0	157.0	−13.5	−17.3
10	Metal mining................	5	109.5	127.9	131.2	−14.4	−16.5
11	Anthracite mining...........	⎫	100.2	155.2	204.3	−35.4	−51.0
12	Bituminous coal and lignite mining....................	⎬ 1	126.0	162.2	166.5	−22.3	−24.3
13	Crude petroleum and natural gas	1	109.1	111.0	112.3	− 1.7	− 2.8
14	Non-metallic minerals, except fuels......................	3	123.4	151.2	156.4	−18.4	−21.1
49	Public utilities................	2	144.5	190.6	e	−24.2	e
42	Communications..............	2	120.3	148.4	e	−18.9	e
40	Railroads[f]	2−	119.8	148.5	157.9	−19.3	−24.1
41–47	Other transportation[g]...........	6+	125.3	140.9	e	−11.1	c
15–17	Contract construction..........	h	107.9	114.2	e	− 5.5	e
01–09	Agriculture[d]..................	10	138.6	166.7	188.6	−16.9	−26.5
70–89	Services[g]......................	12	110.4	118.5	119.0	− 6.8	− 7.2
50–59	Trade.......................	2	115.3	122.1	e	− 5.6	e

[a] Source: Except where otherwise noted, figures come from Technical Note No. 2, "Productivity and Output in the Postwar Period" by Thomas A. Wilson, published in Study Paper No. 21 (*Postwar Movement of Prices and Wages in Manufacturing Industries* by Harold M. Levinson) and *Supplementary Technical Material to the Staff Report* by George W. Bleile and Thomas A. Wilson. This joint document was part of the "Materials prepared in Connection with the Study of Employment, Growth, and Price Levels for Consideration by the Joint Economic Committee, Congress of the United States" (86th Congress, 2nd Session, January 30, 1960). This source indicates that the output and man-hour series on which the above indices are based are not strictly comparable and that the indices for a particular industry may therefore be in considerable error. Columns 5 and 6 are obtained by dividing Column 2 by Columns 3 and 4 respectively, multiplying the quotient by 100, and subtracting 100.0.

[b] Plus signs indicate that the industry division also includes parts of one or more 200-order industries not included in the count. Minus signs indicate that it excludes parts of one or more 200-order industries included in the count.

[c] Based on a Federal Reserve output index for manufacturing using 1954 value added weights and an index of total man-hours derived from published BLS data on employment and average weekly hours per man.

[d] BLS index of real value added per man-hour. See *Trends in Output per Man-Hour in the Private Economy, 1909–1958.* Bulletin No. 1249, U. S. Department of Labor, December 1959, Table 1.

[e] Data for Column 4 not available.

[f] Indices represent "Revenue traffic per man-hour" instead of "output per man-hour."

[g] Indices represent "net national income originating per man" instead of "output per man-hour."

[h] Not included in 200-order industry classification.

Derivation of Gross Primary Employment Decreases per Million-Dollar Increase in Imports in 1958 Prices[a]

Code Number	Title	Price Indices[b] (1947 = 100) 1953	Price Indices[b] (1947 = 100) 1958	Ratio of 1958 to 1953 Prices	Gross Employment Decreases per $1 Million Measured in 1953 Prices	Gross Employment Decreases per $1 Million Measured in 1958 Prices
		(1)	(2)	(3)	(4)	(5)
1	Meat animals and products............	91.2	95.0	1.042	95.84	91.98
8	Vegetables and fruits..................	89.3	97.8	1.095	224.45	204.98
13	Lead and zinc mining.................	87.6	90.0	1.027	164.85	160.52
21	Meat packing and wholesale poultry.....	94.7	97.2	1.026	107.99	105.25
22	Processed dairy products..............	103.1	96.3	.934	54.27	58.10
24	Grain mill products...................	95.9	91.6	.955	51.15	53.56
27	Sugar................................	105.0	110.9	1.056	67.38	63.81
28	Alcoholic beverages...................	114.2	121.9	1.067	85.39	80.03
29	Tobacco manufactures.................	120.2	132.4	1.101	69.99	63.57
30	Spinning, weaving, and dyeing..........	89.9	80.6	.897	136.41	152.07
31	Special textile products................	128.1	123.3	.963	106.85	110.96
34	Apparel..............................	97.1	98.8	1.017	195.41	192.14
35	House furnishings and other non-apparel..	96.0	94.3	.982	134.91	137.38
38	Plywood.............................	116.7	105.0	.900	139.24	154.71
40	Wood containers and cooperage........	126.2	124.9	.990	166.64	168.32
41	Wood furniture.......................	117.5	125.3	1.066	170.72	160.15
45	Paper and board mills.................	132.2	149.8	1.133	84.29	74.40
46	Converted paper products..............	108.1	123.4	1.142	114.88	100.60
49	Industrial organic chemicals............	111.2	112.5	1.012	79.41	78.47
51	Synthetic rubber.....................	124.3	125.3	1.008	65.20	64.68
52	Synthetic fiber.......................	109.8	105.6	.962	91.32	94.93
54	Drugs and medicines..................	83.1	80.6	.970	118.58	122.25
56	Paints and allied products.............	112.3	129.6	1.154	90.55	78.47
59	Vegetable oils........................	72.2	64.5	.893	71.12	79.64
61	Miscellaneous chemical industries	111.2	118.6	1.066	105.32	98.80
65	Tires and inner tubes.................	127.9	153.3	1.199	92.07	76.79
66	Miscellaneous rubber products..........	126.3	147.0	1.104	117.26	100.74
67	Leather tanning and finishing..........	88.2	87.1	.988	80.10	81.07
69	Footwear, except rubber...............	116.6	127.4	1.093	178.58	163.38
70	Glass................................	136.6	169.1	1.238	115.75	93.50
73	Pottery and related products...........	121.9	137.5	1.128	189.43	167.93
79.1	Carbon steel works and rolling mills.....	155.0	208.0	1.342	90.79	67.65
79.2	Alloy steel works and rolling mills, except stainless..........................	155.0	208.0	1.342	93.50	69.67
79.3	Stainless steel works and rolling mills....	155.0	208.0	1.342	96.61	71.99
85	Primary zinc.........................	105.0	98.2	.935	95.40	102.00
88	Primary aluminum, including alumina....	143.3	167.8	1.171	62.72	53.56
89	Aluminum rolling and drawing.........	141.3	180.3	1.276	79.51	62.31
93	Tin cans and other tinware.............	140.8	169.0	1.200	106.10	88.42
94	Cutlery..............................	124.5	143.4	1.152	122.70	106.51
95	Tools and general hardware............	147.0	197.2	1.341	130.39	97.23
103	Lighting fixtures......................	118.2	130.6	1.105	138.36	125.21
105	Metal barrels, drums, etc..............	140.3	181.7	1.295	103.93	80.26
106	Tubes and foils.......................	130.3	156.6	1.202	100.62	83.71
116	Machine tools and metalworking machinery.............................	153.0	199.5	1.304	109.05	83.63
118	Special industrial machinery...........	132.9	161.9	1.218	137.54	112.92
123	Industrial machinery, n.e.c.............	132.9	161.9	1.218	123.42	101.33
127	Ball and roller bearings................	124.2	150.1	1.209	125.86	104.10
131	Motors and generators	123.7	143.0	1.156	129.23	111.79
132	Transformers........................	129.1	154.7	1.198	112.85	94.20
133	Electrical control apparatus............	136.8	181.7	1.328	114.47	86.20

[a] Sources: Columns 1 and 2 are based on Bureau of Labor Statistics wholesale price information. Column 3 = Column 2 ÷ Column 1. Column 4 from Column 1 of Table 3.2. Column 5 = Column 4 ÷ Column 3.

[b] Price indices are weighted by the 1953 value of output of accepted sub-industries, expressed in 1947 prices, except where otherwise noted.

Table G.3 (continued)

Code Number	Liberalized Industry	Price Indices[b] (1947=100) 1953	Price Indices[b] (1947=100) 1958	Ratio of 1958 to 1953 Prices	Gross Employment Decreases per $1 Million Measured in 1953 Prices	Gross Employment Decreases per $1 Million Measured in 1958 Prices
	Title	(1)	(2)	(3)	(4)	(5)
134	Electrical welding apparatus............	128.7	159.4	1.239	102.03	82.35
135	Electrical appliances...................	110.5	112.3	1.016	134.30	132.19
136	Insulated wire and cable...............	130.1	125.4	.964	99.71	103.43
138	Electric lamps........................	137.8	166.9	1.211	109.48	90.40
139	Radio and related products.............	95.5	96.2	1.007	155.15	154.07
141	Communication equipment.............	132.9	161.9	1.218	132.53	108.81
142	Storage batteries.....................	123.4	139.6	1.131	96.09	84.96
143	Primary batteries.....................	118.3	164.0	1.386	118.12	85.22
145.1	Passenger cars and light trucks..........	130.2	152.9	1.174	124.48	106.03
145.2	Heavy trucks and buses................	130.2	152.9	1.174	113.90	97.02
145.3	Motor vehicle parts and accessories......	130.2	152.9	1.174	103.59	88.24
148	Aircraft and parts....................	132.9	161.9	1.218	119.80	98.36
152	Motorcycles and bicycles..............	132.9	161.8	1.217	129.43	106.35
154	Optical, ophthalmic, and photo equipment	115.8	129.2	1.116	128.26	114.93
156	Watches and clocks...................	109.0	119.0	1.092	137.54	125.95
157	Jewelry and silverware.................	101.1	108.0	1.068	136.76	128.05
158	Musical instruments and parts..........	116.2	130.1	1.120	135.38	120.88
159	Toys and sporting goods...............	115.7	118.0	1.020	157.86	154.76
160	Office supplies.......................	98.4	106.8	1.085	134.79	124.23
161	Plastic products......................	126.1	107.1	.849	123.05	144.94
162	Cork products........................	119.6	132.2	1.105	88.16	79.78
164	Miscellaneous manufactured products....	111.3	123.1	1.106	157.31	142.23
	Minimum..........................	72.1	64.5	84.9	51.15	53.56
	1st quartile...........................	108.6	107.6	101.6	94.45	80.66
	Median.............................	121.0	129.8	111.0	114.68	99.70
	3rd quartile.........................	131.2	160.6	120.6	134.85	124.72
	Maximum..........................	155.0	208.0	138.6	224.45	204.98
	Interquartile range...................	22.6	53.0	19.0	40.40	44.06
	Interquartile range÷median...........	18.7%	40.8%	17.1%	35.2%	44.2%

Appendix Table G.4

Projected Average Annual Changes to 1965[a]

	1955–1957 Average	1959	1965 Projection	Average Annual Per Cent Change to 1965 from	
				1955–1957	1959
	(1)	(2)	(3)	(4)	(5)
1. Gross national product (billions of 1959 dollars)......	450.4	479.5	633.0	3.9	4.7
2. Annual hours per civilian employed.................	2153[b]	2106[b]	2038[b]	−0.6	−0.5
3. Civilian employment (million persons)...............	64.2	65.6	73.7	1.5	2.0
4. Annual man-hours of civilian employment (billions)....	138.2[c]	138.2[c]	150.2[c]	0.9	1.4
5. Gross output per civilian man-hour ($ in 1959 prices)	3.26	3.47	4.21	2.9	3.3
6. Gross output per civilian employed ($ in 1959 prices)..	7016	7309	8589	2.3	2.7

[a] Source: *National Economic Projections, Series 1960*, National Planning Association (Washington, D. C., 1960), Table 2. The 1965 projection is the "Judgment Model," one of several projections presented in the source publication.

[b] Based on following average hours worked per week: 41.4 in 1955–57, 40.5 in 1959, and 39.2 in 1965.

[c] Computed as the product of Lines 2 and 3.

Estimated Number of Employees Normally Leaving Liberalized Industries Compared with Gross Employment Decreases[l] Due to Liberalization[a]

Liberalized Industry Code Number	Title	Assumed Monthly Separation Rate[b] (Per Cent)	Per Cent of Employees Leaving in 12 Months[c]	1953 Employment in Liberalized Industry[d] (In thousands)	Assumed 1959: 1953 Employment Ratio	Estimated 1959 Employment in Liberalized Industry[e] (In thousands)	Number of Employees Leaving[f] (In thousands)	Gross Employment Decrease in Liberalized Industry from Liberalization[g] (Number)	Import Increase That Can Be Absorbed by Employees' Leaving[h] (In millions of 1953 dollars)
		(1)	(2)	(3)	(4)	(5)	(6)	(7)	(8)
1	Meat animals and products	n.a.	n.a.	676.3	n.a.	n.a.	n.a.	74.38	n.a.
8	Vegetables and fruits	n.a.	n.a.	480.7	n.a.	n.a.	n.a.	193.62	n.a.
13	Lead and zinc mining	1.6	17.59	17.4	.691	12.0	2.11	128.35	16.4
21	Meat packing and wholesale poultry	1.0[i]	11.36	217.2	.940[i]	204.2	23.20	24.41	950.4
22	Processed dairy products	n.a.	n.a.	52.9	n.a.	n.a.	n.a.	25.49	n.a.
24	Grain mill products	1.3	14.54	36.8	.945	34.8	5.06	16.90	299.4
27	Sugar	n.a.	n.a.	32.2	n.a.	n.a.	n.a.	46.17	n.a.
28	Alcoholic beverages	j	j	106.2	j	j	7.79	43.21	180.3
29	Tobacco manufactures	1.3	14.54	88.1	.861	75.9	11.04	42.54	259.5
30	Spinning, weaving, and dyeing	1.5[i]	16.59	642.6	.815[i]	523.7	86.88	97.57	890.4
31	Special textile products	1.5[i]	16.59	51.2	.815[i]	41.7	6.92	73.57	94.1
34	Apparel	2.3[i]	24.37	701.4	.983[i]	689.5	168.03	133.87	1255.2
35	House furnishings and other non-apparel	2.3[i]	24.37	64.4	.983[i]	63.3	15.43	47.74	323.2
38	Plywood	1.5[i]	16.59	39.1	1.063[i]	41.6	6.90	80.93	85.3
40	Wood containers and cooperage	1.5[i]	16.59	48.0	.683[i]	32.8	5.44	93.87	57.9
41	Wood furniture	1.7[i]	18.59	142.6	1.025[i]	146.2	27.18	102.76	264.5
45	Paper and board mills	1.1[i]	12.43	162.0	1.060[i]	171.7	21.34	39.99	533.6
46	Converted paper products	1.7[i]	18.59	186.3	1.036[i]	193.0	35.88	59.62	601.8
49	Industrial organic chemicals	1.1	12.43	99.6	1.026	102.2	12.70	35.19	360.9
51	Synthetic rubber	1.1[i]	12.43	10.0	1.026[i]	10.3	1.28	19.25	66.5
52	Synthetic fiber	j	j	71.9	j	j	3.68	55.10	66.8
54	Drugs and medicines	1.0	11.36	89.7	1.137	102.0	11.59	52.29	221.6
56	Paints and allied products	.8[i]	9.18	60.8	1.018[i]	61.9	5.68	42.09	134.9

[a] Source: *Employment and Earnings*, Annual Supplement issues (U. S. Bureau of Labor Statistics). Data for Column 1 come from Vol. 5, No. 1 (July 1958), Table SB-2, data for 1953 employment for Column 4 from Table SA-1 of same issue, and 1959 employment for Column 4 from Table SB-1 of Vol. 6, No. 11 (May, 1960).

[b] This rate is intended to represent normal separations other than discharges and layoffs. It is the sum of the annual average of monthly rates for quits and "miscellaneous separations, including military" for whichever of the years 1954 through 1957 this sum for the specified industry was lowest.

[c] Computed by subtracting figure in Column 1 from 100 per cent, to get percentage of original number of employees remaining after one month, raising this percentage to the 12th power to get the number remaining after one year if none of the employees leaving is replaced, and subtracting the percentage remaining from 100 per cent.

[d] From Column 1 of Appendix Table D.1.

[e] Column 5 equals Column 3 times Column 4.

[f] Column 6 equals Column 2 times Column 5.

[g] Represents decrease per $1 million increase in imports, valued at domestic ports in 1953 prices. From Line 2, Appendix Table F.1.

[h] Column 8 equals Column 6, converted from thousands to units, divided by Column 7.

[i] The figure for the liberalized industry was not available so the figure for a larger industry containing it (or, in a few cases, a figure for one or more smaller industries which it contained) was used.

[j] Employment figures for 1959 were obtained directly but are not available for publication. Separation rates are withheld to prevent inference of employment figures. For alcoholic beverages, employment figure used is the sum of employment in distilled, rectified and blended liquors, and malt liquors.

Liberalized Industry		As-sumed Monthly Separation Rate[b] (Per Cent)	Per Cent of Employees Leaving in 12 Months[c]	1953 Employment in Liberalized Industry[d] (In thousands)	Assumed 1959: 1953 Employment Ratio	Estimated 1959 Employment in Liberalized Industry[e] (In thousands)	Number of Employees Leaving[f] (In thousands)	Gross Employment Decrease in Liberalized Industry from Liberalization[g] (Number)	Import Increase That Can Be Absorbed by Employees' Leaving[h] (In millions of 1953 dollars)
Code Number	Title	(1)	(2)	(3)	(4)	(5)	(6)	(7)	(8)
59	Vegetable oils	.7[i]	8.10	23.1	1.266[i]	29.2	2.37	20.58	115.2
61	Miscellaneous chemical industries	.7	8.10	31.4	1.735	54.5	4.41	35.77	123.3
65	Tires and inner tubes	.8	9.18	97.0	.850	82.4	7.56	44.68	169.2
66	Miscellaneous rubber products	1.1	12.43	170.4	1.026	174.8	21.73	76.62	283.6
67	Leather tanning and finishing	1.0	11.36	46.4	.788	36.6	4.16	62.50	66.6
69	Footwear, except rubber	2.0	21.52	232.5	.996	231.6	49.84	132.58	375.9
70	Glass	.8[i]	9.18	144.7	1.022[i]	147.9	13.58	86.73	156.6
73	Pottery and related products	1.1	12.43	45.4	.862	39.1	4.86	163.22	29.8
79.1	Carbon steel works and rolling mills	.7[i]	8.10	495.0	.799[i]	395.5	32.04	51.36	623.8
79.2	Alloy steel works and rolling mills, except stainless	.7[i]	8.10	64.8	.799[i]	51.8	4.20	53.75	78.1
79.3	Stainless steel works and rolling mills	.7[i]	8.10	29.5	.799[i]	23.6	1.91	72.82	26.2
85	Primary zinc	.8[i]	9.18	11.4	.856[i]	9.8	0.90	36.29	24.8
88	Primary aluminum, including alumina	1.1[i]	12.43	19.6	.703[i]	13.8	1.72	29.95	57.4
89	Aluminum rolling and drawing	1.1[i]	12.43	39.1	.703[i]	27.5	3.42	43.85	78.0
93	Tin cans and other tinware	1.1[i]	12.43	55.7	1.076	59.9	7.45	42.11	176.9
94	Cutlery	.8	9.18	17.3	.839[i]	14.5	1.33	82.01	16.1
95	Tools and general hardware	1.5	16.59	39.1	.839[i]	32.8	5.44	89.16	61.0
103	Lighting fixtures	1.1[i]	12.43	54.5	1.203	65.6	8.15	66.70	122.2
105	Metal barrels, drums, etc.	1.1[i]	12.43	10.0	1.042[i]	10.4	1.29	42.89	30.1
106	Tubes and foils	1.1[i]	12.43	5.5	1.042[i]	5.7	0.71	43.95	16.2
116	Machine tools and metal-working machinery	1.0[i]	11.36	157.6	.780[i]	122.9	13.96	62.90	221.9
118	Special industrial machinery	1.1	12.43	104.0	.874	90.9	11.30	84.98	133.0
123	Industrial machinery, n.e.c.	1.0[i]	11.36	33.6	.910[i]	30.6	3.48	55.66	62.5
127	Ball and roller bearings	.9[i]	10.27	58.5	1.040[i]	60.8	6.24	94.46	66.1
131	Motors and generators	.9[i]	10.27	129.3	.998[i]	129.0	13.25	73.76	179.6
132	Transformers	.9[i]	10.27	45.4	.998[i]	45.3	4.65	60.50	76.9
133	Electrical control apparatus	.9[i]	10.27	88.4	.998[i]	88.2	9.06	67.39	134.4
134	Electrical welding apparatus	.9[i]	10.27	8.0	.998[i]	8.0	0.82	31.10	26.4
135	Electrical appliances	1.4[i]	15.56	53.9	.639	34.4	5.35	52.61	101.7
136	Insulated wire and cable	1.4[i]	15.56	62.3	.532	33.1	5.15	43.90	117.3
138	Electric lamps	1.4[i]	15.56	21.2	1.140	24.2	3.77	72.74	51.8
139	Radio and related products	1.8	19.58	363.7	1.128[i]	410.3	80.34	80.46	998.5
141	Communication equipment	1.6	17.59	66.1	1.128	74.6	13.12	91.95	142.7
142	Storage batteries	1.4[i]	15.56	17.3	.532[i]	9.2	1.43	46.52	30.7
143	Primary batteries	1.4[i]	15.56	12.3	.532[i]	6.5	1.01	80.39	12.6
145.1	Passenger cars and light trucks	1.1[i]	12.43	604.3	.788[i]	476.2	59.19	32.67	1811.8

Liberalized Industry		As-sumed Monthly Separation Rate[b] (Per Cent)	Per Cent of Em-ployees Leaving in 12 Months[c]	1953 Employ-ment in Liberal-ized In-dustry[d] (In thousands)	As-sumed 1959: 1953 Employ-ment Ratio	Esti-mated 1959 Employ-ment in Liberal-ized In-dustry[e] (In thousands)	Number of Em-ployees Leaving[f] (In thousands)	Gross Employ-ment Decrease in Liberal-ized In-dustry from Liberal-ization[g] (Number)	Import Increase That Can Be Ab-sorbed by Employ-ees' Leav-ing[h] (In millions of 1953 dollars)
Code Num-ber	Title								
		(1)	(2)	(3)	(4)	(5)	(6)	(7)	(8)
145.2	Heavy trucks and buses.	1.1[i]	12.43	124.2	.788[i]	97.9	12.17	32.90	369.9
145.3	Motor vehicle parts and accessories...........	1.1[i]	12.43	99.3	.788[i]	78.2	9.72	32.81	296.2
148	Aircraft and parts......	1.5	16.59	817.4	.943	770.8	127.88	76.31	1675.8
152	Motorcycles and bicycles	1.0[i]	11.36	9.3	.894[i]	8.3	0.94	67.66	13.9
154	Optical, ophthalmic, and photo equipment.....	.9[i]	10.27	97.0	1.059[i]	102.7	10.55	83.92	125.7
156	Watches and clocks.....	1.1	12.43	29.3	.709	20.8	2.59	94.82	27.3
157	Jewelry and silverware..	1.4[i]	15.56	78.3	.856[i]	67.0	10.43	90.95	114.7
158	Musical instruments and parts................	1.8[i]	19.58	10.7	1.192	12.8	2.51	97.42	25.8
159	Toys and sporting goods.	1.8[i]	19.58	92.5	1.042	96.4	18.88	100.12	188.6
160	Office supplies..........	1.8[i]	19.58	18.6	1.381[i]	25.7	5.03	87.41	57.5
161	Plastic products........	1.8[i]	19.58	85.1	1.433[i]	121.9	23.87	77.79	306.9
162	Cork products.........	1.8[i]	19.58	2.4	1.182[i]	2.8	0.55	48.61	11.3
164	Miscellaneous manufac-tured products.......	1.8[i]	19.58	69.3	1.182[i]	81.9	16.04	77.21	207.7

Index